# Phila
# & the Pennsylvania
# Dutch Country

John Spelman

# Contents

PENNSYLVANIA

EXCURSIONS
p171

NEW JERSEY

PENNSYLVANIA
DUTCH COUNTRY
p181

PHILADELPHIA
p51

MARYLAND

DELAWARE

# Destination: Philadelphia & the Pennsylvania Dutch Country

Ben Franklin slept here, and you can too. Then arise to find dozens of colonial sites, the oldest continually occupied street in the country, a thriving gallery scene and a staggering number of bars and restaurants packed with patrons, all crammed within Philadelphia's small downtown extents. Where else can you peer at Franklin's grave, design a custom-made handbag, eat the planet's best banana bread pudding and party 'til 3am?

In Philly, the old and new exist cheek by jowl, each complementing the other. Respect for history and a flourishing present combine to create unique urban neighborhoods whose material landscapes reflect every period of the nation's growth since before it was founded. Compared with other cities, Philadelphia lacks bourgeoisie pretensions, in part because of its former status as the 'Workshop of the World.' The city's blue-collar roots manifest themselves in tightly knit, somewhat provincial neighborhoods that ring the center of the city. Traditions remain important, as exemplified in the Mummers Parade, and rabid enthusiasm over local sports is nearly ubiquitous.

Beyond the city, southeastern Pennsylvania offers a variety of attractions. Most unique is the Pennsylvania Dutch Country, the home of a large Amish population, containing miles of immensely picturesque farmland that sustains this religious sect that eschews violence and technology. History buffs will be glad to know that Valley Forge and Washington's Crossing are merely moments away by car, while Gettysburg is a longer but worthwhile excursion.

Welcome to the City of Brotherly Love, where colonial history meets contemporary cool. Get a civics lesson at the **National Constitution Center** (p62), stroll through leafy **Rittenhouse Square** (p73) and attend a rousing symphony at **Kimmel Center** (p70). Shop for sausages and pastries at the **Italian Market** (p81), cycle through lovely **Fairmount Park** (p83) and dine at one of Philadelphia's stellar **restaurants** (p103). Outside the city, smell the roses at **Longwood Gardens** (p176), go wine-tasting in **Chadds Ford** (p177) or browse for antiques in quaint **New Hope** (p175). Visit the Amish and Mennonite communities in Pennsylvania Dutch Country and the Civil War battleground of **Gettysburg** (p197).

Splash in the fountain at Eakins Oval in the Parkway area (p74) under the watchful eye of George Washington

Browse the book bindery room in Franklin Court (p57), where Benjamin Franklin lived and worked

View the enchanting light-trimmed rowing clubs of Boathouse Row (p84) on the bank of the Schuylkill River

RICHARD CUMMINS

Admire stately Fairmount Waterworks (p84), seen here with the impressive Philadelphia Museum of Art (p77) in the background

RICHARD CUMMINS

Pay your respects to the Liberty Bell (p58), the enduring symbol of Philadelphia freedom

Explore Independence Hall (p57), the revolutionary birthplace of the United States

LEE FOSTER

RICHARD CUMMINS

Stroll picturesque Elfreth's Alley (p62), the oldest residential street in the country

Play on lively South Street (p78), lined with quirky shops and colorful murals

RICHARD CUMMINS

RICHARD I'ANSON

Groove to the sounds of a street musician performing in Old City (p60)

RICHARD I'ANSON

Shop for unique Amish crafts like this colorful quilt for sale in Bird-In-Hand (p191)

RICHARD CUMMINS

Visit Valley Forge (p173), where George Washington's troops spent a harsh winter before defeating the British

Wander the restored structures at Brandywine Battlefield (p177), site of a bloody and nearly disastrous loss for the revolutionary forces

RICHARD CUMMINS

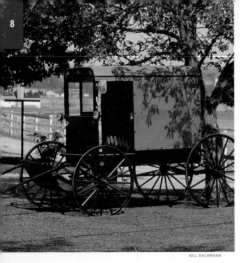

BILL BACHMANN

Ride a buggy (p192) like this traditional
Amish carriage

Meet a friendly Amish farmer in
Intercourse (p190)

BILL BACHMANN

Discover a simpler way of life on the farms of Pennsylvania Dutch Country (p181)

RICHARD I'ANSON

# The Authors

## JOHN SPELMAN

John Spelman was born in Providence, Rhode Island. He earned his BA in cultural geography from Clark University, where his mentors, Martyn Bowden and David Venturo, taught him to write. Upon graduating, John ended 22 years of cushy New England living and moved to San Francisco with $800 and no job prospects, eventually becoming a nameless face in the cartography department of Lonely Planet's Oakland office. In the course of working there, John would be sent back to the East Coast to coauthor Lonely Planet's *New England*.

With his full-time employment as a cartographer coming to an end, John again returned to the East Coast and became a student at Harvard's Graduate School of Design, earning a master's degree in the history of architecture. A few months later he began work on this book. Much of John's nonacademic knowledge of Philadelphia comes from his twin brother, who has lived in the city for several years, maintaining unkempt floor space in the neighborhood of Francisville. Numerous visits and the general process of twinly osmosis have yielded great affection for Philadelphia. The rest of John's expertise comes from one of the most fruitful research periods an author could hope for.

## CONTRIBUTORS

### RON AVERY

Ron Avery wrote the History chapter (p39). He is a native Philadelphian and retired newspaper reporter who is now a tour guide, lecturer and teacher of Philadelphia history at several adult schools. He has written three books about Philadelphia covering the city's history, its most intriguing crimes and its offbeat places.

### FRANCINE MAROUKIAN

Francine Maroukian wrote the Food chapter (p31). She started her New York food career by working for Sheila Lukins at The Silver Palate. In 1983, she opened a private catering business and for several years directed special events for Dean & DeLuca at the Guggenheim Museum. Named one of the best caterers in Manhattan by *Town & Country*, she was contributing food editor at *Family Life* (1992–1999) and has also written for *Esquire, Self, Utne Reader, O, Redbook, Fast Company* and *Travel & Leisure*. She is the author of *Town & Country's Elegant Entertaining, Esquire Eats: How to Feed Your Friends and Lovers* and *Chef's Secrets: America's Best Bare All.*

# JOHN'S TOP PHILADELPHIA DAY

It's Tuesday. Bike in hand, I buy some fruit at the Italian Market (p81) and head over to the Last Drop (p112) on Antique Row to read the paper and drink some coffee. After a couple of hours I depart, admiring Rittenhouse Square (p71) en route to the Philadelphia Museum of Art (p77), where I briefly consider a run up the steps until my coolness-preservation instincts kick in. Getting my fill of Duchamp and furniture, I walk out the backside of the museum and survey the Schuylkill River, Boathouse Row (p84) and the ancient Fairmount Waterworks (p84).

Now feeling peckish, I ride to nearby Rose Tattoo Cafe (p113) to eat mushroom soup in a greenhouse. This accomplished, it's time to visit Old City (p60), where I lock up the bike, grab another cup of coffee and wander around pastoral Independence National Historical Park (p55). When nobody's looking, I kiss Carpenters' Hall (p56). I then buy a bottle of wine and head over to Tartine (p115) or Django (p116), where I meet a friend for one of Philly's best BYOB meals. Now it's time to ride to the Standard Tap (p136) in Northern Liberties for an evening of beer, unless there's an irresistible rock show at the North Star (p140) or an R5 Productions (p140) show in the basement of the First Unitarian Church. I finish the day around 3am at the Center City Pretzel Co (p116) in South Philly, where I shove a hot one down my esophagus before staggering home.

## Essential Philadelphia

- **Rittenhouse Square** (p71) Watching well-dressed crowds from a bench
- **Schuylkill River Trail** (p100) Eyeballs enjoying scenic scenes while feet are pushing pedals
- **Bob & Barbara's** (p135) Catching a Ping-Pong or drag show while holding a can of Pabst and a shot of headache
- **Italian Market** (p81) Buying weird cheeses, sausages and pastries
- **Mütter Museum** (p72) Ogling preserved pathologies

# City Life

# City Life

## PHILADELPHIA TODAY

Somehow, suddenly and very recently, Philadelphia became cool. Rapid change has transformed Center City from the wayward capital of a defunct 'Workshop of the World' to a place teeming with stellar restaurants and comfortable cafés. This transformation comes as the legacy of former mayor Ed Rendell, now governor of Pennsylvania. In the early '90s Rendell took the reins of a dirty city on the brink of bankruptcy. At that time the WC Fields line 'I'd rather be dead than live in Philadelphia' might have seemed apt, depending on your taste. Rendell saw beauty beneath decades of crust and began to polish the city vigorously. His swan, as they say in Philadelphia, emerged as a beautiful princess.

Rendell aggressively promoted the historic city as a marginally forgotten treasure sandwiched between New York and Washington, DC. Under his mayorship, vacant Center City buildings were reinhabited, streets were cleaned and massive brick-and-mortar investments got underway. An impressive list of newly constructed buildings includes the Kimmel Center, the National Constitution Center, the Liberty Bell Center, the Independence Visitor Center, a giant convention center and two new athletic stadiums. The construction of these places and other renewal projects pumped giant gobs of dough into the city's economy. As Center City revived, an endless series of bars, restaurants and clubs opened, and each success made Philadelphia that much more attractive as a travel destination. Center City's architectural heritage benefited, with many old buildings finding new life and new people to admire them.

This renaissance hasn't solved all of the problems caused by Philadelphia's famous 600,000-person depopulation, which began in the 1960s, but it did make Center City into a supremely beautiful and livable urban center, an oasis almost unimaginable in 1990. And all that earlier misfortune means that it's still pretty inexpensive.

Though Philadelphia might seem to be mostly about Center City (Penn's original city, about 2 sq miles), the 1854 annexation of the surrounding towns means that the original 2 sq miles are now 159 sq miles. Think of Philadelphia as a place with extents so large that it contains both its city and its suburbs. While most of these other 157 sq miles aren't frequented by tourists, they obviously make up a defining part of Philadelphia.

Many of these neighborhoods have somewhat depressing stories. Urban blight is a problem, particularly in North Philadelphia. There are around 60,000 derelict or abandoned buildings throughout the city, and this number swells when you add empty lots to the mix. Crime, a poor school system and lack of opportunity are issues that you can't spin positively and are a real part of the city, even if they are invisible from downtown Philadelphia.

However, some neighborhoods outside of Center City – in particular Manayunk and Northern Liberties – have benefited from the city's renaissance. New development has occurred throughout University City, and friendly corridors of shopping and entertainment have been established in an area once deprived of things to do. Penn alums returning for reunion have trouble believing the changes, as do people who actually live in the city. Not all are impressed, with some locals seeing the modifications as attempts to gentrify and disrupt their community.

## Hot Conversation Topics

If you were in line at a cheese steak shop in Philadelphia, you might hear some of these issues arise:

- The Linc is nice, but they've got to be kidding with the $7 beers.
- If they move the Barnes Museum to the parkway, will we still need to make reservations a month in advance?
- I wish they'd move the Rocky statue back in front of the Art Museum.
- For a city on such a rebound, you'd think they'd fix up SEPTA so its slogan, 'We're getting there,' doesn't sound like an apology.
- I'll take an American wit onions.
- Who's playing at the Khyber tonight?
- I wish Rendell was still mayor.

# CITY CALENDAR

Philadelphia's nicest months, September and October, are also the city's busiest. Other popular times to visit include Thanksgiving, New Year's and university graduations in May. During prime tourist season, prices are higher, lines are longer and parking is more difficult.

Summer months can also find the city crowded, though this is offset by a weekend exodus of Philly's residents, many of whom escape summer's heat and humidity by fleeing to the South Jersey Shore. For more information on public holidays, see p207.

Philadelphia stages an exhausting array of festivals, concerts and events. Listed here are the major events, but a complete listing would irritate anyone concerned with deforestation. Use this as a guide but also check with the folks at the Independence Visitor Center for more complete listings. Other good references are the two weekly papers – *City Paper* and *Philadelphia Weekly* – and the tourism website, www.gophila.com.

## JANUARY & FEBRUARY

The biggest party in town is the indescribable Mummers New Year's parade. These two months have the biggest chance of significant snowfall in Philadelphia, the coldest temperatures (26°F on average) and the fewest festivals.

### MUMMERS PARADE

January 1 is the day to see many thousands of men and women strut around in fancy handmade costumes with makeup and banjos. See p81 for details.

### BLACK HISTORY MONTH

In February events and exhibits all around the city celebrate African American history. The **African American Museum in Philadelphia** (p71) and the **Independence Visitor Center** (p55) are both good resources for information.

## MARCH

The average high jumps to 51°F. Easter Sunday brings out tentative forays to backyards for Chestnut Hill egg-hunters.

### THE BOOK AND THE COOK

☎ 312-965-7676; www.thebookandthecook.com

Cookbook authors and Philadelphia's top chefs team up for 10 days to create inspiring prix-fixe menus in restaurants all over town. There's also a kitchen expo so you can buy that essential gadget.

### PHILADELPHIA FLOWER SHOW

☎ 215-988-8899; www.theflowershow.com

The world's largest and most prestigious flower show makes for a spectacular week, unless you have allergies.

## APRIL

If it didn't already happen on some unusually warm March day, spring-happy residents switch to short-sleeve shirts at the first possible opportunity. Buds and blooms also appear, with average highs around 62°F.

### PENN RELAYS

☎ 215-898-6145; www.thepennrelays.com

One of the world's oldest, largest and best amateur athletic carnivals, Penn Relays has been held for over 100 years on Franklin Field at the University of Pennsylvania in late April.

### PHILADELPHIA ANTIQUE SHOW

☎ 215-387-3500; www.philaantiques.com

More then 50 dealers and their objects gather for the country's premier show of American antiques and decorative arts.

### PHILADELPHIA FILM FESTIVAL

☎ 215-733-0608; www.phillyfests.com

This two-week festival shows hundreds of flicks in venues all over town.

## MAY

May is an exceptionally comfortable and pretty month. Flowers and trees say hello. The mean daily temperature hovers around 64°F, and average highs make it to 77°F.

### DAD VAIL REGATTA

☎ 215-542-1143; www.dadvail.org

The largest collegiate regatta in the US draws thousands of rowers and spectators to the Schuylkill River.

## Top Five Idiosyncratic Seasonal Events

Though the famous Mummers Parade has long been the reigning champ of bizarre Philadelphia events, other occasions also approach sublime weirdness.

- **Bloomsday** ( ☎ 215-732-1600; www.rosenbach.org) On June 16, the day on which the hero from *Ulysses* makes his odyssey through Dublin, scores of readers read James Joyce's story on the steps of the Rosenbach Library, where the original manuscript lives.
- **Lord & Taylor Holiday Light Show and Organ Concerts** ( ☎ 215-241-9000) Head over to John Wanamaker's old store (see boxed text on p155) for a light show so opulent and a massive organ so splendid that you'll probably want to relocate to Philadelphia after experiencing this traditional event. Performances occur hourly from Thanksgiving through New Year's Day.
- **Mummers Parade** About 25,000 instrument-wielding Italian Americans strut around in millions of sequins in this spectacular New Year's Day parade (see boxed text p81).
- **Peoplehood** On the last weekend of October, the folks at Spiral Q (p87) organize an all-city giant puppet parade. If you look willing, you just might find yourself wearing a massive rabbit head and hanging out with a cowboy troupe.
- **Terror Behind the Walls** The Eastern State Penitentiary (p76) sets up a haunted house that succeeds in terrifying, in part because it occupies a massive derelict prison.

### PHILADANCO!
☎ 215-387-8200; www.kimmelcenter.org/resident/philadanco.php
This dance troupe from West Philly attained international acclaim and tours most of the year. Catch them at the Kimmel Center each spring.

### PHILADELPHIA OPEN HOUSE TOURS
☎ 215-928-1188
From Society Hill to the suburbs, kind Philadelphians open their historic homes for public viewing.

## JUNE
School's out and festival season begins. Philadelphians concur that this is a great time to be in the city, though the last week or so can be a bit sticky, which is when some folks flee to the shore. The average monthly high is 81°F.

### ODUNDE
☎ 215-732-8508; www.odunde.org
One of the country's largest and oldest African American festivals, Odunde draws over 200,000 spectators to South Street. Derived from a West African spirit festival, the event features a boatload of food vendors, dignitaries, dancers, stilt walkers and two stages for daylong performances.

### PRIDE DAY
☎ 215-875-9288; www.phillypride.org
The LGBT Pride Parade and Festival is held every June during International Gay Pride Month.

### WACHOVIA US PRO CYCLING CHAMPIONSHIP
☎ 215-965-7676; www.firstunioncycling.com
The world's top cyclists race up and down the east side of the Schuylkill River on one of America's most exciting courses. It's 14.4 miles, done five times.

## JULY
By now sidewalks shimmer in the heat and sweltering Philadelphians wade in Logan Circle's Swann Fountain, unless there's a thunderstorm. July is the rainiest month, and the average high hits 86°F. Water ice vendors are happy.

### SUNOCO WELCOME AMERICA
☎ 215-770-5883; www.americasbirthday.com
Philadelphia celebrates its special relationship to Independence Day with fireworks and more during the first week of the month.

## AUGUST
With average highs around 84°F, Swann Fountain remains full for the first half of the month. The second half sees some cooling and the return of vacationers from the Jersey Shore.

### PENNSYLVANIA DUTCH FESTIVAL
☎ 215-922-2317
Get ready for buggy rides, bluegrass music and more centered on the Reading Terminal Market during the first week of the month.

## PHILADELPHIA FOLK FESTIVAL
☎ 215-242-0150; www.folkfest.org
For nearly 50 years this annual baby has been presenting three days of awesome stuff. It's held at Old Poole Farm in Schwenksville in late August. Call to find out about camping.

# SEPTEMBER
Fall colors begin to strut their stuff toward the end of the month, and the mild weather (high 77°F and low 61°F) makes this an excellent time for a visit. Football season begins early in the month.

## PHILADELPHIA FRINGE FESTIVAL
☎ 215-413-1318; www.pafringe.org
From serious dance and theater to uncouth vaudeville and drag acts, the highly acclaimed Fringe Festival puts on hundreds of shows in a two-week period. The whole city gets involved, and the dozens of venues in which shows might occur include the beautiful Arden Theater and the ratty space beneath the Benjamin Franklin Bridge.

# OCTOBER
Expect to feel the return of chilly breezes intermixed with some warm days – highs around 66°F and lows about 49°F. By the end of the month the trees in Fairmount Park look their autumn-colors best. This is the most active month for tourists.

## BATTLE OF GERMANTOWN
☎ 215-848-1777; www.cliveden.org
Up to 1000 reenactors come from thousands of miles away to camp out and redo this famous battle. As hard as Washington's troops try, they seem to lose every year.

## FALL FOR THE ARTS FESTIVAL
☎ 215-247-6696; www.chestnuthillpa.com
Chestnut Hill's annual fall festival features more than 100 artists and craftspeople, and an open house at Woodmere Art Museum. Loads of face painting, food and beer are in store.

## OUTFEST
☎ 215-875-9288; www.phillypride.org
With a mechanical bull, lots of rainbow flags and four city blocks closed to traffic, this is the nation's largest celebration of Coming Out Day.

## PHILLY URBAN LEGEND AWARDS
☎ 215-748-2360; www.urbanbeatmovement.com
Attending this somewhat underground gathering of Philly's best hip-hop performers immediately gives you street cred. The 2003 ceremony featured Lady B, Dj Miz, Crazy Dee, Disco Rat and others.

## RELEASE THE BATS
☎ 215-732-1600; www.rosenbach.org
Having received a commission to interpret Bram Stoker's *Dracula*, the Rosenbach Museum will be presenting special events around Halloween until at least 2005. With the help of Spiral Q, the museum will be organizing a spooky procession of costumed characters, including a colossal 22ft Nosferatu.

# NOVEMBER
It's getting darker and colder – the average low is 40°F – though the emergence of holiday decorations and lights warm up Rittenhouse Square.

## PHILADELPHIA MARATHON
☎ 215-683-2070; www.philadelphiamarathon.com
On the second or third Sunday of the month, Fairmount Park fills with tired, sweaty people and those who like to watch them run.

## THANKSGIVING DAY PARADE
☎ 215-581-4502; www.boscovs.com/parade
The country's oldest Thanksgiving parade gathers its floats and bands for a walk along Market St and Benjamin Franklin Parkway.

# DECEMBER
Erstwhile pedestrians bite the bullet and take SEPTA as frigid temperatures (low 31°F) arrive, along with some snow. Christmas lights are everywhere.

## CHRISTMAS TOURS OF HISTORIC HOUSES
☎ 215-763-8100; www.philamuseum.org
Trimmed with candles and wreathie goodness, the 17th-century mansions in Fairmount Park invite you to visit.

## NEW YEAR'S EVE FIREWORKS
☎ 215-922-2386; www.pennslandingcorp.com
Ring in the New Year on the waterfront, and bring your gloves.

# CULTURE

## IDENTITY

According to the 2000 census, 43% of Philadelphia's population is African American, 43% is non-Latino white, 8.5% is Latino and 4.5% is Asian. A small percentage of residents classify themselves as 'other.' An increasingly vocal gay community has become more pronounced in recent years.

Philadelphia's African American population began growing in the 1790s, when free blacks were attracted to Philadelphia's supportive abolitionist community and to the rare existence of black schools and institutes. Not that life was easy for blacks in old Philly: bigotry, hatred and violence were the norm. Suitable jobs did not exist. This did not change much until WWII, when the city's factories opened their doors to black workers. Thousands moved to Philadelphia to take advantage of new employment opportunities in skilled labor. Unfortunately such opportunity lasted for only a decade.

By the early 1960s postindustrialism began putting the hurt on Philadelphia. Most manufacturing jobs disappeared, either to the Sunbelt or overseas. Along with the jobs, 600,000 people fled, dropping the city's population from over 2 million in 1950 to 1.5 million today. For many who remained, the decision to stay was compulsory: their finances would not permit them to leave. A huge number experienced terrible poverty.

Simple traditions, economic hardship and lingering prejudice keep Philadelphia racially divided, even today. Historically, there has been a strange dichotomy between the multicultural, tolerant and inclusive character of Center City and Philadelphia's often Balkanized neighborhoods, though this trend has been diminishing over the last decade, particularly in West and South Philadelphia.

## LIFESTYLE

Most Philadelphians settle into a lifestyle that revolves around their neighborhood. This is somewhat of a generalization, but your buddy who lives in Rittenhouse Square will probably be somewhat reluctant to walk 20 minutes across town to have dinner with you in Old City. Forgive him. This pattern exists everywhere, from Francisville to Fishtown.

Center City itself is populated mostly by professional types with a decent-sized number of students bringing up the rear. Excepting Society Hill, Center City doesn't contain many families. Though Center City might seem like the main part of Philadelphia, most of the city's citizens don't live here, opting instead for cheaper rents or home ownership in peripheral neighborhoods. Peripheral-living cool kids tend to own cars. Many Philadelphians work downtown; many more have found jobs outside of the city, commuting to suburban office developments like those near King of Prussia or across the river to Trenton, New Jersey.

Row houses remain the principal housing type. Row-house apartments are narrow and usually three stories tall. On the first floor you'll find a kitchen and living area. Bedrooms lie on the floors above, often with a couple of rooms on each floor. The narrowness of row homes makes them difficult to subdivide, which means many apartments have three to five bedrooms and a similar number of roommates.

## SPORTS

Philadelphia's professional and college sports teams enjoy an enthusiastic following, whose devotion in some cases borders on psychosis. There are three major venues – Citizen's Bank Park, Lincoln Financial Field and the Wachovia Center – all clustered on S Broad St in South Philadelphia. Lincoln Field and Citizen's Bank Park are both brand-new stadiums, christened in 2003 and 2004, respectively, with the former

### Lowdown

**Population** 1.5 million
**Time zone** East Coast Time (EST; GMT-5 hrs)
**3-star room** Around $120
**Hours of wine & liquor stores** 9am-9pm Mon-Sat
**Cheese steak** $5.50
**Subway token** $2
**Essential drink** Yuengling lager ($2.50)
**No-no** Don't say you're from Jersey, even if you are.

home to the National Football League's Philadelphia Eagles (or the 'Birds') and the latter housing Major League Baseball's Philadelphia Phillies. The Wachovia hosts the NBA's Philadelphia 76ers (also called the 'Sixers') basketball team and the NHL's Philadelphia Flyers hockey team. If any one of these teams approaches the possibility of a national championship, the city practically shuts down in gleeful anticipation. Only the oldest, most disciplined bartenders will be able to maintain their composure enough to keep their eye off the tube and tend to their flock of customers.

City sports involve more than the big leagues. Philly hosts the annual Army-Navy college football game, and Penn and Temple often field competitive college teams of all varieties, though local media tend to focus on men's football and basketball, overlooking stuff like lacrosse, tennis and hurdling. Additionally Philadelphia is home to the world's oldest and largest track meet, the Penn Relays, plus the famed Dad Vail Regatta and the nation's longest cycling race – the Wachovia US Pro Cycling Championship.

## Top Five Media Websites

The following addresses will help you get the lowdown on whatever might be happening in Philadelphia.

- **www.gophila.com** – A must for visitors, this site provides extensive information about special events, hotel packages and more.
- **www.citypaper.net** – Read how the mayor is helping and hurting the city, what's up in the galleries and who's rocking the Khyber.
- **www.philly.com** – Find out the latest analysis of the next Eagles game at this site, home to the *Philadelphia Inquirer* and the *Philadelphia Daily News*.
- **www.phillyimc.org** – Come here for respectable news from a noncorporate source, organized by one of the most active Independent Media Centers in the country.
- **http://philadelphia.citysearch.com** – This site contains an exhaustive list of the city's sites, restaurants and hotels, with up-to-the-minute descriptions and hours.

For those who prefer to participate rather then spectate, scenic trails along the Schuylkill and Wissahickon provide miles of gorgeous opportunity for cyclists, runners, walkers and roller bladers. Some spots, especially on the Wissahickon, are so serene that you will forget that you're in the fifth-largest city in the US. Or you can just spend hours walking around Center City. And don't forget to ice-skate in the winter.

# MEDIA

Philadelphia has two major dailies: the reasonably respectable *Philadelphia Inquirer*, which occasionally picks up a national award, and the plucky tabloid the *Philadelphia Daily News*, which does not.

The city's most prominent locally owned free weekly, the *City Paper*, is an excellent source for local news as well as arts and entertainment coverage. Nearly as good is the *Philadelphia Weekly,* another alternative paper of similar focus. Both papers provide extensive entertainment reviews and listings.

*Philadelphia Magazine* is the city's glossy monthly. The monthly newsprint, *The Philadelphia Independent,* lies around coffee shops and galleries, waiting for its stories about Philadelphian oddities to be read.

# ECONOMY & COSTS

Ever since the postindustrial economy hit Philadelphia, the city's economy has been struggling. Manufacturing met an untimely demise, a quarter of the population fled, half of downtown shuttered up and Paulie was begging Rocky for work. A dramatic turnaround in the 1990s brought new properity to flagging Center City. Though manufacturing looks like it will never recover, new jobs have been coming out of the now supercharged tourism trade, mostly in the service industry. Philadelphia's biggest employer is the University of Pennsylvania. Numbers two and three are the city government and local utility companies, respectively. In the last decade, large construction projects have also generated jobs.

For now, most of the city's prosperity remains concentrated in its center. Outlying neighborhoods often (but not always) suffer under abysmal economic circumstances. While success in the center has caused some developers to turn their eyes toward revitalization of dodgier sections of town, many residents worry about being supplanted through the tentacles of gentrification.

Travelers coming to Philadelphia will find lodging to be their most costly expense. Unless you plan to see the ballet each night, food will likely come second. A 'two-star' day, including lodging and three meals, will come to about $120. A 'three-star' day

### Philadelphia Radio Stations

**WXPN 88.5 FM** U Penn's excellent station; indie rock and eclectic

**WHYY 90.9 FM** National Public Radio; news and talk

**WKDU 91.7 FM** Drexel University's radio station

**WXTU 92.5 FM** country

**WYSP 94.1 FM** popular music, rock; live Eagles games

**WOGL 98.1 FM** oldies, baby

**WUSL 98.9 FM** (known as Power 99) Hip-hop, R&B

**WPLY 100.3 FM** (known as Y100) Top 40

**KYW 1060 AM** all news, all the time

totals around $165, and a 'four-star' day runs in the vicinity of $325 ($220 hotel, $60 dinner, $25 lunch and $20 breakfast). These numbers are approximations and are based on single-person occupancy. Costs will decrease if you share a room with a travel partner or if you find a great lodging deal (see 'Brave New Rooms,' p164). Costs will increase if you are traveling during a period when hotel occupancy rates are high, or if you go for a suite instead of a traditional room.

Those who want to cut costs will be glad to know that most sites in Independence National Historical Park are free, and that many museums often have deals where admission rates are reduced. While such information is noted in our listings of sites, also check with the Independence Visitor Center for the latest on deals in Philadelphia.

# GOVERNMENT & POLITICS

Philadelphia politics, historically dirty, took an interesting turn in the fall of 2004, when an FBI bug turned up in Mayor John Street's office, shortly before the mayoral election. Street supporters smelled a conspiracy and rallied to secure an overwhelming victory over Sam Katz, the Republican challenger.

Much of the city votes along race lines, and since African Americans are both the largest ethnic group and fairly well empowered and organized, they are well represented in elected offices throughout Philadelphia. This, plus the fact that Philadelphia's blue-collar manufacturing roots persist even though the industry does not, means that voters are heavily Democratic and Independent.

The city government consists of a mayor and a council of 17 members, all of whom are elected for four-year terms. Councilors meet at City Hall at 10am on Thursday. Meetings are open to the public and can be either exquisitely dull or quite interesting depending on how excited you get over rules of order. The government of Philadelphia's website is www.phila.gov.

Though it doesn't technically count as formal city politics, Philadelphia is pumped that Ed Rendell, its former mayor, is now serving a term as governor of Pennsylvania. The city is licking its collective chops over having such prominent representation in Harrisburg, where the state budget gets hammered out.

While Philadelphia is fairly liberal, this contrasts with the rest of the state. Prevalent conservatism is reflected in the oft-repeated joke that Pennsylvania consists of Philadelphia and Pittsburgh, with Alabama in the middle.

# ENVIRONMENT

In early 1682, just before William Penn arrived in his new colony, his commissioners were searching up and down the Delaware River for a site suitable for a capital city. They chose a site just upriver from the confluence of the Delaware and the Schuylkill, and began to survey a town according to Penn's instructions. In October, Penn arrived and immediately extended the plan all the way to the Schuylkill, running roughly parallel 2 miles to the west.

This decision was fateful for the future Philadelphia, a city on the great flat between two rivers. The wide Delaware has served as both the hard edge of the city and, for a long time, as its commercial focus in Philadelphia's role as one of the most important ports in the country. The Schuylkill, on the other hand, has been a soft boundary, guiding the city's growth as it extended inland, just as Penn so wisely anticipated. Today, now that shipping has moved away from the congested city center, the shore of the Delaware has become a focus for recreation, most recently in the ongoing development of the tourist attractions at Penn's Landing.

## GREEN PHILADELPHIA

Philadelphia is half green and half brown. In the green corner is enormous Fairmount Park, around 4000 acres. Once on the periphery of the city, the park has become central as Philadelphia has grown in size, and it is so large – allegedly the nation's biggest urban park – that most Philadelphians are unable to explore the whole thing. The forest around Wissahickon Creek is notable for its remote terrain, where no cars are allowed. In Center City two of Penn's original squares, Washington and Rittenhouse, remain used for their original grassy purposes, and Independence National Historical Park provides more pastoral acreage in the downtown area. Throughout the city, community gardens have been springing up to replace abandoned lots.

However, Philadelphia scores low marks for environmental awareness. This trend is historic, beginning with the original settlers ignoring Penn's plans for a 'green country town.' While they nominally retained his pattern of five squares, they disregarded his more important call for minimum lot sizes, building so closely together that Philadelphia had almost unmatched urban density. Though the colonial city's festering dirt streets covered in pig manure have long been paved over, today many places in town are less than tidy. Littering is a big problem; head down to Passyunk Ave and 9th St in South Philly, and you'll see piles of old cheese steak wrappers and complementary detritus clogging gutters and sidewalks. Walk through Fairmount Park, and the lush green lawns will be sullied by more then one discarded paper cup. Though a recycling program exists, it is inconvenient and many Philadelphians only reluctantly participate.

## URBAN PLANNING & DEVELOPMENT

Philadelphia's urban innovations didn't end with Penn's plan. When the Parks Movement got underway in the middle of the 19th century, Philadelphia was at the forefront. New York had its Central Park and Boston its Fenway, but between them came Philadelphia's own Fairmount Park, which was first established in 1855. Like the other two, it was also designed in part by the great park designer Frederick Law Olmsted. Fairmount, split into east and west sections, hugs the shores of the Schuylkill just north of the city center. The park was an immediate success and served as the site of the 1876 Centennial Exposition, which was visited by over 10 million people. Over the years, the Fairmount Park Commission extended its holdings into a full park system of 8900 acres, so that no resident of Philadelphia is more than a mile from one of its parks. (For information on the parks system, go to www.phila.gov/fairpark or www.nlreep.org.)

The last major addition to Fairmount Park was the Benjamin Franklin Parkway

### How Much?

Average taxi ride $5

Hoagie $5

One hour of parking $6

24 hours of parking $15

Average rock show cover $8

Average mid-range dinner entrée $17

Cup of coffee $1.50

Pretzel 75¢

Movie ticket $8.50

Water ice $1

of the 1920s, a product of the City Beautiful movement connecting the park to the center of the city. Between the foundation of the park and its completion with the parkway, a great change had come to the center of the city. In 1860 downtown Philadelphia (Penn's original plan) had a population of 138,000, which was over 24% of the city's total; by 1930 the downtown had only 56,000 residents, which amounted to only 2.9% of the city as a whole. The suburban sprawl and decline of the center that struck so many American cities hit Philadelphia early and hard.

The city was down but not out, and bringing the story up to the present is largely the history of an inspired recovery. Starting in the early '50s, Philadelphia became a test case for the intelligent restoration and recovery of a major urban center. Many people were involved in this work, but the most important was the legendary city planner Edmund Bacon. In the 1940s Bacon served as director of the Philadelphia Housing Association, which is now the city's largest landlord. Then he was director of the city's Planning Commission from 1949 until his retirement in 1970. Bacon rehabilitated Society Hill, developed the Penn Center, and generally rebuilt the

## The Original American Grid

If its location between the rivers gave the city its shape, it was another idea of Penn's that gave it its character: Philadelphia has long been recognized as the prototype for the gridded cities that have become an American trademark. It isn't that Philadelphia was the first grid in the Colonies – New Haven, Connecticut, for instance, was planned on a grid some 40 years earlier. But New Haven had only eight blocks and a central common; Philadelphia's original plan accounted for 176 blocks with five park squares. It was the most ambitious urban plan in the New World.

Penn's decision for a grid has had a nearly endless impact over the years. Though we are used to the grid now, its broad, straight streets and regular lots were unmatched in early America, and found many imitators. Over a century later, the famous grids of New York and of Thomas Jefferson's design for the whole western part of the country both drew from Penn's ideal. The success of Penn's system may be judged by the fact that as the city grew, his original grid was expanded to cover an area many times its original size – but it is that center that is the core of America's gridded cities, from Chicago to Tulsa.

city on an east-west axis along its spine at Market St. Some of Bacon's projects have since come under criticism (like the Penn Center, which didn't create a viable neighborhood and instead created an office jungle that becomes desolate and empty at night), but generally his work is still esteemed as a major move forward for American planning.

Bacon's work happened under the sponsorship of Mayor (and later Senator) Joseph Clark; in the last 10 years his legacy has carried on under the patronage of (former mayor) Governor Rendell, whose Avenue of the Arts on Broad St is the north-south complement to Bacon's Market St. And just as Bacon had the Penn Center, Rendell's plan has created its great contribution in the Kimmel Center for the Performing Arts, designed by architect Rafael Viñoly, which opened in 2001.

# Arts

# Arts

Philadelphia's arts have the capacity to satisfy everyone's taste. Those interested in fantastic architecture or outdoor sculpture need walk for only a few blocks in Center City to be impressed. Folks keen on 19th-century impressionism will be pleased to know that the Philadelphia Museum of Art contains an excellent collection and that the esteemed Barnes Foundation will probably be moving from the suburbs to Philadelphia's Museum District. Those who prefer more current fare should check out one of the city's many galleries, the Institute for Contemporary Art (ICA) or the Fabric Workshop, where the world's newest work frequently turns up to be pondered. Don't forget to admire some of the city's many colorful outdoor murals as you move from site to site.

## Top Five Art Museums & Galleries

- **Philadelphia Museum of Art** (p77) So awesome, it's like visiting 10 museums
- **Pennsylvania Academy of Fine Arts** (p76) Many periods of American painting in a Furness building
- **Institute for Contemporary Art** (p87) Changing exhibits of artists such as Polly Apffelbaum, Greg Lynn and rocker Patti Smith
- **Nexus** (p63) An old-school gallery in Old City
- **Vox Populi** (p69) What'll those crazy kids think of next?

Beyond visual arts, Philadelphia's music scene is rich and longstanding. Jazz has been thriving here since the 1920s, and today there are at least a dozen places to catch a live combo or crooner. Local soul and hip-hop have earned national recognition, helping coin a genre – the 'Philly Sound.' DJs spin for their steady followings, numerous rock clubs fire up their amps every night and the Philadelphia Orchestra and the Curtis Institute do great stuff with their armies of well-dressed people mastering instruments with strings. Distributed to over 150 stations across the globe, the popular radio program 'World Cafe' (www.worldcafe.org) is produced on Penn's campus.

Theater and dance are strong as well. The ballet skillfully leaps around the country's oldest grand opera hall. Theatrical productions range from traveling Broadway shows to critically acclaimed avant-garde performances at the Arden Theater. Other events to look for are the city's annual Fringe Festival, film screenings at one of several art houses and any classical music performance at the shiny new Kimmel Center.

## VISUAL ARTS

Philadelphia's visual art world has grown large enough to occupy several distinct areas throughout the city. The museum district contains a cluster of top-tier art repositories: the Rodin Museum (p78), the Pennsylvania Academy of the Fine Arts (p76) and the Philadelphia Museum of Art (p77) – the country's third-largest fine arts museum, featuring the world's largest collection of Marcel Duchamp's work, including *Nude Descending a Staircase (No 2)* and the notorious painting on glass *The Bride Stripped Bare by Her Bachelors, Even (The Large Glass)*. The museum's modern and contemporary collections hold pieces by Picasso, O'Keeffe, Matisse, de Kooning, Pollock and just about anyone making an appearance in core art history textbooks. There are scores of rooms dedicated to other periods and cultures, supporting collections of Indian and Himalayan art, European decorative art, early American furniture, 5000 years of East Asian art and much more.

While these three museums comprise what has long been regarded as one of the continent's top art destinations, Philadelphia's art universe is about to expand to even more impressive proportions. The relocated Barnes Foundation and the new Calder Museum are expected to open their doors along the Benjamin Franklin Parkway within the next five years. The Barnes Foundation, presently located a few miles north of Philadelphia, features the world's largest private collection of impressionist, postimpressionist and early French modern paintings, and contains more works by Cézanne than any gallery in France. The future Calder Museum will represent all three generations of Philadelphia's sculpting Calder family, though you don't have to wait for it to open to see their work – just go for a walk outside and keep your eyes open. Consult the 'Culture Files' at www.gophila.com for a list of important outdoor sculptures around town.

In Old City, more then 40 galleries comprise another major Philadelphia art destination. While you can visit at any time, the gallery district is most lively on **First Fridays** (p62), when the evening streets fill up with crowds stumbling from one opening to the next. Lately the gallery scene has experienced significant spatial growth, with newer studios opening on the fringes of Chinatown.

Philadelphia also features the Mural Arts Program, a body established by the city in 1984 to redirect the efforts of misguided graffiti artists. The program became hugely successful and, as it evolved, has attracted participants from all kinds of urban realms. Today over 2000 murals exist throughout Philadelphia, giving the city the distinction of having the largest collection of public murals in the country. New murals are made only after their sponsor submits a successful proposal in a competitive application process, where the backer must demonstrate community support of the project. Guided **mural tours** (p54) occur regularly, and the Independence Visitor Center can provide a map outlining self-guided walking, biking and driving tours.

# ARCHITECTURE

Philadelphia has been a major American city almost since the day it was founded, so it has had the chance to make an important contribution to almost every period in American architecture (though some of these contributions have worn away). The area's earliest settlers were Swedish colonists, who arrived even before Penn founded the province. You can still see their architecture in the core of **Gloria Dei** of 1698–1700 (with later additions), Pennsylvania's oldest standing church.

The English colonial period left a greater legacy in the form of some excellent Georgian-style architecture. Most famous is Edmund Woolley's State House (1731–53), better known as **Independence Hall** (p57). **Christ Church** (1727–34; p61) is equally fine, demonstrating the high level of accomplishment among these frontier builders. 'Builders' is the correct term, because architecture as a profession didn't really exist in the colonies; instead, master craftsmen and gentleman dabblers split the duty of architectural design. The Carpenters' Company, a local guild, had almost complete control of Philadelphia's building into the early 19th century. The results are easy to see; many of Society Hill's houses (such as the **Powel House**; p65) date from this period. These city houses are complemented by the 18th-century mansions that are preserved in Fairmount Park.

Architecturally, perhaps Philadelphia's highest point came in the early 1800s, when it was the country's most important city and an emerging hotbed for the new Greek Revival style. The style was pioneered here by Robert Mills and his mentor, Benjamin Latrobe. Little of their Philadelphia work still stands, but their style may be seen in Frederick Graff's **Fairmount Waterworks** of 1812–22, which Latrobe probably helped design.

Latrobe and Mills were followed by three of Philadelphia's finest architects: William Strickland, John Haviland and Thomas Ustick Walter, all Classicists. Strickland was a student of Latrobe, and his Second Bank of the US (1818–24) and Merchant's Exchange (1832–33) show his mastery at creating a monumental urban scene. Haviland's **Eastern State Penitentiary** (1823–36; p000) and Franklin Institute (now the Atwater Kent Museum; 1825) show an austere solemnity in keeping with his Quaker clients. TU Walter had a more decorative and engaging style, as seen in his **Portico Row** (1831–2; see 'Row Houses' boxed text p25) and Founder's Hall of Girard College (1833–47).

As the Greek Revival style fell from favor, the Gothic Revival and other romantic styles replaced it. The master of these styles in Philadelphia was John Notman, whose **Athenaeum**

## Artists Are Running the Store by John McInerney

Philadelphia's artists have taken things into their own hands and organized some of the city's best places to see great contemporary art. The Old City area is a sure bet to find the most galleries in one spot, and great finds can be gleaned throughout the city. Start in the heart of Old City's gallery district with **Nexus** (p000), a free incubator for emerging artists for over 30 years.

Just a few blocks south of Old City, **Spector Gallery** (Map pp228-9; ☎ 215-238-0840; www.spectorspector.com; 510 Bainbridge St; ☻ 2-6pm Thu-Sat) showcases some of the best young local artists in town. Check out Jim Houser's painted skateboards, Ben Woodward's folksy animal paintings, Tom Lessner's homage portraits to Philly sports legends and Daniel Sadler's beautifully nostalgic Shabitat light sculptures.

In Chinatown, many of the aforementioned artists are part of **Space 1026** (p71), an artist collective that defies simple categorization. Founded by a group of Rhode Island School of Design grads, 1026 is an informal work-studio, print shop and gallery. Exhibitions focus on a national network of young artists, including shows by legendary wheat paster Shepard Fairey (of Andre the Giant fame) and trash-art sensation Bobby Puleo. But most popular are 1026's themed shows, including the flip book festival (yes, just like in grade school), the edible art show and the annual prom. Space 1026 specializes in First Friday openings that differ from your usual wine-and-cheese soirée (think Pabst Blue Ribbon and hoagies) and that last a while, so get there late.

Down the street **Vox Populi** (p69) is the city's strongest artist-run space that shows the work of its own members, including established artists Joy Feasley and Tristin Lowe. Vox was one of the first groups to move into Old City in the 1980s but has continued to press outward with their current location in Chinatown's Gilbert building. They share the building with a host of nonprofits including fellow cooperative **Asian Arts Initiative** (Map pp222-3; ☎ 215-557-0455; www.asianartsinitiative.org; 1315 Cherry St, 2nd fl East; ☻ by appt).

Philly is also known for its sculptors, such as Kait Midgett, who curates shows at **Project Room** (Map p230; ☎ 215-413-3101; 960 N 9th St; ☻ by appt) while installing works around town. Openings take place in a space reminiscent of a German-beer-garden-turned-old-taxi-garage. Next door is the relatively new and mysterious **Table Space** (Map p230; ☎ 215-923-0419; 948 N 8th St; ☻ 6-9pm Mon & Wed, 1-4pm Sun, or by appt), which specializes in experimental film and music along with more traditional exhibits of contemporary art.

For details on events and openings, new hot spots and the latest gossip from around the scene, visit the artist-run nonprofit website www.inliquid.com.

(1845–47; p65) and many churches (in particular, St Marks of 1847–49 and the Holy Trinity of 1856–59) cover the range of these styles. But before he built his finest buildings, he made an even greater contribution to Philadelphia – the Laurel Hill Burying Ground (1836), one of the forerunners of the American Parks Movement.

In the period directly after the Civil War, one figure loomed over all architecture in Philadelphia: Frank Furness. His vivid, frenetic and muscular architecture is like no one else's before or since in the world. His masterpieces were the Pennsylvania Academy of the Fine Arts (1872–76), the Hockley House (1875) and the Furness Building at the University of Pennsylvania (1888–90). Only one building of this period in Philadelphia can stand with his work: John McArthur Jr's **City Hall** (1871–1901; p70), one of the greatest masonry buildings in the country and a highly personal version of the French Second Empire style.

Around the turn of the 20th century, Philadelphia took part in the national flowering of academic and Beaux Arts architecture. National firms like Burnham & Co and McKim, Mead and White built excellent buildings in the city – respectively, the Girard Trust Co (1905–08) and stately department store **John Wanamaker's** (1902–11; p155). The most important buildings of this time were the two great museums. The University Museum (1893–1926) was a collaboration of many of the city's finest architects: Wilson Eyre, Frank Miles Day and Cope & Stewardson. Even more impressive, though, was Horace Trumbauer's masterpiece, the **Philadelphia Museum of Art** (1916–28; p77).

Philadelphia was not a major player in Modernism, although it did contribute one early masterpiece: Howe and Lescaze's **Philadelphia Savings Fund Society (PSFS) building** (p99), one of the earliest office towers in the country. Philadelphia had nothing comparable until 1964, when IM Pei built his Society Hill Towers as part of planner Edmund Bacon's project to revive that flagging district; this achievement was much more successful than his efforts at Penn Center.

The greatest recent contribution to Philadelphia's architecture is Rafael Viñoly's new **Kimmel Center** (p70), a building that soundly characterizes the current compromise between architectural modernism and its postmodern critics. Only time will tell if the Kimmel Center can hold its own with the monumental and civic-minded tradition of its near neighbors, McArthur's City Hall and Furness' Academy of the Fine Arts.

## Row Houses

William Penn's original plan for the city instructed that every house should be placed 'in the middle of its plat, as to the breadth way of it, that so there may be ground on each side for gardens or orchards'; even a passing acquaintance with Philadelphia's row houses will convince you that not all of Penn's rules were followed to the letter.

As the cities of America first grew and had to house ever greater numbers of people, they had two European models to choose from: the English city, with its continuous rows of individual houses, and the Continental city, with its development of the multiple-dwelling apartment house. During colonial times the decision was a snap, and the major cities of Boston, New York and Philadelphia all followed the English style. Yet in the 19th century almost every American city switched over to the Continental-style apartment house, such as the tenement houses of New York. Of the biggest cities, Philadelphia alone stuck to the row house, which has since become the emblem of the city's typical streetscape. (Next was Baltimore, and some smaller places like Richmond, Virginia, followed Philly's lead.)

Look for three major types of row house: old individual and double houses, monumental rows and, as you move toward the edges, the smaller and later worker's row houses. The best individual houses are in Old City and especially on Society Hill, with its outstanding collection of late-18th-century brick houses. New York and Boston once also looked like this, but they've built office towers and tenements where all their 18th-century houses once stood. (Sorry, Boston, Society Hill was all built when Beacon Hill was still a cow pasture.)

By the mid-19th century, individually financed houses gradually gave way to whole speculative rows, where at times a whole block of houses would be built at once to make an impressive, unified effect. These rows, common in the Center City from about 9th St on, are usually of three stories plus a raised basement and are made of brick or brownstone. A famous example is architect TU Walter's Portico Row (1831), on the south side of Spruce St between 9th and 10th Sts.

Just beyond the center and extending in all directions is a landscape full of late-19th-century and early-20th-century row houses, sometimes built individually and sometimes built in seemingly endless identical profusion. These are typically narrower than the more monumental row houses of Center City and are often only two stories plus a raised basement. They are sometimes built of brick and sometimes of wood. Beneath their seeming monotony, these houses contain a wealth of detail and personality. Small as they often are, they sure beat the tenement houses they were up against, and they alone continued the old English tradition of urbanism in major American cities.

# THEATER

Although it's often overshadowed by New York City, Philadelphia's charged theater scene deserves attention. You'll be engaged and rewarded by performances at the **Arden** (p126) and **Wilma** (p127) theaters, both of which are thriving under stellar artistic direction. Each of these theaters stages avant-garde and contemporary work in addition to more staid revivals. North of Center City, find the **Freedom Theatre** (p126), whose annual production of *Black Nativity* pleases crowds in a mansion once owned by Philadelphian thespian Edwin Forrest.

The fairy-tale work of the **Mum Puppettheatre** (p126) combines the realms of fantasy, beauty and darkness to create oft-eerie shows that appeal to both children and adults. If it happens to be playing in town, absolutely do not miss a show of the local **Pig Iron Theatre Company** (p127), whose bizarre combinations of vaudeville, clowning and silence result in something between hilarity and surrealism.

One word of caution: look before you leap at the **Walnut Street Theatre** (p127). While it does hold the honorable distinction of being the longest-operating theater in the country, shows seen here can sometimes be second-rate. Read a review before making an investment on a ticket.

# CLASSICAL MUSIC & OPERA

Classical music in Philadelphia is exciting. Excellence persists at the **Philadelphia Chamber Music Society** (p129), the **Philadelphia Orchestra** (p129) and with the students at the **Curtis Institute** (p129). The orchestra and the Chamber Music Society perform in the brand-new **Kimmel Center** (p129), a beautiful and acoustically superior venue that dominates the Avenue of the Arts in terms of both its size and in the variety and quality of the acts that play inside. In the summer, outdoor performances occur at the **Mann Center** (p129).

The best thing about the Philadelphia opera scene is the late Mario Lanza (who managed to combine the uncombinable: movie stardom and opera singing). That said, while the **Opera Company of Philadelphia** (p129) has two excellent venues in which to perform – the Kimmel Center, with its stellar acoustics, and the **Academy of Music** (p69), with its stellar opulence – it consistently has trouble staging decent shows. Unless some unusual programming happens, a visitor's best bet is to skip the city's signature opera company and listen to a recital at the Curtis Institute or check out one of the **Delaware Valley Opera Company's** (p129) informal summer shows on the lawn of a Wissahickon Park mansion.

# DANCE

Of its dozens of dance companies, Philadelphia has several that demand attention. The world-class **Pennsylvania Ballet** (p128) consistently stages awe-inspiring performances with some pieces of the contemporary variety and others like the *Nutcracker*. The meritorious troupe dances in the beautiful Academy of Music.

Internationally known, **Philadanco!** (p128) is a troupe that began in Philadelphia in the 1970s. It features many of the country's leading African American dancers and is a resident company at the Kimmel Center. The modern dance accomplished by this group is highly sought after, thus their touring absence from the city for most of the year. Catch them if you can.

Seeing dance can be a tricky business, since most companies and venues put on shows intermittently and they last for only a few days. Be sure to check the schedules of the **Painted Bride** (p63), Wilma, Kimmel Center, **Annenberg Center** (p128), the Academy of Music, the **University of Pennsylvania** (p87) and the Fringe Festival to see what's what. When skimming the listings, make a note to look for performances by **Koresh** (p128), a small Philadelphia company that puts on some sweetly choreographed avant-garde stuff.

## Philly Fringe Festival

Nicely resisting urges to swap out Fs for Phs (as Philadelphians often do), the **Fringe Festival** ( ☎ 215-413-9006; www.pafringe.org) transforms Old City into a terrain packed with every kind of artistic spectacle. Over 700 artists – thespians, dancers, musicians, painters, poets and freaks – inhabit the neighborhood for two weeks in August and September, performing wherever space allows. Whether in the basement of a crumbly warehouse, a synagogue, a professional theater or on the sidewalk, expect to see nearly everything. A mime? No problem. The Tiny Ninja Theater Company performing *MacBeth?* Done. Raunchy late-night cabarets? Please do not worry; your back has been covered.

The festival is a great way to check out local hip-hop and theater troupes, such as ToTM Rd and the Pig Iron Theater Company. Performances, of which there are dozens each day, range from super-serious to completely frivolous, and many are excellent for children.

# LIVE MUSIC

While Philly produces noises of all kinds – it's even home to a goth label, Ferrett Records – the town is most famous for its jazz culture, the Philly Soul Sound of the '70s and, today, its contributions to hip-hop. We should also mention that doo-wop used to be a big deal in South Philly (and Mario Lanza still is).

## JAZZ

Philly's been into jazz since the genre's earliest days. Two of the scene's earliest notables include Eddie Lang, who sometimes played behind Bing Crosby, and Joe Venuti. Post-WWII Philadelphia saw scads of greats emerge, particularly African Americans associated with the bebop movement. Dizzy Gillespie, Philly Joe Jones, John Coltrane, Grover Washington Jr, Doc Gibbs and Stanley Clarke represent only a partial list and give insight into Philly's significance for the development of jazz.

The legacy lives on in formal programming by the folks at the Kimmel Center, the **Clef Club** (p139) and Painted Bride, as well as in numerous smoky clubs throughout the city. See the Entertainment chapter for more information.

## THE 'PHILLY SOUND' & R&B

The 1970s saw what has become known as the 'Philly Sound' popularize R&B throughout the nation. Groups like the Temptations, Harold Melvin & the Blue Notes, the O'Jays, Patti LaBelle, Dusty Springfield, the Delfonics and others began producing hit after chart-breaking hit. The defining players who created this new sound were African American–owned Philadelphia International Records and Sigma Studios (still active in Philadelphia). What differentiated the Philly Sound from other kinds of R&B was complicated layering of vocals, stirring melodies and complex instrumentation that often involved several dozen musicians. The music they produced, rooted in soul music, was exceptionally rich and served as a bridge to the evolution of disco.

According to Sigma, the other factor that shaped the Philly Sound was the circumstances of the recording. All the musicians would play simultaneously, in the same room, with all microphones recording not only the instrument to which it was dedicated, but also everything else. Now that's some rich-sounding noise.

## HIP-HOP

Philly's contributions to hip-hop go way beyond Will Smith and DJ Jazzy Jeff. The Roots are the city's current incarnation of respectable superstardom, and the recent work of syrupy Boyz II Men represents Philadelphia's attempts at the other end of the star spectrum.

Though these famous groups are on everyone's radar, many more lesser-known talents perform and record throughout the city. Musiq Soulchild, Jill Scott, Jaguar Wright, Eve and others are currently active in Philadelphia, and several clubs have dedicated hip-hop evenings. Among the most highly regarded are Black Lily and Beat Society, both held at the **Five Spot** (p141) in Old City. Black Lily hosts emerging female hip-hop talents and has

### Top 10 Philly CDs

- *The Ultimate Blue Notes* – Harold Melvin & the Blue Notes. The core group of early '70s soul, this band formed the bedrock of Philly Sound.
- *The Ultimate O'Jays* – O'Jays. This recent collection of another classic Philly R&B band makes you look cool.
- *Philadelphia Songs* – Denison Witmer. Some local alt-rock hipsters claim this evokes the city's mood better than any recent album.
- *Greatest Hits* – DJ Jazzy Jeff & the Fresh Prince. Aristotle, step aside. Without Philadelphia we would never have learned that 'Parents Just Don't Understand.'
- *I Love Rock'n'Roll* – Joan Jett. Don't mess around with a hits collection; go straight for the first number-one album of the Czaress of Eastern Pennsylvania rock.
- *Greatest Hits* – Patti LaBelle. Enough said.
- *Philadelphia* – Neil Young. From the soundtrack to the movie, this is the best CD with the city's name in the title.
- *Legacy – Greatest Hits Collection* – Boyz II Men. Sure it's hokey and dated, but hey, it's BOYZ II MEN!
- *Things Fall Apart* – Roots. Check out this classic hip-hop album from 1999.
- *Young Americans* – David Bowie. Davy cleaned off his glam makeup for this mid-'70s Philadelphia-inspired album. When Davy does it, it has to be cool.

won national regard. Beat Society showcases producers, who sometimes battle each other. Largely, Philly hip-hop distinguishes itself from the old-school gangsta work coming out of New York by being a little more experimental and more willing to take risks at live shows. Even so, Philadelphia has a bit of an exaggerated inferiority complex when it compares itself to its northern neighbor.

# ROCK

Unfortunately, Philly's rock scene isn't as active as its hip-hop or DJ worlds. Some blame the lack of venues and the corporate control of those that do exist; others note that ambitious bands make the move to New York to get noticed. That said, several excellent venues exist, particularly counter-cultural **R5 Productions** (p140), one of the few non–Clear Channel spots; **North Star** (p140), a small, pretty club booking bands like Bishop Allen; **The Fire** (p140), a rockin' dive bar; and the dirty **Khyber** (p140), where the Strokes were in residence when they made it big.

Though it's been a while since a Philly band garnered national attention, current local favorites include An Albatross, the Trouble with Sweeney and Laguardia. Rock fans should be sure to check out the listings in our Entertainment chapter, and for truly underground sounds, keep your eyes peeled for flyers advertising last-minute warehouse shows.

# FILM & TV

In part because so much of its architectural heritage is preserved, Philadelphia has been used to film numerous movies that take place elsewhere. The Eddie Murphy hit *Trading Places* (set in New York) did much of its shooting here, as did *Beloved*, an Oprah Winfrey vehicle (set in Cincinnati). Martin Scorsese's *The Age of Innocence*, starring Michelle Pfeiffer, pretended Philly's Academy of Music was a New York opera house.

While Philadelphia has provided a great backdrop for many movies, a very tender few actually take place here. Among them are *Rocky,* directed by John Avildsen and written by Sylvester Stallone, the uplifting story of a blue-collar-loser-cum-boxer who surmounts incredible odds.

A less-compelling blue-collar story can be had in 1959's *The Young Philadelphians*, directed by Vincent Sherman, starring Paul Newman as an avaricious social climber (once working-class, now a lawyer) who temporarily forgets his values. *The Philadelphia Story*, directed by George Cukor and filmed in 1940, is a Hollywood classic about Philadelphia's upper crust, featuring a gaggle of stars including Katharine Hepburn, Cary Grant and James Stewart, who won an Oscar for his performance. Considered by some to be exploitative, Jonathan Demme's *Philadelphia* stars Tom Hanks as a gay lawyer, educated at Penn, who suffers injustice, redemption and AIDS before dying.

Between all the time traveling, Terry Gilliam's eerie *Twelve Monkeys,* starring Bruce Willis and Brad Pitt, is all about Philadelphia. Scenes from the future are set beneath the city's empty streets, and a virus killing almost all of the earth's population was released here 25 years earlier. M Night Shyamalan's *The Sixth Sense* of 1999 stars Bruce Willis playing a Philadelphia child psychologist. The muted tones of *The Sixth Sense* gave way to Tarkovsky-esque evocations of the natural in Shyamalan's *Signs,* filmed in Bucks County.

Also check out *Witness*, a Harrison Ford thriller telling the tale of an urban detective protecting an Amish tyke and a love interest while hiding in bucolic Lancaster County. Watch out for that silo!

## Yo, Rocky!

As unoriginal as it sounds, your visit to Philadelphia will be substantially enhanced when accompanied by a viewing of *Rocky*, the city's most famous film. Written by and starring Sylvester Stallone, this classic story of a second-rate, aging Italian American boxer perfectly captures the mood and spirit of Philadelphia – and the American city in general – in the bleak bicentennial year during the dank 1970s: despair, hope for the underdog, resilience and quiet dignity.

When a publicity stunt pits an amateur Rocky Balboa against Apollo Creed, heavyweight champion of the world, the blue-collar Balboa becomes the unlikely symbol and hero of a defeated, depopulated and deindustrializing Philadelphia. The weeks preceding the film's match are full of legendary scenes of our man from South Philly working out on the city's streets: his winter runs through the Italian Market; his ascendance of the steps of the Philadelphia Museum of Art; his beating of frozen carcasses in a meat plant; and the climatic, beautifully choreographed bout in the Spectrum. These scenes plus many others provide a glimpse into an older, grittier version of Philadelphia. The heart-warming movie won an Academy Award for best picture in 1976.

## A Very BiG TeA PaRtY

Back in 1998 Philadelphians watching DUTV (Drexel University's educational access station) witnessed the birth of a scrappy 'alternative lifestyle TV show' that has somehow managed to become popular. This tiny cable access show about 'cooking, crafts and anarchy' first appeared in irregular, unannounced three-minute intervals, later became discovered by the area PBS station (WYBE) and is now broadcast nationally on the Dish Network's Free Speech TV (FSTV). The show, BiG TeA PaRtY, is hosted by a political vegetarian whose colorful clothes, outrageous personality and offbeat humor combine with supremely low-budget props and low-tech support to attract an unlikely mainstream following.

The host, Elizabeth Fiend of the band More Fiends (performing the music behind the show), teaches a diverse audience how to compost, how to organize a clothing swap and how to make veggie cheese steaks (recipe follows, per Ms Fiend's generosity). In show No 13, Fiend explains the nutritional merits of eating chestnuts as well as how to use a digital pitch shifter to talk like Satan. And she does it all while wearing rhinestone glasses, green fakefur and vivid rainbow-oriented dresses that tire your eyes as they sift through competing focal points.

The popularity of the show has made Fiend into a quirky local celebrity. Her bizarre outfits make her instantly recognizable, and she's appeared with weatherman Al Roker as an invited guest on the Travel Channel's 'Roker on the Road.' To join the growing cult following, which includes a pretty diverse range of people, and to learn about the merits of political activism, join Fiend and her friends on their extensive website, www.BiGTeAPaRtY.com, or catch them on Free Speech TV. And be sure to eat your vegetables.

### Elizabeth Fiend's Recipe for Philly Cheese Fakes

This yummy vegetarian Philly cheese steak is made out of wheat meat, a meat substitute invented by Buddhist monks. Make your own wheat meat from wheat gluten or buy it ready-made at the health food store.

1. Thinly slice 1lb of wheat meat, two green peppers and one large onion.
2. Put all on a baking sheet sprayed with olive oil.
3. Mix in a healthy dose of soy sauce, ketchup, garlic powder, sage and a dash of cayenne pepper.
4. Bake for 15 minutes at 350°F, mix it up and bake another 15 minutes.
5. Shape the 'meat' on the baking tray to size of your hoagie rolls.
6. Melt American or vegan cheese on top while lightly toasting the hoagie rolls.
7. To serve, the 'pros' in Philly open the roll and use it to scoop up the 'steak' (only wimps use a spatula).

Several of Hollywood's most prominent celebrities hail from Philadelphia. Bill Cosby, Will Smith and Kevin Bacon were all raised in the area (and Kevin Bacon's dad, an urban planner, helped shape it). Sly Stallone, though born elsewhere, spent many years living in Philly before using it as the gritty setting of *Rocky* (and *Rocky II* and *Rocky III* and *Rocky V*), filmed in a remarkable 28 days.

Though Philly has lately been reduced to being the backdrop for mediocre contemporary television shows, it's imperative for TV and music history buffs to know that Dick Clark's *American Bandstand* originated from the City of Brotherly Love.

# LITERATURE

Philadelphia boasts several contemporary writers who are either from the area or now choose to reside here. Among them is John Edgar Wideman, a tremendously respected author who founded Penn's African American Studies program and wrote a prize-winning novel, *Philadelphia Fire*, about the MOVE firebombing. He's the only author to win the PEN/Faulkner Award twice. Other writers include obnoxious yet likable Neal Pollack, of the McSweeney's crew, and Mat Johnson, whose childhood rearing in sketchier parts of Philly have informed his recent novels. Following are select reviews of some of this group's work, as well as a few other novels set in the area.

*Philadelphia Chickens* (Sandra Boynton and Michael Ford, 2002) – An amazingly cute children's book and CD package that tells the fictive tale of an 'imaginary musical revue' and features songs performed by Kevin Bacon and his brother (both from Philly), Meryl Streep and Eric Stoltz.

*The Corrections* (Jonathan Franzen, 2001) — Winner of the National Book Award in 2001, this dark, grim and sometimes hilarious novel focuses on the mundane foibles of a midwestern suburbanite attempting to reassemble her family for Christmas as her husband dies of Alzheimer's; much of the book takes place in Philadelphia, home to two of her dysfunctional adult children.

*Bee Season* (Myla Goldberg, 2001) — The four members of the Philadelphia Naumann family become weirdly challenged following the unexpected success of 4th-grader Eliza, who suddenly finds herself a competitor in the National Spelling Bee.

*Good in Bed* (Jennifer Weiner, 2001) — This popular chick-lit writer dishes out a story about an overweight reporter and her ex-boyfriend's revealing sex column that's half stupid and corny, and half charmingly entertaining. Read the first five pages and see if you can pass it up.

*The Cattle Killing* (John Edgar Wideman, 1997) — Set during Philadelphia's yellow fever outbreak of 1793, this riveting story tells the tale of African Americans who risked their lives to care for the sick, and were then falsely blamed and murdered for starting the epidemic.

*Philadelphia Fire* (John Edgar Wideman, 1991) — Winner of the PEN/Faulkner Award, this novel features an African American protagonist who returns to the city of his youth to write the gut-wrenching story of the MOVE firebombing.

*Drop* (Mat Johnson, 2000) — Written by a native of Northwest Philly, this is a revealing, funny story about a guy desperate to leave Philadelphia, the city that he hates.

*Benjamin Franklin* (Edmund S Morgan, 2002) — Written by an esteemed Yale historian whose studies involve ongoing archival work with all of Franklin's letters, this biography is both fun to read and academically excellent.

*Benjamin Franklin: An American Life* (Walter Isaacson, 2003) — Published on the heels of Morgan's biography, this bio is a bit longer, and lingers more on the personal details of Franklin's life.

# Food

# Food *by Francine Maroukian*

Many first-time visitors to Philadelphia are astonished to discover such a multifaceted food scene, but what they don't know is that the city's culinary vitality and diversity all come down to this: location, location, location. As one of the largest freshwater ports in the world, Philadelphia was a major hub of production and distribution – 'Workshop of the World' – as well as a key immigration destination. Boatloads of skilled laborers from Eastern and Western Europe as well as East Asia emptied into the city, creating a patchwork of ethnic neighborhoods, each dotted with its own bakers, butchers and corner grocers. This tendency toward small, Mom-and-Pop–style food shops and restaurants still exists today. Philadelphia's unique geographical position – suspended between a fruitful countryside and nearby fresh water, bays and the Atlantic Ocean – also keeps the city supplied with a wide range of quality ingredients.

Philadelphia, frequently the focus of national-magazine attention, also intrigues food mavens because it is a city of culinary contrasts. Although the robust, workingman fare for which Philadelphia is best known has roots in the city's dominant German and Italian heritage (between these two legacies, be prepared to enter a sausage-making mecca), the urban fathers were Francophiles who patterned the city (at least architecturally) on Paris. This explains the city's emphasis on fine dining and continued success of restaurants like **Le Bec-Fin** (p111), Georges Perrier's bastion of five-star French cuisine. On the restaurant's 30th anniversary in 2003, Georges Perrier became the longest continually working French chef-owner in this country.

As in most ethnic communities, food figures heavily into holiday celebrations, particularly in a city where neighborhood and family ties remain strong. The Easter, Thanksgiving and Christmas holiday lines at the **Reading Terminal** (p34) and **Italian Market** (p35) form early, and shoppers systematically check off their long lists: fresh turkeys and smoked hams from neighboring farms, Italian pastries and bread from neighborhood bakeries. In Philadelphia's Chinatown, established in the late 19th century and still a bustling cultural and economic community center, Chinese New Year is celebrated with the same culinary gusto.

## STAPLES & SPECIALTIES

In a city of such diversity, it's only natural to find a wide range of specialty foods. But what makes Philadelphia's regional specialties so remarkable is that many of them are singular experiences. Go ahead

## Best Local Cookbooks

- *City Tavern Cookbook: 200 Years of Classic Recipes from America's First Gourmet Restaurant,* by Walter Staib with Beth D'Addono (1999, Running Press)
- *Georges Perrier Le Bec-Fin Recipes,* by Georges Perrier with Aliza Green (1997, Running Press)
- *Philadelphia Flavor: Restaurant Recipes from the City and Suburbs,* by Connie Correia Fisher et al (2000, Small Potatoes Press)
- *The White Dog Cafe Cookbook: Recipes and Tales of Adventure from Philadelphia's Revolutionary Restaurant,* by Judy Wicks et al (1998, Running Press)
- *The Frog Commissary Cookbook,* by Steven Poses, Anne Clark and Becky Roller (1985, Doubleday)
- *Ceviche: Seafood, Salads, and Cocktails with a Latino Twist,* by Guillermo Pernot (2001, Running Press)
- *Susanna Foo Chinese Cuisine: The Fabulous Flavors and Innovative Recipes of North America's Finest Chinese Cook,* by Susanna Foo (2002, Houghton Mifflin)
- *The Reading Terminal Market Cookbook,* by Ann Hazan et al (1997, Camino Books)
- *The Philadelphia Italian Market Cookbook: The Tastes of South Ninth Street,* by Celeste A Morello (1999, Jefferies & Manz)
- *The Metropolitan Bakery Cookbook: Artisan Breads, Pastries, and Desserts from Philadelphia's Premier Bakery,* by James Barrett and Wendy Smith Born (2003, Rodale Press)

and tell anyone who lives there that you had a cheese steak in some other city, and they'll set you straight: Philadelphia cheese steaks can't be duplicated. There's no sense trying to find one, nevertheless eat one, anywhere else in the country.

# CHEESE STEAKS

Cheese steaks – like the ones from **Tony Luke's** (Map pp220-1; ☎ 215-551-5725; www.tonylukes.com; 39 E Oregon Ave; ✆ 6am-midnight Mon-Thu, 6am-2am Fri & Sat) – are wrapped in foil, brown-bagged and sold through windows at stands. While they are not fast food, they are definitely quick eating – it's the discussions about where to find the best that are endless. The fact that cheese steaks 'belong' to Philadelphia is the only thing that everyone in the city agrees upon. The quest for the 'best' is more contentious, having to do with 'roots,' neighborhood loyalty and other intangible issues – some too subtle, too subjective to explain. And then there's the patience required to scrutinize every detail: is the roll crusty enough (without being brittle) and the interior soft but still substantial? Should the meat be thinly sliced or almost shaved? If shaved, should the American cheese be chopped into the meat with the side of the spatula (sort of like scrambled eggs), or should the cheese cover the meat to melt and ooze down? Is it better to lay the melted meat/cheese combo in the roll using the spatula, or use the partially split roll like a baseball mitt to pick it up? Luckily, this is the kind of talking that can be done with your mouth full.

# HOAGIES

Just when you thought you could stop obsessing over a sandwich, a second significant example of Philadelphia's culture on a roll enters the picture – hoagies. Named for the Italian factory workers at the Hog Island shipyards who brought the oversized sandwiches for lunch, hoagies are another hot-button topic. But this time, the controversy is not so much about the filling – a layering of Italian sliced meats like prosciutto, sopressata and coppa with provolone, assorted condiments, oil and oregano-flavored vinegar – it's about the roll. The hands-down Philadelphia favorite is from **Sarcone's Bakery** (p117), a 9th St institution and home to what many claim is not only the best bread in the city but in the world. (You can also get a stellar hoagie made with one of these rolls from Sarcone's Deli, a few blocks away.) The arrival of the *Banh mi*, a sort of Vietnamese version of the hoagie (a wheat and rice flour baguette layered with pork and a pickled vegetable mixture) is just another example of the city's cultural diversity and culinary experimentation.

# WATER ICE

Water ice is another Philadelphia phenomenon: a candied syrup (artificial flavors or natural fruit juice) combined with water and sugar and put in a batch freezer to make a dense flavored ice. Typically served in a little paper cup (with a small plastic spoon), water ice is for sale over the counter in small neighborhood spots like **John's** (p116) and available in several standard flavors, like cherry, chocolate and lemon, with a wider variety offered depending on the season and the source.

# TASTYKAKES

There's a reason why Tastykake, another Philadelphia hometown favorite with a national cult following, has been around since 1914: these compact, individually wrapped cakes were one of the earliest convenience foods. A staple in every worker's lunch pail and school kid's brown bag, Tastykakes have a trans-generational nostalgic appeal. From Krimpets and Kandy Kakes to Creamies or Chocolate Cupcakes (topped with chocolate icing that peels right off in one delicious disc when refrigerated), Tastykakes – 'the cake that made mother stop baking' – are still available at every supermarket and corner grocer as well as by mail order (☎ 800-33-TASTY; www.tastykake.com), a great source of comfort to homesick, transplanted Philadelphians everywhere.

# POTATO CHIPS

Fact: potato chips are America's number one savory snack. Fact: Pennsylvania is the country's number one potato chip producer. As a result, Philadelphia, with its easy access to the hub of highways running along the northeast corridor, is situated on the edge of the 'potato chip belt': a network of factories, many family-owned with roots that can be traced to the region's German settlers.

Unlike the potato chips that are available nationally (produced and distributed by snack-food conglomerates with facilities scattered all over the country), potato chips from smaller companies tend to stay within their own locale, making them some of America's last real regional foods. Like other American regional foods (small-batch smokehouse bacon, for example), these chips are seasoned to reflect a regional spice-palate, like Philadelphia's crab boil-spiced chips, a singularly homegrown flavor that seems exotic to those who live outside of the area.

Another aspect of the Philadelphia area's potato chip legacy is kettle chips, a regional development gone national. Instead of a continuous fryer process that automatically turns out a constant stream of 'regular' light, flat chips, kettle chips are made by a slower, batch-by-batch method, to produce what the Amish call a 'hard bite.'

Look for these regional brands on the shelves: Utz, Herr's, Diffenbach's, Nibble Wit Gibbles, Ray and Kay's, Martins, Bickel's and Zerbes. Note: you can even tour the factory at **Herr's** ( ☎ 800-63-SNACK), the family-owned and -operated local brand dominating the Philadelphia market, which makes not only potato chips but pretzels, tortilla chips and other snacks as well.

# MARKETS

You can't be a great food town without great food markets, and Philadelphia has two of the oldest in the country. If there's such a thing as fusion cooking, there has to be 'fusion shopping,' and these markets exemplify the range of Philadelphia's ethnic culinary community.

## READING TERMINAL MARKET

This 75,000-sq-foot collection of 80 stalls, directly descended from Philadelphia's colonial open-air and shed markets, was established in 1892 on the lower level of the great Reading Terminal (home to the largest single arch train shed in the world and renovated as the Pennsylvania Convention Center). This covered **public market** (Map pp222-3; ☎ 215-922-2317; www.readingterminalmarket.org; 12th & Arch Sts; ☺ 8am-6pm Mon-Sat) draws about 90,000 people a week (about 4.8 million a year), and on any given day you can find people shopping for local ingredients like free-range chickens and farmstead cheese, standing in line for lunch options like tacos from 12th St Cantina or a hoagie from Spartaro's, or just roaming the aisles, food-struck. While the market is open year-round, during the growing season, farmers from neighboring communities sell fresh-picked produce (much of it organic) and flowers from the Pennsylvania countryside in carts located around the center court. The court provides seating for about 200; total market seating exceeds 800.

Four of Philadelphia's signature foods can also be found at market booths in their most perfect versions:

**Soft pretzels** – These are not the standard hard-baked variety, although those are also plentiful in this area. Philadelphia soft pretzels, sold at every convenience store as well as by street vendors, are chewy twists of salted baked bread. At Fisher's Soft Pretzels, you can watch the Amish counter women skillfully roll and flip the dough into the familiar winged shape, and then you can eat a pretzel still warm from the oven. You will find none better, anywhere in the city – except maybe at **Center City Pretzel Co** (p116).

**Vanilla ice cream** – Fifth-generation, family-owned and -operated Basset's Ice Cream, the oldest ice cream company in America (established 1861), is the sole remaining original Reading Terminal merchant. In 1893 Basset's opened a store here and moved the production facilities into the basement. The factory has since moved, but you can still sit at the original marble counter and get a double dip of Philadelphia's trademark vanilla, distinguished by the dark specks of ground vanilla bean versus today's commonly used vanilla extract.

**Scrapple** – If you can bring yourself to view scrapple more as a tribute to the ingenuity of Philadelphia's hard-working and frugal farm communities and less as a mixture of pork scraps (and we are talking about all kinds of scraps) and cornmeal mush, it will be easier to enjoy a fried slab alongside some eggs at the market's Down Home Diner.

**Amish specialties** – The market is also a one-stop source for many other Amish specialties: sticky buns, shoofly pie (a spiced concoction of molasses and brown sugar in wet- or dry-bottom versions, so named because the sticky surface of the pie attracted flies), *fastnachts* (a kind of doughnut), farm meats (like Lebanon bologna, a spiced, aged beef bologna), as well as jams, preserves and vegetable relishes like Chow Chow (a pickled mélange).

While at the Reading Terminal Market, don't miss the well-stocked and knowledgably staffed Fosters Gourmet Cookware, the amazing $5 lunch at Little Thai Village, DiNic's roast pork and provolone sandwiches dripping au jus, soothing subgum wonton soup from Sang Kee's, or Hope's Royale cookies – loaded with chocolate, nuts and coconut – from the Pennsylvania General Store. You can even find bread pudding made from Philadelphia's legendary hoagie rolls at Andro's Prepared Foods.

Food – Markets

# ITALIAN MARKET

A historic open-air market and the oldest such market in the country, the Italian Market (p104) is as noted for its food as for native son Rocky Balboa's famous training run along 9th St in the 1976 film *Rocky*. Much is made of the up-in-neon-lights, Vegas-excitement at Pat's (p116) and Geno's (p116) warring cheese steak stands, on the south side of the market and the apparent end point of many collegiate road trips. But the joy of this market is in its 'everyday-ness': shopping for basics like cheese and olives at Di Bruno's and Claudio's, fresh pasta and other red-sauce standards at Talluto's, fresh fish from Anastasi's, and specialties like venison sausage and alligator cutlets at Di Angelo's, a treasure trove of wild game. The new cultural influences in the market show up in Mexican taquerias like La Veracruzana (p117) and Plaza Garibaldi as well as small strip malls of Vietnamese grocers and restaurants on Washington Ave.

Woven into the fabric of the Italian Market are many long-lived family-owned stores. When immigrants took old-world skills and turned them into businesses, they passed down not only their trade but their traditions, and the exchange that comes with selecting and selling food remains a way of expressing that community tie. Not that much has changed in Philadelphia's Italian Market. Vendors hawk wares in the street, and fires blaze from barrels during the winter months. Two family-owned and operated jewels that you don't want to miss are:

**Fiorella Sausage** (Map pp228-9; ☎ 215-922-0506; 817 Christian St btwn 8th & 9th Sts) Fourth-generation brothers Dan and Eddie Fiorella stand behind a low, long wooden counter all day and weigh terrific sweet and hot Italian pork sausage, curling the links into paper-lined boxes. The walls are lined with photographs of the generations who have gone before them (number five waits

## The Remarkable Culinary Collection of Chef Fritz Blank

*Chef de cuisine et proprietaire* Fritz Blank's astounding library and workshop of gastronomy is housed on several floors above **Deux Cheminées** (Map pp222-3; ☎ 215-790-0200; www.deuxchem.com; 1221 Locust St), his classical French restaurant in a Frank Furness–designed townhouse. The library's approximate 12,000 volumes include written manuscripts and rare cookbooks, American home-cooking classics (in all editions), colorful regional books (including 3000 community cookbooks), and hundreds of campy 1940s and '50s ingredient-driven product pamphlets (eg, 'Great America Chefs Cook with Campfire Marshmallows'). You'll also find a wide range of culinary ephemera (old menus and restaurant memorabilia) and contemporary cookbooks that other culinary scholars may dismiss as celebrity-chef novelties. You can spread out at the wide wooden worktables and even use the Xerox machine. Or you can eat in one of the smaller library rooms (for eight to 12 guests) surrounded by about 2500 Italian and French cookbooks, a richly rewarding experience on many levels. Call for an appointment or reservation.

35

in the wings and works on the weekends), but the only counter decoration is a functional antique brass and bronze National cash register (dated 1901). No 'cross merchandising' containers of grated cheese and boxes of dry pasta – these guys sell just sausage.

**Isgro Pasticceria** (Map pp228-9; ☎ 215-923-3092; 1009 Christian St btwn 10th & 11th Sts) You'll be beguiled by the sugary-sweet baking smell hanging in the air, and even more excited when you step inside this pristine, century-old bakery with cannolis, tray after tray of tender butter cookies, and biscotti that have stood the test of time.

# THIRD PLACES

Although Philadelphia is often billed as a city of neighborhoods, even more so it is a city of subcultures. You can see traces of the city's multicultural roots in the proliferation of European-style 'third places' (like the Parisian sidewalk café, Italian gelateria and German biergarten) that have always provided those walk-to refuges between work and home.

## PUB CULTURE

At one time there were over 100 breweries in a section of Philadelphia known as Brewerytown, evidence of the strong German heritage. As an extension of the brewing industry, pubs sprang up all over the city, providing working men with a pint, some cheap hearty food and a little recreation. Further, Philadelphia, home to most of the early American dartboard manufacturers, was the first US city to 'hang a dartboard,' and boasts the oldest dart league in the country.

There are new versions, like **Standard Tap** (p136) and **North 3rd** (p118), but the standard bearer is still **McGillin's Old Ale House** (p132), a picturesque pub set along the slender alley of Drury St with an off-the-beaten-path sense of discovery. Although it is Philadelphia's oldest pub, McGillin's has changed hands only twice since it opened in 1860 – and both times within the same family. As testimony to its authenticity, all the licenses (from 1860 to current) are posted behind the bar. Another wall is covered with signs from downtown department stores that have gone out of business, including the 1910 bronze plaque from John Wanamaker's, the old Woolworth and Gimbel's signs, as well as the original Strawbridge and Clothier 1860 plaster 'seal of confidence,' donated by Francis Strawbridge himself.

## COFFEE CULTURE

In these days of chain coffee shops on every corner, Philadelphia still retains many independently owned coffeehouses, most of them subscribing to the mismatched-furniture-and-scattered-newspaper aesthetic. But the epicenter of the city's coffee subculture is also the chicest: **La Colombe** (p109), a simple but warmly inviting room dominated by a solid wood turn-of-the-century bar, converted into a customized coffee station. With a length of 28ft (or 12 to 14 espresso drinkers, shoulder to shoulder), the bar serves 1200 to 1500 people a day. Partners Jean-Philipe Iberti and Todd Carmichael started their café-cum-roasting-business in 1994 using a 15-kilo Vittoria roaster and now turn out 470 metric tons a year from their Philadelphia factory. With four blends sold nationally, La Colombe is the coffee choice of some of the country's most discriminating chefs, like Daniel Boulud and Jean Georges Vongerichten.

## THE BYOB CULTURE

Since liquor and wine distribution in Pennsylvania is run by the state and restaurateurs pay the same amount as retail customers (with their only discount being the 7% sales tax), it might seem that the BYOB movement grows out of restriction. But it's actually about choice. At **Django** (p116), home to the most sought-after BYOB reservations in town, chef-owners Amy Olexy and Bryan Sikora made a conscious decision not to apply for a liquor license, believing that wine lists can be too confining. Instead, they strive to provide a food forum for customers who wish to bring wine that reflects their personal interests.

Opening a restaurant without the expense of a liquor license and bar inventory requires less start-up money, which can mean fewer – or no – investors to please. As a result, a BYOB is often more of a personal statement for the chef-owner, and in some cases, that statement not only shapes the cuisine but also the culture of the restaurant. At **Dmitri's** (p115), the grandfather of Philadelphia's BYOB movement (and probably still the most popular), located in an old pharmacy, Dmitri Chime's decision to put the kitchen behind the existent counter impacted the menu (by limiting cooking methods) and created a community crossover with the **New Wave Café** (p135), a bar across the street where you can have a drink until your table is ready.

# PHILADELPHIA'S RESTAURANT RENAISSANCE

In the early 1970s Philadelphia began to undergo what is often described as a 'restaurant renaissance' – but 'explosion' might be a better word. Although the city was already home to a richly diverse food scene, small quirky restaurants (like Frog, Astral Plane, Wildflowers and Lickety Split) started to spring up in old brownstones and renovated storefronts. With mismatched chairs and china, limited seating and adventurous seasonal menus, these restaurants broke with the traditional model of fine dining to become part of a bigger culinary revolution. Drawing on Philadelphia's wide range of ethnic ingredients, these chefs – many of them owners as well – took far-flung flavors and brought them together in experimental ways, creating what we now call 'fusion' cuisine, while a generation of Americans who had been exposed to European travel – the tip of the baby boomer iceberg – began to understand that fancy food could be found in funky places.

There are a handful of people credited with starting this renaissance, but most roads lead back to Peter von Stark, a local chef who met chef Georges Perrier on a trip to France. Von Stark brought Perrier back to Philadelphia and together they opened La Panetiere in a small townhouse on Spruce St. Later, when La Panetiere moved to Locust St, Perrier stayed in the old location and opened **Le Bec-Fin** (p111), his award-winning French dining establishment (which later moved again, to its current home on Walnut St).

But the emotional undercurrent of the renaissance is best explained by Steve Poses, who, at age 26, invested $35,000 to open Frog, one of the early entries in Philadelphia's restaurant renaissance: 'I thought that food was a good way to define a community, and I wanted to create a place for people to come together.'

Frog's church-pew seating, recycled green marble table tops (salvaged from an old soda fountain) and equally eclectic fusion French menu informed the city's dining scene for the next decade, and this influence can still be found in the smaller restaurants of today, particularly owner-operated BYOBs.

The success of innovators like Poses and their ability to draw suburban diners into the city also attracted restaurateurs with more money to spend. The next wave of places was more polished, like Neil Stein's glorious adaptive re-use of an art deco brokerage house for **Striped Bass** (p111), Mark **Vetri's** (p113) eponymous townhouse location, and the newest sleek jewel box, **Salt** (Map pp222-3; ☎ 215-545-1990; 253 S 20th St).

Beyond the food, a major factor in drawing national attention to Philadelphia's dining scene today is the diversity of design, as exemplified by Stephen Starr. But as different as these new restaurants might look, their roots are firmly planted in the renovated storefronts of the city's earliest renaissance.

## The Book & the Cook

Once a year (usually around the third week of March; visit www.thebookandthecook.com for exact dates), Philadelphia hosts a 10-day celebration of collaborations between cookbook authors and restaurateurs. A menu is selected from each cookbook and prepared by the partnering restaurant's staff under the supervision of the author, who then does a meet-and-greet during the meal. Although cookbooks are available at each location, the result is much more intimate than a standard book signing. With about 75 collaborations, food writers, workers and lovers create a citywide culinary community, with each restaurant hosting what feels like an individual dinner party with each cookbook author being the guest of honor. Some of the past stellar collaborations have been between Craig Claiborne and **Le Bec-Fin** (p111), Bobby Flay and Jack's Firehouse, and Lydia Bastianich and Savona.

# All-Starr Weekend

It's possible to visit Philadelphia for a long weekend, eat each meal in a different Stephen Starr restaurant, and still have a few left over. Starr, a former concert promoter and comedy club owner, is a supercharged combination of urban planner and party planner, opening restaurants with such appeal that he is able to draw suburbanites into parts of the city they have never seen before. His witty design sense is on display in every project, typically in the form of inventive lighting that verges on magical illumination.

Starr, who likens himself to a music industry 'A-and-R' guy, is a pop-culture fan and frequently describes his restaurants in terms of movies and television shows. Although each production is a flawless reincarnation of a certain period or place, these are not theme restaurants – Starr is more committed to design than that. With an approach that is both cerebral and artistic, Starr creates complete environments. Although he attends to every detail (right down to the branded, wrapped chopsticks at POD), the showman in him doesn't want you to see the effort. There's a playfulness and a lightness attributable to Starr's theatrical background. You may be going to Oz, but you rarely see the Wizard.

## Friday Night

**POD** (p121) If George and Jane Jetson opened an Asian fusion place, it would look like POD: a sushi conveyor belt, molded rubber furniture that lights up when you sit down, and poured high-gloss white resin walls. But it is surprisingly comfortable as well as quiet (thanks to the foam ceiling). The waitstaff's orange/powder blue uniform is by designer Todd Oldham.

## Friday Late Night

**El Vez** (Map pp222-3; ☎ 215-928-9800; 121 S 13th St) Starr describes El Vez as 'a gritty East LA-meets-Tijuana Taxi vibe.' The kitschy decor features Day of the Dead images, a homage to '70s Cha Cha sensation Charo, and low-rider–inspired button-tufted velvet upholstered booths. Margaritas are shaken tableside.

## Saturday Lunch

**Continental** (p106) Starr took the retro route with a stainless steel diner retooled as a martini bar and a mod, '60s *Catch Me If You Can* look: olive-shaped halogen lamps are suspended over the booths, and the olive green banquettes have pimento-red trim.

## Saturday Night

**Buddakan** (p107) Starr makes a play on East-West culture in a former post office, using smooth dark wood in a way that recalls a boardroom more than a dining room. There's a long communal table suggestive of a conference table, with a 10ft, gold leaf Buddha seated at the head, glowing like some sort of mystical CEO.

## Saturday Late Night

**Tangerine** (Map pp226-7; ☎ 215-627-5116; 232 Market St) Part nightclub, part restaurant, totally fabulous. A long candlelit entrance leads to a seductive inner-sanctum dining room, where light filtered through hanging filigreed lamps turns the ceiling into a starry night sky, and votive candles, tucked into dozens of tiny niches, flicker like the twinkling lights of a distant city.

## Sunday Brunch

**Jones** (p113) Imagine that the Brady Bunch went over to Rob and Laurie Petrie's for Sunday brunch – that's Jones. Rough stone walls, swivel chairs, wall-to-wall carpet and a fieldstone fireplace, plus a Starr touch: many of the tables are fitted with reassuring little nightlights.

## Sunday Dinner

**Alma de Cuba** (p109) The bar scene is so hot it's almost tropical: a strategically lit, painted tin ceiling, visible through the black wood slats (like the roof of tobacco-drying barns), creates a saturated red glow, and hazy black and white images of Cuban street scenes are projected onto the white walls.

## Whenever You Can

**Morimoto** (p113) There is no finer convergence of Starr power than this collaboration with Iron Chef Masaharu Morimoto and designer Karim Rashid. The subject of a James Beard–award-winning Food Network special (documenting every step from conception and construction to the opening), Morimoto is stunningly beautiful, with surfaces so round and smooth that the result is almost liquid. Long glass-top tables are aglow with electric candle lamps and framed by opalescent benches with interior tube lighting that shifts from blue and green to fuchsia, causing the entire restaurant to change color under an undulating bamboo ceiling.

**Angelina** (Map pp226-7; ☎ 215-925-6889; 706 Chestnut St) Starr is at his opulent, over-the-top best, from the floating ceiling bearing a reproduction of Giorgione's reclining nude, *Sleeping Venus*, to the patterned toile wallpaper and giant framed Italian landscapes hanging over each booth.

**Striped Bass** (p111) In December 2003, Starr bought Neil Stein's famed seafood restaurant, Striped Bass. According to news reports, he's planning on keeping the name and decor (with a few cosmetic touch-ups) and will reopen early in 2004.

# History

# History *by Ron Avery*

Probably no American city is so drenched in history. The scars left by cannon and musket balls that flew during the 1777 Battle of Germantown are still visible on the walls of the colonial mansion known as Cliveden. A few blocks away, guides point out the faded bloodstains of a British general who bled to death on the floor of another historic house.

In Philadelphia, some homeowners have archaeological digs in their own backyards. Worshippers at Kesher Israel Synagogue sit where Vice President John Adams once listened to a lecture series by scientist Joseph Priestly; the synagogue was then a church. And it's not a joke when a small child asks, 'Guess what president's house I live in?' – he and his family do indeed live in the house once occupied by former Virginia congressman and fourth US president James Madison.

There are an estimated 2000 buildings still standing from the 18th century. Countless 19th-century homes and commercial buildings survive. About 150 museum houses are open to the public in the city and surrounding suburbs. There's no way to ignore history in this town.

## RECENT PAST

Back in 1903, muckraking journalist Lincoln Steffens characterized Philadelphia as 'corrupt and contented.' Exactly 100 years later, Philadelphia voters seemed to reaffirm Steffens' assessment by overwhelmingly reelecting a mayor undergoing an FBI investigation. The accidental discovery of an FBI bugging device in the City Hall office of Mayor John Street only weeks prior to the November 2003 election simply made Street a more sympathetic figure to Philly voters, some of whom suspected a Republican conspiracy. The largest unions supported Street, as did the national Democratic Party, which sent former president Bill Clinton and former vice president Al Gore to Philadelphia to drum up support for Street. A potential disaster became an asset for the mayor.

Regardless, Democrat Street was expected to win because 75% of all registered voters in the city are Democrats. The last Republican mayor was elected in 1948. One-party rule is an old tradition in Philadelphia. In Steffens' day an all-powerful GOP machine ruled the city with no opposition. Republicans even paid rent for Democratic headquarters – just to maintain the appearance of a rival. Fifty years ago everything flip-flopped when the Democrats took over.

While Philadelphia's political history is a bit sordid, its prominence in American history is a source of great civic pride.

## FROM THE BEGINNING

Philadelphia was a planned city, born in 1682. It was the creation of idealistic English Quaker William Penn, who borrowed the name from antiquity; it's Greek and means 'brotherly love.' The name *Pennsylvania* honors Penn's father, Admiral Sir William Penn, and was chosen by King Charles II. Penn hated the name – he suspected (correctly) that everyone would assume he had immodestly named the colony in his own honor.

But before delving into Penn's life and the Quaker philosophy that guided the founding of his colony and capital city, we must first give some space to prior denizens of the region.

| TIMELINE | 1681 | 1682 | 1700 |
|---|---|---|---|
| | British King Charles II grants William Penn 45,000 sq miles of land and names it Pennsylvania, in honor of Penn's father. | Penn arrives in the new colony aboard the ship *Welcome*, one of 23 shiploads of immigrants to arrive in the first year. | There are more than 2000 residents in Philadelphia. |

The first inhabitants were the Lenape Indians, a generally peaceful people who inhabited parts of New York, New Jersey, Pennsylvania and Delaware. Like other tribes, the Lenape were decimated by European diseases and pushed ever westward by settlers and government policy. Now calling themselves 'the Delaware Indians,' remnants of the tribe are settled in Oklahoma and Canada.

## DUTCH & SWEDISH COLONIES

The first Europeans to claim the region were the Dutch, who made it part of their New Netherland colony. They attempted to create a settlement in 1631 on the Delaware Bay, near the present site of Lewes, Delaware. It lasted less than a year. All 28 Dutch settlers were massacred by the Indians in a dispute that has never been totally clear to historians. After this bloody debacle, Dutch colonial effort was concentrated along the Hudson River and Manhattan Island. Still, Dutch fur traders did visit the area frequently.

The vacuum along the Delaware River was exploited by Sweden, which was looking to get into the colonization game. So smack in the middle of New Netherland, the Swedes created New Sweden.

In 1638 about 60 to 70 Swedes sailed up the Delaware and built a fort and small settlement at the present site of Wilmington, Delaware. Needless to say the Dutch were not happy about this development. During the next 17 years, the two sides fought several bloodless 'wars' over who owned the land along the Delaware River. A show of force by either the Dutch or the Swedes always led to a quick surrender.

The problem for Sweden was not simply Dutch claims to the area – Swedes just didn't want to immigrate to such a remote wilderness. Land was plentiful in Sweden, and there were no persecuted religious groups longing for a place to worship in peace. No more than 500 Swedes immigrated, and most of those were petty criminals, army deserters, debtors or malcontented Finns under Swedish domination. These settlers did have large families, so there were probably more than 1000 Swedes spread along the Delaware River when Penn arrived.

One reminder of the Swedes today is Gloria Dei (Olde Swedes') Church in the Queen's Village section of South Philadelphia. Dating to 1700, this perfectly preserved gem is the oldest church in Pennsylvania. Another lasting contribution of the Swedes and Finns was the introduction of the traditional notched-log cabin to the New World.

## WILLIAM PENN & THE QUAKERS

With New England developing in the north, and Maryland and Virginia to the south, Britain consolidated its North American holdings by taking the Dutch areas with a show of naval force. In 1664 a large British fleet appeared in the waters off Manhattan. The Dutch surrendered without firing a shot, and all Dutch lands in North America – including what are now New Jersey, Delaware and Pennsylvania – came under English rule.

Meanwhile in Great Britain, a new religious sect calling itself the Religious Society of Friends was rapidly gaining converts and infuriating the establishment. Founder George Fox sprang from humble origins, but he was a charismatic figure and a powerful speaker. Fox urged a return to 'primitive Christianity' without clergy, dogma, ceremony or the trappings of churches. He preached that there was a spark of God within every man; therefore war and killing were forbidden, and all men were equal – adherents refused to bow or remove their hats to social superiors. Worship consisted of silent meditation in plain, unadorned meetinghouses. The name 'Quaker' was used as a term of derision by detractors, but the Friends embraced it. There are still more than 100 Friends meetinghouses in the region but no more than 15,000 Quakers in today's metropolitan population of five million.

| 1701 | 1723 | 1732 | 1774 |
|------|------|------|------|
| Penn issues liberal Charter of Privileges, granting religious freedom. | Benjamin Franklin, a 17-year-old runaway from Boston, arrives in Philadelphia. | Construction begins on the Pennsylvania State House (Independence Hall). | The First Continental Congress meets at Carpenters' Hall to protest British policies. |

This simple faith based on pacifism and equality captivated William Penn, the 23-year-old son of a wealthy high-ranking British naval officer. To his father's dismay, Penn became a loud and eloquent spokesman and leading Quaker. During his life, Penn wrote and published more than 100 pamphlets, tracts and books, mostly on religion. He was jailed or fined on several occasions for his public preaching of Quakerism.

When his father died, Penn inherited estates in England and Ireland as well as an IOU for about £16,000 that the admiral had loaned to King Charles II. In 1681 Penn petitioned the crown for a grant of land in America to discharge the debt. It didn't take long for the king to agree. Penn was granted 45,000 sq miles of mostly forested land stretching from the west bank of the Delaware River to the Allegheny Mountains, making the 37-year-old Quaker the world's largest private landowner.

It would be wrong to think that Penn sought the colony only as a refuge for persecuted Quakers. In fact, Friends were free to practice their faith in tolerant Rhode Island and newly founded Carolina. Two Quakers already owned half of New Jersey, and Penn was involved in drawing up a liberal constitution for the colony of West Jersey.

But Penn was personally ambitious and wanted to engineer his own 'holy experiment,' putting Quaker principles into everyday practice. He was a good real estate promoter, selling land to fellow Quakers, speculators and persecuted German religious sects. But he was a poor money manager and thus spent most of the next 36 years until his death (1718) in England trying to get his finances in order while ruling Pennsylvania through a series of appointed deputies. One of his biggest headaches was a border dispute with the Calvert family of Maryland. That dispute ended 81 years later when two British surveyors, Charles Mason and Jeremiah Dixon, laid out a 230-mile dividing line.

Despite all his woes, including a stint in debtor's prison and a crippling stroke, the proprietor of Pennsylvania left an indelible mark on the colony. Most important was Penn's commitment to religious tolerance and the promotion of what is known today as 'diversity.' Colonists poured into Pennsylvania from England, Wales, Germany and Ireland. The melting pot included French Huguenots, Scotch-Irish and handfuls of Swiss, Italians, Dutch and Swedes. By the time of the Revolutionary War, Philadelphia had more than a dozen Protestant churches, two Catholic churches, a Jewish congregation and many Quaker meetinghouses in and around the city.

Further, Penn was a rare colonist who saw Native Americans as 'noble and intelligent' rather than 'godless savages.' His dealings with the Indians were so fair that Pennsylvania enjoyed an unprecedented 70 years of peace with the native tribes.

Another Penn contribution was Philadelphia's pioneering design – it was the first American city laid out on a grid pattern of wide, straight streets crossing at right angles.

# BENJAMIN FRANKLIN & THE GROWTH OF THE CITY

Philadelphia grew rapidly from a muddy quagmire to a large, cosmopolitan city. Factors behind its rapid growth included the city's busy port and its hard-working Quaker entrepreneurs. (It is often said that 'the Quakers came to America to do good and they did well.') The region was blessed with wonderfully fertile soil that made eastern Pennsylvania and Delaware the first 'bread basket of America.' Philadelphia was also blessed with a young runaway from Boston named Ben Franklin.

One cannot underestimate Franklin's endless contributions to his adopted city. The list includes America's first hospital, fire company, fire insurance company, lending library and scientific think tank (the American Philosophical Society). They all continue to this day. He successfully pushed for street paving, street lighting (with whale-oil lamps) and street cleaning. Franklin was behind the establishment of militia and a nondenominational college that grew to become the University of Pennsylvania.

| 1775 | 1776 | 1777 | 1787 |
|---|---|---|---|
| Fighting breaks out in Massachusetts as the Second Continental Congress convenes at the State House. | Independence is declared by the Continental Congress meeting in the State House. | Nine-month occupation of city by the British Army begins. The Continental Army winters at Valley Forge. | The US Constitution is hammered out by delegates meeting at Independence Hall. |

## The Inventor

It was 6am and, because his 'domestic negligently omitted, the evening before, to close the shutters,' Ben Franklin was amazed at the bright sunshine flooding into his Paris bedroom. In an amusing essay in the *Journal of Paris,* the American diplomat mathematically calculated the enormous savings in candles if only the 100,000 late-sleeping residents of Paris would rise with the sun and retire to sleep earlier. We're still saving candles, although it was decades after Ben's early-to-bed-early-to-rise suggestion that America finally adopted his bright idea of daylight saving time.

Perhaps no American before or since can match Ben Franklin for the quality and quantity of his new ideas, practical suggestions, scientific discoveries and inventions.

Franklin loved swimming; he even gave swimming lessons as a young man. Not surprisingly, he invented swim flippers for his feet and paddlelike extensions for his hands. Long before his kite-and-key experiment, Ben became the world's first windsurfer. While floating on his back, he used a large kite to pull him across a lake.

He found it tedious to put on one pair of spectacles for reading and to constantly have to switch to another pair of eyeglasses for distant viewing. So he invented the bifocal lens.

For a long time Franklin pondered fireplaces. Wood was becoming scarce and expensive around growing American cities. Worse, most of the heat in a fireplace goes right up the chimney. Franklin observed that those sitting in front of a fire have their fronts 'scorched' and their rears 'froze.' His solution, of course, was the invention of the Pennsylvania fireplace, better known as the Franklin stove. It recirculates the heated air, warms an entire room and saves loads of firewood. In addition 'it cures most smoky chimneys and thereby preserves both the eyes and furniture.' Soon wise consumers everywhere were using the Franklin stove.

Franklin was a man with an insatiable curiosity. Standing at the rear of a large crowd that was listening to a famous street preacher, he wondered how many people could hear the human voice. He backed up until he could no longer hear the speaker. With a few measurements and some quick math, Franklin proved that 30,000 people can hear a good loud voice.

Franklin's brain also pondered the cause of the common cold, the origin of marsh gas, the behavior of oil on water, lead poisoning, a cure for insomnia and why a canal boat moves faster when the water gets deeper.

Fascinated by electricity, he became the world's top scientist, endeavoring to figure out what the mysterious force was and how it could be used. His first practical application for electricity was killing turkeys and chickens. He said electric slaughtering made their flesh quite tender. Franklin gave us many of the words we use today in electricity: positive, negative, conductor, nonconductor, battery, grounding. His kite-and-key experiment led to the lightning rod, which has saved uncounted thousands of buildings. Proving that lightning was, indeed, a form of electricity was a giant step toward scientific thinking. Franklin contradicted practically every clergyman in America, who preached that lightning strikes on a house or a person were God's punishment for some hidden sin.

By the late 1760s Philadelphia was the largest city in North America, with about 25,000 residents. It was the colonial center of the arts, science and medicine. Colonial Philadelphia was a good place for ambitious 'leather apron' craftsmen like Franklin, as well as progressive thinkers, religious minorities and those seeking to make their fortune in trade and commerce.

# BIRTHPLACE OF THE AMERICAN REVOLUTION

As tensions mounted with England over its taxation policies, Philadelphia leaders, including lawyer John Dickinson, articulated American grievances. Franklin was dispatched to London to try and heal the rift. In the fall of 1774, delegates from 12 of the colonies gathered at the newly built Carpenters' Hall to protest the harsh measures imposed on Boston. The First Continental Congress petitioned the king and voted to boycott all British goods.

When war broke out the following year, the struggle was led by representatives of all 13 colonies meeting in the Pennsylvania State House, later nicknamed 'Independence Hall.' In this splendid example of Georgian architecture, patriot leaders declared independence

| 1790–1800 | 1793 | 1832 | 1844 |
| --- | --- | --- | --- |
| Philadelphia is the nation's capital while Washington, DC is under construction. | More than 5000 die in yellow fever epidemic. | Matthias Baldwin builds the first American railroad locomotive. | Anti-Catholic rioting sees churches burned. |

in 1776 and drew up a constitution for a new nation in 1787. And Philadelphia would be the capital of the new nation from 1790 to 1800 while Washington, DC was under construction.

The city and its suburbs house many of the most well-known and powerful symbols and sites of the American Revolution: Carpenters' Hall, Independence Hall, the Liberty Bell, Valley Forge, Betsy Ross House, Christ Church, Washington's Crossing (in Bucks County) and Fort Mifflin. Founding fathers, including George Washington, John Adams, Thomas Jefferson and Alexander Hamilton, spent years in Philadelphia during the Revolution and during the city's 10-year stint as the national capital.

As the largest rebel city and the seat of the revolutionary government, Philadelphia was attacked by the British Army and held for nine months during 1777 and '78. Major battles

## The Liberty Bell

Ask the two million annual visitors to the Liberty Bell why it is famous and 80% will shrug their shoulders. Some 18% will say because 'it is a symbol of liberty' but not know exactly why. And 2% will say the bell rang on July 4, 1776, to announce the signing of the Declaration of Independence.

Well, the Old State House Bell – now known as the Liberty Bell – is, indeed, a universally recognized symbol of American independence. But it did not ring on July 4.

As a matter of fact, the Continental Congress voted for independence from Great Britain on July 2, 1776. The vote was 12 colonies for the break, with New York abstaining while it awaited instruction from home. (It soon joined in the vote.) On July 4, Congress issued an eloquent explanation to the world of why it was breaking ties to Britain. One wise historian has described the Declaration of Independence as 'a press release.'

The Liberty Bell did not ring on July 2 either.

However, on July 8, all of the city's church bells rang for hours to announce a public reading of the declaration. No one can say for sure if the State House Bell joined the chorus. There is doubt, because the wood steeple was very rotted at the time, so it may have been too dangerous to ring the bell for hours on end.

The bell did not become a beloved symbol of freedom until the late 1830s – some 60 years after the Revolution.

But first a brief history of the bell: Pennsylvania's colonial Assembly ordered the bell from an English foundry in 1752. A biblical inscription on the bell reads, 'Proclaim Liberty throughout all the land unto all the inhabitants thereof.' Since no one in 1752 knew a revolution was coming, historians believe the verse commemorates William Penn's liberal constitution for the colony of Pennsylvania called 'the Charter of Privileges.'

The first time the bell was rung, it cracked. The bell was broken up and recast by local foundry owners, Pass and Stowe, who put their names on it. The new bell's sound was so poor that Pass and Stowe recast it again. The third casting is the Liberty Bell we see today.

The bell may have cracked in 1845 (no one is sure of the date). A repair was made by drilling out the hairline crack. This is the famous visible crack. A newspaper account tells us the thin hairline crack continued to expand, finally silencing the bell for good on Washington's birthday, February 23, 1846.

So why is the bell famous?

In the late 1830s those working to abolish slavery began using the image of the bell in their literature and referring to the Old State House Bell as 'the Liberty Bell.' Abolitionists liked its inscription proclaiming liberty 'to ALL the inhabitants.'

But what really made the bell an icon was a fanciful tale that appeared in the *Saturday Courier Magazine* in 1847 by writer George Lippard. The fictional story tells of an elderly bell ringer waiting in the belfry on July 4, 1776 – doubtful that Congress had the nerve to break with Britain. Finally, the old man's cute, little grandson – who had been listening to the great debate at the door – shouts 'Ring, Grandfather, ring.'

This tale was taken as truth and soon reprinted in newspapers and 19th-century history books. It is doubtful that the Liberty Bell would be today's famous symbol of liberty and independence without obscure George Lippard and his tale of the old bell ringer.

| 1854 | 1856 |
| --- | --- |
| The city grows from 2 sq miles to 129 sq miles in city-county consolidation. | The first Republican presidential convention is held at Musical Fund Hall. |

around Philadelphia included Brandywine (the largest battle of the Revolution in numbers of participants), Germantown, Paoli and the bloody siege of two American forts on the Delaware River. In December 1777, Washington and his ill-supplied army settled into winter quarters at Valley Forge, about 25 miles west of the city.

Psychologically one of the most important battles of the Revolution occurred about 40 miles north of Philadelphia in Trenton, New Jersey. Patriot morale was at a low ebb when a desperate Washington crossed the Delaware River about 7 miles north of Trenton in the teeth of a raging blizzard on Christmas night, 1776. The sunrise attack took 1000 German mercenary soldiers, known as Hessians, by total surprise. With a minimal loss of American life, Washington captured 900 enemy soldiers.

## CAPITAL OF A NEW NATION

The years following the Revolution were a glorious period for the city; it was both the American capital and state capital. Although New York City was the temporary national capital when George Washington was sworn in as president in April 1789, Philadelphia was a frontrunner to become the permanent capital. However, a political deal was struck with Virginia and Maryland concerning unpaid debts from the Revolutionary War. As a result, the new capital city was to be built on the Potomac River. To appease Philadelphia, it was made the temporary capital while the new federal city was under construction.

George Washington's presidential house is gone but buildings that hosted the US Congress and Supreme Court still stand, as do the First and Second Banks of the United States. Visitors in the late 18th century commented on the city's impressive architecture, cultural institutions and the opulent lifestyles of its upper class. Probably the largest fortunes in early America were amassed by merchants Robert Morris (who lost it all), William Bingham and French-born shipping mogul Stephen Girard.

But it was during this same period, when Philadelphia was the nation's capital, that it suffered its greatest calamity. An epidemic of yellow fever killed 5000 in a few months, shutting down the city. Those who could afford it fled for healthier places.

## A CITY OF FIRSTS

Moving into the 19th century, Philadelphia quickly lost its preeminence in population, finance and shipping to New York City. Instead, it became a city noted for its quiet conservatism. It wasn't until 1833 that a Merchants Exchange building replaced taverns as the venue for conducting business and trade. More than any other American city, Philadelphia developed a true aristocracy based on old bloodlines rather than wealth. Intermarried family dynasties – with names including Biddle, Cadwalader, Wharton, Wister, Pew, Chew, Morris, Norris, Pepper, Lewis, Penrose and Ingersoll – provided leadership in business, culture, charity, law, politics and medicine right into the 20th century. As Mark Twain observed: 'In Boston they ask, How much does he know? In New York, How much is he worth? In Philadelphia, Who were his parents?'

Early in the 19th century the seeds of a great industrial city were being sown. Philadelphia was a national leader in the manufacture and use of steam engines, and an early textile industry began shifting from hand looms to factories well before the Industrial Revolution. John Fitch built the world's first steamboat and chugged up the Delaware River in 1786. Matthias Baldwin built America's first railroad locomotive in 1832; the Baldwin Locomotive Company would grow to become the world's largest builder of locomotives and the city's largest industrial firm.

There is no doubt that Philadelphia was the center of early American science and medicine. Ben Franklin was founder and first president of the nation's first learned and

| 1871 | 1876 |
|---|---|
| A 30-year construction project begins on City Hall. | The nation celebrates its 100th anniversary with the Centennial Exhibition. |

scientific society, the American Philosophical Society (whose third president was Thomas Jefferson). This was the 'think tank' where the best minds in the nation could consult with their peers. Before heading west, explorer Meriwether Lewis spent a full month in the city consulting with the society's members, purchasing scientific instruments, medicine and tons of supplies. When the Lewis and Clark expedition ended, Jefferson forwarded many artifacts to the society, and member Charles Willson Peale displayed the expedition artifacts – along with the sensational reconstruction of a mastodon – in his renowned natural history museum. There are still trees growing in Philadelphia from seeds sent back by Lewis and Clark. Most of the explorers' journals are housed at the society's headquarters, next to Independence Hall.

One of Philadelphia's nicknames is 'City of Firsts.' Historians have listed more than 500 Philly firsts, ranging from America's first bottle of root beer and Thanksgiving Day parade to the creation of the world's first all-electronic computer, ENIAC, developed at the University of Pennsylvania during World War II. Philadelphia boasted the nation's first hospital, first medical school (at the University of Pennsylvania), first mental hospital, first pharmacy school and first medical society. All of these institutions flourish to this day.

The nation's first large municipal water system was built along the banks of the Schuylkill River in the first decades of the 19th century. The Fairmount Waterworks was not only a pioneering industrial site but also one of early America's most beautifully landscaped gardens. After Niagara Falls, the Waterworks was the most popular subject for artists of the early 19th century. Following years of restoration, it is again one of Philadelphia's premier beauty spots.

The Philadelphia Stock Exchange was America's first, founded in 1790, although New York's soon eclipsed it. In the first national census of 1790, New York City was slightly larger than Philadelphia (but with the contiguous municipalities of Southwark and Northern Liberties added, Philadelphia was bigger). Its number two status throughout the 19th century would give Philadelphia a lingering inferiority complex. No one can deny that New York City is more dynamic, but Philadelphians have always believed that their city is more civilized, more cultured and more livable.

# IMMIGRATION & THE CIVIL WAR

Like New York City, sections of Philadelphia became crowded with poor Irish Catholic immigrants, leading to conflict with Protestant 'nativists.' The resentment led to bloody riots in 1844, with many deaths and the destruction of two Roman Catholic churches. A full-scale battle was fought between militia men and about 2000 Protestants attacking St Philip Neri Catholic Church in Southwark.

It was a lawless era. Gangs of young thugs ruled the slums. Historians have identified 50 gangs, including the Killers, Blood Tubs and Schuylkill Rangers. There were violent anti-black riots as well as attacks and harassment of abolitionists.

The lawlessness was brought under control in the years after 1854, when all of Philadelphia County was consolidated in one large city and a 900-man police force was created to patrol the consolidated city. With the stroke of a pen, Philadelphia grew from William Penn's original 2 sq miles to its current 129 sq miles. For many years, Philadelphia was the nation's largest city in area, until New York City went through the same consolidation progress in 1898.

When it came to the struggle to abolish slavery, there was an ironic dichotomy in 'the City of Brotherly Love.' The Quaker-led Pennsylvania Abolition Society, founded in 1775, was the first in the nation. Pennsylvania was also first to abolish slavery, with a gradual emancipation law in 1780. Philadelphia was a hotbed of anti-slavery agitation as the nation moved toward civil war. But the working class was decidedly bigoted and considered the abolitionists a bunch of radical lawbreakers.

| 1901 | 1907 |
| --- | --- |
| The first New Year's Day Mummers Parade is held on Broad St. | Demolition of 1000 structures begins to create Benjamin Franklin Parkway. |

Still, a new political party dedicated to preventing the spread of slavery in the West held its first presidential nominating convention at Philadelphia's Musical Fund Hall in 1856. The new Republican Party chose California's John C Fremont as its first presidential candidate.

When the South seceded in 1861, the masses rallied to the Union cause. But the city's upper class tended to be either anti-war or pro-Southern due to longtime family and business ties to Dixie; Philadelphia's huge textile industry was closely tied to southern cotton.

During the Civil War, Philadelphia was a major center of manufacturing of uniforms, weapons, blankets and fighting ships. About 90,000 men enlisted in Philadelphia units. The city was also a center for treating the sick and wounded after the creation of two huge army hospitals with a combined total of 7000 beds. Forty miles south of the city, Fort Delaware on Pea Patch Island in the Delaware River became a notorious prison camp for captured Confederate soldiers. The fort is now an interesting historical site, and there are two fine Civil War museums in the city today.

## Philadelphia's Immigrants

The first large wave of immigrants from the 1820s through 1850 was the Irish. The only two ethnic groups to settle in Philadelphia in large numbers at the end of the 19th century were Italians and Jews. Relatively small numbers of Slavs, Poles, Greeks and other Eastern Europeans chose Philadelphia.

Because most jobs in Philadelphia required some skills, British and German craftsmen continued to arrive into the 1920s. A good cricket match with a visiting English team could attract 15,000 fans even in the 1920s.

A Puerto Rican community established itself in North Philadelphia in the 1950s and '60s. More recently, thousands of Asian immigrants from Cambodia, Vietnam, China and India have settled in the city.

# INDUSTRIAL MIGHT

Philadelphia emerged from the Civil War as America's leading industrial city. More than in any other American city, the Industrial Revolution of the late 1800s was seen here in full flower. By the end of the century the city housed more than 7000 factories, mills and small workshops. Textiles was the largest industry, but there was a wonderful diversity of products coming out of Philadelphia: false teeth, umbrellas, Turkish cigarettes, beer, watch cases, machine tools, bathtubs and banjos.

The Pennsylvania Railroad connected the city to the entire East Coast and Midwest, and would grow into the world's largest corporation in the 20th century. The Reading Railroad made Philadelphia the world's leading exporter of coal coming from northeastern Pennsylvania and shipped in barges.

Unlike New York's multifamily tenements, Philadelphia housed its booming working class mostly in individual two- and three-story brick row houses – a traditional architectural style rooted in the 18th century. About 4000 houses were built annually, selling for $1000 to $2500. As a result Philadelphia had the highest rate of home ownership and the lowest density per housing unit of any industrial city in the US. The brick row house is still the most common form of housing, and the city has perhaps the oldest housing stock of any city in the nation today.

The wealth created by the Industrial Revolution manifested itself in several grand projects. Philadelphia's enormous (600 rooms), wildly ornate City Hall took 30 years to complete (1871–1901) and cost double its original estimate. Philadelphia opened America's first municipal zoo in 1874. In the late 1860s it developed one of the nation's largest and most scenic city parks. About 4000 acres on both sides of the Schuylkill River, plus the scenic gorge of the Wissahickon Creek, form the heart of the Fairmount Park system.

| 1918 | 1926 |
|---|---|
| A Spanish flu epidemic kills 15,000 residents. | The Benjamin Franklin Bridge, then the world's longest suspension bridge, opens. |

For the 100th birthday of the nation, Congress authorized the city to hold a grand fair, the Centennial Exhibition in Fairmount Park. The city has not thrown such a successful party since. Ten million visitors – a quarter of the nation's population – attended the big blowout. Spread across 285 landscaped acres were 249 buildings. Just about every state and 50 foreign nations exhibited their wares, as did most major manufacturers. Fairgoers were wowed by the introduction of Alexander Graham Bell's telephone and the 2500-horsepower Corliss steam engine, which drove scores of labor-saving machines. The only major exhibition building that survives is the former art museum, an architectural jewel now known as Memorial Hall.

The years after the Civil War also marked the beginnings of an all-powerful Republican Party political machine that would rule the city until 1952. Lincoln Steffens' 1904 classic study *Shame of the Cities* details a place where all city employees paid kickbacks to the GOP and no one expressed shock when a district with fewer than 100 registered voters cast 252 votes. It was a time when most of the Republican bosses were also contractors bidding and getting city work. The most prominent 'contractor bosses' were brothers – William, George and Edwin Vare, who grew up in poverty on a South Philly pig farm and died millionaires. All three held public offices, and together they ran the city GOP machine. Starting with a trash-hauling business, the Vares set up several other firms including street paving. Between 1888 and 1928 they won 280 city contracts worth more than $28 million. That figure more than doubled when contracts with the telephone and gas companies were added.

In 1924 Bill Vare won a US Senate seat but never took office. A lengthy Senate investigation of voter fraud in Philadelphia concluded that only one vote in eight was not tainted by fraud.

Philadelphians tolerated the corruption and political shenanigans because the city was generally prosperous. The party machine provided jobs for the unemployed, furnished coal in the winter for the poor and fixed minor brushes with the law. All that was asked in return was party loyalty. The power of Philadelphia's GOP machine meant it could control statewide elections, thanks to all those registered Republicans and an additional 30,000 to 80,000 phantom voters.

Along with general prosperity, there was also conflict and tragedy in the first decades of the 20th century. A strike by streetcar motormen in 1910 led to warfare on the streets, pitting strikers and their sympathizers against replacement workers and overburdened police. Twenty-nine deaths were recorded during the 66-day strike. It required the heavy presence of state police and the swearing in of 3000 'special police' to end the bloodshed and rioting. The strike ended with the promise of a gradual pay raise from 23¢ to 25¢ per hour.

Tragedy struck again in 1918 when a worldwide epidemic of the so-called Spanish flu left 15,000 Philadelphians dead. Historians say no other American city was hit harder by the deadly virus. On the worst day of the outbreak, 754 people died in the city. The morgue had room for about 30 bodies.

# THE '20S THROUGH THE '50S

In the roaring '20s Philadelphia had more than its share of gangster activity brought on by Prohibition. There were scores of whiskey stills in the city and thousands of illegal speakeasies. To bring about some law and order, the city persuaded Marine Corps hero Major General Smedley Darlington Butler to take a leave of absence from the service to become the city's top cop. The no-nonsense two-time winner of the Congressional Medal of Honor did such a good job of reforming the police and was so zealous in enforcing Prohibition (10,000 arrests for illegal sales or bootlegging in one year) that the politicians were thrilled to get rid of the too-honest leatherneck.

| 1950 | 1951 |
|---|---|
| The population of the city reaches a high point of two million. | Independence National Historical Park is created. |

During the boom years of the 1920s the broad Benjamin Franklin Parkway leading to a huge new art museum was completed. In 1926 the Benjamin Franklin Bridge (then called the Delaware River Bridge) opened to traffic. The first bridge connecting central Philadelphia and New Jersey held the title of world's longest suspension bridge for a couple of years.

The city tried to duplicate the great success of the 1876 Centennial Exhibition with a 150th sesquicentennial celebration in South Philadelphia in 1926, but it was plagued by problems and failed to lure big crowds.

Philadelphia weathered the Great Depression of the 1930s somewhat better than other cities because of the diversity of its industry. World War II was like a spring shower to the city's industrial economy: factories and textile mills sprang to life again, and more than 3500 businesses produced war supplies. The US Naval Ship Yard had 30,000 employees working 'round the clock.

In 1948, the city scored a coup by hosting both the Republican and Democratic presidential conventions, plus the third-party convention of Progressive Party candidate Henry Wallace. But both major parties had such unpleasant experiences that it wasn't until 2000 that the GOP returned to nominate George W Bush. In 1948 hotel rooms were so scarce that some delegates commuted daily from Trenton and Atlantic City. Worse, Convention Hall in West Philadelphia was not air-conditioned during one of the hottest summers on record. More than 100 Democrats collapsed of heat exhaustion.

Philadelphia's industrial might continued into the 1950s, with firms churning out everything from rugs to television sets. The 1950s census showed Philadelphia's population at an all-time high of two million. Yet the power of the GOP political machine was broken in 1952 by Democratic reformers. Since that year, Republicans have failed to elect a single mayor or local congressperson.

## Further Reading

- *A Concise History of Philadelphia* by Ron Avery (1999, Otis Books) A brief history of the city from its founding to the end of the 20th century
- *The Perennial Philadelphians: The Anatomy of an American Aristocracy* by Nathaniel Burt (1963, Little Brown) A very readable city history told through an examination of Philadelphia's upper-crust families
- *William Dorsey's Philadelphia and Ours* by Roger Lane (1991, Oxford University Press) A fine account of the city's African American community in the 19th and 20th centuries
- *Life and Times in Colonial Philadelphia* by Joseph J Kelly (1973, Stackpole Press) A lively, humanizing, anecdote-packed history of early Philadelphia
- www.ushistory.org: website operated by the private Independence Hall Association, filled with material on Philadelphia, its historic sites and the Revolutionary War

# DECLINING FORTUNES

Philadelphia, like many other industrial cities, saw a mass exodus of industry in the decades following World War II. The huge textile industry disappeared, first moving to cheaper labor markets in the South, then abroad.

By the 1960s there were clear patterns of decline. Old industries closed or relocated. Some firms moved to modern industrial parks in the suburbs, but most just folded and died. Gone are the old industrial giants, including Philco, the Pennsylvania Railroad, the Budd Company, Jack Frost Sugar, Curtis Publishing and the US Naval Ship Yard. Even the Pennsylvania Railroad, once the world's largest corporation, went bankrupt in 1970. Population declined rapidly. Once-stable blue-collar neighborhoods started to crumble, while the outlying suburbs boomed.

| 1952 | 1987 |
|---|---|
| The long reign of the Republican Party ends; Democratic domination begins. | A new city skyline takes shape as Liberty Place One becomes the first building higher than City Hall. |

All the news coming out of Philadelphia in the 1970s and '80s seemed to be negative. The reign of ill luck included two deadly confrontations between police and a radical group called MOVE in 1978 and 1985. Legionnaires' disease made its first appearance during a convention of the American Legion in 1976. A new organized-crime boss, 'Little Nicky' Scarfo, unleashed a tide of bloody mob warfare in the 1980s that continued for a decade. Controversial Mayor Frank Rizzo's two terms in the '70s were marked by racial polarization, constant political battles and the largest tax increases in Philadelphia's history. Thousands signed recall petitions to oust Rizzo, but his allies on the Board of Elections rejected the petitions.

Even the city's lauded bicentennial was a disappointment; a few small museums were established, but there was no major celebration aside from ceremonies and fireworks on July 4. Mayor Rizzo ensured that nothing would happen by guaranteeing that no neighborhood would be forced to accept a fair or exposition; no area wanted one in its backyard, so nothing happened. In addition, Rizzo killed any chance of a big celebration when he said he would need thousands of federal troops to keep the peace because of threats from radicals to parade.

Since 1950 the city has lost 500,000 residents – 25% of its population – and nearly 300,000 industrial jobs.

# A CITY REBORN

While Philadelphia's population continued to decline in the 1990s, the decade saw major development and renewed energy at the city's core. Many old neighborhoods were gentrified, and residential neighborhoods close to downtown boomed. A new city skyline took shape as several gleaming skyscrapers sprouted in defiance of an old tradition that no building would be taller than 548ft City Hall.

New theaters were built, including the impressive glass-enclosed Kimmel Center for the Performing Arts, providing a new state-of-the-art home for the famed Philadelphia Orchestra. A $500-million convention center opened in 1993. New museums, hotels, restaurants and clubs created a feel of liveliness and fun in the downtown scene. A restaurant renaissance that started in the 1970s hit full stride, attracting the attention of foodies worldwide.

Most of the credit for the Center City boom goes to two-term Mayor Ed Rendell, a dynamic cheerleader for Philadelphia. Rendell had good ties with President Clinton. More importantly, he was an expert at mobilizing private philanthropy for civic projects, such as the Constitution Center and the Kimmel Center.

Most important for its future, the city has preserved a great deal of its historic buildings and early architectural gems, providing an interesting mix of the old and the modern. The old buildings, historic areas, leafy squares, plethora of statues, monuments, public art and museums give Philadelphia the look and feel of a European city.

Philadelphia was, and remains, a national center of science, medicine and higher education which forms the new base of the city's economy, along with an expanding hospitality industry. On weekends the streets of Center City are filled with suburbanites and downtown professionals strolling the sidewalks and filling the clubs, theaters and the many new sidewalk cafés. William Penn's 'holy experiment' is thriving.

1993

The new $500-million Pennsylvania Convention Center opens.

# Neighborhoods

# Neighborhoods

Philadelphia's neighborhoods present a range of interesting opportunities, from the staid to the bizarre. Most of the places worth visiting are located in or around Center City, the town that William Penn planned back in the 17th century. Here, particularly in Independence National Historical Park, you'll find all of that revolutionary-era history you so deeply crave. Within this park, seek out Philadelphia's twin powerhouse attractions: the Liberty Bell, symbol of abolition and freedom, and Independence Hall, where both the Constitution and the Declaration of Independence were signed. Speaking to its global importance, Independence Hall holds esteem as a World Heritage Site. In the USA the only other works built by Westerners to earn this distinction are Jefferson's Monticello and the Statue of Liberty.

Beyond such colonial offerings, Philadelphia's neighborhoods present a range of world-class museums devoted to art. For buffs and generalists with only one day, a visit to the Philadelphia Museum of Art, the Institute for Contemporary Art in University City or the Pennsylvania Academy of the Fine Arts is essential and rewarding.

For those interested in less highfalutin' attractions, Philly's got numerous other destinations. Most popular is the Mütter Museum, where the strong-stomached stare at freakish pathological specimens while their friends wait in the lobby. Who's ready for some of John Wilkes Booth's neck? Others interested in a fascinating relic of history and an innovative piece of prison architecture should head to pleasantly derelict (it adds to the charm) Eastern State Penitentiary, built in 1829. If that doesn't grab you, don't worry. There are hundreds of other things to do here, from sunning in Fairmount Park to screaming at a Flyers game. Between seeing the sights, don't miss taking part in Philadelphia's renowned restaurant scene or knocking one back in some excellent bars.

This book's exploration of neighborhoods begins with Independence National Historical Park, a green L-shaped lawn separating the Old City district from Center City. From here you move into Old City, explore its alleys, galleries and nightlife, and then pop south into quiet, residential Society Hill. Then go east, crossing the interstate to see the waterfront area of Penn's Landing. From this spot, look across the Delaware River (Washington crossed it

> ## Top Five Free Philly Attractions
>
> - **Independence Hall** (p57) Check out the building where they signed all those documents.
> - **Liberty Bell** (p58) It's got a crack, and it might just be what brought you to this fair city.
> - **City Hall** (p70) Go up the tower for an unbeatable view of Philadelphia.
> - **Fireman's Hall** (p62) Don't ask to slide down the pole.
> - **Franklin Court** (p57) Learn that Franklin was born in Boston, check out his printshop and ponder his inventions.

much farther upstream) to Camden, New Jersey. Thinking fondly of Bruce Springsteen, you cross back over the highway to explore Center City, Philadelphia's downtown.

Beginning with the Avenue of the Arts, discover the city's high-end performance spaces, see if the ballet has any tickets left and then check out Chinatown. Heading directly south, explore Washington Square West and then move west in search of stylish Rittenhouse Square. This accomplished, go north to take in the museum district, which is organized around Benjamin Franklin Parkway. Catching a cab, race down to South Street, get a tattoo and then continue your travels in South Philly, the large and largely Italian American neighborhood south of Center City.

Hop another cab north to hipster-heavy Northern Liberties. Driving through, plan your evening and then ask the cabbie to take you to Fairmount Park, the largest urban park in the States. Feeling ready for some learnin', cross the Schuylkill River and buy some books in University City, home to the University of Pennsylvania. Panting and tired, agree to wrap up your city coverage tomorrow, when you'll visit the historic sites of Germantown, the cute shops of Chestnut Hill and the nightlife of Manayunk, all between 5 and 10 miles from downtown.

# ITINERARIES

## One Day

Begin the day with pancakes at **Blue in Green** (p112) on Jeweler's Row. Head over to the **Independence Visitor Center** (p55) to pick up free tickets to **Independence Hall** (p57) and to ask a ranger about possible special events and tours. Walk across the street to check out the **Liberty Bell** (p58), and then move on to Independence Hall. Revive your colonial spirits with lunch at the **City Tavern** (p106). Spend the afternoon poking around your pick of Independence National Historical Park's offerings. Have a trendy dinner at one of Steven Starr's nearby restaurants; **Jones** (p113) is particularly good for kids. If you aren't tuckered out, check out a rock show at the **Khyber** (p140), or hire a cab to take you **Ortlieb's Jazzhaus** (p139) or **Bob & Barbara's** (p135). Still feeling lively after 2am? Time for another cab ride and a South Philly cheese steak at **Pat's** (p116) or **Geno's** (p116), where you will make one of life's hardest choices: electing to eat at one over the other.

## Two Days

Cover the one-day itinerary. Your second day brings you out of Old City and over to Rittenhouse Square. Agonize over the gruesome displays of early medical science at the macabre **Mütter Museum** (p72). Settle your stomach by strolling around regal **Rittenhouse Square** (p73), and then grab a people-watching lunch at either **Rouge** (p110) or **Bleu** (p110). Depending on your preference, hit the neighborhood's classy shops, have a punk-rock reunion with kitschy **South Street** (p78) or enjoy the vast **Philadelphia Art Museum** (p77). Grab an early dinner at a BYOB – try **Tartine** (p115), **Audrey Claire** (p110) or **Tre Scalini** (p118) – and then have a major league evening watching the Flyers, Sixers, Eagles or Phillies in South Philly. Post-game, have a dive-bar drink at the **Philadium** (p135).

## Three Days

After two days on foot, it's time to rent a bike and explore **Fairmount Park** (p83). Grab a free map from the folks at **Trophy Bikes** (p146) and ride along the east side of the Schuylkill River to Manayunk, checking out **Boathouse Row** (p84) and bridges along the way. In **Manayunk** (p89), grab a stellar cup of coffee at **La Colombe** (p121). After a refreshing drink, stroll the cute downtown before riding back to the city, with a possible biking detour around the Wissahickon. Return the bike and cab it over to Northern Liberties for a meal and a drink at the **Standard Tap** (p136). Spend the remainder of your evening here or check out the DJ at **Aqua Lounge** (p141).

# ORGANIZED TOURS

A variety of tours exists to help you explore the city. They can be booked directly with the operators, through your hotel reception, at the **Independence Visitor Center** (p55) or with a travel agent.

## Walking Tours

Free walking tours are offered by the park rangers at Independence National Historical Park; check with the Independence Visitor Center for the current schedule.

### AUDIO WALK & TOUR
☎ 215-272-5886; 1/2/3/4 people $10/14/16/20; SEPTA 5th St Station, Bus 9, 21, 38, 42, 47
A self-guided audio tour through the historic

square mile. Pick up a CD player and map at the Independence Visitor Center.

### GHOSTS OF PHILADELPHIA
☎ 215-413-1997; www.ghosttour.com; adult/child $12/6; SEPTA 5th St Station, Bus 9, 21, 38, 42, 47
A candlelight tour that asks 'does Benedict Arnold have unfinished business at the Powel House?' Reservations required. Tours depart at 7:30pm from the corner of 5th and Chestnut Sts April through November.

### LIGHTS OF LIBERTY SHOW Map pp226-7

☎ 215-542-3789; www.lightsofliberty.org; 6th & Chestnut Sts; adult/child/student/senior $17.76/12/16/16; SEPTA 5th St Station, Bus 9, 21, 38, 42, 47

Making five moonlit stops in Independence National Historical Park, this hour-long tour about the American Revolution involves five-story projections on the walls of landmark buildings and the voices of Whoopi Goldberg, Walter Cronkite and Charlton Heston. Tours are offered April through October.

### PHILADELPHIA NEIGHBORHOOD TOURS

☎ 215-599-2295; www.gophila.com; 6th & Market Sts; adult/child/student/senior $32/22/27/27; SEPTA 5th St Station, Bus 9, 21, 38, 42, 47

Each Saturday from May through October, these three-hour tours explore Chinatown, South Philly, Society Hill and more. Meet in the Independence Visitor Center.

### POOR RICHARD'S WALKING TOURS

☎ 215-206-1682; www.phillywalks.com; adult/child/student/senior $15/10/10/10

Animated smarty-pants (actually a group of U Penn PhD-in-history students) present a plethora of well-researched tours, covering either the city's 400-year history or focusing on a specialized period. Formerly leading only groups, in summer 2004 they'll begin offering outings for individuals.

### WALK PHILADELPHIA

☎ 215-625-9255; www.centercityphila.org; 6th & Market Sts; adult/student $10/8; SEPTA 5th St Station, Bus 9, 21, 38, 42, 47

This company offers a huge range of specialty architectural tours throughout the city. Stop by the Independence Visitor Center for a brochure outlining their schedule, which runs from April through December.

# Trolley, Bus & Carriage Tours

The 76 Carriage Company (Map pp226-7; ☎ 215-925-8687) and the Philadelphia Carriage Company (Map pp226-7; ☎ 215-922-6840) form a queue at the corner of 5th and Chestnut Sts. Both operate fleets of horse-drawn carriages with a driver-commentator. A 20-minute tour of Independence National Historical Park costs $25 for four people; each additional person costs $6 extra. Longer tours take in Society Hill and Old City. A full hour runs to $70.

### THE BIG BUS COMPANY

☎ 215-965-7676; www.bigbustours.com; 6th & Chestnut Sts; adult/child $22/10; SEPTA 5th St Station, Bus 9, 21, 38, 42, 47

Ride an open-roof double-decker bus for a 90-minute tour of Center City and Fairmount Park. The bus makes 19 stops, including Independence Hall, the Philadelphia Museum of Art and the zoo. You can get off and reboard as often as you like within one full loop.

### MURAL ARTS PROGRAM

☎ 215-685-0754; www.muralarts.org; 6th & Market Sts; adult/child/student & senior $18/10/15; SEPTA 5th St Station, Bus 9, 21, 38, 42, 47

These two-hour sojourns tour one of five city regions, en route discussing local murals, how they are made and how they have helped to change their communities. Reservations are accepted but not required. Tours depart from the Independence Visitor Center on Saturdays from May to October. Reservations are recommended.

### RIDE THE DUCKS Map pp226-7

☎ 215-227-3825; www.phillyducks.com; 6th & Chestnut Sts; adult/child $20/11; SEPTA 5th St Station, Bus 9, 21, 38, 42, 47

Offering unusual land-and-water tours using modified WWII amphibious vehicles, these tours are incredibly popular with families. Daily tours run April through November at varying times (depending on the season) and come with a plastic, bill-shaped duck caller and a phenomenally high-energy driver who will attempt to coerce groups into collectively doing the 'YMCA' song.

## Top Five – Independence National Historical Park

- **Bishop William White House** (p56) Experience 18th-century opulence in this little-changed upper-crust home.
- **Franklin Court** (p57) Learn why Benjamin Franklin was America's first international celebrity.
- **Independence Hall** (p57) Check out the spot where the US Constitution and Declaration of Independence were signed.
- **Liberty Bell Center** (p58) Stare at its crack and learn of its past.
- **Second Bank of the US** (p59) Take a gander at Thomas Jefferson's mug in the National Portrait Gallery, contained in this model of the Parthenon.

# INDEPENDENCE NATIONAL HISTORICAL PARK

Once this park was the backbone of the United States government. Today it is the backbone of Philadelphia's tourist trade. Walk around the park for a few minutes, and you'll see storied buildings in which the seeds for the Revolutionary War were planted and the US government came into bloom. You'll also find beautiful, shaded urban lawns dotted with plenty of squirrels, pigeons and costumed actors.

These days, the park looks spiffier then ever. The Liberty Bell just moved into a much-improved building, a fantastic visitor center opened on Market St and restoration of the Second Bank of the US is underway. The only downer is the barrier that now surrounds the park's top two sites – Independence Hall and the bell – installed as a security precaution.

As old as many of the buildings in the park are, the sylvan environment does not represent a picture of Philadelphia as it existed in the 18th century. The green spaces that now surround many of the park's monuments were created in urban renewal projects in the 1950s, which cleared away 19th- and 20th-century structures (some of them blighted) to highlight the jewels of the revolutionary period. Back when Franklin was postmaster, this area was as densely built as anywhere in the country. The principal exception to this rule was Independence Square, the hallowed ground where the Declaration of Independence was read aloud for the first time.

Opening hours given in the following listings are approximations. These can change at any time based on season, security and budgetary constraints. Most places in the park are open daily from 9am to 5pm, but this can vary by an hour or so, while some hours are extended during the summer and some buildings close on Monday. A few buildings in the park are not open to the public. Admission to the visitor center and the park's buildings is free, as are the walking tours and other activities. The visitor center can give you up-to-the-minute information about when sites are open and closed as well as provide a list of special events occurring around the time of your visit – like meeting with a costumed actor portraying George Washington's slave, Hercules, who tells of the president's domestic life as well as his own flight to freedom; or visiting story-telling generals from both sides of the Revolutionary War, who will try to persuade kids to side with their rivaling causes.

Each site is staffed with well-educated park rangers, most of whom are excellent at answering questions.

## Orientation

This park, combined with the rest of Old City, forms what has been dubbed 'America's most historic square mile.' The L-shaped park is administered by the National Park Service (NPS) and covers 45 acres west of the Delaware River between Walnut and Arch Sts and between 2nd and 6th Sts. Independence Hall and the Liberty Bell are on most visitors' must-see lists, but other sights like Carpenters' Hall and Franklin Court are well worth seeing too. Several sights lie outside the 'L,' in Old City and Center City.

### INDEPENDENCE VISITOR CENTER

Map pp226-7

☎ 215-925-6101; 800-537-7676; www.independence visitorcenter.com; 6th & Market Sts; admission free;
⏱ 8:30am-5pm; SEPTA 5th St Station, Bus 9, 21, 38, 42, 47
For an overview of the park as well as information on Philadelphia, Bucks County and Lancaster County, stop in this excellent center. Inside, the Philadelphia Convention & Visitors Bureau operates a desk that provides tips on the city, maps, attraction brochures, tours and events. A separate desk is staffed by friendly park rangers who answer questions about the park's changing array of special events and who hand out even more maps. This is the desk where you can pick up free tickets to the Liberty Bell, Independence Hall, Todd House and Bishop White House. The visitor center also contains nifty computer terminals that outline lodging and entertainment options in Philadelphia and surrounding counties.

There are continuous free showings of the 28-minute documentary *Independence* (directed by John Huston) about the creation of the USA and also of *The History Channel's Choosing Sides: Young Voices of the Revolution,* a 20-minute film aimed specifically at high-school students.

## BISHOP WILLIAM WHITE HOUSE
Map pp226-7
309 Walnut St; admission free; SEPTA 5th St Station, Bus 9, 21, 42, 57

This is the restored home of Reverend William White, first bishop of the Episcopal Diocese of Pennsylvania. Built in 1786, the house's eight levels reflect 18th-century, upper-class Philadelphia life. Many of the furnishings, including a library of 1000 books, were once owned by the bishop; the remainder are period. Amongst the cool things to be seen are fantastic wallpaper prints, some Argand lamps (very new-fangled, back in the day), and a creative attempt at plumbing involving a long shoot, a bucket and horribly inconveniencing somebody living about 100ft behind the bishop's house.

As with the Todd House, you can visit only as part a park service tour, so get a ticket early in the morning from the Independence Visitor Center.

## CARPENTERS' HALL Map pp226-7
215-925-0167; www.carpentershall.org all.org; 320 Chestnut St; donation requested; 10am-4pm, closed Tue Jan & Feb; SEPTA 5th St Station, Bus 9, 21, 38, 42, 57

Founded in 1724 to teach its members architectural skills, the Carpenters' Company, America's oldest trade guild, had much influence on Philadelphia's development; its members gave advice on building techniques and worked as architects on many projects. This Georgian building, built in 1770 and still owned by the Carpenters' Company, was designed by Robert Smith, a master carpenter and leading light of the group.

Aside from being an important center of creativity for those influential in the shaping of the early American built environment, Carpenters' Hall played a significant role in revolutionary affairs. It served as the site of the First Continental Congress in 1774. Then, in 1775 the hall also hosted a clandestine visit between Benjamin Franklin, John Jay, Francis Daymon and Julien Achard De Bonvouloir, a French spy who met with the revolutionaries at great personal danger. The exhibits are all carpentry-related and include a scale model of the building during its construction, as well as early tools and some Windsor chairs used by delegates to the Continental Congress.

## CONGRESS HALL Map pp226-7
215-597-8974; 6th & Chestnut Sts; admission free; 9am-5pm; SEPTA 5th St Station, Bus 9, 21, 38, 42, 47

When Philadelphia was the nation's capital, this Federal-style building, just west of Independence Hall and originally the Philadelphia County Courthouse, is where the US Congress met from 1790 to 1800. The House of Representatives held their sessions on the 1st floor, and the Senate met above. Here, the Bill of Rights (the first 10 amendments) was added to the Constitution, the US Mint was established, George Washington was inaugurated for his second term, and Vermont, Kentucky and Tennessee were admitted to the Union. Beautifully restored and still outfitted with some original furnishings, the various chambers, offices and committee rooms look much like they did 200 years ago.

## DECLARATION HOUSE Map pp226-7
215-597-8974; 7th & Market Sts; admission free; 10am-4pm; SEPTA 8th St Station, Bus 17, 33, 44, 47

Thomas Jefferson drafted the Declaration of Independence in rooms that he rented on the 2nd floor of this site. The original house, built in 1775 by a bricklayer from Philadelphia named Jacob Graff, was demolished in 1883 and reconstructed in 1975 for the bicentennial. There's an exhibition of Jefferson memorabilia, an eight-minute documentary film about him called *The Extraordinary Citizen*, and replications of his two upstairs rooms with period furnishings including reproductions of the swivel chair and desk he used to write the declaration. To clear space for this reconstruction, the powers that be razed a building designed by Frank Furness.

## Transport
Subway SEPTA services the park at the 5th St Station, on Market St.
Bus The 57 runs from South Philly through the park on its way to Girard Ave in Northern Liberties along 3rd St; it returns on 4th St. Bus 44 enters Center City from the Vine St Expressway at 23rd St, then shoots over to Market St, where it terminates at 5th and Market Sts.
Parking There's a paid parking lot underneath the Independence Visitor Center, if you don't see any open metered spots.

## FRANKLIN COURT Map pp226-7

**Market St btwn 3rd & 4th Sts; admission free; ◷ 9am-5pm; SEPTA 5th St Station, Bus 9, 17, 21, 33, 42, 57**

This complex, a tribute to Benjamin Franklin, is built on the site where he lived and worked. In the 1960s, rundown row houses occupying the site were demolished, creating a clear space for the court. Entry to the court from Market St is through the miraculously preserved brick archway that Franklin and his carriages once used. The court itself is a void occupied by three steel frame 'Ghost Buildings,' designed by Robert Venturi, that outline the long departed shapes of Franklin's house (it was razed by his heirs in 1812) and his print works. Inscribed in the ground throughout the court are quotations from correspondence between Franklin and his wife, Deborah. The evident fuss they made over exactly how to decorate the 'Blue Room' of their house is fairly amusing.

An **Underground Museum**, everything about which proclaims 'I am proud to have been built and designed in the '70s!' sits on the west side of Franklin Court. It displays Franklin's various inventions, revealing just how much this genius managed to contribute to 18th-century science and technology. One gallery presents portraits of the Franklin family and domestic artifacts from their home. Another is equipped with a freakish diorama inhabited by miniature figurines on a motorized floor portraying Franklin engaged in daring acts of diplomacy. There's also a short biographical film and a phone bank (which kids particularly enjoy) where actors give voice to comments made about him by his contemporaries.

Franklin was the nation's first postmaster, and **B Free Franklin Post Office** (☎ 215-592-1289; 316 Market St) is a working post office with period furniture. There isn't much to do there, but you can have a letter postmarked by hand with a stamp bearing Franklin's signature. Upstairs, the one-room, low-budget US Postal Service Museum attempts to illustrate US postal history with an exhibit including Pony Express pouches, originals of Franklin's *Pennsylvania Gazette* and, of course, a model of the space shuttle.

Franklin's **printing office and bindery** (320 Market St) has working demonstrations of reproduction colonial equipment. At **322 Market St** is a replica of an office of the *Aurora & General Advertiser*, a newspaper published by Franklin's grandson.

One of the coolest and least visited spots in the Franklin Court complex is the fireproof building at **318 Market St**, which Franklin designed with inspiration from the Great Fire of London and was one of the rental properties that he built along this street. The Park Service sought to preserve only the original parts of the building, dating from the 18th century. Because the building changed hands so many times and underwent significant structural modification over hundreds of years, the only stuff retained were the walls and roof. In the char marks left by deceased chimneys and in holes created by now absent structural agents, you can read where the original floors were located, the position of stairs, the arrangement of fireplaces and flues, and imprints made by closets, cornices and joists. It's an interesting lesson in the methods and meaning of historic preservation. A gallery in the cellar displays artifacts found in Franklin's privy and well, which you'll note, if you look on the ground outside, were disgustingly close together.

## INDEPENDENCE HALL Map pp226-7

**☎ 215-597-8974; Chestnut St btwn 5th & 6th Sts; admission free; ◷ 9am-5pm; SEPTA 5th St Station, Bus 9, 21, 38, 42, 47**

This World Heritage Site is the birthplace of United States government. It was built between 1732 and 1756 and started life as Pennsylvania State House, the colony's headquarters. At that time it was on the outskirts of the city. The Second Continental Congress met here from 1775 to 1783. The Assembly Room saw a lot of action: the delegates from the 13 colonies met in it to approve the Declaration of Independence (July 4, 1776) and the design of the US flag (1777), the Articles of Confederation (1781) were drafted here, and the Constitutional Convention produced the US Constitution (1787) within its walls. Later the assassinated body of President Abraham Lincoln lay in state here on April 22, 1865.

One of the country's best examples of Georgian architecture, the hall's simple, understated lines show the Quaker influence of Philadelphia's early days. British troops used the furniture in the 1st-floor's two rooms and the large central hallway for firewood when they occupied the city from 1777–78 – what you see today are examples from the period.

The **Supreme Court Chamber** is to your right as you enter. The Pennsylvania coat of arms, dating from 1785, hangs over the judge's chair. It replaced King George III's coat of arms, which was burned outside in Penn Square (near the site of today's City Hall) on July 8, 1776, the day the Declaration of Independence was read in public for the first time. The coat of arms was removed around midday and marched around the city until dark. As summer days are long in Philly and as the extents of the city were still very small, one has to wonder how many taverns Georgie's wooden seal visited before its demise.

The **Assembly Room**, across the hall, is where most of the building's notable events took place, and you can see original fixtures, including the chair George Washington used during the Constitutional Convention. The 2nd floor, unfortunately closed indefinitely due to structural and security concerns, features the Governor's Council Chamber, where royal governors conducted affairs of state; the Long Gallery, where American patriots were imprisoned by the British during the Revolution; and the Committee of the Assembly's Chamber, which has a display of weapons used during the war.

To join a free tour of the building, you need to get a ticket from the NPS desk in the Independence Visitor Center at least a half an hour before heading over to Independence Hall. This allows enough time to walk the two blocks from the information center to the site and to wait in a security line to pass through a metal detector. It's a good idea to get your tickets early (rangers recommend before 2pm but, hey, no guarantees), as they run out on busy days. Tours run every 15 minutes between 9am and 5pm from outside the east wing of the hall. Lasting about 30 minutes, these tours can be crowded, allowing up to 80 guests at a time. During the peak seasons – May through June and late September through October – try to visit early or late in the day.

The **West Wing** of Independence Hall houses a small exhibit containing some blockbuster artifacts: the copy of the Declaration of Independence that was first read to the public (by John Nixon in Independence Square), a copy of the Constitution edited by George Washington, and a copy of the Articles of Confederation covered with Congressman Elbridge Gerry's notations. Also on display is the silver Syng Inkstand, used in the formal signing of both the Declaration of Independence and the Constitution of the United States of America.

## INDEPENDENCE SQUARE Map pp226-7
**Walnut St btwn 5th & 6th Sts**

This historic open space, behind the Independence Hall complex, is where the Declaration of Independence was first read publicly, on July 8, 1776. Today its old shade trees and grassy expanses would add up to a thoroughly enjoyable Arcadian experience were it not for the ring of armed guards and security barriers, which cut across the green in order to encircle Independence Hall and its neighboring buildings. Even so, it remains a pleasant spot to grab a bench.

## LIBERTY BELL CENTER Map pp226-7
☎ 215-597-8974; 6th & Market Sts; admission free;
⏰ 9am-5pm; SEPTA 5th St Station, Bus 9, 21, 38, 42, 47

Philadelphia's top tourist attraction, the famous **Liberty Bell,** is housed in a brand-new building designed to frame the view of the bell in such a way that Independence Hall and blue skies form its backdrop. Commissioned to commemorate the 50th anniversary of the Charter of Privileges (Pennsylvania's constitution enacted in 1701 by William Penn), this 2080-pound bronze bell was made in London's East End by the Whitechapel Bell Foundry in 1751. The bell's inscription, from Leviticus 25:10, reads: 'Proclaim liberty throughout all the land unto all the inhabitants thereof.'

The bell was secured in the belfry of the Pennsylvania State House (now Independence Hall) and tolled on important occasions, most notably the first public reading of the Declaration of Independence in Independence Square. The bell became badly cracked during the 19th century; despite initial repairs it became unusable in 1846 after tolling for George Washington's birthday.

The bell became famous only after slavery abolitionists – who were inspired by its biblical inscription, which they took to symbolize liberty – adopted it in the mid-19th century. In 1976 the bell was moved from Independence Hall for the country's bicentennial celebrations, as the large number of visitors couldn't be accommodated there. It was moved again in 2003 to its current home.

Exhibits in the new building explain how the bell was cast, outline its history as a human rights symbol and explain in great detail its storied past. There's also a noisy interactive display where kids can ring a normal bell and a cracked bell, and listen for tonal differences. After hours, the bell is illuminated and visible from the street.

## NEW HALL MILITARY MUSEUM

Map pp226-7

☎ 215-597-8974; Chestnut St btwn S 3rd & S 4th Sts; admission free; ☺ 10am-4pm peak season, 2-5pm off-season; SEPTA 5th St Station, Bus 9, 21, 42, 57

Located in the building that housed the War Department from 1791 to 1792, this museum displays a hilarious photo comparing tiny brick New Hall to the Pentagon.

Aside from this, revolutionary muskets, pistols, swords and grenades are on view. The museum also features a blunderbuss (a unique-looking firearm), a small display outlining the history of black involvement in the Rhode Island Regiment and exhibits on early naval tactics.

## OLD CITY HALL Map pp226-7

☎ 215-597-8974; 5th & Chestnut Sts; admission free; ☺ 11am-5pm; SEPTA 5th St Station, Bus 9, 21, 38, 42, 47

Built in 1791, Old City Hall was simultaneously home to the government of Philadelphia and the US Supreme Court, which presided here until 1800 while Philadelphia was the nation's capital. You can visit the room used by both of these bodies. When made, the building was considerably lavish for its time. This opulence was part of a failed plan to coax the federal government to remain in Philadelphia by providing it with super-fancy buildings.

In the 1830s rooms on the 2nd floor were leased for the purpose of conducting cases against runaway slaves under the Fugitive Slave Act. In 1901 the local government moved over to Center Square. Today the hall contains a small exhibit on the early Supreme Court (whose members did not enjoy the prestige of their counterparts today), the evolution of the American justice system from its British antecedents and daily life in early Philadelphia.

## SECOND BANK OF THE US Map pp226-7

Chestnut St btwn 4th & 5th Sts; admission free; SEPTA 5th St Station, Bus 9, 21, 38, 42, 57

Modeled after the Greek Parthenon, this 1824 marble-faced Greek Revival masterpiece built by architect William Strickland was home to the world's most powerful financial institution until President Andrew Jackson dissolved its charter in 1836 – he didn't approve of the bank's conservative policies. The building then became the Philadelphia Customs House until 1935, whence it became a museum. The structure was first restored in 1974. It is again under restoration, which is scheduled to be finished in spring of 2004.

Today the bank is home to the **National Portrait Gallery**, housing many pieces by Charles Willson Peale, America's top portraitist at the time of the American Revolution. His subjects were among the most prominent men of the day, including William Clark, Meriwether Lewis, Thomas Jefferson and Joseph Brant, a Mohawk leader involved in the Six Nations of the Iroquis Confederacy who sought Indian autonomy. The Portrait Gallery also includes George Washington's death mask.

Other exhibits include a copy of the 1st edition of the Declaration of Independence (the original is in Washington, DC) and early prints of Philadelphia when it was the nation's capital. The Gallery will be closed until the current restoration is completed in spring 2004. A few of the collection's most important pieces are on display temporarily at the **First Bank of the US**. (p97).

## TODD HOUSE Map pp226-7

S 4th & Walnut Sts; admission free; SEPTA 5th St Station, Bus 9, 21, 42, 57

Built in 1775, lawyer John Todd lived here from 1791 to 1793 before dying of yellow fever during an epidemic that hit the city. His widow, Dolley Payne Todd (1768–1849), later became Dolley Madison, wife of James Madison, the nation's fourth president, who spent time here courting her when she was a widow.

The Georgian redbrick house is typical of a middle-class home in the late 18th century and, though you can't tell by looking at it, a diner used to operate out of the 1st floor in the 1950s. Spotless renovation has been achieved here.

You can visit the house only as part of one of the popular, free park service tours, which occur only a few times a day and can accommodate a maximum of 10 people. To be sure of a spot and to find out precise tour times, get your ticket at the Independence Visitor Center early in the morning.

Neighborhoods – Independence National Historical Park

# OLD CITY

*Eating p105; Shopping p150; Sleeping p162*

Old City picks up where Independence National Historical Park leaves off. Here, too, are scads of excellent sites to visit. Some of them are colonial in nature, such as Benjamin Franklin's grave and Elfreth's Alley, the nation's oldest continually inhabited street (so they say). Others, like the collection of odd equipment displayed at the **Fireman's Hall** (p62), span the ages. The arts are strong in Old City, as is evidenced by the presence of several highly regarded theater and performance venues, notably the **Arden** (p126), the **Painted Bride** (p63) and **Mum Puppettheatre** (p126), as well as by the existence of a strong and densely populated gallery scene. Also here are stacks of bars, clubs and restaurants. Old City is a happening, well-rounded, lively destination: good for kids, grandma and that art student your sister is dating.

Back when Penn was in charge of things, Old City, along with some of Society Hill, *was* Philadelphia. As the city developed, the neighborhood's proximity to the Delaware River inspired the construction of warehouses, factories, banks and stores. When the city's manufacturing center relocated farther west, the neighborhood declined, and it wasn't until the gentrification of Society Hill in the 1970s that people started to look at Old City's dilapidated warehouses as suitable for conversion into apartments, galleries and other small businesses.

Old City's prosperity really began to blossom about 15 to 20 years ago. North of Market St, a gallery district emerged. South of Market, particularly on 2nd St, saw the establishment of dozens of nightclubs and quality restaurants. Before this happened there wasn't that much to do in Old City aside from dropping by **Christ Church** (p61) or catching a rock show at the **Khyber** (p140). The change has been astounding. However, a few of Old City's buildings remain run down, particularly along Front St north of Market and sections of the neighborhood near the infrastructure supporting the Benjamin Franklin Bridge.

## Orientation

Old City ain't that big. It's contained within Walnut and Vine Sts, and Front and 6th Sts. Most of the galleries are on N 2nd and N 3rd Sts. The most popular nightclubs are on S 2nd, S 3rd and Bank Sts. Within the regular grid of major streets, look for a few cobbled alleys.

### ARCH STREET MEETING HOUSE

Map pp226-7

☎ 215-627-2667; 320 Arch St; $1 donation requested; ☽ 9am-5pm Mon-Sat, 1-5pm Sun; SEPTA 2nd St Station, Bus 5, 48, 57

The forbidding wall surrounding this Quaker building was built in 1693 to keep dogs and cats out of the graveyard. The Quakers wanted to get rid of it to make their house more inviting, but authorities deemed it too historic to remove. So despite the look, visitors should feel welcome to drop by.

The Arch Street Meeting House was built in 1804 on land donated by William Penn and is the country's largest Quaker meetinghouse. The furniture is all original and predates the building by 100 years. This is a good place to learn more about the Quakers, who still meet here twice a week. A receptionist answers questions and delivers a talk about the building to those who are interested.

### BENJAMIN FRANKLIN BRIDGE

Map pp226-7

The world's longest suspension bridge when it was completed in 1926 (at a cost of $37 million), this 1.8-mile long, 800,000-ton bridge

## Transport

**Subway** Old City's main subway stop is SEPTA's 2nd St Station, on Market St.

**Bus** The 57 runs from South Philly through Old City on its way to Girard Ave in Northern Liberties along 3rd St; it returns on 4th St. Buses 21 and 42 head east across Center City from University City, along Chestnut St. They turn at 2nd and return along Walnut.

**Parking** There's a paid lot on Front St, just south of Market. There's another paid lot on 2nd near Chestnut. Metered parking can be most easily had on the blocks north of Arch St.

crosses the Delaware River between Philly's Old City and Camden, New Jersey. The bridge, designed by Paul Cret, dominates the skyline here, especially at night when it's beautifully lit – each cable is illuminated by computer in a dominolike effect to follow the trains as they cross. Pedestrians can enjoy a picturesque walk over the bridge during the day, with views of the waterfront piers below. At night, the pedestrian entry closes.

## BETSY ROSS HOUSE Map pp226-7
☎ 215-686-1252; 239 Arch St; suggested donation adult/child $2/1; 🕑 9am-5pm Tue-Sun; SEPTA 2nd St Station, Bus 5, 48, 57

Some uncertainty surrounds Betsy Griscom Ross (1752–1836), an 18th-century upholsterer and seamstress. Although it's now known that she didn't design the American flag, she may or may not have sewn the first US flag for the early federal government. Further mystery: This is either the house where she lived or it's next to the site where her house once stood. Inside the sparsely furnished two-story house (built in 1740 but restored to how it appeared in early 1777), you can see Betsy's sewing machine and other tools. This is the only colonial upholstery shop remaining in the USA, so it's a must-see for modern professional upholsterers.

## CHRIST CHURCH Map pp226-7
☎ 215-922-1695; www.oldchristchurch.org; Church & N 2nd Sts; donation requested; 🕑 9am-5pm Mon-Sat, 1-5pm Sun; SEPTA 2nd St Station, Bus 5, 17, 33, 57

George Washington, Benjamin Franklin and Betsy Ross worshiped at this beautiful Episcopal Church, and the signers of the Declaration of Independence prayed here on July 5, 1776. The church was built in 1744, and its white steeple – which dominated the city skyline at the time – was added in 1754.

## CHRIST CHURCH BURIAL GROUND
Map pp226-7
www.oldchristchurch.org; 5th & Arch Sts; $2/1 adult/child; 🕑 10am-4pm Mon-Sat, noon-4pm Sun, weather permitting, closed Jan & Feb; SEPTA 5th St Station, Bus 57, 48

Buried here are scores of revolutionary-era notables, including the Franklin family, several generals, even more lesser officers, five signers of the Declaration of Independence and a few early mayors. The cemetery was founded in 1719, but the earliest legible stone is from 1723. The area was opened to the public for

the first time in 25 years, and official opening hours are still being worked out; those listed above are merely approximations. After hours, you can easily see the graves of Benjamin and Deborah Franklin from the street. There's a good view of the cemetery from the windows on the 2nd floor of the **US Mint** (p64).

## THE CLAY STUDIO Map pp226-7
☎ 215-925-3453; www.theclaystudio.org; 139 N 2nd St; admission free; 🕑 noon-6pm Tue-Sun; SEPTA 2nd St Station, Bus 5, 48

The completely hip Clay Studio exhibits staid and oddball works in ceramic. The studio has been in Old City since 1974 and is partially responsible for the development of the area's burgeoning gallery scene. On display here are the teapots of Bonnie Seeman, contemporary Chinese ceramics by the Nexus Gallery, wood-fired group exhibits and resident artists' work. Many of the pieces are for sale, and some of them are even affordable.

## CONGREGATION MIKVEH ISRAEL
Map pp226-7
☎ 215-922-5446; 44 N 4th St; admission free; 🕑 services 7:15pm Fri, 8 & 9am Sat & Jewish holidays; SEPTA 5th St Station, Bus 17, 33, 48, 57

Founded in 1740, Congregation Mikveh Israel is the oldest Jewish congregation in Philadelphia and the second oldest in the country. Among the artifacts on display here is a letter from George Washington to the congregation,

---

## Top Five – Old City

In addition to the spots listed below, this neighborhood's collective nightlife gets an honorable mention. See the Entertainment chapter for more information.

- **Christ Church** (p61) See the architectural masterpiece in which Washington and other Revolution-era figures prayed.
- **Elfreth's Alley** (p62) Take a stroll down the alley reputed to be the country's oldest continually occupied residential street.
- **Fireman's Hall** (p62) Check out three centuries worth of fire-fighting equipment.
- **Mum Puppettheatre** (p126) Allow your belief to be suspended as you enter a bizarre world.
- **National Constitution Center** (p62) Learn about the principles intended to guide this country in a surprisingly dramatic museum.

thanking them for their congratulations to him on his becoming president.

## DREAM GARDEN Map pp226-7

☎ 215-238-6484; 601 Walnut St; admission free; ☾ 7am-6pm Mon-Fri, 10am-1pm Sat; SEPTA 5th St Station, Bus 9, 21, 42, 57

This vividly colorful stained-glass mural by the studios of Louis Comfort Tiffany contains over 100,000 pieces and is almost 50ft long. Made in 1916 according to the designs of Maxfield Parrish, this piece is best viewed in morning light. It's hidden in the lobby of the Curtis Publishing Company building.

## ELFRETH'S ALLEY Map pp226-7

Btwn Front & 2nd Sts; SEPTA 2nd St Station, Bus 5, 48

Believed to be America's oldest continually occupied residential street (1713), this picturesque alley, named for a blacksmith who lived here, connects N Front St with N 2nd St. Along the narrow alley, 33 privately owned houses date from 1728 to 1836.

The small **Mantua Maker's Museum House** (Map pp226-7; ☎ 215-574-0560; No 126; adult/child $2/1; ☾ 10am-5pm Mon-Sat, noon-5pm Sun March-Oct), which is also called Elfreth's Alley Museum, has period furniture, changing exhibits and guided tours. A couple of the houses (Nos 110, 114, 112) taped little signs in their windows describing the history of their occupants. Read the signs but don't knock on any doors.

## First Fridays

Between October and July Philadelphia's art scene revs up for First Friday. On the first Friday of each month the 40-plus Old City galleries, showrooms and cooperatives stay open until 9pm or 10pm. Young artists, students and other onlookers hang out and enjoy the exhibits in spaces that get filled to the brim with well-dressed urban types. Many of the galleries put out complimentary wine, beer and snacks. Among the more discerning galleries are **Nexus** (p63), **The Clay Studio** (p61), The Temple Gallery, Muse, Third Street Gallery and collaborative **Space 1026** (p71).

Don't forget to visit **Vox Populi** (p69); though it isn't in Old City, its exhibits are usually pretty fun. While popular, they won't make you feel like a sardine, which is both a charming and irritating aspect of the Old City experience.

For details call the **Old City Arts Organization** ( ☎ 215-625-9200; www.oldcityarts.org; 230 Vine St).

## FIREMAN'S HALL Map pp226-7

☎ 215-923-1438; 147 N 2nd St; ☾ 10am-5pm Tue-Sat; SEPTA 2nd St Station, Bus 5, 48

This restored 1876 firehouse is a museum that portrays the history of fire-fighting in America with terrific memorabilia and restored early models of pumpers and rolling stock. It's an excellent stop for anyone of any age.

The 1st floor deals with the early days, showing bucket brigades and the rise of an organized volunteer department led by Ben Franklin in 1736. It also houses several large fire trucks (horse-drawn, people-drawn, motorized and steam-powered). The 2nd floor details the inception of the paid department, with models of early equipment and fire-fighting techniques. Brass name plaques list those Philadelphians who died in the line of duty. Other exhibits include a fireboat wheelhouse and a re-creation of the typical living quarters of early professional firefighters.

## LIBRARY HALL Map pp226-7

☎ 215-440-3400; 105 S 5th St; admission free; ☾ 9am-5pm Mon-Fri; SEPTA 5th St Station, Bus 9, 21, 42, 57

This building contains the research library and offices of the American Philosophical Society. The site on which the library sits was originally home to the first subscription library in the USA. The Library Company of Philadelphia, a forerunner of the Library of Congress, was later founded here in 1789, remaining until 1888, when the building was demolished. The present building was constructed in 1959, and its facade is an exact reproduction of the original.

Only the lobby of Library Hall is open to the public. It hosts changing, thematic exhibits largely about the history of the library and the splendor of its collections. Depending on when you visit, you might see an 18th-century manuscript covering some aspect of American Indian linguistics, a 1st edition of Darwin's *The Origin of Species* or some items from Franklin's personal library. The remainder of the building is open only to researchers with legitimate need to use the library's collections.

## NATIONAL CONSTITUTION CENTER

Map pp226-7

NCC; ☎ 215-409-6600; www.constitutioncenter.org; 525 Arch St; adult/child $6/5; ☾ 9:30am-5pm Mon-Fri, 9:30am-6pm Sat & Sun; SEPTA 5th St Station, Bus 17, 33, 44, 47, 48, 57

Somehow or other, this brand-new museum accomplishes the impossible: it makes

Neighborhoods – Old City

the United States Constitution sexy and interesting for a general audience. It's a good thing, too, since, as the folks at the NCC will tell you, fewer than 6% of American citizens can name the basic freedoms guaranteed by the First Amendment.

Housed in a massive building whose scale is intended to overwhelm, the museum contains a 350-seat theater in the round, where an enveloping screen and single live actor colorfully discuss the evolution of the Constitution through history. Other exhibits include a blue screen that creates the illusion of visitors being sworn in as president, interactive voting booths, and Signer's Hall, which contains lifelike bronze statues of the signers in action. There's also an Internet café where you can go online to register to vote or email your representative, perhaps to make a reservation at the **US Mint** (p64).

## NATIONAL MUSEUM OF AMERICAN JEWISH HISTORY Map pp226-7

☎ 215-923-5986; www.nmajh.org; 55 N 5th St; SEPTA 5th St Station, Bus 17, 33, 48, 57

This museum once operated out of a small building adjacent to Mikveh Israel, built for the bicentennial. Now the former building is being replaced by a much larger six-story structure that will be devoted to telling the story of the role of Jews in American history. The new museum is due to open in 2006. In the meantime efforts are underway to house a small exhibit outlining the American Jewish experience somewhere in the vicinity of Mikveh Israel; call for details.

## NEXUS FOUNDATION FOR TODAY'S ART Map pp226-7

☎ 215-629-1103; 137 N 2nd St; admission free; ⏰ noon-5pm Tue-Sun; SEPTA 2nd St Station, Bus 5, 48

Over 25 years old, this cooperative is Old City's most prominent gallery, and exhibits the work of members and invited artists. Past shows have included 'Iron On,' which displayed T-shirts for love (meaning people who love T-shirts really appreciated the exhibit) and T-shirts for sale (meaning they could then demonstrate their love in spending cash) as well as the work of William Cromar. Often artists who exhibit here attain national recognition.

## PAINTED BRIDE ART CENTER

Map pp226-7

☎ 215-925-9914; www.paintedbride.org; 230 Vine St; gallery admission free, performances $10-25; ⏰ 10am-6pm Tue-Fri; noon-6pm Sat; SEPTA 2nd St Station, Bus 5, 48, 57

A multipurpose art facility, the Painted Bride offers a dedicated gallery space with a changing array of progressive visual artists, such as photographers Amie Potsic and Neila Kun. The Bride, of Philly's older contemporary house of culture, also books a full calendar of in-your-face dance, spoken word and jazz. Spalding Gray did gigs here.

**Tops for Children**

Little squirts love Philly, and here's why:

- **Franklin Institute** (p76) This place reigns as champion of interactive displays. Walk through a giant heart and ride a steam train.
- **Independence National Historical Park** (p55) While just about anything in this park – including the bell and the hall – are good for kids, the little ones especially like Franklin Court.
- **Please Touch Museum** (p78) Giant toys allow children to pretend to drive a bus or to shop for groceries.
- **The Academy of Natural Sciences** (p76) Romp with dinosaurs and a roomful of live butterflies and dig for fossils.
- **Ride the Ducks** (p54) Tour Old City in an amphibious vehicle with a plastic duck caller.
- **Independence Seaport Museum** (p66) Quickly learn about the water or whatever else and then explore the pièce de résistance – the submarine.
- **Mum Puppettheatre** (p126) Even if you don't have a kid, this place kicks butt.
- **Eastern State Penitentiary** (p76) Not great for the littlest guys, but those a bit older dig this creepy place.
- **New Jersey State Aquarium** (p67) Most kids like to look at large glass tanks full of slippery objects.
- **Philadelphia Zoo** (p84) In addition to taking a gander at exotic animals, you can ride in a tethered balloon.
- **Prince Musical Theater** (p127) This venue occasionally programs events like a Wizard of Oz sing-along.
- **Walnut Street Theatre** (p127) America's oldest theater frequently stages plays for children.
- **Spiral Q Puppet Theater** (p87) Who doesn't want to see a colorful warehouse full of giant parade costumes?

Neighborhoods – Old City

## PHILADELPHIA MERCHANTS EXCHANGE Map pp226-7

3rd & Walnut Sts; admission free; 🕑 8am-4:30pm Mon-Fri; SEPTA 2nd St Station, Bus 21, 42, 57

Another beautiful piece of architecture, this Greek Revival building stands out from its Federal and Georgian brick neighbors with its semicircular Corinthian portico and lantern tower. William Strickland, who was also responsible for the nearby Second Bank of the US, designed it in the 1830s. The country's first stock exchange opened here in 1834 and operated until the Civil War. During the 19th century, the area immediately around the exchange was the city's primary transportation hub and a terminus for several omnibus routes. There is a small, free exhibit on the 1st floor explaining the history of the exchange, why Greek Revival architecture was associated with democratic ideals, and biographical information on Strickland. The remainder of the building is closed to the public.

## PHILOSOPHICAL HALL Map pp226-7

☎ 215-440-3400; 104 S 5th St; admission free; 🕑 10am-4pm Wed-Sun Mar–Labor Day, 10am-4pm Thu-Sun Labor Day–Feb; SEPTA 5th St Station, Bus 9, 21, 42, 57

Behind Old City Hall is Philosophical Hall (built 1786–89), home of the American Philosophical Society, which was founded in 1743 by Benjamin Franklin and is the USA's oldest learned society. Past members have included Thomas Jefferson, Marie Curie, Thomas Edison, Charles Darwin and Albert Einstein. The society is still active in many fields, including medicine, computers, literary studies and quantum physics.

In 2001 the American Philosophical Society opened Philosophical Hall to the public for the first time since the beginning of the 19th century. Exhibits rotate frequently and have included 'Stuffing Birds, Pressing Plants, Shaping Knowledge,' which explained the development of 18th- and 19th-century natural history and presented specimens once used in the famed natural history museum that Charles Wilson Peale organized back in the early 1900s. Another exhibit explored – through the display of bizarre scientific instruments used from 1750–1875 – how the Enlightenment's culture of science impacted the growth of early America.

## US MINT Map pp226-7

☎ 215-408-0112; www.usmint.gov; Arch & N 5th Sts; admission free; SEPTA 5th St Station, Bus 17, 33, 48, 57

The US Mint, opposite Christ Church Burial Ground (of which there is a good view from the 2nd floor), is the world's largest mint and the fourth one built on this site; the current building dates from 1969. It makes coins (including over one million Lincoln pennies a day) and medals, performs designing and engraving, and processes mutilated coins.

Philly's mint is one of two in the country that provides tours (the other is in Denver), though tours are free and ridiculously hard to arrange. To be admitted, guests must obtain sponsorship from their local congressional office and then jump through a series of bureaucratic hoops. The process takes about a month. More information on this can be had at the mint's website. If you manage to get inside and past security, you can watch the coinage operation from a long, glass-enclosed gallery.

# SOCIETY HILL

*Sleeping p163*

Residential headquarters for well-heeled Philadelphians, the quiet streets of Society Hill provide some of the shadiest, safest and most pleasant strolling opportunities this side of the Delaware. Society Hill's picturesque, private feel makes it a popular destination for horse-drawn-carriage operators and baby-stroller pushers. The neighborhood is best represented by a prominent citizen: Eli the well-groomed pug.

Eli lives in a Federal-style row house on 4th St near Spruce, which is selling for $2.7 million dollars. Every day, he gets up and is walked through the grounds of IM Pei's Society Hill Towers, huge structures that helped to successfully gentrify the neighborhood back in the '70s. On his morning circuit he stops at a café, which is frequented more by families with children then by ultra-cool hipsters. After vigorously chowing a bagel, he heads home so his owners can do some work from their upstairs office.

In the evening, he hobbles down even more residential streets en route to Washington Square, a center for Philadelphia's dog-walking community.

A visit to Society Hill will reveal a landscape dominated by 18th- and 19th-century architecture interspersed with contemporary homes attempting to blend into the older fabric. Aside from walking, most of the attractions in this neighborhood involve visits to old congregations and historic houses. The area underwent major restoration during the 1960s and '70s, when it saw Pei's towers rise. It takes its name from the Free Society of Traders, a group of businesspeople who settled here with their families in 1683 at the behest of William Penn.

## Transport

**Subway** Society Hill is slightly removed from the subway and uses SEPTA's 2nd St Station, on Market St.
**Bus** The 12 meanders east from University City, mostly along Locust St. It enters Society Hill along Pine St, hits 3rd St and departs the neighborhood along Spruce before jumping up to return along Walnut St.
**Parking** There are paid parking lots along Lombard near 2nd.

## Orientation

Society Hill has excellent boundaries. On the north edge is lively South St, and to the south is livelier Old City. Go west and you hit Washington Square; go east and there's the freeway, Penn's Landing and the Delaware River. More precisely, Society Hill lies between S 6th and S Front Sts and Walnut and Lombard Sts, straddling Independence National Historical Park.

## ATHENAEUM Map pp226-7

☎ 215-925-2688; 219 S 6th St;
www.philaathenaeum.org; free admission; ☼ 9am-5pm Mon-Fri; SEPTA 2nd St Station, Bus 21, 42, 90
John Nottam's Gothic Revival building houses a member-supported library specializing in architecture and design. Scholars and other interested parties can request access to the library, while anyone may tour the historic site museum and its exhibitions.

## OLD ST JOSEPH'S CHURCH Map pp226-7

☎ 215-923-1733; 321 Willings Alley; admission free; SEPTA 2nd St Station, Bus 9, 21, 42, 57
This is the site of the city's first Roman Catholic Church, built in 1733 when Catholic services were strictly banned in Britain and its empire. Nevertheless, William Penn tolerated all faiths in his colony, though as a precaution the church was purposely hidden from view by an alley and courtyard. Its pastor dressed as a Quaker when traveling around the city. Irish

and German craftsmen and domestic staff dominated the original congregation. For a while, it was the only Catholic Church allowed to practice by law in the English-speaking world. The current church was built in 1839. Check at the rectory daily between 10am and 4pm about visiting the church when services aren't being held.

## PHYSICK HOUSE Map pp226-7

☎ 215-925-7866; 321 S 4th St; adult/child $3/2; ☼ 11am-2pm Thu-Sat; SEPTA 2nd St Station, Bus 9, 21, 42, 57
Built in 1786 by Henry Hill, a wine importer who kept City Tavern well-stocked, this is the only freestanding, Federal-style mansion remaining in Society Hill. After Hill died in one of Philly's frequent yellow fever outbreaks, the building became home to the father of American surgery, Dr Philip Syng Physick (history's biggest victim of unfunny puns). Andrew Jackson went under his knife. Restored in the 1960s, the house is one of the few sites still displaying original neoclassic furnishings. Hours expand slightly in peak season, and entry includes a guided tour.

## POWEL HOUSE Map pp226-7

☎ 215-627-0364; 244 S 3rd St; adult/child $3/2; ☼ noon-5pm Thu-Sat, 1-5pm Sun; SEPTA 2nd St Station, Bus 9, 21, 42, 57
Home to Samuel Powel, the mayor of Philadelphia at the time the boys declared independence, the Powel House frequently served as a meeting place for the revolution's top brass. Washington, Adams and Franklin were all entertained at the mayor's house, which John Adams found exceptionally well-appointed.

Such appointments have been largely retained or restored, and today's visitors can see firsthand what the quality of life was like for the wealthiest colonial patriots. The admission price gets you a tour of the garden and house, including the room in which the Washingtons celebrated a wedding anniversary. Reservations are recommended.

# PENN'S LANDING

*Sleeping p163*

Back in its heyday, Penn's Landing was a very active port area until that activity moved farther south down the Delaware. Severed from the rest of the city by the interstate highway, the area then existed as an underused, unattractive and uninhabited stretch of land for most of the 1960s and '70s. Recognizing that a valuable waterfront area was being wasted, local leaders moved to make the site an attractive destination, resulting in the establishment of the Independence Seaport Museum, a Hyatt Regency and the Great Plaza, which provides a venue for outdoor events and festivals.

Most of the action in today's Penn's Landing involves boarding submarines, strolling along the water's edge and buying cotton candy from a vendor whenever a festival occurs. The view east across the water can be pretty, particularly when it involves capturing the Benjamin Franklin Bridge at sunrise. The view west to the highway is the opposite of pretty, an issue that Mayor Street has decided to confront. Proposals to cap the interstate and build on top of it are being floated.

Also in progress is an expanded and renovated **International Sculpture Garden**, part of which was moved to allow construction of the Hyatt. The garden, run by the Fairmount Park Art Association, includes sculptures from India, Korea, British Columbia, Indonesia and Costa Rica, as well as Columbus Monument, a 106ft-high obelisk. Some of the sculptures are currently in storage, but will be reinstalled when the new garden is ready; call ☎ 215-546-7550 or visit www.fpaa.org for an update.

North of Penn's Landing and the Benjamin Franklin Bridge you'll find another sliver of land similarly separated from the rest of Philadelphia by I-95. This bit contains several monumentally sized nightclubs and the Festival Pier, which provides even more space for outdoor events.

Several of the sights listed below can be viewed at a discounted rate if you purchase a Ship's Pass (adult/child/senior $19/13/15), which gets you access to the **Independence Seaport Museum** (p66) and its ships, plus a ferry ride on the River Link Ferry to Camden, NJ, where you can tour the *Battleship New Jersey* (p67). A similar package, the River Pass (adult/senior/child $21.50/21/15.50), gets you access to the Independence Seaport museum, its ships, the **New Jersey State Aquarium** (p67) and a ferry ride between them. Both of these specials are available April through November.

## Orientation

Short and lean, Penn's Landing sits between I-95 and the Delaware River. Its northern edge lies around Market St, and its southern edge is in the vicinity of South St. An information center with a public bathroom is just south of the Seaport Museum.

### INDEPENDENCE SEAPORT MUSEUM

Map pp226-7

☎ 215-925-5439; 211 S Columbus Blvd; www.phillyseaport.org; adult/child/senior $8/5/6.50, admission free 10am-noon Sun; ☉ 10am-5pm; Bus 12, 25, 76

This kid-friendly museum offers a range of exhibits and interactive displays. Sound a series of signals such as foghorns and a steam whistle, or climb into an immigrant's steerage compartment. The 'What Floats Your Boat' portion of the museum provides insight into the history of ship construction and the scientific principles behind buoyancy,

## Transport

**Subway** SEPTA hooks up to Penn's Landing at 2nd St Station.

**Bus** The 25 runs along the west side of the Delaware River. The 42 traverses Center City along Chestnut St, hits Penn's Landing and heads back across the city on Walnut St.

**River Link Ferry** Runs every 40 minutes from 9am to 5pm between Penn's Landing and the Camden Waterfront.

**Parking** There are paid lots on Columbus Blvd near Market St and on Columbus Blvd near Chestnut St.

displacement and wind-propelled sails. Another exhibit explains the history of Philadelphia's port activity; a series of aerial views of the city from the 1680s to the present show its growth from the perspective of the Delaware. One of the more interesting displays is a collection of seemingly unrelated nautical-themed artifacts, such as a massive ship's carpenter's screwdriver and various complicated implements. Your admission ticket also gains you access to board the nearby American warships *USS Becuna* and *USS Olympia*.

**USS Becuna** In 1944 this Balao-class submarine was originally built of welded steel in Groton, Connecticut, and became the flagship submarine of General MacArthur's Southwest Pacific Fleet. During World War II it destroyed three Japanese vessels and patrolled the Java and China seas as well as the coast of the Philippines. In 1951 the *Becuna* underwent substantial modifications, reemerging in its updated form as a Guppy 1A–class ship. During the Korean and Vietnam Wars, she sailed in the Mediterranean before being decommissioned in 1969.

**USS Olympia** One of the US navy's first steel ships, the *Olympia* was commissioned in 1892. She became one of America's most distinguished warships, principally because of her role as Commodore Dewey's flagship in 1898's Battle of Manila Bay during the Spanish-American War. The results of this decisive battle saw the Spanish fleet – largely considered superior to their American adversaries – crippled for the duration of the war and revealed the United States as an emerging world power. Following the Spanish-American War, the *Olympia* performed minor operations near Turkey and Panama, and served as a training vessel for new cadets. During World War I, the ship patrolled the waters off the United States' East Coast; at the end of the war, she carried the body of the Unknown Soldier from France to Arlington National Cemetery before being decommissioned in 1922.

### THE IRISH MEMORIAL
Map pp226-7; Front & Chestnut Sts; www.irishmemorial.org; Bus 25, 42
Dedicated to the victims of the 'Great Hunger' that claimed a million Irish lives between 1845–1850 and caused a million more to emigrate to the US, the centerpiece of this memorial is a huge sculpture by Glenna Goodacre, who designed the Vietnam Women's Memorial in

Washington, DC. The massive bronze sculpture (30ft long, 12ft wide and 12ft high) depicts 35 life-sized figures in a thematic progression from starvation to emigration. The statue was dedicated in November 2003, and future plans for the site include gardens and interpretive stations.

### VIETNAM VETERANS MEMORIAL
Map pp226-7; Columbus Blvd & Spruce St; Bus 12, 25, 76
Dedicated in 1987, this memorial honors the 80,000 Philadelphians who served in the Vietnam War, including the 642 who died. The black Missing in Action flags fly alongside the Stars and Stripes.

## Across the River
Waving at Penn's Landing from the opposite shore of the Delaware River is the waterfront of Camden, New Jersey. Over yonder, you can check out two big sites that are ideal for kids: the *Battleship New Jersey* and the New Jersey State Aquarium.

### NEW JERSEY STATE AQUARIUM
Map pp226-7
☎ 856-365-3300; www.njaquarium.org; 1 Riverside Dr; adult/student/child/senior $14/12/11/11; ☉ 9:30am-4:30pm Mon-Fri, 10am-5pm Sat & Sun; River Link Ferry
This massive facility features eight big displays including a coral station of colorful Caribbean fish, a shark tank and an archway where you can pass under schools of fish. The Ocean Tank exhibit gives you a (simulated) glimpse of Hudson Canyon, a deep chasm that lies 35 miles off the coast of New Jersey. The aquarium gets quite crowed on weekends.

### BATTLESHIP NEW JERSEY
Map pp226-7
☎ 856-877-6262; www.battleshipnewjersey .org; Riverside Dr; adult/child/senior $12.50/8/8 ☉ 9am-5pm Apr-Sep, 9am-3pm Oct-Mar; River Link Ferry
Tour the USA's most decorated battleship. The basic tour covers much of the ship, including a look at the living quarters of officers and sailors. Lay out a few more dollars and you can take the two-hour Firepower Tour, in which you'll see even more of the ship, participate in a simulated missile launch and have the opportunity to crawl in a 16-inch gun turret.

# CENTER CITY

*Eating p107; Shopping p152; Sleeping p164*

Philadelphia's center of creativity, commerce, culture and just about everything else, this is the engine that drives the city. It contains the city's tallest buildings, the financial distinct, big hotels, museums, concert halls, shops and restaurants. At its physical center, where Market and Broad Sts cross, sits Penn Square and City Hall, which is covered in Alexander Milne Calder's sculptures and topped with a ridiculously large statue of William Penn. The municipal government clusters around this 548-ft-tall Second Empire monolithic building, and during business hours this area is filled with people in suits and skirts scurrying hither and thither. During the day, City Hall allows visitors to take a free ride to the top of the building's tower. Inches below Penn's giant feet, excellent views and orientation to the city are afforded.

Looking northwest, see the Benjamin Franklin Parkway stretching diagonally towards the Philadelphia Museum of Art and Fairmount Park beyond it. Travel away from City Hall along this path and you enter a district full of hotels, office buildings and parking lots. Pass through Logan Square and the rotary that surrounds it to find shorter buildings, green park spaces and Philadelphia's Museum District. This northwest corner of Center City is lively during the day but relatively empty (read: mildly unsafe, but mostly unfun) at night.

Turn to the northeast and it will be impossible to miss identifying the Pennsylvania Convention Center, which takes up four blocks and occupies the old Reading Railroad train shed. Beneath this monstrous building, find the colorful **Reading Terminal Market** (p34). Just past the convention center is Chinatown, small and almost always open for business and food.

Take a southeast gander to behold the neighborhood of Washington Square West, whose streets closest to Washington Square contain numerous bars, a hospital district and lovely redbricked Jeweler's Row. The half of Washington Square West closest to Broad St contains numerous residential alleys and Philadelphia's centralized gay neighborhood, locally referred to as the Gayborhood.

Look directly south and your eyes will follow the line of the Avenue of the Arts (Broad St) to the glass-domed Kimmel Center. Many of Philadelphia's most prestigious cultural performances are held along this stretch of road.

Finally turn to face the Rittenhouse Square District. You won't be able to see the square because numerous tall buildings will be blocking your view. That's because everyone wants to live or work near this pretty urban oasis. Hurry down the elevator, find your path to the square and get ready for lunch.

In the following pages, Center City is broken into the following subcategories: Avenue of the Arts, Chinatown & Around, Rittenhouse Square, Washington Square West and Parkway & Museum Area.

## Orientation

Center City matches the extents of Penn's original city. Its northern and southern edges are Vine St and South St, respectively, while the eastern and western edges are the Delaware River and the Schuylkill River, respectively. The area is 2 miles wide from river to river, and 1 mile from Vine St to South St.

With the exception of Benjamin Franklin Parkway, nearly every street is part of a grid. North-south streets are mostly numbered, except for Broad St, the main north-south street (and the equivalent of 14th St), and Front St (the equivalent of 1st St). Market St is the main east-west route and divides the city's center between north and south. North of Market St, street addresses are labeled 'N'; south of Market, they take an 'S.' This means that 31 N 2nd St and 31 S 2nd St are on the same road, with Market St halfway between them.

Technically, Center City includes Old City, Society Hill and South Street, but since these neighborhoods are so distinct, we've given them equal ranking and their own headings.

## THE FABRIC WORKSHOP & MUSEUM

Map pp222-3

☎ 215-568-1111; www.fabricworkshopandmuseum
.org; 1315 Cherry St, 5th fl; suggested donation
adult/child $5/2; ⏰ 10am-6pm Mon-Fri, noon-4pm
Sat; SEPTA 13th St Station, Bus 27, 32, 38, 44, 48

On one level, check out a bunch of resident
artists and interns creating and then
transforming the bizarre into art. Above it is
a museum of changing fabric- and texture-
based exhibits, variously featuring the work
of folks like Robert Venturi, Denise Scott
Brown, Robert Morris and Nancy Rubins. A
representative exhibit includes 'RN: The Past,
Present and Future of Nurses' Uniforms,'
which presents historical artifacts, the 'ideal'
uniform of the present (hundreds of nurses
were surveyed to determine this result) and
futuristic items like the Inter-Galactic Nurse.

## MASONIC TEMPLE Map pp222-3

☎ 215-988-1910; www.pagrandlodge.org; 1 N Broad
St; donation requested; ⏰ tours 11am, 2pm & 3pm
Tue-Fri, 10am & 11am Sat; SEPTA 13th St Station, Bus
27, 32, 38, 44, 48

This temple is the headquarters of the Grand
Lodge of Free & Accepted Masons of Pennsylvania.
Some of the founding fathers, including George
Washington, were members, and the temple
library and museum contain letters and books
from their period. The seven lodge halls, elaborate
and freakishly mythical, are designed in different
architectural styles: Corinthian, Egyptian, Gothic,
Ionic, Norman, Oriental and Renaissance. Guided
tours last 45 minutes.

## VOX POPULI Map pp222-3

☎ 215-568-5513; www.voxpopuligallery.org; 1315
Cherry St, 4th fl; admission free; ⏰ noon-6pm Wed-
Sun; SEPTA 13th St Station, Bus 27, 32, 38, 44, 48

A cooperative gallery founded to support the
work of emerging artists, Vox Populi instantly
makes visitors feel like hip art-world insiders,
perhaps because there isn't much signage
directing them to the gallery. Membership to
the co-op changes annually; each month these
Voxers display their work, often laced with
droll pop overtones. This is one of the most
significant spaces for Philly's young artists, and
First Fridays (p62) are particularly fun here.

# AVENUE OF THE ARTS

From the Ballet to the Clef Club, many of
Philadelphia's most important houses of
culture line up on either side of the Avenue

## Transport

**Subway** The Broad St Line runs directly underneath
the Avenue of the Arts. Depending on your stop, use
City Hall, Walnut-Locust or Lombard-South station.
**Bus** The 40 crosses Broad at South, heading east. It
returns on Lombard. Bus 12 crosses Broad at Locust,
heading east; it returns on Walnut.
**Parking** There's a parking lot near the Bellevue, on
Locust near Broad.

of the Arts (aka Broad St). Dominated by
theaters, tall office towers, campus buildings
and grand music halls, the Avenue of the
Arts lacks a sizable residential community.
The thoroughfare's focus is clearly on
performance; this is the place to catch
Broadway shows, live chamber music, the
Philadelphia Orchestra and more.

As it has been ever since Penn planned
Philadelphia, Broad St is one of the widest
in town. This width sets buildings father
apart, creating a grandly sized space
that helps give the Avenue of the Arts a
slightly formal feel. As the avenue heads
to South Philly, building heights decrease
and the regality is lost. You'll know when
the Avenue of the Arts becomes merely
Broad St when you begin to see heaps
of unticketed cars parked illegally in the
middle of the road.

The Broad St art scene got its start back
in the 1850s when the city's grand opera
house, the Academy of Music, was built.
At the time the Broad St site was chosen
because it was a relatively quiet place on the
edge of the densely built part of the city,
where noise would be less likely to disturb
performances.

## Orientation

This one's easy: the Avenue of the Arts is
Broad St, south of Market St. At its north
end is City Hall, and its southern end
becomes less artful around Fitzwater St.

## ACADEMY OF MUSIC Map pp222-3

☎ 215-893-1955; www.academyofmusic.org; Broad &
Locust Sts; tour $5; tickets $5-155; ⏰ box office open
1hr before performance; SEPTA Walnut-Locust Station,
Bus 9, 12, 21, 27, 32, 42

The oldest grand opera house still used for its
original purpose, the neo-baroque Academy
of Music, designed by LeBrun and Runge

Neighborhoods – Center City

## Top Five – Avenue of the Arts

- **City Hall** (p70) Take in a panoramic view of Philadelphia atop a giant masonry tower.
- **Kimmel Center** (p70) Listen to some classical tunes at this brand-new concert hall.
- **McGillin's** (p132) Toast your friends near the fireplace of Philadelphia's oldest bar.
- **Pennsylvania Ballet** (p128) Watch this impressive troupe dance in America's oldest grand opera house.
- **Wilma Theater** (p127) Check out an avant-garde production at this hip playhouse.

in 1855, hasn't changed much since it first opened. The beautiful murals on the ceiling still exist, though the 5000lb chandelier is no longer raised and lowered by hand, much to the delight of today's stage workers. Tours of the building occur throughout the year, and reservations are required; for more information, call ☎ 215-893-1935.

The Academy, now managed by the Kimmel Center, is home to **The Opera Company of Philadelphia** (p129) and the **Pennsylvania Ballet** (p128). It also stages Broadway shows. The main box office is at the Kimmel Center.

### CITY HALL Map pp222-3

☎ 215-686-9074; www.phila.gov; Broad & Market Sts; admission free; ⏰ 9:30am-4:30pm Tue-Fri; SEPTA 13th St Station, SEPTA 15th St Station, Bus 27, 32, 33, 44

One of Philadelphia's architectural highlights, City Hall is purported by some to be the country's largest municipal building. Completed in 1901, it took 30 years to build. By the time of completion, the excessively ornamental building of French influence had shifted in popular taste from being totally fashionable to completely passé. Whatever your taste, it's darn weird to see a Victorian skyscraper.

The elaborately designed building was constructed without a steel framework, so the 22ft-thick granite walls at the base support the central tower. City Hall was the city's tallest building until the completion of Liberty Place in 1987, and is the world's tallest building without steel-framed construction. AM Calder's 27-ton, 37ft-high bronze statue of William Penn crowns the 548ft-high City Hall. Before Liberty Place, a 'gentlemen's agreement' had limited the

height of Philadelphia's buildings to Penn's hat. Now City Hall no longer dominates the Philadelphia skyline.

Free tours of the interior are at 12:30pm from room 121. You can also visit the observation deck of the tower for a magnificent view of the city from 40 floors up. From the northeast corner, take the elevator to the 7th floor and follow the red line to the waiting area. You get your ticket here and then are escorted in another elevator to the deck. These trips can be crowded but you can go to the waiting area and book a time. Note that 10am to noon is usually reserved for school or other special groups.

### KIMMEL CENTER FOR THE PERFORMING ARTS Map pp222-3

☎ 215-790-5800; www.kimmelcenter.org; Broad & Spruce Sts; $18-80; ⏰ 10am-6pm (open later on performance evenings); SEPTA Walnut-Locust Station, Bus 9, 12, 21, 27, 32, 42

Very few pieces of architecture achieve instant critical recognition as superior works. Luckily for Philadelphia, the Kimmel Center just might deserve inclusion in this group. Rafael Viñoly's design is a stunning technological and aesthetic achievement. The shell of the building is a 400ft-long vaulted ceiling made of glass through which visitors watch expanses of cloud pass overhead. Contained within this shell are two theaters with exemplary acoustics and sight lines: **Verizon Hall**, a 2500-seat, cello-shaped concert hall, and the **Perelman Theater**, containing 650 seats and a rotating stage.

Opened in 2001, the Kimmel Center hosts numerous jazz, pop, classical, choir, dance, theater and family-entertainment performances, and is the principal home of **The Philadelphia Chamber Music Society** (p129). Free tours are conducted Tuesday through Sunday at noon, 1pm and 2pm.

## CHINATOWN & AROUND

The fourth-largest Chinatown in the USA, Philly's version has existed since the 1860s. Chinese immigrants who built America's transcontinental railroads started out west and worked their way here.

Today's Chinatown remains a center for immigrants, though now many of the neighborhood's residents come from Malaysia, Thailand and Vietnam in addition to every province in China. Though it does hold a few residents, the tone of Chinatown is thoroughly commercial. At street level you'll find restaurants, Chinese bakeries, shops full of Hello Kitty merchandise and stores devoted to supporting the day-to-day practice of living (eg, hardware stores).

The easiest way to explore the culture of the neighborhood is through its food. During the day, casual markets materialize on the sidewalks. At night, dozens of restaurants and specialty food stores fill up with hungry Joes looking for a cheap bite. The small neighborhood is also home to one of the city's better rock venues, the Trocadero (p141), and artists are attracted to bargain rentals on Chinatown's edge.

Lately the city government has seemed out to get Chinatown. Construction of the nearby Convention Center seriously threatened its survival. More recently there was talk of building one of the new sports complexes here until more sensible heads lobbied successfully to keep them in South Philadelphia.

## Orientation

Philadelphia's eight-block Chinatown lies between N 8th and N 11th Sts and Vine and Arch Sts. There are at least five restaurants along every street.

### THE AFRICAN AMERICAN MUSEUM IN PHILADELPHIA Map pp222-3
☎ 215-574-0380 ext 224; www.aampmuseum.org; 701 Arch St; adult/child/student/senior $6/4/4/4; ☾ 10am-5pm Mon-Sat, noon-5pm Sun; SEPTA 8th St Station, Bus 47, 48

This museum contains one of the country's best collections on black history and culture. Its work explores African American heritage through slavery, emancipation, the civil rights movement and beyond. Exhibits have included

## Transport

**Subway** SEPTA's 11th St Station enjoys picking up and dropping off people on Market St.

**Bus** The 47m, originating in South Philly, crosses Chinatown using 9th St, before heading north along 7th. Eastward-bound bus 48 crosses town along Market St. The western return crosses the city and Chinatown along Arch St.

**Parking** Street parking shouldn't be too challenging, especially north of Race. If it is, don't fret – a paid lot exists at Race and 11th.

## Top Five – Chinatown

- **The African American Museum in Philadelphia** (p71) Explore some of America's best exhibits on black heritage.
- **Charles Plaza** (p108) Dine on some of the finest fake meats ever made.
- **Ray's Cafe and Teahouse** (p108) Enjoy exotic coffee, elaborately prepared.
- **Reading Terminal Market** (p104) Eat every possible kind of food in this ancient market hall.
- **Trocadero** (p141) Take in some rock at this lively club.

an outstanding collection of photojournalism documenting Dr Martin Luther King Jr and another outlining the history and symbolism of black dolls (for example, black china dolls were 'intended to be the slave and servant playmates of white dolls'). There's also a renowned gift shop selling craftwork.

### CHINESE FRIENDSHIP GATE Map pp222-3
N 10th St btwn Cherry & Arch Sts; SEPTA 11th St Station, Bus 23, 47, 48, 61

A decorative arch built in 1984 as a joint project between Philadelphia and its Chinese sister city, Tianjin, the multicolored, four-story Friendship Gate is Chinatown's most conspicuous landmark.

### SPACE 1026 Map pp222-3
☎ 215-574-7630; www.space1026.com; 1026 Arch St; admission free; ☾ First Fridays & by appt; SEPTA 11th St Station, Bus 23, 47, 48, 61

On the edge of Chinatown, this cooperative gallery and studio is run by a group of artists (many from Rhode Island School of Design) who present fantastic exhibits of other peoples' work on First Fridays (p62). Some past shows include Andrew Kuo's screen prints, the work of installationists employed by the ICA (p87) and a flipbook festival. For the daring, it's pretty easy to drop by the studio during the week; someone friendly is awake by noon. Be sure to check out their store of silk-screen items – all cool, all for sale.

## RITTENHOUSE SQUARE

Philadelphia's most fashionable neighborhood, the residential areas bordering the namesake square are totally chic, containing the most expensive apartments in

## Transport

**Subway** SEPTA's Market-Frankford line runs along this neighborhood's northern border, and the Broad St line runs along its eastern edge. 19th St Station, on Market St, is the closest station to the square itself.

**Bus** Buses 9, 21, and 42 run across town, entering the Rittenhouse Square District heading east along Chestnut St. They return along Walnut St.

**Parking** Street parking can be a challenge near the square. Your best bet is to park around Pine St and hike in. A garage exists at Walnut and 21st, though there are many more.

the city. But since this is Philly, even the most expensive apartments remain plausibly affordable, at least when compared with the rates charged in other major American cities. This makes for an interesting street scene: nattily dressed business people, young ladies in thrift-store clothes, the descendants of Philadelphia's former aristocracy, myriad students, and kids smoking dope in the park.

At all hours Rittenhouse Square is lively. The square itself is one of few urban parks that feel completely safe at night, largely because it's in constant use by people coming to enjoy 24-hour diners, sidewalk restaurants, shopping, a few slick bars and the beauty of the square itself.

The pretty district offers more then just the square. Walnut St, Chestnut St and the streets connecting them are packed with big department stores, cool boutiques and plenty of urbanity. The subdued south side of the neighborhood comes with numerous quiet streets and alleys. Here the taller buildings closer to the business district give way to smaller residential row houses, and fine strolling can be accomplished among the late-19th-century brownstones. Back here you'll find a few cute BYOBs tucked in amongst the housing stock.

As the buildings suggest, the district was settled around the end of the 19th century by Philadelphia's aristocratic class. Though Penn allocated space for the square when he planned the city 250 years earlier, it wasn't much more then a patch of grass until the upper crust started building their mansions, some of which still exist (one now houses an Anthropologie store). Paul Cret molded it into its present City Beautiful form in 1913.

# Orientation

The Rittenhouse Square district's northern edge is Market St, the southern edge is South St, the eastern side is the Avenue of the Arts and the western side is the mighty Schuylkill River (which you need to pronounce correctly: *skoo*-kuhl). The grid exists here as elsewhere, though the paths of several streets are temporarily interrupted by Rittenhouse Square. A few alleys exist to get you on your toes or to hide from the cops.

## CIVIL WAR LIBRARY & MUSEUM
Map pp222-3
☎ 215-735-8196; 1805 Pine St; adult/child/senior $5/3/4; ☷ 11am-4:30pm Tue-Sat; Bus 17, 40

Highly recommended for Civil War buffs, this three-story building contains one of the country's most comprehensive Civil War libraries and museums. The former houses over 12,000 volumes plus manuscripts and other archival material, while the latter boasts some unique artifacts, including items – such as the stuffed head of Old Baldy – that belonged to Generals Grant, Sherman, Meade and Mulholland. A gallery of changing exhibitions deals with different aspects of the war.

## MÜTTER MUSEUM Map pp222-3
☎ 215-563-3737 ext 242; www.collphyphil.org/ muttpg1.shtml; 19 S 22nd St; $8; ☷ 10am-5pm; SEPTA 22nd St Station, Bus 7, 9, 21, 42

Everyone loves a 50lb distended colon! That's precisely what you get here, in the College of Physicians of Philadelphia's museum. This collection of pathological and anatomical specimens and medical artifacts was started

## Top Five – Rittenhouse Square

- **The Curtis Institute of Music** (p129) Check out impossibly talented students performing at their recitals.
- **Le Bec-Fin** (p111) Judge for yourself whether or not this is America's best restaurant.
- **Lombardi's** (p109) Do it right at America's first pizzeria.
- **Mütter Museum** (p72) Don't try to avoid the king of odd museums, even if medical pathologies make you queasy.
- **Rittenhouse Square** (p73) Watch the fashionable crowds from a bench at this beautiful urban square.

in the late 19th century to educate medical students. It features a fascinating but often gruesome collection of exhibits, including the double liver shared by 19th-century Siamese twins Chang and Eng Bunker, the tumor removed from President Cleveland's cancerous jawbone, and numerous skeletons of dwarves and unusually tall people. Another display features various items swallowed by patients.

## PHILADELPHIA ART ALLIANCE

Map pp222-3

☎ 215-545-4302; www.philartalliance.org; 251 S 18th St; admission free; ⏰ 11am-5pm Tue-Sun; SEPTA 19th St Station, Bus 2, 12

Though the forbidding exterior of this stately mansion (built 1906) on Rittenhouse Square discourages entry, folks are very welcome to visit the Philadelphia Art Alliance. Back in the '30s Frank Lloyd Wright, Le Corbusier and Martha Graham spoke here. Andrew Wyeth and Bauhaus instructor Josef Albers also enjoyed exhibitions at the Art Alliance. Today it exhibits an eclectic body of work and hosts a regular calendar of lectures.

## RITTENHOUSE SQUARE Map pp222-3

The most popular, famous and prestigious of the city's squares – laid out by William Penn and with entrances designed in 1913 by Paul Cret – is named after David Rittenhouse, the local 18th-century astronomer, mathematician and clockmaker. Surrounded by fancy apartment buildings, hotels and restaurants, the square features a fine collection of statues as well as a children's wading pool and numerous wooden benches. It's popular with city workers and tourists alike, all who come here in fine weather to rest under the shade of the trees, read, enjoy a sandwich or drink, or feed the squirrels, occasionally enjoying the faint operatic sounds emerging from the lungs of students inside the nearby Curtis Center.

## ROSENBACH MUSEUM & LIBRARY

Map pp222-3

☎ 215-735-1600; www.rosenbach.org; 2010 Delancey St; adult/child $5/3; ⏰ 11am-4pm Tue-Sun; Bus 33, 12, 40

Housed in a sumptuous 19th-century townhouse on one of the city's loveliest streets, this small museum contains a top collection of rare books and manuscripts. The original, hand-written manuscript of James Joyce's *Ulysses* is on permanent display, as are the first four pages of Bram Stoker's *Dracula* and most of Joseph Conrad's manuscripts. The

collection also includes paintings by Canaletto and original illustrations by author Maurice Sendak. Guided tours occur on the hour, and last 75 minutes.

See the City Calendar (p13) in the City Life chapter for information on the annual Bloomsday celebration.

# WASHINGTON SQUARE WEST

A mixture of high-end and low rent, the character of Washington Square West varies greatly block by block: some are down-and-dirty, others ritzy; some are packed full of cheap bars, and others contain big hospitals devoid of life at night.

Market and Chestnut Sts pass through this neighborhood from Old City toward City Hall. As you leave the golden halo of Independence National Historical Park, things get momentarily dingy. Some of the buildings along these commercial roads are empty, while others are filled with Rite-Aid pharmacies and cheap electronics stores. Soon, though, this dinginess is replaced by another golden halo, this time cast by Howe and Lescaze's PSFS building and by the new life that the convention center across the street gives to the neighborhood. Nearby is the city's oldest bar, McGillin's (p132).

The northern blocks of Washington Square West are mostly full of early skyscrapers and department stores installed when this area was a major banking hub. Move a bit to the south, and the buildings get shorter. Sansom and Walnut Sts contain the 'hood's primary shopping options, which are largely old and weird. Don't miss having pancakes at Blue in Green (p112) along Jeweler's Row.

The southwest quadrant of Washington Square West contains a confusing network of cobblestone alleys lacing between Broad and 12th Sts. This cute, quiet, tree-lined

Neighborhoods – Center City

## Transport

**Subway** SEPTA's Market-Frankford line runs along this neighborhood's northern border, and the Broad St line runs along its eastern edge.
**Bus** The 9, 21, and 42 buses run across town, entering Washington Square West heading east along Chestnut St. They return along Walnut St.
**Parking** Why not use the lot on 11th St near Locust?

oasis is home to Philadelphia's Gayborhood, which cornered the market on Washington Square West's best real estate. Within these alleys, especially along Camac St, find ancient members-only organizations for artists such as the Plastics Club and the Philadelphia Sketch Club, as well as an extremely rare sight: a street paved with wood.

## Orientation

The northern edge of this neighborhood is Market St, and the southern edge is South St. The eastern boundary is 7th St and Washington Square Park; to the west is Broad St. Within this district, the Gayborhood runs north-south between Walnut and Pine Sts. East-west, it sits between Broad and 12th. Find all those crazy alleys in here.

### ATWATER KENT MUSEUM Map pp222-3
☎ 215-685-4830; www.philadelphiahistory.org; 15 S 7th St; adult/senior/child $5/3/3; ☽ 10am-5pm Wed-Mon; SEPTA 8th St Station, Bus 47, 48

Over 300 years of the city's social history and local culture are represented at this museum. Its collection of more than 75,000 artifacts – including military uniforms, dolls, model ships and radios – are used to depict ordinary daily life in Philadelphia's past. At the rear of the 1st floor is a children's display devoted to cheese steaks. Other exhibits include one about Philly as the Workshop of the World and another about William Penn. You can take a gander at the famous wampum belt made by the Lenni Lenape, which uses beads to depict a chubby Penn holding hands with an Indian as a symbol of friendship.

---

Atwater Kent acquired the Norman Rockwell Museum's exhibits when that museum closed, and there is a permanent exhibition of Rockwell's work on the 2nd floor. The old Greek Revival building that the museum occupies was the original home of the Franklin Institute back when it was a progressive research center and not a museum.

### PENNSYLVANIA HOSPITAL Map pp222-3
☎ 215-829-3270; www.uphs.upenn.edu/paharc; 800 Spruce St; admission free; ☽ 9am-5pm Mon-Fri; Bus 12, 47

Founded in 1751 by Benjamin Franklin and Dr Thomas Bond, Pennsylvania Hospital was the country's first hospital. A booklet offering a self-guided walking tour is available from the information desk/welcome center in the ground-floor lobby of the modern section of the hospital. Make an advance appointment for a guided tour.

Entry to the old part of the hospital is on 8th St. Here the Pine Bldg has been in continuous use since 1755. Inside you'll find the History of Nursing Museum, Historic Library of Pennsylvania Hospital (containing important collections on the history of medicine) and North America's oldest surgical amphitheater for medical students. Outside, in front of the west wing of the Pine Bldg, is the tranquil Physick Garden, where plants used in the 18th century as herbal remedies are grown.

### WASHINGTON SQUARE Map pp222-3
Walnut St btwn 6th & 7th Sts

On the northwest edge of Society Hill, this square is one of those in William Penn's original city plan, and its shaded benches offer a peaceful respite from a day's sightseeing. The Tomb of the Unknown Soldier is the country's only monument to the unknown American and British dead of the Revolutionary War.

The square was once an upper-class residential district, and in the 19th century Philadelphia's publishing industry became concentrated in the surrounding offices. These days there's a mix of apartments as well as various offices and small businesses. It's an excellent spot to watch for pugs.

## PARKWAY & MUSEUM AREA

Back in 1907 Philadelphia decided that the new urban designs inspired by the World's Columbia Exposition in Chicago looked pretty darn good. So Philly's city fathers

---

### Top Five – Washington Square West

- **Antique Row** (p156) Search for dusty trinkets and odd finds among the many shops.
- **Last Drop** (p112) Spend two hours with coffee and hipsters at this cool café.
- **Morimoto** (p113) Eat extraordinary sushi with TV's Iron Chef.
- **Pennsylvania Hospital** (p74) Stroll the venerable grounds of the nation's first hospital.
- **Washington Square** (p74) Pet the dogs in one of Penn's original squares.

---

installed a sort-of Parisian boulevard, the Benjamin Franklin Parkway, running diagonally from the northwest quadrant of Center City through to Fairmount Park. Gathered around this attempt at monumental City Beautiful planning are many of the city's most visited museums. During the school year, big yellow buses perpetually hover in front of places like the Franklin Institute and the Academy of Natural Sciences, dumping off kids to get some learnin'. During the summer, the kids and yellow buses are still present, now coming from camp programs.

City Beautiful grandeur along the parkway exists exclusively at its terminal points. At one end of the parkway is the enormous Philadelphia Museum of Art, perched upon a hill. At the other end, the large frogs and turtles of Alexander Stirling Calder's Swann Memorial Fountain perpetually spit water in Logan Square. Both the art museum and Calder's fountain create the kind of enjoyable, noble civic spaces called for by the parkway's City Beautiful aspirations. Rocky Balboa's view from the steps of the art museum remains inspirational, and a summertime afternoon spent wading among the water-spouting creatures in the large fountain is a favorite Philadelphia treat. Nobody – including the police – seems to care that this activity is technically illegal.

An additional, visually boring section of the boulevard runs limply from the fountain to City Hall. This middle portion of the parkway comes off half-baked. The buildings along its sides aren't very orderly and make a poor physical match for the broad road. The north side contains mostly residential apartment buildings and a few park spaces, and the sloppy southern edge is hard to discern, controlled more by ramps connecting Philadelphia to I-676 then by Paul Cret and Jacques Gréber's design. Future plans may restore a bit of the unachieved monumentality: a new museum devoted to Philadelphia's three sculpting Calders is in the works, and current talks suggest that the financially unstable Barnes Museum will be moving here as well. Should this happen, the Benjamin Franklin Parkway would rank as one of the world's leading art destinations.

The northern section of this neighborhood stretches up along Pennsylvania Ave. This is a mostly residential area, where affluence is concentrated in the blocks

closest to the Schuylkill. As one moves north of Fairmount and east of 21st St, the quality of the housing stock takes a precipitous decline and eventually becomes representative of the poverty that exists throughout large expanses of Philadelphia. Within the realm of the less grungy blocks, don't miss taking a tour of the impressive, castlelike Eastern State Penitentiary. Experience its bleak immensity, totally differently from that frilly City Beautiful stuff. Though it's now considered cool to live across the street from this empty prison, it must have felt pretty grim to sit on one's porch and stare at that sucker back when it was operational. This section of town is also home to a rockin' rock club, **North Star** (p140).

South of the parkway are a few museums – especially every five-year-old's dream, the Please Touch Museum – that don't front the big road. You'll also find a few sleepy blocks of lovely residential row homes nestled behind the museums and west of the blocks that hold some of Philadelphia tallest skyscrapers.

## Orientation

Try to contain your surprise as you read that the Benjamin Franklin Parkway shapes the orientation of this neighborhood. Penn's uniform grid extends north from Market St up to Green St. The diagonal parkway interrupts it, creating a quick, direct artery to Fairmount Park and I-676. North of Green the grid remains somewhat regular, but occasional diagonals like Poplar St and Fairmount Ave exist as potentially confusing items.

The western edge of this neighborhood is Fairmount Park and the Schuylkill River, and the southern edge is Market St. The eastern and northern boundaries are soft. If you find yourself on Broad St or in Francisville, know that you are elsewhere.

## THE ACADEMY OF NATURAL SCIENCES Map pp222-3

☎ 215-299-1000; www.acnatsci.org; 1900 Benjamin Franklin Parkway; adult/senior/child $9/8.25/8; ☼ 10am-4:30pm Mon-Fri, 10am-5pm Sat & Sun; Bus 33, 38, 48, 76

The country's oldest natural history museum was founded in 1812, though the building itself dates from 1868. It has a terrific permanent 'Discovering Dinosaurs' display on the 1st floor, complete with computer videos and reconstructed skeletons. The museum also features 'Outside In' (a hands-on nature center for kids on the 3rd floor); separate halls on Africa, Asia and North America; and a hot and humid butterfly room where you can mingle with live specimens from rain-forest environments. You can even go on a 'dig' for fossils in a simulated New Mexico field station.

## EASTERN STATE PENITENTIARY

Map pp222-3

☎ 215-236-3300; www.easternstate.org; 22nd St & Fairmount Ave; adult/student/child $9/7/5; ☼ 10am-5pm Wed-Sun Apr 16–Nov 30; Bus 7, 33, 48

The forbidding exterior of this 1829 prison was designed to frighten would-be criminals into rethinking their illegal thoughts. Prisoners had to deal with an even scarier interior: the facility was guided by 'progressive' Quaker beliefs in reform through strict isolation.

When it was built, Eastern State was the most expensive building in the USA and the most famous prison in the world. Today admission to the giant, crumbling castle includes an audio tour, special guided tours and changing art installations. Start in the Old Visitor's Room and stroll through the decaying cell blocks, prison greenhouse and death row. Don't miss Al Capone's cell and, if you can, check out the annual Halloween event (p14).

## FRANKLIN INSTITUTE SCIENCE MUSEUM Map pp222-3

☎ 215-448-1200; http://sln.fi.edu; 222 N 20th St; Science Center adult/child/senior $12.75/10/10, Imax $8, Science Center & Imax adult/child/senior $16.75/14/14; ☼ Science Center 9:30am-5pm, Mandell Center 9:30am-5pm Sun-Thu, 9:30am-9pm Fri & Sat; Bus 33, 38, 48, 76

Founded in 1824, the world-class Franklin Institute Science Museum moved into this four-story Greek Revival building in 1934. The museum pioneered the hands-on science concept that is so widespread nowadays.

In the **Science Center** you can walk through a 4-ton, two-story papier-mâché replica of a beating heart. Other working devices demonstrate various aspects of electricity (of course) and physics; the train-related exhibits (including a ride on a steam train) are especially popular with children. You'll also find a giant pinball machine here. Downstairs, the **Fels Planetarium** has a computer-driven look at the cosmos plus laser shows and astronomy exhibits. The **Mandell Center**, a 1991 addition to the museum, traces the development of computers, telecommunications and space travel into the near future, and examines environmental concerns.

For an additional charge, check out the excellent **Tuttleman IMAX Theater**. Housed in a four-story dome, the theater features a 79ft movie screen that surrounds the audience.

## PENNSYLVANIA ACADEMY OF THE FINE ARTS Map pp222-3

☎ 215-972-7600; www.pafa.org; 118 N Broad St; adult/senior/student/child $5/4/4/3; ☼ 10am-5pm Tue-Sat, 11am-5pm Sun; SEPTA 13th St Station, Bus 27, 32, 38, 44, 48

The Pennsylvania Academy of the Fine Arts was founded in 1805 and boasts a prestigious art school and museum, both of which are the nation's oldest. Its home is a masterwork of Victorian Gothic architecture designed by Frank Furness and George Hewitt, built in 1876. Their typically frenetic design features whacked-out floral motifs, stained glass, exposed iron beams, big skylights, excessive polycromy and numerous kinds of marble.

The academy's collection of American paintings and sculpture displays work from the country's foundation to the present, and includes pieces by such noted early American painters as Robert Henri, Benjamin West, Charles Wilson Peale, Gilbert Stuart and Thomas Eakins. The intelligently organized museum chooses to show pieces from its collection that work in concert to provide a comprehensible glimpse into the development of American art.

Guided tours are available daily at 1pm (Wed, Sat, Sun) or 12:30pm (Tue, Thu, Fri) and are included in the admission fee.

## PHILADELPHIA MUSEUM OF ART

Map pp222-3
☎ 215-763-8100; www.philamuseum.org; Benjamin Franklin Parkway & 26th St; adult/senior/student/child $10/7/7/7, pay-what-you-wish Sun; 🕙 10am-5pm Tue, Thu, Sat & Sun, 10am-8:45pm Wed & Fri; Bus 32, 38, 43, 76

The country's third-largest art museum is home to over 300,000 paintings, sculptures, drawings, prints and decorative arts. Many of the major artists of the 19th and 20th centuries are represented in its collection of mostly Asian, European and US art. Architecturally, the museum consists of three Greek-style 'temples' with fluted columns supporting a blue-tiled roof topped by bronze griffins.

In the Great Stair Hall, just past the 1st-floor entrance, stands the 1892 statue of the nude huntress Diana by Augustus St Gaudens; it was brought here from New York in 1932 after being saved from the demolished Madison Square Garden.

Museum highlights include the 19th-century European and impressionist galleries, featuring the work of Brancusi, Degas, Renoir, Manet and Van Gogh. There are galleries for special exhibitions, and other permanent exhibition galleries include American Art, Early-20th-Century Art, Contemporary Art, Japanese & Chinese Art, Near Eastern & Asian Art, Medieval & European Art, Arms & Armor, European Art 1500–1700, English Period Rooms, European Art 1700–1850 and American Period rooms. The museum also features complete buildings, including an Indian Hindu temple and a Japanese Buddhist temple from Nara.

## Barnes Foundation

Back in 1922, Dr Albert Barnes started a philanthropic foundation to expose the common man to education and art. Born and raised in a working-class neighborhood in Philadelphia, Barnes made his fortune inventing and manufacturing an antiseptic product, and began collecting the work of French masters. In his factories, Barnes, a nice guy, would hang these works and hold discussions about art with his employees. What began as an exercise for his factory workers evolved over the next few decades into the world's largest private collection of impressionist, postimpressionist and early French modern paintings.

The Barnes Foundation contains works by Cézanne (more of his work than in all the galleries of France, in fact), Degas, Matisse, Manet, Monet, Modigliani, Picasso, Renoir, Rousseau and Seurat. Pause here, and reread that list. This is a mind-blowing collection, especially considering it was assembled by a single guy. Aside from these paintings, there is art and craftwork from around the world, including antique furniture, ceramics, handwrought iron and Native American jewelry. The gallery also provides an educational program on the world's different artistic traditions.

Barnes, educated as a medical doctor at U Penn, was fascinated by psychology, and this led him to organize the foundation's pieces in a curious manner. Unlike most museums, which typically organize works by period, artist or style, Barnes grouped works according to composition. Depending on the shapes involved, you might find a piece by Horace Pippin mounted next to an ornamental doorknob, which would in turn be placed next to an example of African folk art.

When Barnes died, he intended for his gallery to exist precisely as he left it. But lately, due to political wrangling in the city and financial trouble at the foundation, the gallery is likely to be moved from its present home to the museum district on Benjamin Franklin Parkway. However, this may not happen; even if it does, the relocation will take a year or two to get underway.

For now, you can visit the **gallery** ( ☎ 610-667-0290; www.barnesfoundation.org; 300 N Latches Lane, Merion; $5; 🕙 9:30am-5pm Fri-Sun Sep-Jun, 9:30am-5pm Wed-Fri Jul & Aug; SEPTA R5 Merion Station, Bus 44) in its original home, about 5 miles from downtown. Due to a court-ordered limitation on visitors, reserve a tour 45 to 60 days in advance.

If you're driving, follow the Schuylkill Expressway northwest and turn left at the City Ave turnoff. Follow City Ave, then turn right onto Lancaster Rd; Latches Lane is the fourth turn on the left.

Particularly worthwhile are Wednesday and Friday nights between 5pm and 8:45pm, when there are live music performances, films, talks, guided tours, food and drink. Before heading into the museum, reflect on Rocky's famous run of the city-facing steps and check out the slick polycromy along the roof's entablature and accenting the capitals of columns.

## PLEASE TOUCH MUSEUM  Map pp222-3

PTM; ☎ 215-963-0667; www.pleasetouchmuseum.o rg; 210 N 21st St; $9; pay-what-you-wish 9-10am Sun; ⏱ 9am-4:30pm Labor Day–Jun, 9am-5pm Jul–Labor Day; Bus 33, 38, 48, 76

Designed for children seven years of age and younger, this highly regarded museum emphasizes learning through playing. Its interactive exhibits feature a mock TV studio with a working camera, a real SEPTA bus and a miniature supermarket where kids can select

groceries, operate a register and restock items. In the Sendak area, children meet oversize creatures from books such as *Where the Wild Things Are.*

Outside is a science park, jointly administered with the Franklin Institute Science Museum. It's an interactive learning area where exhibits include a miniature golf course and a radar detector.

## RODIN MUSEUM  Map pp222-3

☎ 215-763-8100; www.rodinmuseum.org; Benjamin Franklin Parkway & N 22nd St; suggested donation $3; ⏱ 10am-5pm Tue-Sun; Bus 7, 32, 38, 43, 48

A must-see for many, this noteworthy museum contains the largest collection of Auguste Rodin's sculptures outside of Paris. These include his famous *The Burghers of Calais* and *Gates of Hell,* as well as a bronze cast replica of *The Thinker.* Audio tours cost $5.

# SOUTH STREET & AROUND

*Eating p114; Shopping p155; Sleeping p168*

Though general use of the adjective *funky* is vague and nondescript, it fits when discussing the character of South Street. Why? Because all of the various, conflicting definitions of *funky* apply to this neighborhood. It's simultaneously cool, seedy, weird, trendy, unfashionable and bad-smelling. Teenagers really love it, and tourists and the homeless do, too. Artists and punks affectionately remember scenes from previous years, and parents enjoy taking their kids for colorful walks, possibly to the pedestrian bridge crossing over to Penn's Landing. Hipsters want to be cool enough to dislike popular South Street but can't help being drawn to the numerous record shops, the art-supply store and the Whole Foods grocery. Dirty-looking cheapskate eateries thrive, as do more expensive BYOBs creating unusual food. South Street is largely commercial, particularly east of 10th St. It's a popular place for a night out on the town, but if you go, don't drive – the traffic and the lack of parking spaces are maddening.

South Street got its start as a cool place when a ramp for the freeway was slated to bulldoze the street. Rents for the doomed area dropped to just above zero, and artists and squatters were attracted to it. After several years, the ramp scheme was dropped but rental rates remained low because the neighborhood had become a ghost town, and then a center for burnouts and the '70s youth culture. Artists tend to breed coolness, and they did so here. Galleries began to open, as did an underground punk club (started by the same guy who now runs Bar Noir; p132). Before becoming the city's preeminent restaurateur, Stephen Starr also opened a club during the late '70s.

Immediately below South Street near the Delaware River is Queen's Village, a pleasant residential district hiding a couple of great restaurants and bars that are off most tourists' radars. Colonial-architecture buffs should know that Queen's Village, at one time outside of Philadelphia's city limits, was settled around the same time as Old City. Down here, colonial row homes still exist, and in numbers much greater than in Old City. Because the area was outside of William Penn's jurisdiction, the streets here are much narrower, following a settlement pattern more typical of other early American cities. The intimate spaces created by the narrower streets and closer houses afford vast adorableness. If you liked Elfreth's Alley, check out its bigger brothers throughout Queen's Village.

# Orientation

South Street runs from river to river. Its five blocks closest to the Delaware contain the counterculture stores, clubs, restaurants and bars that everyone finds so attractive. Move west, and things get dingier and less populated. Cross west of Broad St and reward yourself by going to **Tritone** (p139), **Bob & Barbara's** (p135) or **Ron's Ribs** (p115).

Colonial Queen's Village lies south of South St and east of 3rd St.

## HEAD HOUSE SQUARE Map pp226-7
### 2nd & Pine Sts; Bus 40, 57

Between Pine and South Sts, this attractive square is named after the fire-engine houses, called 'head houses,' built in the early 19th century. With cupolas, alarm bells and a fire officers' social club upstairs, the head house at 2nd and Pine Sts escaped demolition and was restored. The shed between Lombard and Pine Sts was one of several built in 1745 for street trading; also restored, it's home to an open-air craft market on summer weekends.

## MOTHER BETHEL AME CHURCH
Map pp228-9

☎ 215-925-0616; 419 S 6th St; admission free;
☽ office 10am-4pm Mon-Fri, museum by appt
Tue-Sat & after services Sun; Bus 12, 57

Founded by two local freed slaves in 1787, this is South Street's major historic building and is regarded as the birthplace of the African Methodist Episcopal (AME) order. Benjamin Rush, a signer of the Declaration of Independence and among the first white revolutionaries to speak out against slavery, defended this church and provided

## Top Five – South Street

- **Bob & Barbara's** (p135) Pound 'em back at this amazing dive bar: Ping-Pong on Tuesday, drag show on Thursday.
- **Fluid** (p141) Dance with the cool kids at this super-hip club.
- **Mother Bethel AME Church** (p79) Check out Richard Allen's church, once a center of abolitionist activity.
- **Tartine** (p115) Enjoy the finest in French country cooking at this little bistro.
- **TLA** (p141) Listen to some rock 'n' roll in a former movie theater.

## Transport

**Subway** SEPTA's Lombard-South St Station is located on Broad St.
**Bus** The 40 runs east along South St and returns west along Lombard St.
**Parking** Metered parking will be easy to find except east of 5th St, where you should use the lots that are recommended for Society Hill, on Lombard near 2nd.

it with financial support. As a stop on the Underground Railroad, the church and its pastor, Richard Allen (entombed within the church), hid hundreds of fugitive slaves prior to the Civil War. During the war itself, the church served as an important recruiting station for the Union Army.

The church and its congregation contributed many firsts to African America's history. This is the oldest piece of real estate owned by American blacks. Other contributions are the nation's first black periodical and first black insurance company.

The present church is the fourth one built on this site; it dates from 1889 and was restored in 1987. The original structure was an abandoned blacksmith's shop that was hauled to this spot from a distant location, which explains why the church uses an anvil as its symbol. Most of the congregation now live in West Philadelphia but still worship here.

## ST PETER'S CHURCH Map pp228-9
☎ 215-925-5968; 3rd & Pine Sts; admission free;
☽ 8am-4pm; Bus 12, 57

Robert Smith, also responsible for Christ Church (p61) and Carpenters' Hall (p56), built this beautiful church from 1758–64 (though people started using it in 1761, when Christ Church was unable to cater to the growing Anglican congregation). Apart from the mid-19th-century steeple, the church looks much as it did when George Washington and his family worshiped here. Buried in the graveyard are artist Charles Wilson Peale and the chiefs of seven Indian tribes who died in Philly during the 1793 smallpox epidemic when meeting with Washington for a peace council. Guides are on site to answer questions 11am to 3pm Saturday and 1pm to 3pm Sunday.

## ISAIAH ZAGAR HOUSE Map pp228-9
### 826 South St

If you've spent more then a day in Philadelphia, you probably noticed the work of Isaiah

Zagar. He's the guy responsible for the scores of murals and mosaics made from bits of broken mirrors and ceramics, fused together with brightly colored grout. Most pieces feature unusual protrusions made from found objects such as bicycle wheels, dolls' heads or discarded bottles.

While you can find his work covering the exterior of the **Painted Bride** (p63), in the

bathrooms of the **Last Drop** (p112) and in national museums and galleries, the epicenter of Zagar's world is right here on South Street. His house is a bizarre man-made garden, where passersby gawk at a freakish fantasy world from the sidewalk. At least 20 of his murals enliven buildings within a block's distance of his home street. He's been transforming the area since 1968.

# SOUTH PHILADELPHIA

*Eating p116; Shopping p156*

South Philly rules. If nothing else, it birthed the cheese steak. It also bakes most of the hot, stuffable pretzels found in food trucks all over town. Of course, the neighborhood involves much more then these tasty, steaming items. Spreading over several blue-collar square miles, this gritty chunk of land contains serious 24-hour diners far removed from the comfortable green spaces around Independence Hall. This is real urban America, as yet untainted by bourgeoisie ambitions. Down here, most sidewalks come without trees (considered dirty because they shed their leaves), litter collects in many gutters (is it not dirty, too?) and cars ignore traffic laws. Drive down Broad St and you'll see cars parked in the median for as far as the eye can see. Look down a narrow cross-street, particularly around the Melrose Diner, and you'll see rows of them double parked, using an unclear system of organization. (Don't attempt to join the fray. A mystical protocol is at work, and only those from South Philly understand it).

Culturally the experience of South Philadelphia is shaped by its inhabitants, traditionally immigrants from Italy and their descendants. The treeless concrete sidewalks contain stacks of plain brick row houses, auto-body shops and unpretentious restaurants where the portions are big and the sauce is red. Most of the area's sites – the Mummers Museum, the Mario Lanza Museum and the Italian Market – reflect the neighborhood's Italian American experience, and the Italian Market exists as a ritual undisturbed since the end of the 19th century.

Recent times have seen new waves of immigrants arrive, particularly from Mexico and Southeast Asia. Taquerias and expansive Vietnamese markets have sprung up along Washington Ave. The Vietnamese enclave is particularly well developed around 8th St.

## Orientation

Bordered by Washington Ave to the north and by the Delaware and Schuylkill Rivers to the east, south and west, South Philly is large. In the far south are the Veterans and First Union Spectrum sports stadiums, and in the north are most of the neighborhood's other attractions.

### GLORIA DEI (OLDE SWEDES')
### CHURCH Map pp228-9
☎ 215-389-1513; Columbus Blvd & Christian St; donation requested; 🕙 9am-5pm Apr-Oct, other times by appt; Bus 25, 63

Philadelphia's original settlers were Swedish Lutherans, and this is the site of their first church (1643). The original log structure was replaced

in 1700 by the current brick version, which is the oldest church building in Philadelphia. A graveyard and several other 18th-century buildings surround the church, squeezed between I-95 and Christopher Columbus Blvd.

### Transport
**Subway** SEPTA's Broad St line runs down the middle of this big neighborhood, all the way to the stadiums.
**Bus** The 23 runs south along 12th and north along 11th. Bus 47 runs south along 8th and north along 7th. The 2 runs north along 16th and south along 17th. Bus 64 runs west from Pennsport to Grays Ferry along Federal St, and returns east along Ellsworth and Washington.
**Parking** Street parking is the thing.

# Mummers Parade

Said to be the country's oldest continual folk festival, the **Mummers Parade** ( ☎ 215-965-7676; www.mummers.org) has mysterious origins. It may have originated from a Swedish and Finnish custom of celebrating a 'second Christmas' with wandering minstrels, or from the English Mummery Play, a kind of burlesque with harlequins dressed in silk and satin. In German, *Mummerkleid* means 'fancy dress' and *Mummenspiel* means 'masquerade,' so maybe that's where the name came from. Regardless, Philadelphia's first Mummers appeared in the 1700s parading in the Washington Ave area, and the bands grew in size until, in 1901, an official site – at Broad St from South Philadelphia to City Hall – was ordained for the parade.

Each New Year's Day more than 25,000 participants, mostly heterosexual men, gussy up in outrageous costumes replete with sequins, feathers and makeup. Women dress up too, and they all strut their way along Broad St. They're accompanied by bands that are traditionally limited to accordions, saxophones, drums, violins, banjos, bass fiddles, glockenspiels and clarinets.

As with Mardi Gras, the extravagant costumes are the highlight of the show. Mummers, members of clubs that represent different city neighborhoods, spend all year (and a lot of money) designing and creating their costumes, not to mention practicing the music and choreographing their routines. Each year features different themes, such as fairy tales or Broadway shows.

The parade starts at 7am and can last as long as 12 hours. Despite the low temperatures, there's always a large, enthusiastic and often hard-drinking turnout. If you miss the parade, you can catch the Mummers bands playing at the **Mummers Museum** (p81) and at other special performances. To catch them in all their glory, though, you really need to see them on New Year's Day.

The parade's theme song is 'Oh Dem Golden Slippers,' written by James Bland (1854–1911) in 1879. He was born of free African American parents in Flushing, New York, and studied at Howard University. He worked for a while as a page in the House of Representatives and later became a successful minstrel in England, where he gave a command performance for Queen Victoria. He wrote about 700 songs, including 'Carry Me Back to Old Virginny,' but was credited with only 37. Around the turn of the 20th century he settled in Philadelphia, where he died in poverty.

## ITALIAN MARKET Map pp228-9
**9th St btwn Christian St & Washington Ave; Bus 27, 40, 43**
This is the country's largest outdoor market. The stalls and specialty shops offer sights, sounds and smells rarely found in this age of supermarkets and gourmet stores. Many vendors close up shop on Sunday and Monday, and the market's pace builds up during the week to the busiest days of Friday and Saturday. The market offers a wide selection of items at low prices, and locals regularly travel miles to shop here. The Easter and Christmas holiday seasons are especially good times to visit, though the place is Deadsville on the big days themselves.

As well as the street stalls and the many butchers – where you can get a sausage that's 10% garlic by volume – on S 9th St, look out for **D'Angelo Brothers**, specializing in sausage and pâté; **Di Bruno Bros** with their cheese and olive selection; **Talluto's**, a traditional Italian deli; and **Fante's Kitchen Wares Shop** (p157).

## MARIO LANZA MUSEUM Map pp228-9
☎ 215-238-9691; 712 Montrose St; admission free;
☺ 10am-3pm; Bus 47, 63
Local legend and international celebrity Mario Lanza (1921–59) was born Freddie Cocozza

nearby at 634 Christian St. The museum is on the first floor of the Columbus House within a homey room dedicated to Lanza's vocal talents. It's full of photos, stills from his films, posters and other memorabilia. Films of his performances are also shown.

## MUMMERS MUSEUM Map pp228-9
☎ 215-336-3050; http://riverfrontmummers.com/
museum.html; 1100 S 2nd St; adult/child $2.50/2;
☺ 9:30am-5pm Tue-Sat, noon-5pm Sun, closed Sun
Jul & Aug; Bus 4, 57
Those who really want to feel like they traveled to a foreign city would do well to stop in here. The Mummers Museum explains the history and culture of Philadelphia's most colorful citizens, who spend every day of the year planning, designing costumes and practicing for their New Year's Day parade (p13): an enormous masquerade. Exhibits include some of their extravagant costumes, photographs, a video of the most recent parade and a digital clock that counts down the days to the next January 1. If you're lucky, you may catch one of the string bands rehearsing. Weather permitting, there are free, outdoor string-band concerts on Tuesday from May to September.

### SAMUEL S FLEISHER ART MEMORIAL
Map pp228-9

☎ 215-922-3456 ext 318; www.fleisher.org; 709-721 Catherine St; admission free; ⊙ 11am-5pm Mon-Fri; Bus 40, 47

On a side street and with an easy-to-miss door, this school and its exhibition spaces frequently get overlooked. Come here to check out exhibitions that might explore art created by architects or display the sculpture of Warren Holtzman. One of the buildings in the Fleisher compound is a Romanesque Revival church designed by Furness. Check out the sanctuary, which houses stained glass windows by Lafarge, a mural by Robert Henri and many 14th- to 16th-century sculptures. Welcome to the dark ages. The staff also offer free art lessons.

# NORTHERN LIBERTIES
*Eating p118*

A working-class neighborhood for as long as anyone can remember and a one-time brewery district, Northern Liberties has emerged as a destination for hipsters in the know over the last few years. The neighborhood has shifted from a somewhat dangerous place to a gritty center of cool. How did this happen?

Old City, directly to the south, attained its own prosperity in the early 1990s, which popularized that area and spurred piecemeal redevelopment up the Delaware waterfront and into Northern Liberties. Meanwhile, a gaggle of artists, musicians and spendthrifts fled the increasingly expensive neighborhoods to the south and came to Northern Liberties. A few bars opened to cater to this new crowd, and suddenly the area came to be seen as a comely bargain. Cool venues attracted cool people, which in turn attracted more venues. Now, instead of being able to merely watch some jazz at Ortlieb's and pound a few drinks at Liberties, you can have Sunday brunch in a bunch of newly opened bars and restaurants. On this day, it is nearly impossible to find any kind of purveyor of food or liquid that isn't serving mimosas with elaborate crepes or omelets.

Northern Liberties' recent fortune is only a few years old. While property values are way up and significant change has definitely occurred, the neighborhood remains – for the moment at least – a fringe destination. The region is grimy, a bit seedy and a tad polemicized. Some longtime residents are worried that Northern Liberties will eventually grow too successful and, ultimately, too gentrified. Whether or not this happens, adventurous visitors are encouraged to enjoy some of the city's best nightlife offerings – Ortlieb's (p139), **Standard Tap** (p136) and **Aqua Lounge** (p141) – while they last.

Most of the changes to the Northern Liberties scene involve the establishment of restaurants and bars. There aren't too many conventional tourist sites, aside from the two mentioned on the next page.

## Orientation

Northern Liberties lies north of the dead zone created by the infrastructure of I-676 and south of a grungier neighborhood called Fishtown. The southern edge is generally considered to be Spring Garden Ave; the northern edge is Girard Ave. I-95 creates the eastern boundary, and 6th St makes the western one. Hipsters' efforts have saturated 2nd and 3rd Sts as well as bits of Girard Ave. The remainder of the neighborhood maintains its postwar seediness. The farther west you move, the more likely you should be traveling with another person.

### EDGAR ALLAN POE NATIONAL HISTORIC SITE Map p230

☎ 215-597-8780; www.nps.gov/edal; 532 N 7th St; admission free; ☉ 9am-5pm Wed-Sun; Bus 43, 47

Poe, America's noted 19th-century horror-story writer, penned 'The Black Cat' among others while he lived in the modest brick house on this site from 1843–44. In the museum next door there's information and an audiovisual presentation on the man and his work.

### Transport

**Bus** The 43 runs along Spring Garden St, and 57 runs from South Philly through Old City on its way to Girard Ave in Northern Liberties along 3rd St; it returns on 4th St. Bus 15 runs across town on 15th St.

**Parking** Park on the street. The commercial sections of 2nd and 3rd are the safest and most populated.

### NATIONAL SHRINE OF ST JOHN NEUMANN Map p230

☎ 215-627-3080; www.stjohnneumann.org; 1019 N 5th St; admission free; ☉ 7:30am-6pm Mon-Sat, 7:30am-5pm Sun; Bus 15, 57

Entombed in a glass case in front of an altar, the preserved body of the USA's first saint resides at the St Peter's Catholic Church. Born in 1811, St John Neumann served as a Catholic bishop, founded the nation's first archdiocesan school system and established an order of nuns. He was canonized in 1977 and pilgrims from all over the world have flocked here ever since.

# FAIRMOUNT PARK

*Eating p119; Sleeping p168*

Welcome to the nation's largest urban park, many times the size of New York's Central Park. Its embryo was created during the early 1800s, as miles of land on either side of the Schuylkill were purchased to prevent private owners from dumping waste into the river. Pure goods were needed, because around that time the Fairmount Waterworks began operations downstream to provide drinking water to Philadelphia. Over time, the park grew to its current vast size.

Today Fairmount Park is popular with city residents and is a great place for a picnic, a stroll or a run. It contains several noteworthy attractions, all of them beautiful. The grounds and buildings of the old waterworks (1811) have recently been restored and are open to the public. Nearby check out Boathouse Row, whose postcard-pretty, mostly Victorian buildings house numerous rowing clubs who make constant use of the calm, still river (rendered so by the dramatic dam of the waterworks). Also within the park are several colonial estates, open for tours, whose wealthy inhabitants turned their keys over to the city during the 19th century when the city needed the land on which stood their riverside mansions. Other attractions are a Japanese teahouse, a big zoo and thousands of acres of remote grounds. Depending on which area of the park you're in, litter can be a problem, as can safety at night.

## Orientation

Fairmount Park covers nearly 14 sq miles – 10% of the city's land. The southern section, roughly the shape of South America, stretches some 4 miles northwest from the Philadelphia Museum of Art to the Falls Bridge, near Manayunk. Most of the park is divided by the Schuylkill River into East and West Fairmount Park. Northwest from East Falls, the park stretches along Wissahickon Creek (a tributary of the Schuylkill River) past Chestnut Hill.

Neighborhoods – Fairmount Park

## Transport

### BOATHOUSE ROW Map p225
**Kelly Dr near the Fairmount Waterworks; Bus 76**
Another major Philly landmark, this is home to the 'Schuylkill Navy,' a collection of rowing clubs renowned for their distinctive Tudor-style Victorian buildings on the east bank of the Schuylkill River. These buildings, dating from the late 19th and early 20th centuries, are a lovely enough sight during the day, but after dark are illuminated to marvelous effect. See the Spectator Sports (p144) and Outdoor Activities (p146) sections under Sports, Health & Fitness in the Entertainment chapter for more information.

### FAIRMOUNT WATERWORKS Map pp222-3
☎ 215-685-4908; www.fairmountwaterworks.org; 640 Waterworks Dr; ☺ 10am-5pm Tue-Sat, 1-5pm Sun; Bus 76
A National Historic Engineering Landmark, this beautiful Greek Revival complex was built in 1815 and was designed to pump 4 million gallons of water daily from the Schuylkill River to a reservoir on the site now occupied by the Philadelphia Museum of Art. It was closed in 1909 due to pollution and reopened in October 2003 after a lengthy and thorough restoration.

On the site, which was Philadelphia's biggest tourist attraction when it was first built, sits an interpretative center where you can learn the story of the Schuylkill, the history of the Waterworks and lessons in the responsible development of our natural environment.

### JAPANESE HOUSE & GARDENS
Map pp 220-1
☎ 215-878-5097; www.shofuso.com; near Belmont Ave & Montgomery Dr; adult/child $2.50/2; ☺ 10am-4pm Tue-Fri, noon-6pm Sat & Sun May-Oct; Bus 38
A gift of the American-Japan Society of Tokyo, the traditional 17th-century-style upper-class Japanese house (or *Shofu-so*) in West Fairmount Park provides a peaceful retreat from the city bustle. Originally built for an exhibit in New York's Museum of Modern Art, the house was later moved to its site in Fairmount Park.

Designed by Junzo Yoshimura with construction directed by Heizaemon Itoh the 11th (descended from a family with 350 years of traditional Japanese building experience), the house is stunning in its apparent simplicity.

Set in beautiful Japanese gardens beside a stream, notice the remarkable harmony of proportion between house and garden. You can also enjoy tea ceremonies and origami demonstrations here. As the house and gardens reflect conditions of 17th-century Japan, it's not for those using a wheelchair.

The house and gardens are part of the 22-acre **Horticultural Center** (☎ 215-685-0096; ☺ 9am-6pm), which you enter via Horticultural Dr off Belmont Ave.

### PHILADELPHIA ZOO Map p225
☎ 215-243-1100; www.philadelphiazoo.org; 3400 Girard Ave; adult/child $15/12 peak, $10 off-peak; ☺ 9:30am-5pm Feb-Nov, 11am-4pm Dec & Jan; Bus 76
The 42-acre zoo in West Fairmount Park is the country's oldest, having opened in 1874. It houses over 1800 mammals, birds, reptiles and amphibians. Despite its age and Victorian touches, the zoo has been modernized and features natural habitats, not just cages, for many of its 'stars.' The primate house, destroyed by fire in 1995, was reopened in 1999 on the zoo's 125th anniversary.

Seasonal events include animal rides, swan-boat rides and a 400ft aerial view of Fairmount Park attained by climbing aboard a tethered balloon (this costs extra). Parking in the zoo's lot costs $7.

## EARLY AMERICAN HOMES
Back when the city was small and yellow fever outbreaks occurred regularly, many of Philadelphia's wealthiest families built themselves estates near the (then) distant banks of the Schuylkill River. These summer retreats, built during the late 18th and early 19th centuries, were close enough to the city for merchants to oversee business operations but far enough away to escape the city.

Several of these mansions and grounds have been preserved and today lie within the boundaries of Fairmount Park. Generally they're open Tuesday or Wednesday to Sunday from 10am to 4pm, though the hours sometimes vary, so call ahead. Admission costs $3 per house. For more information, check out the website www.philamuseum.org/collections/parkhouse.

## CEDAR GROVE Map p101
☎ 215-763-8100
A three-story house with a gambrel roof, this mansion began its life in 1746 and underwent numerous structural changes as several generations of prominent Philadelphian families lived here. Today the house remains furnished with pieces that reflect the changing patterns of 150 years of fashion, from the work of early Pennsylvanian cabinetmakers to Rococo chairs.

## LAUREL HILL Map p101
☎ 215-627-1770; E Edgely Dr; ☾ Jul–mid-Dec
Built in the 1760s, this house began its life as a purely Georgian creature. The strict symmetry did not last long; it was erased in the early 19th century with the construction of two additions: a one-story ell and a two-story octagonal wing. Laurel Hill, sitting atop a bluff overlooking the Schuylkill, occupies the most dramatic setting of Fairmount's mansions.

## LEMON HILL MANSION Map p101
☎ 215-232-4337; Sedgeley & Lemon Hill Dr; ☾ Apr–mid-Dec; Bus 76
A neoclassical mansion with oval rooms, Lemon Hill was built in 1800 and owned by Henry Pratt. Lemon Hill is named for the impressive citrus trees that grew in the greenhouse of Robert Morris, who owned the estate before Pratt. He was forced to sell his property to escape his creditors.

## MOUNT PLEASANT Map p101
☎ 215-763-2719; Mt Pleasant Dr
Described by John Adams as 'the most elegant seat in Pennsylvania,' Georgian-style Mt Pleasant (1763–64) was built by a wealthy Scottish privateer and owned for a time by infamous traitor Benedict Arnold. Inside there's Chippendale furniture and other ornate woodwork.

## STRAWBERRY MANSION Map p101
☎ 215-228-8364; Strawberry Mansion Dr; ☾ Feb-Dec; Bus 7, 39, 54, 61
The largest house in the park, Strawberry Mansion features a Federal-style main section

built in the 1790s, with disproportionately large Greek Revival wings added in the 1820s. It was purchased in 1871 to be part of the growing Fairmount Park, and a steamboat landing was built on the riverbank near this mansion. As the property quickly became a popular destination, an in-mansion restaurant was established that served strawberries and cream to the crowds – hence the name.

Today the main attractions are an antique toy exhibit; the mixture of Empire, Federal and Regency furniture; and Tucker porcelain.

## SWEETBRIAR Map p101
☎ 215-763-8100; ☾ Jul–mid-Dec; Bus 15
A fantastic example of American neoclassical architecture, Sweetbriar was built in 1797 by Samuel Breck, a merchant who had been educated in France. (The Marquis de Lafayette was entertained at Sweetbriar.) Breck's close relationship with European taste manifested itself in design decisions throughout the house. Check out the so-called Etruscan room.

## WOODFORD Map p101
☎ 215-229-6115; 33rd & Dauphin Sts; Bus 7, 39, 54, 61
Begun in 1756, this Georgian mansion was built in several stages and completed in the 1770s. It contains a wonderful collection of colonial furniture and decorative art. Ownership changed hands several times: it was first owned by William Coleman, a pal of Franklin's who sold it to a Quaker merchant, Alexander Barclay, who passed it over to his brother-in-law, David Franks. Franks made the unfortunate decision to support the crown during the Revolutionary War. Whoops. The home was taken from him following the USA's success.

---

## Top Five – Fairmount Park

- **Boathouse Row** (p84) Bring a picnic and watch the scullers.
- **Fairmount Park** (p83) Get lost in America's largest urban park.
- **Fairmount Waterworks** (p84) Explore this newly restored wonder.
- **Philadelphia Zoo** (p84) Check it out: African lions! There are balloon rides too.
- **Sweetbriar** (p85) Live it up touring this 18th-century estate.

# UNIVERSITY CITY & WEST PHILADELPHIA

*Eating p119; Shopping p157; Sleeping p168*

West of the Schuylkill River, many of the treats worth visiting are within the vicinity of University City, which got its start in the late 19th century when the University of Pennsylvania moved across the river from its smaller origins in Center City. The university dominates the neighborhood, contributing many of the region's significant architectural sites and museums. The Ivy League school, along with nearby Drexel University, gives the area 30,000 students and a corresponding demand for cultural activity, nightlife and cheap eats. This demand, plus the city's contemporary revitalization efforts, has resulted in a gradual but noticeable change in University City's urban landscape.

Surrounding the district of University City is the much larger neighborhood of West Philadelphia. With some exceptions, this is a community that has experienced hard times almost continually since the Great Depression. It's largely populated by blue-collar African Americans who got the very short end of a very long stick when the city's manufacturing jobs began disappearing after World War II. Depending on where you go, you might find a pretty enclave of large Victorian houses, delicious dirt-cheap food, and a bar called The New Third World Lounge, whose name offers exaggerated and hilarious commentary.

For most of the last several decades, University City suffered from its position within blighted West Philly. Directly across the street from Penn, it wasn't very hard to find a house boarded shut or falling down. Now in the midst of a comeback, University City has spruced itself up. The pedestrian-friendly streets near the campus have attracted a pair of movie theaters, numerous national retailers (EMS, the Gap etc), boutique shops and a bunch of restaurants as part of the city's recent (past five years) food revolution.

Making inroads into the areas of West Philly bounding University City are hipsters, gutter-punks and students, none of whom want to pay the more expensive rents that Center City landlords demand. Typically these neighborhoods have a gritty, down-home feel, with residents lounging on their stoops in the heat of the summer. This grittiness is reflected in the existing bar choices – you'll be hard pressed to find anything upscale. Safety is a concern here – the greater your distance from the campuses, the more caution you should exercise. Women especially may not want to walk around alone at night. The grittiness is interspersed with the occasional genteel street lined with large shade trees.

## Orientation

The extents of University City are principally shaped by the nucleus created by Penn and Drexel's campuses. Generally University City is considered to contain these campuses, the commercial hot spots extending from the campuses, and the neighboring residential areas, which provide most of the cheap apartments that all those students need. Like most other places in Philadelphia, the streets here are organized around a grid that's oriented to the cardinal compass points.

West Philly is bounded to the east by the Schuylkill River and to the west by Cobbs Creek, which forms the border between Philadelphia and Delaware County. The northern edge extends to Fairmount Park, and the indistinct southern edge lies somewhere around the neighborhood of Kingsessing.

While the ubiquitous grid covers most of West Philly, there are a couple of diagonal avenues that can cause some confusion. Baltimore Ave is particularly tricky, as south of this diagonal the grid shifts in its orientation.

### 30TH ST STATION Map p225

☎ 215-349-3147; 30th St at Market St; admission free; ☻ 24hr; SEPTA 30th St Station, Bus 21, 30

Built by Graham, Anderson, Probst & White in 1934, this station deserves a visit even if you're not catching a train. The massive neoclassical station's main concourse, with its refined ceiling treatment, is one of Philly's most romantic public spaces. The grand exterior, with its Corinthian columns and its beautiful nighttime floodlighting, can be seen across the river from JFK Blvd and Market St Bridge. The station's south side is an attractive place for a quick snack – though your options will mostly be chain eateries – and is where people often just hang out, sometimes playing chess. This is also the busiest train hub in America outside of New York City.

Amtrak cars and SEPTA's regional trains run out of this station; SEPTA's local subway service operates from near this station, meaning you have to physically exit the building to use the subway. Note that SEPTA's 30th St Station is not the same as this grand 30th St Station.

## THE INSTITUTE FOR CONTEMPORARY ART Map p225

ICA; ☎ 215-898-7108; www.icaphila.org; 118 S 36th St; adult/senior/student $3/2/2, admission free 11am-1pm Sun; 🕑 noon-8pm Wed-Fri, 11am-5pm Sat & Sun, closed Sun in summer; SEPTA 36th St Station, Bus 21, 30

Philadelphia's only contemporary art museum, the ICA's claim to fame is Andy Warhol, whose first important show was held here. In its 40-year history the museum has displayed the works of Robert Mapplethorpe, Robert Morris, rocker Patti Smith and Charles LeDray (thousands of his tiny sculptures). Because the ICA has no permanent collection, its remarkable exhibits change perpetually, which means that you have no excuse not to drop by each time you visit Philly. Regular admission grants visitors free access to special events, which includes a lecture series on contemporary art.

## SLOUGHT FOUNDATION Map p225

☎ 215-746-4239; www.slought.org; 4017 Walnut St; admission free; 🕑 11am-6pm Wed-Sat; SEPTA 40th St Station, Bus 30, 40

Expect to get a heaping helping of serious theory during a visit to this academic, highbrow gallery. In a nutshell, this foundation supports worthy projects that might not otherwise

## Transport

**Subway** The Market-Frankford line runs out to 69th St, along Market.

**Trolley** The 10 emerges from underground tracks paralleling the Market-Frankford line after 33rd St Station and travels along Lancaster Ave. The 13 emerges after 37th St Station and travels southwest along Baltimore Ave.

**Bus** The 21 heads west along Walnut St, arrives at 63rd St and returns along Chestnut St.

**Parking** Lots surround Amtrak's 30th St Station. Also look for one at Walnut and 37th. Once you get two blocks away from Penn's Campus, street parking is easy.

receive attention. Occupying a former bank, the Slought screens films, offers public discussions and organizes exhibits that might explore the art of the youth of West Philadelphia or present the sculpture of Michael Gitlin and Michael Zansky. The Slought is also involved in quirky archival work, which has included study of Oliver Cromwell's 17th-century edict dissolving parliament. Contemporary poets often present work here.

## SPIRAL Q PUPPET THEATER Map p225

☎ 215-222-6979; www.spiralq.org; 3114 Spring Garden St, 2nd fl; $5; 🕑 10am-4pm Mon-Fri; Bus 38, 43

A workshop that spends half its time celebrating and instigating harmonious community life and the other half protesting political injustices, Spiral Q accomplishes these objectives through ancient traditions of outlandish parade and pageantry. At the museum you'll find the products of their labor: a roomful of community-made giant puppets (6ft human heads, an enormous papier-mâché matador, a cardboard school of fish masks, cardboard costumes and more glitter and paint than in the rest of North America combined). If you look willing, there's a good chance that the infectious charmers at the museum will get you to lend a hand to whatever project is being made. Note that the opening hours vary. And winter visitors beware: the rickety museum occupied a former warehouse and doesn't have any heat.

## UNIVERSITY OF PENNSYLVANIA Map p225

U Penn; ☎ 215-495-7000; SEPTA 36th St Station, Bus 21, 30, 40, 42

Philadelphia's contribution to the Ivy League traces its roots to Benjamin Franklin's Public Academy of Philadelphia, which opened its doors in 1751. The first classes were held in a warehouse on 2nd St near the Delaware River. In 1755 the academy was incorporated, received the power to confer college degrees and subsequently changed its name to the College, Academy and Charitable School of Philadelphia. The fifth-oldest college in the colonies, it stood out from its antecedents because they were concerned with the education of religious figures, while Penn's curriculum focused on nonsectarian instruction. The college became the nation's first university in 1779 and moved to this 260-acre campus, west of the Schuylkill, in the 1870s.

Neighborhoods – University City & West Philadelphia

The central portion of the campus, **Levy Park** (also known as The Green) is well landscaped and provides comfortable, shady spaces to laze about in the summer. During the school year, competition for these shady spots greatly increases with the arrival of Penn's 23,000 students. The campus's earliest structures are largely Gothic Revival and help to complete the overall picturesque effect.

### UNIVERSITY OF PENNSYLVANIA'S THE ANN & JEROME FISHER FINE ARTS BUILDING Map p225

**220 S 34th St; SEPTA 36th St Station, Bus 21, 30, 40**

Generally referred to as the Furness Building – after its designer, architect Frank Furness – this building, completed in 1891, made many contributions to innovative library design. Take a gander at the reading room, which is several stories tall and is beautifully lit by a series of clerestory windows and skylights. Though entrance to this room is permitted only to those wielding Penn library cards, you can hoof it up to the 4th floor to observe the library through some windows.

Contained inside the Fine Arts Building are two worthwhile art galleries. The visual arts **Arthur Ross Gallery** (Map p225; ☎ 215-898-2083; www.upenn.edu/arg; 220 S 34th St; admission free; ☽ 10am-5pm Tue-Fri, noon-5pm Sat & Sun) presents the work of Penn's students and faculty. Every few months the gallery shuts down to change the exhibitions. The small **Kroiz Gallery** ( ☎ 215-898-8323; www.upenn.edu/gsfa/archives; 220 S 34th St; admission free; ☽ Tue-Fri 10am-5pm, Sat noon-5pm) contains the design school's archives. Here you can ponder some of Louis Kahn's drawings and check out changing exhibits, which might show old

drawings by Paul Philippe Cret and others who exemplify Penn's Beaux Art traditions.

### UNIVERSITY OF PENNSYLVANIA'S COLLEGE HALL & UNDERGRADUATE ADMISSION Map p225

☎ 215-898-7507; College Hall; ☽ admissions office 9am-5pm Mon-Fri; SEPTA 36th St Station, Bus 21, 30, 40, 42

Finished in 1873, College Hall was the first building to occupy the present site of the University of Pennsylvania. Back then Penn was small enough to need only one building to house all of the campus's activity. Today College Hall contains a handful of the university's more important administrative offices including undergraduate admissions, which organizes campus tours. These tours depart weekdays at 11am and 2pm, expect during February and May, when they are offered at 2pm only.

College Hall may also be the model for the mansion of the Addams Family, whose cartoonist and creator, Charles Addams, was a Penn alum.

### UNIVERSITY OF PENNSYLVANIA'S INFORMATION DESK Map p225

☎ 215-898-4636; 3417 Spruce St; ☽ 7-1am daily during school year, 7am-8pm Mon-Fri during breaks; SEPTA 36th St Station, Bus 21, 30, 40, 42

Located on the 1st floor of Penn's Houston Hall and staffed by friendly students, the desk offers maps and information.

### THE UNIVERSITY MUSEUM OF ARCHAEOLOGY & ANTHROPOLOGY Map p225

☎ 215-898-4000; www.upenn.edu/museum; 3260 South St; adult/child/senior/student $8/5/6/6, admission free Sundays; ☽ 10am-4:30pm Thu-Sat, 1-5pm Sun, closed Sun in summer; SEPTA 36th St Station, Bus 21, 30, 40

This world-renowned museum contains interesting permanent exhibits and a wide range of changing exhibitions. Its archaeological treasures hail from ancient Egypt, Mesopotamia, the Mayan peninsula, Asia, Greece, Rome, Africa, Polynesia and North America. Highlights include one of the world's largest crystal balls (a 55-pounder that may have belonged to the Empress Dowager of China); samples of the oldest writing ever found, from Sumer; bronzes from Benin, in Nigeria; and a 12-ton granite Sphinx of Ramesses II, circa 1293–1185 BC, from Egypt.

# MANAYUNK

*Eating p121; Shopping p157*

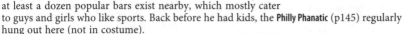

With its steep hills and Victorian row houses overlooking the Schuylkill River, Manayunk – from a Native American expression meaning 'where we go to drink' – still remains a good spot to accomplish this activity. Other then drinking, visitors are also permitted to eat and shop. If they're very lucky (most aren't), a decent rock show will be playing at the **Grape St Pub** (p140). If not, they comfort themselves with knowledge that at least a dozen popular bars exist nearby, which mostly cater to guys and girls who like sports. Back before he had kids, the **Philly Phanatic** (p145) regularly hung out here (not in costume).

During mornings and afternoons spent in this former textile-manufacturing neighborhood, many Philadelphians enjoy pleasant afternoon strolls along gentrified Main St – a National Historic District with chic boutiques, art galleries, restaurants and bars. A more natural experience can be had wandering along the former towpath beside the Manayunk Canal. Here you can check out remnants from the foundations of the old factories and locks that made this urban village into a thriving, if small-scale, manufacturing center, back before train lines usurped canal routes.

## Transport

**Train** Take the SEPTA Norristown R6 suburban train to Manayunk Station.

**Bus** The 61 begins at Walnut and 9th Sts, travels northwest along Ridge Ave, connects with Main St and travels into Manayunk.

**Car** From Fairmount Park, follow Kelly Dr north into Manayunk. Several well-marked parking lots exist on Main St.

## Orientation

Manayunk lies about 4 miles northwest of downtown, along the east side of the Schuylkill River. The commercial activities of the neighborhood exist along Main St, which runs parallels to the river. Matching the path of Main St are the elevated tracks of SEPTA's R6 train, one block to the northeast, running over Cresson St. The neighborhood is hilly, and the elevated parts are mostly residential. The flatter lowlands contain stuff for visitors.

### MANAYUNK CANAL Map p230
**SEPTA Norristown R6, Bus 61**

Back before railroads took over the transportation scene, canal systems like this one in Manayunk were a primary means of moving cargo in the first half of the 19th century. Today the Manayunk system is in picturesque ruins, and you can take in the scene by strolling along its former **Tow Path**, peering at rail lines, derelict canal locks, old textile mills, remnants of buildings, and birdies and fishies.

# CHESTNUT HILL

*Eating p123; Shopping p159; Sleeping p169*

Prosperous and darling, this neighborhood looks much like the railroad suburb it was 100 years ago, only with more boutique shopping and people wearing contemporary clothes. Those who live here tend to be young families who sought and found a safe, quiet enclave not too far from downtown. This village boasts an older mode of life: the grocery store still runs monthly tabs and offers delivery, the town is still organized around the train station, the Women's Exchange still serves afternoon tea and one of the most exciting recreational activities is eating an ice cream cone. Other options include stopping by for the annual crafts fair or bird-watching in the Wissahickon Valley, where 167 kinds of feathered buddies live. The small town contains an astounding number of artisan bakeries.

Chestnut Hill got its start in the colonial period as a farming community that operated some preindustrial mills along the Wissahickon Creek. Both British and American forces marched along the town's main road as they went to and from the Battle of Germantown. The town underwent serious change in the 1880s when Henry Howard Houston bought large tracts of land to develop for wealthy families. Over several decades, a few hundred beautiful homes were built (and many survive) in styles ranging from Queen Anne to the Arts and Crafts movement. Most of these homes are stone, made from schist quarried in the Wissahickon. Though you'd never guess it when checking out all of the bakeries, vernacular colonial homes and stone Victorian mansions, Chestnut Hill actually helped to birth postmodern architecture with the **Vanna Venturi House** (p91).

## Transport

**Train** Take the SEPTA R8 suburban train and get off at Chestnut Hill West. Alternatively take the SEPTA R7 suburban train and get off at Chestnut Hill East. Go left on Bethlehem Pike for a couple of blocks to reach town.

**Bus** The 23 originates in South Philly on 11th St, heads north, turns left onto Germantown Ave and travels to Chestnut Hill.

**Car** Several well-marked parking lots exist on Germantown Ave.

# Orientation

Chestnut Hill is organized around Germantown Ave, its main commercial road. Its western boundary is Wissahickon Park. Head south on Germantown Ave and you hit the neighborhood of Mt Airy.

### VISITORS CENTER Map p231

☎ 215-247-6696; 8426 Germantown Ave; ☽ 8:30am-5pm Mon-Fri, 10am-3pm Sat; SEPTA R8 Chestnut Hill West, SEPTA R7 Chestnut Hill East, Bus 23

Stop by this tiny visitors center to pick up the usual assortment of maps, brochures and advice. The center also sells the *Architectural Guide and Map of Chestnut Hill,* produced by the Chestnut Hill Historical Society.

### CHESTNUT HILL HISTORICAL SOCIETY Map p231

☎ 215-247-0417; www.chhist.org; 8708 Germantown Ave; ☽ 10am-5pm Mon-Fri; SEPTA R8 Chestnut Hill West, SEPTA R7 Chestnut Hill East, Bus 23

On the 1st floor of one of the area's many stone Victorian houses is a small exhibit of old photographs showing Chestnut Hill back when it was a black-and-white bourgeoisie town instead of today's full-color version. For $6 you can buy copies of the historical society's notable 'Architectural Guide and Map of Chestnut Hill.' It shows all the streets in town as well as the precise locations of 80 of Chestnut Hill's more significant pieces of architecture and a picture of each building. Also for sale are several history and picture books about Chestnut Hill and nearby Germantown.

The society organizes a few architectural tours ($12) each season; visit the website for more information.

### MORRIS ARBORETUM Map p231

☎ 215-247-5777; www.upenn.edu/arboretum; 100 Northwestern Ave; adult/student/senior/child $8/6/6/3; ☽ 10am-4pm; Bus L

The beautiful, rolling landscape of the arboretum's 92 acres will impress even those uninterested in gardening. It's so awesome that it's Pennsylvania's *official* arboretum. There are thousands of exotic trees, some well-designed winding paths, natural streams and plenty of isolated spots. Kids love the swan pond and the Garden Railway display, which features detailed miniatures of historic buildings and places made entirely of natural materials (leaves, twigs, roots) with G-scale trains racing by.

The admission price includes a guided tour; these are offered Saturday and Sunday

## Top Five – Chestnut Hill

- **McNally's Tavern** (p138) Eat a Schmitter beneath stacks of pewter mugs.
- **Morris Arboretum** (p90) Pet the trees and flowers.
- **Shopping** (p159) Buy cute stuff along Germantown Ave.
- **Woodmere Art Museum** (p91) Check out NC Wyeth and the rest of the gang.
- **Women's Exchange** (p124) Have tea in their garden.

at 2pm. In addition to the hours noted above, the arboretum is open until 5pm on weekends April through October.

## VANNA VENTURI HOUSE Map p231
**8330 Millman St; SEPTA R8 Chestnut Hill West, SEPTA R7 Chestnut Hill East, Bus 23**
This is it: postmodernism, found in the house Robert Venturi built for his mom in 1963. As any architectural text will tell you, things just haven't been the same since. Do you see the clever references to popular building typologies and conventions? Can you find meaning in that archlike thing over the front door? It's a private house, so gawk only from the street.

## WOODMERE ART MUSEUM Map p231
☎ 215-247-0476; www.woodmereartmuseum.org;

9201 Germantown Ave; adult/student/senior/child under 5 $5/3/3/free; ⌚ 10am-5pm Mon-Sat, 1-5pm Sun; Bus L
Housed in one of Chestnut Hill's larger Victorian mansions with a dang pretty mansard-topped tower and 6 acres of land, the original core of this museum's collection is an eclectic grouping of oriental rugs, paintings, sculpture and European decorative art presented in old galleries and parlors. Woodmere focuses its efforts on displaying the work of Philadelphia area artists, past and present. Among those represented are NC Wyeth, Daniel Garber, Thomas Pollock Anshutz and Benjamin West. The museum maintains a children's gallery and offers a changing schedule of kid-oriented programs. It sometimes hosts classical music concerts in its rotunda.

# GERMANTOWN
*Eating p124*

For travelers Germantown presents a few exciting options, most of them tied to tumultuous moments in its history. The site of Philadelphia's only revolutionary battlefield, Germantown existed back in those days as a remote country retreat for the upper crust, who used it to flee from outbreaks of yellow fever or to escape the city's oppressive summer heat. When George Washington was president and serving his term in Philadelphia, he joined the migration of the wealthy; thus Germantown became the de facto capital of the country. Germantown is also famous as an early center of abolitionist activity, and the town later became an important stop on the Underground Railroad. Harriet Tubman would lead freed slaves along the Wissahickon to a Germantown Ave station, the Johnson House, which still stands today.

Presently an identity crisis looms over Germantown. It contains some excellent history-related attractions, but these seem disconnected from the daily life of the place. The underused monuments (which, by the way, means that you'll easily get your money's worth of a tour guide's attention) sit along a seedy commercial corridor featuring a profusion of shops and businesses (check-cashing places, convenience stores, pawn shops, hair-braiding salons, cheap breakfast joints with Styrofoam plates and plastic forks, and a Western Union) with plenty of pedestrian traffic, at least during the day. While it is healthier than many of Philadelphia's most blighted spaces, the underside of this low-rent distinct is that there is a substantial amount of crime.

Even so, though you'll find some derelict buildings along Germantown Ave, you'll also find large sections containing blocks of well-loved, well-preserved Victorian mansions on grassy lawns and tree-lined streets – a clear reminder of Germantown's days as a supremely affluent community. Though hard to predict, gentrification seems about ready to plan a march down Germantown Ave from the direction of nearby Chestnut Hill, just like all those revolutionary troops did back in the day – a prospect over which residents have conflicting feelings.

## Orientation
Germantown's slightly hilly topography, its position well outside Philadelphia's original boundaries and the fact that settlement began long before Jefferson kicked off his famous survey all explain why a uniform grid doesn't exist. Gently curving Germantown Ave runs more or less southeast to northwest and is the main drag for this neighborhood – most sites are on it or near it. Head southeast on the road and you chart a course through North Philly;

## Transport

**Train** Take the SEPTA R7 suburban train and get off at Germantown Station. Go left on Chelten Ave for a couple of blocks to reach town, an activity not enjoyed at night.

**Bus** The 23 originates in South Philly on 11th St, heads north, turns left onto Germantown Ave and travels to Germantown.

**Car** Plenty of street parking exists. Germantown Ave is fairly safe, especially as you get closer to Mt Airy.

head northeast and you pass through Mt Airy on the way to tony Chestnut Hill. The area north of the avenue is sketchy. Land to the south benefits from close proximity to the Wissahickon River and contains some of those Victorian mansions, particularly on Tulpehocken St and Walnut Lane.

### GERMANTOWN HISTORICAL SOCIETY & VISITORS CENTER
Map p231

☎ 215-844-1683; 5501 Germantown Ave; ⓨ museum 10am-4pm Tue & Thu, 1-5pm Sun; visitor center 10am-4pm Tue-Fri; Bus 23

Displaying cannon balls from the Battle of Germantown, paintings by Peale, dolls, period clothing, and plenty of photographs and etchings of the changing town, the historical society's museum well presents the story of Germantown's four centuries. Learn about the town's German roots, its role as an abolitionist hotbed and its development as one of the nation's first commuter suburbs. While the place is mostly a museum, the sort-of visitors center makes an effort to orient travelers and can provide brochures detailing area attractions.

## EARLY AMERICAN HOMES

### CLIVEDEN Map p231

☎ 215-848-1777; www.cliveden.org; 6401 Germantown Ave; ⓨ 1-4pm Thu-Sat Apr-Dec; adult/child/senior/student $5/2/3/3; SEPTA R7 Germantown Station, Bus 23

During the Battle of Germantown, 125 British troops barricaded themselves within Cliveden. Though damaged during the battle, the Georgian house survived well enough for Benjamin Chew's descendants to live in it for 200 years. Aside from looking for musket

holes and Affleck sofas during a house tour and wandering about the shady grounds (and onetime battlefield), visitors can also check out an exhibit near the gift shop that details the lives of Chew's slaves, one of whom was Richard Allen, who later founded **Mother Bethel AME Church** (p79) and became a leading abolitionist. Call to inquire about numerous special events, including a reenactment of the battle.

### DESHLER-MORRIS HOUSE Map p231

☎ 215-842-1798; 5442 Germantown Ave; admission free; ⓨ 1-4pm Fri-Sun or by appt; SEPTA R7 Germantown Station, Bus 23

George Washington and family lived in this house when a yellow fever epidemic hit Philadelphia in 1793. He must have become fond of the place, for he returned again in the summer of 1794, when humid heat in Philly made the president too hot. Much of the house is authentically George. The wood floors he walked on are still there and in good shape. A few Washington-owned artifacts lie about (if you're lucky, you might get to hold his silver tankard) as do items from the family who built the house. Interesting pieces include decorative tiles around fireplaces, a peculiar ceramic chicken feeder, a wooden Noah's Ark play set and a Rembrandt Peale portrait. A tour – led by an incredibly knowledgeable woman who's been running them for around 20 years – takes you through house and garden.

### EBENEZER MAXWELL MANSION
Map p231

☎ 215-438-1861, 215-438-0133 special events; 200 W Tulpehocken St; adult/child $3/2; ⓨ 1-4pm Fri & Sat Apr-Dec; SEPTA R7 Germantown Station, Bus 23

Nearly bulldozed in the '60s, this Victorian-Gothic mansion, built of stone and slate, sits in a neighborhood that still looks much like it did back in the last half of the 19th century. House tours (included in the admission price) of the restored building reveal a parlor full of Rococo furniture and a kitchen full of old-school gadgetry. Outside, the site maintains two styles of 19th-century garden. Around Halloween the creepy-looking building hosts ghost walks (adult/child $10/5).

### GRUMBLETHORPE Map p231

☎ 215-843-4820; 5267 Germantown Ave; admission free; ⓨ 1-4pm Tue, Thu & Sun; SEPTA R7 Germantown Station, Bus 23

Built in 1744, this opulent colonial home

exemplifies Germantown's residential architecture from the middle of the 18th century. Like many of the other area homes from this period, Grumblethorpe – a stone house made for Philadelphia's prominent Wister family – was originally used as a summer retreat. A tour of the restored house includes a look at the workshop from which Charles Johes Wister made many contributions to the fields of astronomy, horticulture and meteorology.

### JOHNSON HOUSE Map p231

☎ 215-438-1768; www.johnsonhouse.org; 6306 Germantown Ave; adult/child/senior/student $5/2/3/3; ♥ Thu & Fri by appt, 1:30, 2:30 & 3:30pm Sat; SEPTA R7 Germantown Station, Bus 23

Philadelphia's only accessible and intact Underground Railroad site, the Johnson House (1768) was owned by a Quaker family who began operating it as a station by 1858. According to local lore, both Harriet Tubman and William Still visited the house as they conducted hundreds of escapes to freedom. House tours discuss the building's architectural and social history (Mamie Eisenhower had tea here when the Women's Club of Chestnut Hill owned the house, and it has scars from the Battle of Germantown), its role in the Railroad (you'll see the 3rd-floor hiding place) and a discussion of American slavery and abolitionism.

### STENTON Map pp220-1

☎ 215-329-7312; www.stenton.org; 4601 N 18th St; adult/senior/student $5/4/4; ♥ 1-4pm Tue-Sat Apr-Dec, by appt Jan-Mar; Bus 23

This sophisticated Georgian structure – the plantation home of William Penn's secretary, James Logan – was made of brick in the 1720s. It is a beautiful home, populated with many pieces of furniture made by Philadelphia's finest colonial cabinetmakers, and little changed since the 18th century. Three generations of Logans lived on the estate until 1899, when the National Society of the Colonial Dames of America was given the task of preserving the estate.

### UPSALA Map p231

☎ 215-842-1798; 6430 Germantown Ave; admission free; ♥ 1-4pm Thu & Sat; SEPTA R7 Germantown Station, Bus 23

Part of the 'American side of the street' during the Battle of Germantown, the front lawn of this Federal-style home was used by Washington's soldiers to position the cannons they would eventually fire at the poor Georgian-styled home across the street. The house was built in 1795, well after the battle.

### WYCK Map p231

☎ 215-848-1690; www.wyck.org; 6026 Germantown Ave; adult/senior/student/family $5/4/4/10; ♥ noon-4:30pm Tue & Thu, 1-4pm Sat Apr–mid-Dec or by appt; SEPTA R7 Germantown Station, Bus 23

Preserved with such intelligent care that *Pennsylvania Heritage* published a glossy article about it, Wyck (1689) was continually inhabited by members of the same Quaker family for nine generations. Though notable events have occurred here (the British used it as a field hospital during the Battle of Germantown), Wyck is more interesting as a reflection of different moments of American life at home. Inside, find over 100,000 artifacts – books, natural history specimens (one of the owners was a founder of the Franklin Institute), textiles, children's toys and cartloads more. Outside, find a garden with about 30 kinds of roses, some grown from plantings of the original flowers, arranged in the same pattern for 175 years.

---

## Top Five – Germantown

- **Cliveden** (p92) Visit a house that was bombarded during the Revolutionary War.
- **Deshler-Morris House** (p92) Explore a house that George Washington rented while he was president.
- **Johnson House** (p93) Tour Philly's only accessible Underground Railroad station.
- **Rib Crib** (p124) Masticate some tangy take-out.
- **Wyck** (p93) Check out this fabulously preserved 17th-century home.

# ELSEWHERE IN THE CITY

Although most Philadelphia attractions are contained in a compact area, this is a huge, sprawling city, with some choice attractions laying far beyond the standard tourism zones. If you have time (and a car), it's worth your while to venture out to these notable spots.

## THE CHURCH OF THE ADVOCATE

☎ 215-236-6773; www.churchoftheadvocate.org; 1801 W Diamond St; admission free; ❤ 9am-5pm; SEPTA Susquehanna-Dauphin Station; Bus 33, 39

Inside this Episcopalian church you'll find a series of impressive, vividly colorful paintings (1973–76) by two Philadelphia artists, Walter Edmonds and Richard Watson, outlining the black religious experience from slavery to the present. This revolutionary church, built in 1890, provided a peaceful and protective haven to the civil rights movement, largely because of the leadership of Reverend Paul Washington. In 1968 the church was home to the Third Annual National Conference on Black Power, and in 1970 the Black Panthers held a large convention here. When racial tensions were high in the '60s, this church was the site of negotiation and resolution. Today the surrounding neighborhood is pretty rough.

## THE WAGNER FREE INSTITUTE OF SCIENCE Map pp220-1

☎ 215-763-1299; 1700 W Montgomery Ave; admission free; ❤ 9am-4pm Tue-Fri by appt; SEPTA Cecil B Moore Station, Bus 2, 3

This forgotten natural history museum sits quietly unused in decrepit North Philadelphia. Those who make an appointment to visit find more then preserved starfish and bones from the mid-19th century; they find a museum that never modernized yet somehow didn't close shop. The objects and labels in the ancient glass and wood display cases haven't been moved in over 100 years. By deed and by trust, nothing can be added or augmented.

## WOODMONT MANSION

Woodmont Rd; admission free; ❤ 1-5pm Sun Apr-Oct

God lived in Philly, or so said Father Divine, who claimed to be the physical embodiment of Jesus. Thousands believed him and joined his Peace Mission Movement in the early 20th century. For a time the cult was considerably wealthy, as is evidenced by their enormous château-style mansion, Woodmont. Guests are welcome to visit 'The Mount of the House of the Lord' and to view the Shrine of Life, which contains the body formerly used by Father Divine (God). Whatever one feels about his cult, Father Divine's peace movement, once influential, helped foster support for racial equality in the 1920s and '30s.

Visitors must dress according to the international modesty code, which is outlined in the Sleeping chapter (p161). Note that the mansion temporarily closes for the last week in April and the first week in May.

You need a car to visit the mansion. Exit the Schuylkill Expressway at Conshohocken. Take Rte 23 east, turn right on Spring Mill Rd and then turn left on Woodmont Rd.

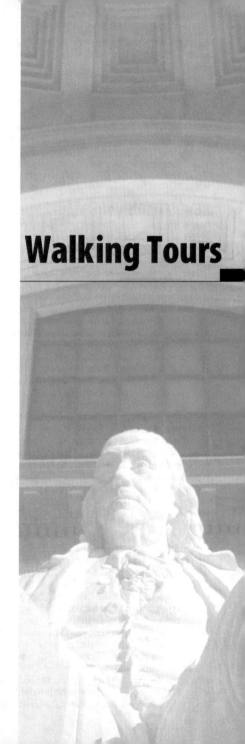

# Walking Tours

# Walking Tours

Philadelphia is one of America's most walkable cities. The 2 sq miles of Penn's original city are flat, picturesque and loaded with history. Knowing this, we've provided a few walking tours that will help you amble with purpose. One tour explores the colonial and revolutionary sites in Old City and Society Hill, and another navigates you past some of downtown Philly's finest architecture.

We also provide a tour for those interested in a strut through South Philly's Italian Market. If you like to bike, definitely don't pass up our ride down the Schuylkill River and beyond.

## REVOLUTIONARY RAMBLE

*Neighborhoods p55; Eating p105; Shopping p150; Sleeping p162*
Much of old Philadelphia is best explored on foot. The following suggested walking tour covers Independence National Historic Park and takes in sections of Old City and Center City.

Start at the **Independence Visitor Center** 1, where you can pick up information on the historic park. Directly across Market St, find the **Liberty Bell Center** 2, housing the cracked yet revered symbol of American independence. If you have time, get in line for a viewing; if not, you'll be able to see the bell from the street later in this tour. Go east along Market St, passing 4th St and arriving

### Walk Facts

**Start** Market and 6th Sts (SEPTA 5th St Station)
**End** Market and 7th Sts (SEPTA 8th St Station)
**Distance** 2 miles

at a group of 18th-century buildings, among which is the **B Free Franklin Post Office** 3; behind them is **Franklin Court** 4, site of Ben Franklin's home and workplace.

Head back west on Market St and turn north on 5th St. Go two blocks to Arch St, on the corner of which is the 1783 **Free Quaker Meeting House** 5. Unlike other Quakers, the Free Quakers supported and fought in the Revolutionary War. Turn west on Arch St to find the brand-new **National Constitution Center** 6 sitting on the north side of this block. Head inside to learn about your rights and to register to vote. Return east on Arch and cross 5th. After a few steps, look for an iron fence in the opening of the brick wall to your right. This is **Christ Church Burial Ground** 7; you should be able to see the graves of Benjamin and Deborah Franklin just a few feet from your position on the sidewalk. Or pop in to say 'hello.' On the north side of Arch St is the **US Mint** 8. Continue east along Arch St, crossing 4th St, to 1804 **Arch St Friends Meeting House** 9. Continue past 3rd St and find the **Betsy Ross House** 10, circa 1740; Betsy Ross might not have lived in this house and she did not design the first flag of the US, but check it out anyway.

Continue east to 2nd St, turn left (north), then right (east) into **Elfreth's Alley** 11, a residential street purported to be the oldest continually operated street in America. On 2nd St just north of the alley is **Fireman's Hall** 12, originally a firehouse (built in 1876) but now a cool museum.

Turn around and head south on 2nd St, cross Arch St and arrive at **Christ Church** 13 (1754), once used by many of the city's early dignitaries. Carry on south over Market and Chestnut Sts, stopping just before Sansom St. Here, glance at the **Thomas Bond House** 14, former home of the cofounder of the Pennsylvania Hospital and now a B&B. A little farther south at the corner of Walnut St is **City Tavern** 15, a reconstruction of the 1773 original, where you can try some of the kinds of food that people like Thomas Jefferson might have eaten. If tired, pop in for a beer, perhaps the one that's brewed per George Washington's private recipe.

Exit and turn right onto Walnut St. At the intersection of 3rd St, view the Greek Revival **Philadelphia Merchants Exchange** 16, designed by William Strickland and built in 1834. Across the street is the 18th-century **Bishop White House** 17, home of Reverend William White, the first Episcopal bishop of Pennsylvania; he lived here from 1787 to 1836. Go north on 3rd St for

half a block to discover the Neoclassic **First Bank of the US 18**, which was constructed in 1797 and served as the country's national bank until 1811.

Cross west through the lawn of Independence National Historical Park past the 1770 **Carpenters' Hall 19**, the site of the First Continental Congress in 1774, and the place where revolutionary leaders met with a French spy. Exit the lawn on 4th St, turn north, go to Chestnut St and turn west. Here is the Greek Revival **Second Bank of the US 20**, home of the National Portrait Gallery. Beside the bank but set farther back is **Library Hall 21**, containing the library of the American Philosophical Society, on the site of the country's first subscription library (1789).

Continue west on Chestnut and cross 5th St. This brings you to several of the most important historical buildings in Philadelphia. The first is **Old City Hall 22**, which served as the US Supreme Court from 1791 (when it was built) to 1800. Behind it is the 1789 **Philosophical Hall 23**, owned by the American Philosophical Society. In the center, **Independence Hall 24**, circa 1756 and a World Heritage Site, is where the Declaration of Independence was adopted and the US Constitution drafted. Beside Independence Hall, at the corner of 6th St, is **Congress Hall 25**, where the US Congress met between 1790 and 1800, when Philadelphia was the nation's capital. Across the street from these legendary edifices you can see the Liberty Bell through a glass window.

Turn left (south) on 6th St and walk to Walnut St. As you do, on your left you pass **Independence Square 26**, where the Declaration of Independence was read publicly by John Nixon for the first time on July 8, 1776.

Turn right (west) on Walnut St. On the corner of 6th St is the former **Curtis Publishing Company building 27**, where the celebrated artist Norman Rockwell delivered his paintings for the cover of the *Saturday Evening Post.* Go inside to find Tiffany's magnificent stained-glass Dream Garden. Opposite is **Washington Square 28**, one of the city's original squares. Continue along Walnut St to 7th St, and then turn north.

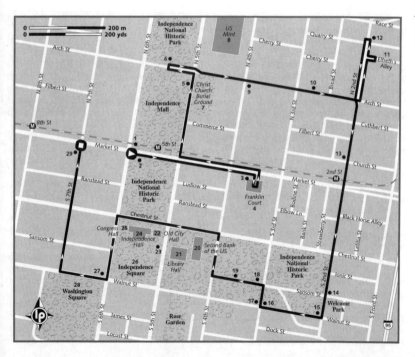

As you head toward Market St, you pass Sansom St, or Jewelers' Row, a retailing remnant from the early 20th century. At the corner of 7th and Market Sts is **Declaration House 29**, also called Graff House, a reconstruction of the house where Thomas Jefferson wrote the Declaration of Independence.

# DOWNTOWN ARCHITECTURE

*Neighborhoods p68; Eating p107; Shopping p152; Sleeping p164*

Philadelphia concentrates much of its important architecture around City Hall. Many of the buildings in this area emerged after the Civil War, when Philadelphia had achieved great prosperity as the 'Workshop of the World.' The works you will see reflect Philly's industrial wealth.

Begin at **City Hall 1**, built between 1871 and 1901 by John McArthur Jr. One of the greatest masonry buildings in the country, City Hall is a highly personal version of the French Second Empire style, topped with an oversized statue of William Penn. Cross John F Kennedy Blvd to 1 N Broad St to see James Windrim's 1873 castlelike **Masonic Temple 2**. Though it might seem unusual to see turrets and battlements on a building in downtown Philly, such flourishes will appear as normal for those who actually venture into the strangeness inside. Go another block north and view one of the finest surviving examples of Frank Furness' architecture, the **Pennsylvania Academy of the Fine Arts 3**, built between 1872 and 1876.

Turn around and head south for one block. Turn east on Arch St and go straight

## Walk Facts

**Start** Market and Broad Sts (SEPTA 15th St Station or City Hall Station, at the intersection of the Market-Frankford and Broad St lines)
**End** Locust and 16th Sts (SEPTA Walnut-Locust St Station)
**Distance** 1.5 miles

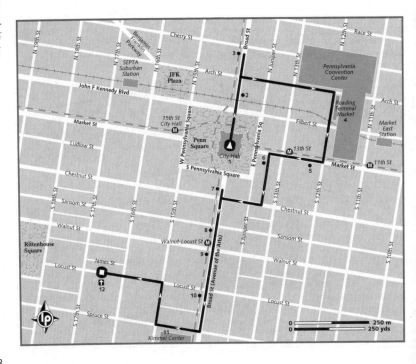

for three blocks, until you arrive at **Reading Terminal Market** 4, where you can enjoy almost any snack you like, some made by Amish vendors. When you leave, realize that you just ate under the former tracks of the Reading Railroad Station, of Monopoly fame.

Head south for two blocks on 12th St, arriving at Market St. On the southwest corner of 12th and Market Sts, stare lovingly at Howe and Lescaze's **Philadelphia Savings Fund Society** 5 (1930), one of the earliest and finest Modernist office towers in the country. Continue west on Market, passing 13th St. On the south side of this block, enter **John Wanamaker's** 6, designed by DH Burnham & Co in the early 1900s and now housing a Lord & Taylor department store. With the possible exception of Marshall Fields in Chicago, this is the grandest department store still standing in the US. Pass though the grand court and exit on Chestnut St, turn west and walk to Broad St. At the northwest corner of this intersection, check out McKim, Mead and White's **Girard Trust Co** 7, circa 1905–08, which should remind you of the Pantheon. Today it's operated as a Ritz-Carlton. If you need a rest and a scotch, go inside to drink one under the rotunda.

Walking south to 140 Broad St, take a gander at the sweeping staircases and mansard roof of the Second Empire–style **Union League** 8, designed by John Fraser in 1864–65. It's one of the few things in town built during the Civil War. Continue south for one block to Napoleon LeBrun and Gustavus Runge's 1855–57 **Academy of Music** 9, the nation's first grand opera house. Continue to Locust St to find the 1902–13 **Bellevue** 10, designed by GW and HD Hewitt. Another block south down Broad brings you to Spruce St, which holds the glass-roofed **Kimmel Center** 11, the city's latest attempt at archiectural greatness, designed in 2001 by Rafael Viñoly.

Go west on Spruce St, and then turn north on 15th St. After one block, turn west on Locust St, and proceed forward for 1½ blocks. At 1625 Locust, find **St Marks Church** 12 (1847–49), by John Notman, Philly's master of Romantic architectural styles.

# ITALIAN MARKET STROLL

*Neighborhoods p81; Eating p116; Shopping p156*

America's oldest and largest outdoor market stretches along 9th St between Christian St and Passyunk Ave. Every day but Monday the sidewalks fill with vendors collectively selling Philadelphia's best and cheapest selection of produce. In between the produce vendors are tables full of cheap and/or weird stuff. One might offer 10 sponges for $1; another may sell miniature gas-powered scooters.

As this walking tour is largely about food, start with lunch and end with dessert. Begin at Reed and Broad Sts, getting in the Italian mood by checking out Diane Keller's awesome mural of **Mario Lanza** 1. Walk one block north on Broad St, and then turn east on Wharton St. Walk five full blocks to Passyunk Ave and witness actual hatred between Philly's biggest cheese steak rivals, **Pat's** 2 and **Geno's** 3. Pat's, which invented the

## Walk Facts

**Start** Broad and Reed Sts (near SEPTA Tasker-Morris stop)
**End** Christian and 10th Sts
**Distance** 1 mile

sandwich in the 1930s, entices customers with promises of 'the original.' Geno's, poaching off Pat's success since the '60s, attracts visitors as a giant peacock might, using colorful, overwhelming lights and signage. Both promise to be the best. Pick one, eat a cheese steak and then head north on 9th St.

After two blocks, turn east on Washington St. Walk for almost a block to find **Center City Pretzel Co** 4. If it's before noon, shell out 30¢ for a hot one and hope to watch the oven in action. If it's after noon, then mentally register this place and return around 1am. In the meantime, return to 9th St and go north; you've just entered the stretch of road with the densest concentration of vendors. After a very short block, check out **Fante's Kitchen Wares Shop** 5, at the intersection of Kimball St. Established in the Italian Market in 1906, this is one of America's finest shops for cooks (professional or not). For many it's reason enough to come to Philadelphia.

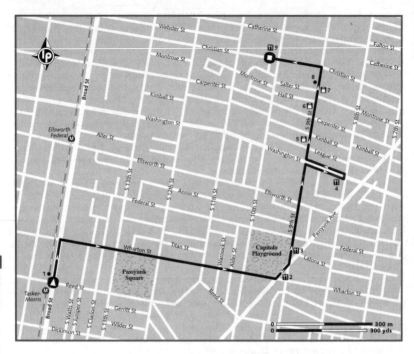

Continue north for two short blocks to **Di Bruno's Brothers 6**, a small shop, here since 1939, with over 400 kinds of cheese. Head north just a few feet, crossing Montrose St. On the east side of the street, check out **D'Angelo Brothers 7** ( ☎ 215-923-5637, 909 S 9th St), a butcher that stocks over 35 kinds of sausages (one of them 10% garlic by volume!) as well as plenty of fresh game and specialty pâté. Look for freshly killed bunnies and pheasants hanging in the window. Across the street, gaze upon South Philly's favorite controversial mayor, **Frank Rizzo 8**, whose mug appears in giant form in another of Diane Keller's murals. It's the most vandalized mural in town.

Walk north for half a block and turn west on Christian St. Walk one block, cross 10th St, and prepare for dessert at **Isgro Pastries 9**, here since 1904. We recommend a cannoli before possibly climbing aboard Bus 23 on 11th St, which runs north to Center City.

## SCHUYLKILL BIKE & BRIDGE TOUR

*Neighborhoods p83; Eating p119; Sleeping p168*

This tour covers sites seen on an 8.5-mile loop along the east and west banks of the Schuylkill River. The loop can be accomplished by runners and roller bladers, but there are a few tempting excursions along the way that you'll need a bike to reach. Along the loop, you'll pass under many bridges dramatically spanning the river. Most of these bridges have informational signs outlining their history somewhere near the bike path. Throughout the ride, the Schuylkill will remain your picturesque companion.

Begin at the **Fairmount Waterworks 1**. This engineering project (1812–15) looks somewhat like the acropolis and once provided drinking water to the entire city.

### Tour Facts

**Start** Near Kelly Dr and Fairmount Ave at the Fairmount Waterworks (SEPTA bus 76)
**End** Near Kelly Dr and Fairmount Ave at the Fairmount Waterworks (SEPTA bus 76)
**Distance** 8.5 miles

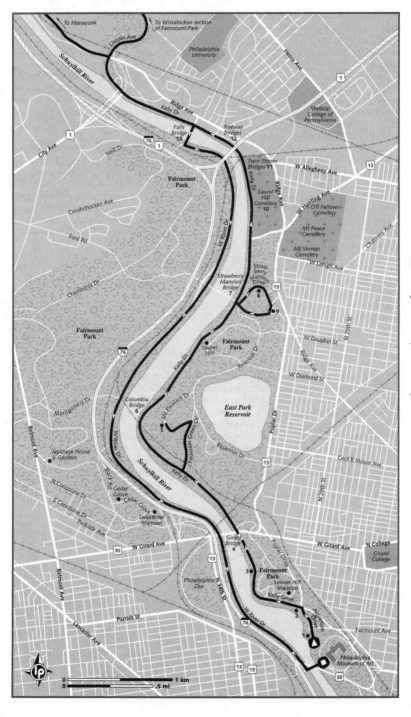

To Manayunk

To Wissahickon section
of Fairmount Park

Lincoln Ave

Schuylkill River

Philadelphia
University

Henry Ave

1

Ridge Ave

Kelly Dr

Medical
College of
Pennsylvania

Falls
Bridge
13

freeway
bridges
12

City Ave

Heill Dr

Twin Stones
Bridges 11

W Allegheny Ave

13

Fairmount
Park

Laurel
Hill
Cemetery
10

W Hunting Ave

Off Fellows
Cemetery

Conshohocken Ave

Ridge Ave

Mt Peace
Cemetery

Chalmers Ave

Ford Rd

Chamounix Dr

W River Dr

Mt Vernon
Cemetery

W Lehigh Ave

Strawberry
Mansion
Bridge
7

Straw-
berry
Mansion
Drive

8

13

9

Fairmount
Park

76

Kelly Dr

Laurel
Hill

Fairmount
Park

Reservoir Dr

W Dauphin St

N 29th St

W Diamond St

East Park
Reservoir

Columbia
Bridge
6

Mt Pleasant Dr

5

Fountain Green Dr

Reservoir Dr

Poplar Dr

13

Montgomery Dr

W River Dr

Black Rd

Schuylkill River

Belmont Ave

Japanese House
& Gardens

Cecil B Moore Ave

N Concourse Dr

Cedar
Grove

Cedar Grove

N 29th St

S Concourse Dr

Sweetbriar
Mansion

Parkside Ave

Girard
Bridge
4

Girard Dr

30

W Girard Ave

W Girard Ave

N College

Girard
College

13

Philadelphia
Zoo

N 34th St

3

Fairmount
Park

Poplar Drive

Lemon Hill
Mansion

Belmont Ave

Lancaster Ave

Parrish St

W River Dr

76

Kelly Drive

2

Aquarium Drive

Fairmount Ave

13

13

13

30

Philadelphia
Museum of Art

0 ————— 1 km
0 ————— .5 mi

It was also Philadelphia's top tourist attraction in the early 19th century. Find the Schuylkill River Trail, a bike path running between the river and the east side of Kelly Dr. Head north – the river will be on your left and the road on your right. In moments you'll encounter **Boathouse Row** 2, a cluster of Victorian buildings where most of the river's sculling activity originates.

Continue along and you'll pass the **Ellen Phillips Samuel Memorial Garden** 3, whose three terraces, built from 1933 to 1961, contain heavy-handed (they look almost Soviet) sculptures such as *The Puritan* and *The Settling of the Seaboard*. Keep going north, and you'll pass under **Girard Bridge** 4, which isn't that exciting unless you dig efficient, modern infrastructure of the small-scale two-lane variety. After about 0.3 miles, Fountain Green Dr will intersect Kelly Dr. Here you may take a detour to view **Mount Pleasant** 5.

Continue for another 0.3 miles on the trail, and you'll pass under **Columbia Bridge** 6, an arching railroad bridge made of concrete and faced with stone. The current manifestation dates from 1921, though this crossing has a long history. The first bridge that allowed trains to span the Schuylkill was located here. Today it marks the finish line for regattas. Ride for another mile and you'll arrive at **Strawberry Mansion Bridge** 7 (1897), one of the first steel-framed bridges in the US. The beautiful bridge once carried trolleys across the river. It was recently restored and now serves pedestrian, equestrian and light vehicular traffic. Its underside is beautifully lit at night. Here you may detour to **Strawberry Mansion** 8 and **Woodford Mansion** 9 by turning east on Strawberry Mansion Dr and following the signs.

Continue north on the trail, passing **Laurel Hill Cemetery** 10. For those interested in garden-like cemetery landscaping, this one, founded in 1836, is famous and well worth exploring. Numerous prominent Philadelphians are buried here, including David Rittenhouse and Frank Furness. After a mile you'll arrive at the **Twin Stones Bridges** 11, two old small guys, each carrying a single railroad track. Next to them, pass under a pair of enormous **freeway bridges** 12 connecting Rte 1 to I-76, whose decks are far overhead. The difference in scale is just plain neat. Continue for about a quarter of a mile, coming to **Falls Bridge** 13, a short span from the late 19th century featuring decorative ironwork along its deck.

Now it's time to make a decision. You may cross the Schuylkill over the Falls Bridge and return to Philadelphia along the west side of the river (4 miles). You'll again pass by all the bridges you've just seen, and you'll see Boathouse Row and the Fairmount Waterworks from an interesting perspective. Or you may forge ahead 2 more miles and have a pleasant lunch in Manayunk (Map p230). If you'd like to add a bit more scenic mileage to your trip, a third choice is to head for the gravel paths of the Wissahickon section of Fairmount Park (Map pp220-1). Things get significantly more rustic here, and no cars are allowed. The Wissahickon contains plenty of birds, bridges and woods.

To get to Manayunk and the Wissahickon, ride along the trail until it ends. Continue on Kelly Dr (you'll be contending with autos) until it hits Ridge Ave; go west on Ridge Ave. For the Wissahickon, you'll make an almost immediate right into the park. For Manayunk, take Ridge Ave to Main St, and ride for about half a mile to cuteness. If you get tuckered out, you can always ride home on the SEPTA's R8 at Manayunk Station.

# Eating

# Eating

Dismiss the notion that Philadelphia eating is mostly about cheese steaks. While this greasy delight still stands as a prominent member of the Philly food family, things have changed in the last 15 years. During the past decade, hundreds of new restaurants have opened in Center City whose fine dining rooms provide a culinary balance to Philly's traditional cheap eats. Philadelphia appears to have a limitless capacity to welcome and lucratively support an army of bistros and BYOBs that fill up quickly on weekends. Philadelphia can also brag about its number of celebrity chefs, which include Susanna Foo, Georges Perrier, Stephen Starr and Masaharu Morimoto – the Iron Chef himself.

On the more relaxed side of things, Philly boasts one of the finest café cultures in America. The city has become prosperous enough to provide cafés with plenty of lounging clients, and land values remain (at the moment) low enough not to drive the independent coffeehouse out of business, as has been the fate of cafés in more expensive cities.

Keep in mind that many of Philadelphia's best eating options are in bars. Places like the **Standard Tap** (p136), **New Wave Café** (p135) and **Nodding Head Brewery** (p133) sling great food in addition to beer.

## How Much?

Eating cheaply in Philadelphia comes easy. Pretzels cost less than $1, a cheese steak around $6 and most stuff coming out of a food truck will be around $5. Chinatown presents many options where you can feast for less than $7. At mid-range eateries you can expect to pay around $8 for appetizers and $15 for entrées. At the peak of the food pyramid, the tasting menus at Le Bec-Fin and Morimoto surpass the $100 mark.

## Tipping

As elsewhere in the USA, tipping is customary in Philadelphia restaurants. Servers expect 15% to 20% of the check total (before tax). Give a little more if the service was exceptional and a little less if it wasn't. Many restaurants add a service charge for parties of six or more; if you're traveling with a gang, check the check before you tip. Tipping is optional at coffee bars and places where you place your own order at the counter.

## Markets & Take-Out

Feel like a picnic? The following vendors can help stock your basket.

### ESSENE Map pp228-9 *Health Food*
☎ 215-922-1146; 719 S 4th St; salad bar $6.99 per lb; ☾ 9am-8pm

At the rear of this health food store is a self-serve cafeteria offering organically grown produce for lunch and dinner. Representative items include tofu curry, paella and various salads, all sold by the pound. This place is a boon for macrobiotics.

### FRESH GROCER Map p225 *Supermarket*
☎ 215-222-9200; 4001 Walnut St; ☾ 24hr

Just west of the University of Pennysylvania, this newfangled place doesn't close.

### ITALIAN MARKET Map pp228-9 *Market*
www.phillyitalianmarket.com; S 9th St from Wharton to Fitzwater Sts; ☾ 9am-5pm Tue-Sat, 9am-2pm Sun

Find exotic cheeses, cheap produce, gourmet prepared items and much more along S 9th St. See p35 for more details.

### READING TERMINAL MARKET
Map pp222-3 *Market*
☎ 215-922-2317; www.readingterminalmarket.org; 12th & Arch Sts; ☾ 8am-6pm Mon-Sat

At this jumble of butchers, produce, Amish delicacies and take-out stands, you can buy anything from a fresh pretzel to a smoothie. On weekends, a boy-genius pounds out jazz on the market's upright piano, sounding like someone five times his age. See p34 for more on the market.

### SUE'S FRUIT Map pp222-3 *Produce*
☎ 215-569-0985; 115 S 18th St; ☽ 6am-6pm Mon-Sat, 8am-4pm Sun

This is a hole-in-the-wall stuffed full of fruits and vegetables.

### WHOLE FOODS Map p228-9 *Supermarket*
☎ 215-733-9788; 929 South St; ☽ 8am-10pm

America's chain of upscale, healthy and mainly organic supermarkets has two outlets; the other branch is in the **Museum District** (Map pp222-3; ☎ 215-557-0015; 2001 Pennsylvania Ave; ☽ 8am-10pm).

# OLD CITY

Most of the restaurants in Old City congregate around Market and 2nd Sts. Things get so hopping that it's sometimes hard to tell what distinguishes a club from a restaurant. More often than not, Old City establishments switch-hit and serve both roles. Stephen Starr's **Continental** (p106) best exemplifies the neighborhood.

## Budget

### THE BOURSE Map p226-7 *Food Court*
☎ 215-625-0300; 5th & Ranstead Sts; $3-7; ☽ 10am-6pm Mon-Sat, 11am-5pm Sun; SEPTA 5th St Station, Bus 17, 33, 48, 57

The spectacular Victorian digs of this architecturally impressive building make it worth a visit even if you're not hungry. The various eateries renting space inside the Bourse food court include **Pains Delicatessen**, **Powerjuicer**, a chocolatier and a Chinese joint dishing out fast-food fare.

### CAROUSEL SHOP
Map pp226-7 *American*
☎ 215-925-3637; 210 S 3rd St; breakfast & lunch mains $2-6; ☽ 7am-7pm; SEPTA 2nd St Station, Bus 17, 21, 33, 42, 76

Everything including the lemonade is homemade in this 27-year-old mom-and-pop operation. Some breakfast sandwiches cost less than $2, and the liverwurst special remains $2.65. They've also got Hershey's ice cream and can whip up milkshakes.

### GIANFRANCO PIZZA RUSTICA
Map pp226-7 *Pizza*
☎ 215-592-0048; 6 N 3rd St; slices $1.75;

☽ 10am-10pm Mon-Thu & Sat, 10am-11pm Fri; SEPTA 2nd St Station, Bus 48, 57, 76

This bare-bones pie shop has no discernible ambience and some of the finest slices in town. It's a great place to power up before getting your drink on at one of the nearby clubs.

### OLD CITY COFFEE
Map pp226-7 *Café*
☎ 215-629-9292; 221 Church St; snacks $2-5; ☽ 7am-8pm Mon-Thu, 7am-10pm Fri, 7:30am-10pm Sat, 7:30am-6pm Sun; SEPTA 2nd St Station, Bus 48, 57, 76

This quiet place, located on a cobbled side street, brews good coffee and stocks cookies and prepared salads. Aside from a few curbside tables, there's not much seating.

### OLDE CITY WRAP SHACK
Map pp226-7 *Juice/Wraps*
☎ 215-577-5948; 146 N 2nd St; wraps $5, smoothies $3.75; ☽ 11am-9pm Mon-Fri, noon-6pm Sat & Sun; SEPTA 2nd St Station, Bus 48, 57, 76

Only 4ft wide, this place really is just a shack. It churns out some excellent juices and smoothies and, if you want to splurge, a few more bucks earns you a great wrap. Though take-out is the norm, these items are best enjoyed on the shack's hammock, stool or plastic chair, possibly with some Dylan tunes wafting out of the aging stereo.

### PETIT 4 Map pp226-7 *Desserts*
☎ 215-627-8440; 160 N 3rd St; ☽ 7am-6pm Tue-Thu, 7am-10pm Fri, 8am-10pm Sat, 8am-6pm Sun; SEPTA 2nd St Station, Bus 48, 57, 76

Sweet tooths will adore this tiny storefront

## Top Five – When You Pay

These are the five best affordable dining options in Philly. Most are BYOBs, so don't forget to stop by the state store before the clock strikes 9pm.

- **Django** (p116) Tables must be booked a month in advance.
- **Dmitri's** (p115) This is an unfairly charming Mediterranean place.
- **Tartine** (p115) This casual bistro serves simple French dishes and mind-blowing mousse.
- **Tequila's** (p110) Expect serious Mexican food, sweet drinks and a wandering magician.
- **Tre Scalini** (p118) Get ready for squid ink pasta and South Philly atmosphere.

and café, where the bakers create scrumptious pastries, cakes, chocolates and other delights. Stop by for afternoon tea, or pick up some gingerbread cookies to go.

## Mid-Range

### ARIANA  Map pp226-7 *Afghan*
☎ 215-922-1535; 134 Chestnut St; lunch mains $6-7, dinner mains $9-14, BYOB; ⏰ 11am-10pm Mon-Thu, 11am-11pm Fri & Sat, 3-10pm Sun; SEPTA 2nd St Station, Bus 17, 21, 33, 42, 76

If you'd like to sit on a cushion in front of a window overlooking Chestnut St, head into Ariana for some choice vegetarian options. While the menu is heavy on pumpkin, spinach, cauliflower and eggplant, there's also lamb topped with almonds, pistachio and rosewater-soaked orange strips.

### CHLOE  Map pp226-7 *Modern American*
☎ 215-629-2337; 232 Arch St; mains $16-22, cash only, BYOB; ⏰ 5-9:45pm Tue-Sat; SEPTA 2nd St Station, Bus 48, 57, 76

Run by a husband-and-wife team, this small and loud place leans heavily toward the cute – they've mounted their wedding bouquet to the wall. Foodwise the compact menu changes seasonally. Call ahead to make sure banana bread pudding is being served; it was modeled after the one God created when the world started. It's so good it shouldn't appear on earth, but there it is. Reservations are not accepted, so expect a wait on weekends.

### CITY TAVERN
Map pp226-7 *Colonial American*
☎ 215-413-1443; www.citytavern.com; 138 S 2nd St; lunch mains $14-18, dinner mains $19-28; ⏰ lunch 11:30am-3pm, dinner 4-11pm Mon-Sat & 3-10pm Sun; SEPTA 2nd St Station, Bus 17, 21, 33, 42, 76

This is a faithful reconstruction of the tavern in which all those revolutionary types did their plotting. Modern-day folks come here to eat dishes that 'interpret and deliver the culinary experience of the 18th century.' So grab a Windsor chair, listen to someone jammin' on the harpsichord and tear into some braised rabbit. All servers appear in period costume. Bonus: our forefathers knew how to make strong punch, and the City Tavern seems to have inherited this tradition. Beer made using Washington's and Jefferson's personal recipes is sold by the bottle.

### THE CONTINENTAL
Map pp226-7 *Modern American/Asian Fusion*
☎ 215-923-6069; 138 Market St; dinner $16-25, small plates $5.50-12; ⏰ lunch 11:30am-3:30pm Mon-Fri, dinner 5-11pm Sun-Wed & 5pm-midnight Thu-Sat, brunch 10:30am-3pm Sat & Sun; SEPTA 2nd St Station, Bus 17, 21, 33, 42, 76

The first of Stephen Starr's creations, the Continental looks like an overly designed, stylized American diner. Despite the look, its black-clad servers dish out short-order 'world tapas,' meaning little plates of lobster mashed potatoes, steamed dumplings, grilled tofu in a too-sweet peanut sauce and swordfish tacos. Check out the impressive list of specialty martinis, and dress your hippest – everyone else does.

### DINARDO'S FAMOUS SEAFOOD
Map pp226-7 *Seafood*
☎ 215-925-5115; 312 Race St; lunch mains $8-12, dinner mains $16-25; ⏰ lunch 11am-3pm, dinner 3-9pm Sun-Thu & 3-10pm Fri & Sat; SEPTA 2nd St Station, Bus 48, 57, 76

If you like eating in a celebrated, brightly lit crab joint minimally decorated with fishing tackle, head over here for fried crab cakes made from the same recipe since 1938. Tourists with kids favor this spot.

### KABUL  Map pp226-7 *Afghan*
☎ 215-922-3676; 106 Chestnut St; mains $10-12, BYOB; ⏰ 4-10pm Mon-Thu, 4-11pm Fri & Sat, 2:30-10pm Sun; SEPTA 2nd St Station, Bus 17, 21, 33, 42, 76

Prompt service and excellent value accompany a range of mushy and delicious lamb, chicken and vegetable dishes. Try the very impressive turnovers stuffed with spiced pumpkin and

### BYOB Phenomenon
Because of Pennsylvania's arcane liquor laws, it's exceptionally hard for restaurants in Philadelphia to get a license to serve booze. A happy consequence of this is that many spots, including some of the nicest in town, allow patrons to 'bring your own bottle' (BYOB) of drink. This is a great boon to thrifty diners, who can eat at a charming bistro and bring some inexpensive wine. The only drawback is that meals might require an added trip to the liquor store, and stores close at 9pm and usually don't open on Sunday. A few places charge a $1 to $2 corkage fee. At most places, however, it's complimentary.

onions served with yogurt. For dessert, order the firnée – it tastes like a sweet custard flavored with pistachio.

## LA LOCANDA DEL GHIOTTONE

Map pp226-7 *Italian*

☎ 215-829-1465; 139 N 3rd St; mains $15-18, cash only, BYOB; ☽ 5-10pm Sun-Thu, 5-11pm Fri & Sat; SEPTA 2nd St Station, Bus 48, 57, 76

Listen politely to the specials – which might include a veal chop stuffed with three cheeses and bacon covered in an apple demi-glace – and then immediately order the gnocchi of the day. Sure, the specials are terrific, but the gnocchi are occasionally perfect. Meals begin with bread and a very oily pesto, and everything is handled by an exceedingly good waitstaff.

## Top End

### BUDDAKAN Map pp226-7 *Asian Fusion*

☎ 215-574-9440; 325 Chestnut St; lunch mains $14-18, dinner mains $20-28; ☽ lunch 11am-3:30pm Mon-Fri, dinner 5-11pm Sun-Thu & 5pm-midnight Fri & Sat; SEPTA 2nd St Station, Bus 17, 21, 33, 42, 76

Glamorously dressed diners sit beside a two-story bronze Buddha, which dominates one of Stephen Starr's best and subtly designed restaurants (except for that Buddha). Entrées such as miso-poached shrimp ($27) or appetizers like tea-smoked spare ribs ($16) hit the spot, and there seems to be wasabi in just about everything. Courses tend to come too fast, making an otherwise nice meal shorter than it should be. The bartenders make some fabulous specialty cocktails.

### LA FAMIGLIA Map pp226-7 *Italian*

☎ 215-922-2803; 8 S Front St; pastas $18-25, mains $26-45; ☽ lunch noon-2:30pm Tue-Fri, dinner 5:30-10pm Tue-Sun; SEPTA 2nd St Station, Bus 17, 21, 33, 42, 76

Decorated with gilded mirrors and ornately framed portraits of old people, the small, formal dining room serves penne with proscuitto, onions and Parmesan or tagliarini sautéed with black and red caviar to a room full of gentlemen in jackets and ladies in black. The wine list is superb.

# CENTER CITY

Back in 1992 about 65 restaurants existed in Center City. In 2004 that number topped 250. We promise, if you look hard enough,

## Top Five – When Others Pay

In anticipation of your visit to Philadelphia, try to write a winning grant proposal that allows you to study 'food culture.' Alternatively, just bring extra cash (or a wealthy friend), as these places are worth the big bucks.

- **Le Bec-Fin** (p111) Some say it's the country's best.
- **Morimoto** (p113) The Iron Chef himself oversees the kitchen.
- **¡Pasión!** (p110) The ceviche is otherworldly.
- **Susanna Foo** (p111) Eat at the place where fusion cuisine was invented.
- **Vetri** (p113) The chef is really handsome, and the ravioli machine must have come with papal blessings.

you'll find anything you want. The majority of Philadelphia's most famous restaurants lie along Walnut St between Broad St and Rittenhouse Square.

# AVENUE OF THE ARTS

Head toward City Hall, and the food gets fancy. Head toward South Philly, and it doesn't.

## BELLEVUE FOOD COURT

Map pp222-3 *Food Court*

☎ 215-875-8350; Broad St at Walnut St; $2-6; ☽ 7am-6pm Mon-Fri, 7am-5pm Sat; SEPTA Walnut-Locust Station, Bus 9, 12, 21, 27, 32, 42

In the basement level of the otherwise beautiful Bellevue building, find this food court, which bills itself as 'gourmet fast food.' There's a Le Bus Bakery, a deli, a pizza place, a sushi joint, Rocco's Famous Italian Hoagies, a soup vendor, a 12th Street Cantina and a few others.

## BROAD STREET DINER Map pp228-9 *Diner*

☎ 215-334-1611; 1135 Broad St; breakfasts & sandwiches $3-6; ☽ 24hr; SEPTA Ellsworth-Federal Station, Bus 27, 32

So what if the desserts are terrible and the place is a tad rough-and-tumble? It's open 24 hours, it looks cool and it's 35 years old.

## FOUNDERS DINING ROOM

Map pp222-3 *French*

☎ 215-790-2814; Broad St at Walnut St; lunch mains $13-15, dinner mains $28-36, 5-course prix-fixe dinner

$85; brunch mains $12-20; ☺ breakfast 6:30-10:30am Mon-Sat, lunch 11am-2pm Mon-Sat, dinner 5:30-10pm Wed-Sat, brunch 10:30am-2pm Sun; SEPTA Walnut-Locust Station, Bus 9, 12, 21, 27, 32, 42

For Philly's best in high-altitude, jacket-required, antiquated dining, take the Bellevue's elevator all the way to the 19th floor for excellent food and a panoramic view. The dining room lies under an ornate plaster, pastel-colored rotunda with a stained-glass oculus; at dinner there's a live trio or piano to which people actually dance.

# CHINATOWN & AROUND

Chinatown contains dozens of restaurants, and most of them don't close until midnight or later. It's a hot destination for late-night cheap eats, particularly at Penang.

## Budget

**PENANG** Map pp222-3                    *Malaysian*
☎ 215-413-2531; 117 N 10th St; mains $5-16; ☺ 11:30am-1am; SEPTA Chinatown Station, Market East Station, Bus 23, 48, 61

Every kind of Philadelphian packs Penang late at night, attracted by giant, cheap dishes (most items cost less than $8) of mango shrimp, plates of ginger duck or steaming bowls of noodle soup served with an abundance of greens.

### RAY'S CAFE AND TEAHOUSE

Map pp222-3                          *Coffee/Chinese*
☎ 215-922-5122; 141 N 9th St; coffees $4-8, mains $6-14; ☺ 9am-9:30pm Mon-Thu, 9am-10:30pm Fri, 11am-10:30pm Sat, 11:30am-9pm Sun; SEPTA Chinatown Station, Market East Station, Bus 23, 48, 61

This eclectic joint serves exotic coffee brewed with elaborate contraptions, some of which are displayed on the counter. Try the iced coffee ($5.50), which takes 12 hours to make using a cold drip and no heat. Foodwise we recommend some very chewy Chinese black mushrooms in a ginger sauce topped with walnuts ($9) for an interesting contrast in texture and taste. If possible, order some dumplings – so good that they are often ordered in place of entrées.

## Mid-Range

### CHARLES PLAZA

Map pp222-3                       *Vegetarian Chinese*
☎ 215-829-4383; 234 N 10th St; lunch specials $6, dinner mains $8-13; ☺ 11:30am-10pm Mon-Thu, 11:30am-midnight Fri, 3pm-midnight Sat, 3-10:30pm

Sun; SEPTA Chinatown Station, Market East Station, Bus 23, 48, 61

At the edge of Chinatown, one of Philly's friendliest hosts (who used to practice Eastern medicine before his move to the USA) has earned himself a pack of regular followers – from grandparents to vegans to Chinese Americans. His flavorful, healthful offerings include sizzling fish and some of the planet's most convincing mock-meats.

**JOSEPH POON** Map pp222-3          *Asian Fusion*
☎ 215-928-9333; 1002 Arch St; rice & noodle dishes $7-14, entrées $12-20; ☺ 11:30am-10pm Tue-Thu, 11:30am-11pm Fri, 3-11pm Sat & Sun; SEPTA Chinatown Station, Market East Station, Bus 23, 48, 61

Hyped-up Joseph Poon is a good spot, but some wonder if the quality of food merits all that buzz. Dominated by seafood and duck, the menu offers traditional stuff like mushroom dumplings as well as more unusual fare such as wok-seared venison with pineapple. Hyperactive Mr Poon, whose motto is 'my kitchen is open and my mind is too,' donates a significant amount of time to various charitable causes in the Chinese American community. He made a celebrity appearance at the recent Liberty Bell move, where he rapidly carved bells out of peppers.

**JOY TSIN LAU** Map pp222-3              *Chinese*
☎ 215-592-4138; 1026 Race St; dim sum items $2-3; dinner mains $7-15; ☺ 11am-midnight Mon-Thu, 11am-1am Fri & Sat, 10:30am-midnight Sun; SEPTA Chinatown Station, Market East Station, Bus 23, 48, 61

Come to Chinatown's most popular dim sum house on a weekend to find scores of Chinese Americans scarfing down tiny steamed dumplings and buns selected from passing carts. While dim sum is served daily until 3pm, Saturday and Sunday mornings are the most crowded times to drop by.

**LEE HOW FOOK** Map pp222-3             *Chinese*
☎ 215-925-7266; 219 N 11th St; dinner mains $10-16, BYOB; ☺ 11:30am-10pm; SEPTA Chinatown Station, Market East Station, Bus 23, 48, 61

Serving sea bass and lemon chicken, Lee How Fook is a traditional, bare-bones Chinatown favorite. Though the place looks a bit seedy, don't fret: it's perfectly safe and delicious.

**VIETNAM** Map pp222-3                 *Vietnamese*
☎ 215-592-1163; 221 N 11th St; mains $9-11; ☺ 11am-9:30pm Sun-Thu, 11am-10:30pm Fri & Sat;

Eating – Center City

**SEPTA Chinatown Station, Market East Station, Bus 23, 48, 61**
The elegance of Vietnam's room almost makes diners forget they are paying next to nothing for their dinner. The spring rolls are consistently peppery and crispy, and the menu is laden with vermicelli, lemongrass and catfish.

# RITTENHOUSE SQUARE

This district contains 'Restaurant Row,' a stretch of Walnut St that houses the city's most highly touted restaurants, including **Le Bec-Fin** (p111), **Susanna Foo** (p111) and **Striped Bass** (p111). Along the square's edges are several alfresco options. Small BYOBs are sprinkled about.

## Budget

**LA COLOMBE** Map pp222-3                    *Café*
☎ 215-563-0860; 130 S 19th St; coffee $1-2; 
✎ 7:30am-6:30pm Mon-Fri, 8:30am-6:30pm Sat & Sun ; SEPTA 19th St Station, Bus 2, 9, 12, 42, 76
The trendy Rittenhouse masses stay caffeinated at this super-hip spot, serving the same coffee as **Le Bec-Fin** (p111).

**LITTLE PETE'S** Map pp222-3 *Classic American*
☎ 215-545-5508; 219 S 17th Sts; $3 minimum; 
✎ 24hr; SEPTA 19th St Station, Bus 2, 9, 12, 21, 42, 76
Packed solid at all hours on weekend nights, Little Pete's is a Philly diner institution serving all kinds of questionable food at prices seemingly less than cost. Eat the onion rings, but never ever get the cherry pie. And don't even think about making our mistake and ordering it with beer.

**LOMBARDI'S** Map pp222-3                    *Pizza*
☎ 215-564-5000; 132 S 18th St; large pizzas $12.50-14.50, cash only; ✎ 11:30am-10pm Sun-Tue, 11:30am-11pm Wed-Sat; SEPTA 19th St Station, Bus 2, 9, 12, 21, 42, 76
Allegedly, America's first pizzeria has two outlets. One is in New York City, and the other, predated by its NYC brother, is right here. The thin-crusted Neapolitan-style pizza keeps Philadelphians happy, though some lament the fact that individual slices aren't available. Diners can eat in or take out.

**MIDTOWN III** Map pp222-3                    *Diner*
☎ 215-567-5144; 28 S 18th St; $3-7; ✎ 24hr; SEPTA 19th St Station, Bus 2, 9, 12, 21, 42, 76
Home to blue-collar types and bleary-eyed Rittenhouse Square revelers, the Midtown III serves eggs, grilled sandwiches and milkshakes in digs that scream 1972. Come for the white Formica, orange stools and dated light fixtures, but avoid the spaghetti.

**SCOOP DEVILLE** Map pp222-3      *Ice Cream*
☎ 215-988-9992; 107 S 18th St; medium cone $3.20; 
✎ 10:30am-9pm Mon-Sat, noon-9pm Sun; SEPTA 19th St Station, Bus 2, 9, 12, 21, 42, 76
Loved by every kid from Philadelphia and every stoner from Penn, this pink ice cream parlor allows you to pick your base ice cream and then choose additives. A contraption blends the mixture together, and a cone is born.

## Mid-Range

**ALMA DE CUBA** Map pp222-3                 *Cuban*
☎ 215-988-1799; www.almadecubarestaurant.com; 1623 Walnut St; mains $19-29; ✎ 5-11pm Mon-Thu, 5pm-midnight Fri & Sat, 5-10pm Sun, bar 5pm-2am daily; SEPTA Walnut-Locust Station, Bus 2, 9, 12, 27, 32, 42
In addition to the menu of modernized Latin entrées, this loungey Stephen Starr house also offers seven kinds of ceviche, such as Maine lobster and crab with orange-habanero sauce, tomatoes and mango ($17). On many nights the bar is a relaxed spot to hang, away from more crowded Rittenhouse destinations. On Wednesday, go to hear Cuban jazz bands.

Eating – Center City

---

### Open All Night

Many of Philadelphia's diners and cheese steak stops stay open all night to provide delight and indigestion.

- **Broad Street Diner** (p107) This classic spot is old and gritty with good black coffee.
- **Geno's Steaks** (p106) In one corner…
- **Pat's King of Steaks** (p116)…in the other corner
- **Little Pete's** (p109) It can't be over-stressed: don't get the pie. But that French toast looks kinda good…
- **Melrose Diner** (p116) In the heart of South Philly and in the heart of South Philadelphians
- **Silk City Diner** (Map p230; ☎ 215-592-8838; 435 Spring Garden St; burgers $5; ✎ 7am-midnight Mon-Thu, 24hr Fri-Sun) Open 24 hours on weekends, this place has tableside juke boxes, malts, neon and hipsters.

## ASTRAL PLANE

Map pp222-3 *Modern American*
☎ 215-546-6230; 1708 Lombard St; mains $13-18;
⊙ 5-11pm Mon-Thu, 5pm-midnight Fri & Sat, 11am-
5pm Sun; SEPTA Lombard-South Station, Bus 2, 17, 40
In a quiet, candlelit room full of niches, dark red
walls, autographed photos of old Broadway
stars and a shrine to *The Wizard of Oz*, it is
imperative that diners taste the pistachio-
crusted salmon with pistachio butter ($17). It
and the silver dessert tray are amazing.

## AUDREY CLAIRE

Map pp222-3 *Modern American/Mediterranean*
☎ 215-731-1222; 20th & Spruce Sts; small dishes
$6-11, bigger dishes $14-20, BYOB; ⊙ 5:45-10pm
Tue-Thu, 5:45-11pm Fri & Sat; Bus 7, 12
Small and precious, Audrey Claire looks like the
restaurant embodiment of a cover from *Real
Simple* magazine. It's customary for groups to
order and share from the amazing assortment
of appetizers – particularly the stellar flat
breads – but you won't lose points in getting
a proper entrée. Try something with the
pomegranate and goat cheese spread.

## BLEU Map pp222-3 *Continental*

☎ 215-545-0342; 227 S 18th St; mains $13-24;
⊙ 11am-11pm Sun-Thu, 11am-1am Fri & Sat; SEPTA
Walnut-Locust Station, Bus 2, 12
Blessed with spectacular frontage overlooking
Rittenhouse Square, this sort-of brasserie
is popular with the see-and-be-seen crew.
Interior decorative touches may make diners
feel like they're eating their shrimp-based
avocado soup inside of a Matisse knockoff. If
available, Bartlett pears wrapped in cured ham
over frisee are cool and refreshing.

## FRIDAY SATURDAY SUNDAY

Map pp222-3 *Classic American*
☎ 215-546-4232; 261 S 21st St; lunch mains $6-9,
dinner mains $15-22; ⊙ lunch 11:30am-2:30pm Tue-Fri,
dinner 5:30-10:30pm Mon-Sat & 5-10pm Sun; Bus 7, 12
The *Miami Vice* feel of this restaurant, now 30
years old, comes from its decorative purple
neon and a 2nd-floor tropical fish tank.
Despite the dated decor, it still manages to
occasionally win 'most romantic dining' in
the weekly newspapers' readers' polls. There's
a middle-aged crowd, filet mignon and an
amazing wine list of more than 160 bottles,
each one (no matter how rare) sold at just $10
above cost.

## MAGAZINE Map pp222-3 *Modern American*

☎ 215-567-5000; 2029 Walnut St; mains $10-18;
⊙ 6-10pm Tue & Wed, 6pm-midnight Thu-Sat; SEPTA
19th St Station, Bus 9, 12, 17, 21, 33, 38, 42
This small place feels half like a grandmother's
formal dining room and half like a bistro,
incongruously appointed with some large
and decent pop art canvases. For unknown
reasons the chef prepares particularly good
duck, so anything with that as an ingredient
is highly recommended. During humid
summers, try the chilled potato leek soup
with duck confit; it has a nice creamy base
with occasional, delicious ducky crunches.
Cocktails are also well made.

## ¡PASIÓN! Map pp222-3 *Latin*

☎ 215-546-6230; 211 S 15th St; mains $18-35;
⊙ 5-10pm Mon-Thu, 5-11pm Fri & Sat, 5-9pm Sun;
SEPTA Walnut-Locust Station, Bus 9, 12, 21, 27, 32, 42
Feel like you've embarked upon a world-
class Caribbean retreat at this 'nuevo Latino'
favorite. Chef Guillermo Pernot – known for
super-fresh, light ceviches – also prepares
mean, flavorful croquetas and sea bass. The
room is friendly, warm and bright.

## ROUGE Map pp222-3 *Continental*

☎ 215-732-6622; 205 S 18th St; dinner $14-25;
⊙ 11:30am-2am; SEPTA Walnut-Locust Station,
Bus 2, 12
Cigar-smoking dames and the fellas who
love them dig the sidewalk seating at
this cramped Rittenhouse Square favorite,
one of the top picks for black-wearing
scenesters who want to be seen. Its
Continental cuisine might seem secondary
to the glancing. Those who snap out of the
moment realize the food they are eating
actually tastes good.

## TEQUILA'S

Map pp222-3 *Modern American/Continental*
☎ 215-546-0181; 1511 Locust St; mains $15-20;
⊙ lunch 11:30am-2pm Mon-Fri, dinner 5-10pm Mon-
Thu & 5-11pm Fri & Sat; SEPTA Walnut-Locust Station,
Bus 9, 12, 21, 27, 32, 42
David, the very friendly owner, hugs all his
regulars while his buddy Oscar sometimes
wanders around performing magic tricks.
This Mexican place is no taqueria: it's a large,
formal dining room with beautiful murals,
dark beams and adobe-esque walls. The
mole is tops.

## WARSAW CAFE

Map pp222-3                    *Eastern European*
☎ 215-546-0204; 306 S 16th St; lunch mains $7-10, dinner mains $14-16; ⏲ lunch 11:30am-2:30pm Mon-Fri & 11:30am-3pm Sat, dinner 5-10pm Mon-Thu & 5-10:30pm Fri & Sat; SEPTA Walnut-Locust Station, Bus 9, 12, 21, 27, 32, 42

Once a guy who used to eat a macrobiotic diet, Marrion, the owner of this place, now turns out the best pierogies, Norwegian strudel, borscht and weinerschnitzel in town. Not that he has much competition, as this cozy spot is the only place of its kind in Center City. Warsaw Cafe prepares a fantastic sauerbraten, using filet mignon instead of usual cheaper cuts, marinated for three days. No knife is required.

# Top End

## BRASSERIE PERRIER Map pp222-3    *French*
☎ 215-568-3000; www.brasserieperrier.com; 1619 Walnut St; mains $24-39; ⏲ lunch 11:30am-2:30pm Mon-Sat, dinner 5:30-10pm Mon-Thu, 5-11pm Fri & Sat, 5-9pm Sun; SEPTA Walnut-Locust Station, Bus 9, 12, 21, 27, 32, 42

Less stodgy then Le Bec-Fin (see below), Georges Perrier's second operation is close enough to the mother ship that the ringleader can pop back and forth as needed. Here French cuisine melds with Italian and Asian influences, and excitingly, there is a diverse fondue menu. Entry doesn't require a jacket but one helps.

## LE BAR LYONNAIS Map pp222-3    *French*
☎ 215-567-1000; 1523 Walnut St; mains $15-30; ⏲ 11:30am-midnight Mon-Fri, 6pm-1am Sat; SEPTA Walnut-Locust Station, Bus 9, 12, 21, 27, 32, 42

For those with thinner wallets or who didn't book a table months in advance, Mr Perrier operates a 'bistro' within Le Bec-Fin. Dining on this side of the fence doesn't require multiple courses but men still must wear a jacket. The caliber of food served here ranks with that in the formal dining area. Steak tartare, anyone?

## LE BEC-FIN Map pp222-3    *French*
☎ 215-567-1000; www.lebecfin.com; 1523 Walnut St; 3-course prix-fixe lunch, $45, 6-course prix-fixe dinner $135; ⏲ seatings 11:30am, 1:30, 6 & 9pm Mon-Fri, 6 & 9:30pm Sat; SEPTA Walnut-Locust Station, Bus 9, 12, 21, 27, 32, 42

Considered by many to be the finest restaurant in the United States, this longstanding establishment blows minds and budgets with its five-star meals. To experience the splendor, make a reservation before you book your hotel, and don't forget to pack a jacket and tie. Says Georges Perrier, the owner, 'I am a perfectionist. I am never satisfied,' though rest assured that you will be. Monday through Thursday a three-course dinner menu is offered for a mere $65.

## STRIPED BASS Map pp222-3    *Seafood*
☎ 215-732-4444; 1500 Walnut St; mains $32-46; ⏲ 11:30am-11pm Mon-Sat, 11am-10pm Sun; SEPTA Walnut-Locust Station, Bus 9, 12, 21, 27, 32, 42

Huge ceilings dwarf the potted trees that break up the space of this beautifully formal and modern dining room, which attracts a distinctly corporate clientele. You may recognize this elegant space as the setting of the anniversary dinner in M Night Shyamalan's Philadelphia-based 1999 film *The Sixth Sense*. Traditional plates of caviar cost $85; a caviar sampler totals $185. There's an oyster bar and entrées such as crisp wild striped bass with artichoke broth. Note: in December 2003, Stephen Starr bought the Striped Bass from longtime owner Neil Stein. Starr says he plans to keep the name and the decor, with minor renovations.

## SUSANNA FOO Map pp222-3    *Asian Fusion*
☎ 215-545-2666; mains $25-40; 1512 Walnut St; ⏲ 11am-11pm Sun-Thu, 11am-1am Fri & Sat; SEPTA Walnut-Locust Station, Bus 9, 12, 21, 27, 32, 42

Elegant and warm with pink and peach tones, Susanna Foo's famous house is one of the originators of Asian-fusion cuisine. For many, what comes out of the back room is the finest Chinese food they'll have in their lives.

# WASHINGTON SQUARE WEST

Whether you're dining in the Gayborhood or lounging at one of the many cafés, Washington Square West aims to please.

# Budget

## 10TH STREET POUR HOUSE

Map pp222-3                    *Breakfast*
☎ 215-922-5626; 262 S 10th St; breakfast mains $2-6, lunch mains $5-6, cash only; ⏲ 7:30am-3pm Mon-Fri, 8:30am-3pm Sat & Sun; SEPTA 11th St Station, Bus 9, 12, 21, 23, 38, 42, 47

Stop by this cute, clean and orange-yellow spot for specialty pancakes and omelets.

If eggs and syrup turn you off, try one of the great vegetarian sandwiches on French bread, featuring sautéed spinach, eggplant and roasted peppers.

### BLUE IN GREEN Map pp222-3 *Breakfast*
☎ 215-923-6883; 719 Sansom St; pancakes $6-9; ☽ 8am-3pm Mon-Fri, 9am-3pm Sat & Sun; SEPTA 8th St Station, Bus 9, 21, 38, 42, 47, 61

Pancake batter (choose from buttermilk, whole wheat, corn or potato) achieves divine form at this narrow joint nestled into Jeweler's Row. The basic pancakes aren't too frilly; just about the fanciest additive is berries. There are eggs and sandwiches, too.

### CAPAGRIO Map pp222-3 *Gelato*
☎ 215-351-0900; 119 S 13th St; small serving $4.50; ☽ 7:30am-8pm Mon-Thu, 7:30am-10pm Fri-Sun; SEPTA 13th St Station, Bus 9, 21, 23, 38, 42

A vividly blue café serving tasty paninis ($3.25 to $6), this place dishes out some mean gelato. Flavors are various and curious.

### EL FUEGO Map pp222-3 *Mexican*
☎ 215-592-1901; 723 Walnut St; burritos $5; ☽ 11am-10pm Mon-Fri; SEPTA 8th St Station, Bus 9, 21, 38, 42, 47, 61

A taqueria that tries very hard to make authentic California burritos, El Fuego turns out good stuff that nearly hits the target. The cooks prepare good guacamole and chips but some of the line crew needs additional tortilla-folding training.

### LAST DROP Map pp222-3 *Café*
☎ 215-893-9262; 1300 Pine St; bagel sandwiches $4; ☽ 7am-midnight Mon-Fri, 8am-midnight Sat & Sun; SEPTA Lombard-South Station, Bus 23, 40

Perhaps the most comfortable café in Philadelphia, Last Drop attracts hipsters in droves. It sits on a corner and has plenty of windows overlooking the street as well as some outdoor seating. Inside, the place is very pretty, with tall ceilings and nice tables spaced a reasonable distance from one another. Sometimes the dudes pouring the coffee take themselves too seriously.

### MEAN BEAN CAFÉ Map pp222-3 *Café*
☎ 215-925-2010; 1112 Locust St; coffee & eats $1.50-4.25; ☽ 7am-11pm Mon-Thu, 7am-midnight Fri, 8am-midnight Sat, 8am-11pm Sun; SEPTA Walnut-Locust Station, Bus 9, 12, 21, 23, 42

Overlooking an adjoining garden, the Mean Bean boasts some exceptional outdoor seating. In the summer the staff puts out a water dish for dogs and cats. In the winter, café-goers fill up the much smaller interior digs for bagel-and-egg sandwiches, tuna salad, and spinach and broccoli quiche.

### MILLENNIUM Map pp222-3 *Café*
☎ 215-731-9798; 212 S 12th St; ☽ 7am-10pm Mon-Fri, 8am-11pm Sat & Sun; SEPTA Walnut-Locust Station, Bus 9, 12, 21, 23, 42

This gay café's big windows make it a favored spot to grab a coffee, sit in a somewhat uncomfortable metal chair and gaze at the boys and girls passing by on the sidewalk, many of whom are about to get sweaty at the **12th Street Gym** (p147) next door. Millennium keeps informal hours; those listed above are approximations.

### MORE THAN JUST ICE CREAM
Map pp222-3 *Dessert*
☎ 215-574-0586; 1119 Locust St; ice creams & desserts $2.75-7.50, food $5-8; ☽ 11am-11:30pm; SEPTA Walnut-Locust Station, Bus 9, 12, 21, 23, 42

Perhaps serving Philly's largest slice of deep-dish apple pie, this joint whips up desserts that are really difficult to eat solo. Though the ice cream operations overshadow the dining room, there are some good and inexpensive omelets, salads (spinach, Caesar, fresh beet with goat cheese, field greens with salmon etc) and other healthy fare.

# Mid-Range

### EFFIE'S Map pp222-3 *Greek*
☎ 215-592-8333; 1127 Pine St; mains $12-14, BYOB; ☽ 5-10pm Sun-Thu, 5-11pm Fri & Sat; SEPTA Lombard-South Station, Bus 23, 40

It's blessed with a darn charming garden for outdoor eating, and the proprietor of tiny Effie's could be the sultriest Greek woman in the city, aside from Catherine Poneros. The kitchen churns out hearty salads, souvlaki, fish and stuffed chicken with pistachio.

### THE INN PHILADELPHIA
Map pp222-3 *Modern American*
☎ 215-732-2339; 251 S Camac St; brunch mains $8-15, dinner mains $15-25, bar food $9-13; ☽ brunch 11am-3pm Sun, dinner 5:30pm-closing Tue-Sat & 5pm-closing Sun; SEPTA Lombard-South Station, Bus 23, 40

Enjoying one of the prettiest possible locations in Philly, this hidden restaurant lies at the intersection of two narrow, tree-lined alleys in the middle of the Gayborhood. Add an über-cute garden space and six small-scale dining rooms to this geography and you've got an exceptional destination for romantics. Sunday brunch offers six variations of eggs with hollandaise sauce. There's a BYOB option Tuesday through Thursday, or just order from the bar.

### JONES Map pp222-3 *Classic American*
☎ 215-223-5663; 700 Chestnut St; soups & sandwiches $5-8, mains $13-22; ☽ 11:30am-midnight Mon-Thu, 11:30am-1am Fri, 10:30am-1am Sat, 10:30am-11pm Sun; SEPTA 8th St Station, Bus 9, 21, 38, 42, 47, 61
In this Stephen Starr rendition, the design team created a place that tows the line between a family den and a Howard Johnson's. The food attempts clever conventionalism, with grilled cheese sandwiches (thus a somewhat fancy restaurant where it's okay to take kids, as many do), tomato soup, fried chicken and a 'Thanksgiving Dinner,' which so authentically tastes like leftovers that it came lukewarm (not a good thing). As is typical of Starr, the specialty drinks rule.

### MIXTO Map pp222-3 *Colombian/Cuban*
☎ 215-592-0363; 1141 Pine St; breakfast mains $3-7, lunch mains $6-12, dinner mains $14-22; ☽ 10am-11pm; SEPTA Lombard-South Station, Bus 23, 40
Fantastic smoothies (banana, tamarind, blackberry, passion fruit) are the thing to get at Mixto, which also serves dishes laden with cassava, plantains and tamales (which can be bland at times). The room is loud and modern.

## Top End
### MORIMOTO Map pp222-3 *Japanese*
☎ 215-413-9070; www.morimotorestaurant.com; 723 Chestnut St; dinner mains $20-35; ☽ lunch 11:30am-2pm Mon-Fri, dinner 5-11pm Mon-Thu, 5pm-midnight Fri & Sat, 4-10pm Sun; SEPTA 8th St Station, Bus 9, 21, 38, 42, 47, 61
Remember the Iron Chef from television? Well, along with coproprietor Stephen Starr, he runs this restaurant. For truly unsurpassed food, try the chef's multicourse tasting menu (Omakase), which costs $80, $100, $120 or more depending on the volume of food. Reservations are a must.

### VETRI Map pp222-3 *Italian*
☎ 215-732-3478; www.vetriristorante.com; 1312 Spruce St; pastas $18-24, mains $28-38; ☽ 6-11pm Mon-Sat; SEPTA Walnut-Locust Station, Bus 12, 23

To make gnocchi, the chefs at Vetri brought a machine from the Tuscan countryside and restored it from rusty trash to shiny maker of delicious little balls. Both the food and the dining room are pretty, and the wine cellar is stupendous. A five-course tasting menu costs $75 per person; seven courses cost $100 per person.

# PARKWAY & MUSEUM AREA
Looking at art makes people hungry and tired. Though there aren't many options in the immediate vicinity, these three places can help you avoid the cafeteria at the various museums.

### BRIDGID'S Map pp222-3 *Classic American*
☎ 215-232-3232; 726 N 24th St; mains $8-12; ☽ lunch 11am-3pm Mon-Fri, dinner 4:30-11pm Mon-Sat & 4:30-9pm Sun; Bus 7, 48
A cozy bar serving Trappist ales and other fancy beers greets guests up front while a small, romantic dining room with a low-beamed ceiling in the back dishes out fare ranging from gnocchi (do not order) to beer-battered brotola – a light white fish deep-fried into crispy goodness.

### FOUNTAIN Map pp222-3 *Modern American*
☎ 215-963-1500; 1 Logan Square; dinner mains $20-35; ☽ 6:30-10:30pm Mon-Fri, 7am-10pm Sat & Sun; SEPTA 19th St Station, Bus 32, 33, 48, 76
Martin Hamann's paradise at the Four Seasons gives people reason enough to stay at the hotel. Service is spotless, chandeliers are shiny and men are required to wear jackets.

### ROSE TATTOO CAFE
Map pp222-3 *Modern American*
☎ 215-569-8939; 19th St at Callowhill St; lunch mains $7-12, dinner mains $19-25; ☽ lunch 11am-3pm Mon-Fri, dinner 5-10pm Sun-Thu & 5-11pm Fri & Sat; Bus 33
Not a café at all, the Rose Tattoo has three separate rooms, all exceptionally romantic. One of them, for nonsmokers, is a second-level balcony located within a space that feels similar to a greenhouse from the 1920s (an effect created through a combination of iron work, a profusion of flowers, music and antique ceiling fans). The menu offers jambalaya, quiches, hearty salads and a curious dish of shrimp battered with coconut and beer and served with a sweet orange-horseradish sauce. The mushroom soup is

easily the best in town, and the dessert tray should definitely be viewed.

# SOUTH STREET

South Street contains a variety of eating options that reflect the diversity of people who visit. Some of Philadelphia's best BYOBs lie on side streets, catering to tamer crowds from Society Hill and Queen's Village. The thoroughfare itself is packed with cheap eats and cafés where you can find a ton of dyed hair, ripped pants and tattoos.

## Budget

**THE BEAN** Map pp228-9        *Café*
☎ 215-629-2250; 615 South St; coffee $1.50; ☾ 7am-midnight; Bus 40, 47
The personable staff and ample table space of this hipsterish café make it a good retreat from South Street's excessive pedestrian and vehicular traffic. The tables are a tad close together, which is great for eavesdroppers and bad for people who can't help whispering about their embarrassing medical problems.

**CAFE IZMIR** Map pp228-9        *Café*
☎ 267-679-0761; 620 S 9th St; treats $2-5; ☾ 7am-10pm; Bus 40, 47
So comfortable that leaving becomes emotionally difficult, this new, three-room café uses its fireplace to burn actual wood. Furniture is colorful, mismatched and cool. The guys who run the place put sincere energy into making it an unofficial neighborhood cultural center and host an irregular schedule of film screenings, music, belly dancing and more. The coffee is strong, and soups, salads and baked goods are served.

### GIANNA'S GRILLE

Map pp228-9        *American/Vegan*
☎ 215-829-4448; 507 S 6th St; sandwiches $5-7, pizza slices $2; ☾ noon-8pm Tue-Thu, noon-9pm Fri & Sat; Bus 12, 40, 47
The minimal effort expended in decorating this place has the perhaps intentional effect of forcing customers' eyes toward a display case full of attractive and affordable vegan desserts. Aside from desserts, the place offers both actual-meat and fake-meat favorites as well as actual-cheese and fake-cheese specialties.

### ISHKABIBBLE'S EATERY

Map pp228-9        *American*
☎ 215-923-4337; 337 South St; $3-7; ☾ 10am-11pm Sun-Thu, 10am-2am Fri & Sat; Bus 40, 57
Savory, inexpensive dishes like chicken cheese steaks, burgers and veggie burgers get served up for breakfast, lunch and dinner. Fresh cookies are baked on the premises. Order through a window and eat at the pink stools or on the sidewalk.

**JIM'S STEAKS** Map pp228-9     *Cheese Steaks*
☎ 215-928-1911; 400 South St; cheese steaks $5-7; ☾ 10am-1am Mon-Thu, 10am-3am Fri & Sat, noon-10pm Sun; Bus 40, 57
Here since 1939, Jim's is thought by many to be a top contender for Philadelphia's best cheese steak honor. Demonstrative of this, a line runs out the door at almost all hours.

### PINK ROSE PASTRY SHOP

Map pp228-9        *Dessert*
☎ 215-592-0565; 630 S 4th St; cakes $5-6, pies $5; ☾ 8am-10:30pm Mon-Thu, 8am-11pm Fri, 9am-11pm Sat, 9am-10:30pm Sun; Bus 40, 57
At this cute place, doily-like curtains in a pink building, mismatched little tables, fresh flowers and white cabinetry provide the backdrop for consumption of elaborate cakes, tarts and various international pastries. There is also a simple breakfast and lunch menu listing eggs, grilled cheese sandwiches and little else.

**SOUTH STREET DINER** Map pp228-9    *Diner*
☎ 215-627-5258; 140 South St; eggs $3-6, sandwiches $5-7; ☾ 7am-3am; Bus 40, 57
Despite the awning's 24-hour proclamation, this expansive diner shuts down for a few hours in the early morning. The food is only so-so, so don't order anything complicated. A plus is the existence of a fully loaded, rotating dessert display.

## Mid-Range

**AZAFRAN** Map pp228-9       *South American*
☎ 215-928-4019; 617 S 3rd St; mains $13-20, BYOB, corkage $1; ☾ 5-10pm Tue-Thu, 5-11pm Fri & Sat, 4:30-9:30pm Sun; Bus 40, 57
While it may seem that beautiful bathrooms are the main attraction, the food served at this homey place is worth eating. Thick chunks of meat or fish – the definition of fresh – are skewered with sugarcane

and basted with ginger butter. A nicely appointed patio attracts romantics. Who wants caramel flan?

### CEDAR'S Map pp228-9 — *Lebanese*
☎ 215-925-4950; 616 S 2nd St; mains $8-15, sandwiches $3.75-4.25; ⏰ 4-10pm Mon-Thu, 11:30am-11pm Fri & Sat, 5-10pm Sun; Bus 40, 57
This family-run place cooks up stuffed, pickled eggplant with soft pine nuts and spices, various meat kabobs and a *labni*-filled omelet – a thin egg wrapping stuffed with a very garlicky, cheesy filling made of yogurt and seasoned with parsley, onion and mint – that's favored by vegetarians.

### THE DARK HORSE PUB
Map pp228-9 — *English*
☎ 215-928-9307; 421 S 2nd St; mains $14-24; ⏰ dinner 5-10pm Mon-Thu, 5-10:30pm Fri, 11:30am-10:30pm Sat, 11:30am-9pm Sun; bar 11:30am-2am Tue-Sun, 3pm-2am Mon; Bus 40, 57
Head over to the Dark Horse Pub where the English congregate to watch soccer and drink Youngs London Ale. With new ownership, the Anglophone wattage has dimmed a tad – now you can get your rib-eye steak with Creole red beans and rice – but there are still plenty of blood puddings and Stilton cheeses lurking in the wood-paneled corners.

### DMITRI'S Map pp228-9 — *Mediterranean*
☎ 215-625-0556; 795 S 3rd St; mains $14-20; ⏰ 5:30-11pm Mon-Sat, 5-10pm Sun; BYOB; Bus 40, 57
Small and popular, Dmitri's sends guests waiting for a table across the street to **New Wave Café** (p135), where they can enjoy a drink until space is made. Dmitri's is known for intimate tables, excellent fish and waitresses who wear fashionable clogs.

### FAMOUS 4TH ST DELI
Map pp228-9 — *Deli*
☎ 215-922-3274; 700 S 4th St; treats $6-10; ⏰ 7:30am-4pm Mon-Sat, 7:30am-4pm Sun; Bus 40, 57
Usually referred to as 'The Famous,' this deli has been owned and run by the same family for three generations. The friendly waiters will correctly recommend the corned-beef special as a favorite sandwich, though it might be a bad idea to pass up the superb Reuben on a cold day. All meals come on styrofoam plates, and traditionally diners are given complimentary cookies for dessert. The only observable change made

to the ancient dining room is ongoing: a ceaseless accumulation of framed celebrity endorsements.

### FEZ Map pp228-9 — *Moroccan*
☎ 215-925-5367; 620 S 2nd St; mains $9-20; ⏰ 5:30-10:30pm Sun-Thu, 5-10:30pm Fri & Sat; Bus 40, 57
Run by the same family as Cedar's, next door, Fez offers low, cushioned seating, brass serving platters, a hookah or two and occasional belly dancing as entertainment. The seven-course dinner specials are a particularly good value. The vegetarian version ($17) includes *harira* (lentil soup), salads, *bastilla* (a sweet entreé of phyllo pastry), couscous, fruit, mint tea and Moroccan pastries.

### JUDY'S CAFE Map pp228-9 — *American*
☎ 215-928-1968; 627 S 3rd St; mains $12-21; ⏰ 5:30-10pm Sun-Thu, 5:30-11pm Fri & Sat; Bus 40, 57
This gay-friendly establishment has been dishing out stuffed meatloaf, chicken cutlets and mashed potatoes for decades. The real hit of the menu is an appetizer: the baked goat cheese with greens and tomato coulis. It could not be more delicious, nor could it be any bigger. Judy's also makes a great cosmopolitan.

### RON'S RIBS Map pp222-3 — *BBQ*
☎ 215-829-4448; 1627 South St; sandwiches $5, ribs $10-12; ⏰ noon-midnight Mon-Thu, noon-3am Fri & Sat; SEPTA Lombard-South St Station, Bus 2, 27, 32, 40
Run by two African American families since 1945, this place can be smelled from a block away. Get ready for some fiery deliciousness and maybe a side of candied yams, corn bread or cole slaw.

### TARTINE Map pp228-9 — *French*
☎ 215-592-4720; 701 S 4th St; mains $16-26, BYOB, cash only; ⏰ 6-10pm Wed-Sat, 5-9pm Sun & Mon; Bus 40, 57
Run by an old French guy who putters around the dining area when he isn't busy creating some of Philly's finest food, this casual bistro is top-notch in almost every way. A generous and buttery onion tart is topped with deliciously potent sardines, and the lightly sauced Coquille St Jacques lies under a bed of browned gruyère. The mousse with crème anglaise is tremendous. Tartine has an unusual BYOB policy that allows patrons to either bring booze of their own or purchase one of Tartine's select bottles.

## Top End

**DJANGO** Map pp228-9 *Modern American*
☎ 215-522-7151; 526 S 4th St; mains $19-24, BYOB;
🕑 5:30-10:30pm Tue-Sun; Bus 40, 57
A sensory overload comes with every meal at this BYOB. Django combines odd ingredients to make dishes that sound questionable but taste divine. The menu changes monthly, relies on local produce, and might include appetizers like a 'game tart' made of braised boar, venison, onions, pastry, fried quail eggs and *foie gras* sauce. Inside, the restaurant is country-cute and informal. Make reservations at least two weeks in advance for weeknight dining, three weeks for weekends.

**MALLORCA** Map pp228-9 *Spanish*
☎ 215-351-6652; 117-119 South St; tapas $6-10, mains $18-28; 🕑 11:30am-10pm Mon-Thu, 11:30am-11:30pm Fri & Sat, noon-10pm Sun; Bus 40, 57
Serving many lobster-based dishes such as twin tails in an apple champagne sauce, this place also prepares a daily tapas menu. Look to these daily specials for small plates of spicy pork and very tender fish cheeks. If the pretty decor seems strangely familiar, this is because Mallorca has more than one location in Pennsylvania.

# SOUTH PHILADELPHIA

Full of red sauce, garlic and pasta, this neighborhood, traditionally populated by working-class Italian Americans, has lately attracted immigrants from all over Asia and Mexico. You can find great bowls of pho and some giant Vietnamese markets around 11th and Washington Sts. Mexican joints also favor Washington St, and there is even a stand near the cheese steak epicenter.

## Budget

### CENTER CITY PRETZEL CO
Map pp228-9 *Pretzels*
☎ 215-463-5664; 816 Washington Ave; pretzel 30¢;
🕑 midnight-noon Mon-Fri, 1am-noon Sat, 10:30pm-10:30am Sun; Bus 47, 64
Open only in the dark, this place has the freshest pretzels in town. Center City Pretzel is where all the trucks buy their goods from. After paying, stand on the sidewalk and watch hundreds of pretzels emerge slowly from the giant oven.

### GENO'S STEAKS
Map pp228-9 *Cheese Steaks*
☎ 215-389-0659; 1219 S 9th St; cheese steaks $5-6, cash only; 🕑 24hr; Bus 23, 47, 64
With what must be a staggering electric bill, Geno's bright and colorful signage can be seen for miles. Geno's opened opposite **Pat's** (see below) in the 1960s, spawning one of history's greatest turf wars. Some visitors are perplexed by Geno's little Confederate display across the street.

### ISGRO PASTRIES
Map pp228-9 *Bakery*
☎ 215-923-7215; 1009 Christian St; 🕑 8:30am-6pm Mon-Sat, 8:30am-4pm Sun; Bus 23, 47, 63
For cakes and pastries, Isgro has been satisfying Italian American stomachs since 1904. Cannolis are filled to order.

### JOHN'S WATER ICE
Map pp228-9 *Water Ice*
☎ 215-925-6955; 701 Christian St; water ices $1;
🕑 11am-9pm Wed-Mon May-Sep; Bus 47, 63
Tasty water ice – called lemonhead regardless of its flavor – can be found at John's, which has been serving the neighborhood since 1945. Flavors include lemon, cherry, chocolate and pineapple.

### MELROSE DINER
Map pp220-1 *Diner*
☎ 215-467-6644; 1501 Snyder Ave; mains $3-8;
🕑 24hr; SEPTA Snyder Station, Bus 37
Situated in the part of town where everyone double parks, Melrose is a family-owned diner that's been serving American comfort food since 1935. According to some, it 'has its own culture' with vintage '70s interiors and a history of mob-boss clientele. It's a busy place with its own bakery whose cheap desserts are surprisingly good.

### PAT'S KING OF STEAKS
Map pp228-9 *Cheese Steaks*
☎ 215-468-1546; 9th St & Passyunk Ave; cheese steaks $5-6, cash only; 🕑 24hr; Bus 23, 47, 64
Back in 1930 Pat Olivieri invented cheese steaks while operating a hot dog stand on the **Italian Market** (p104). A few years later he opened this place. Perhaps more impressive than the giant crowds who show up after the bars close are the smaller numbers having a steak for breakfast at 9am. Pat's has a fierce and bitter rivalry with neon **Geno's** (see above), across the street.

### SARCONE'S BAKERY Map pp228-9 *Bakery*
☎ 215-922-0445; 758 S 9th St; bread $1-2;
🕑 7:30am-3:30pm Tue-Sat, 7:30am-1pm Sun; Bus 27, 40, 43

Since 1918 practically everyone in South Philadelphia has been coming here for their bread. Arrive before noon or you might find slim pickins.

### TAQUERIA LA VERACRUZANA
Map pp228-9 *Mexican*
☎ 215-465-1440; 908 Washington St; burritos $5, dishes $8-10; 🕑 7am-midnight; Bus 47, 64

South Philly's emerging Mexican population has blessed the city with spectacular *fundido*. The burritos are good, but it's a crime to pass up the simple, cheesy treat.

### VARALLO BROTHERS Map pp228-9 *Bakery*
☎ 215-952-0367; 1639 S 10th St; cannolis $1.50;
🕑 7am-9pm Sep-Jul; Bus 23, 29

A no-frills bakery turning out scads of cannolis, cookies and Italian pastries, Varallo has some tables inside for those who also want a great espresso.

# Mid-Range

### BUTCHER'S CAFE Map pp228-9 *Italian*
☎ 215-925-6200; 901 Christian St; lunch mains $9-12, dinner mains $15-17, BYOB; 🕑 lunch 11:30am-3pm Tue-Thu, dinner 5-9pm Tue-Thu, 5-10pm Fri & Sat, 1-9pm Sun; Bus 23, 47, 63

Meat hooks still cling to the walls in this former

butcher shop, where you can try simple fare like ziti Bolognese. There isn't much for vegetarians.

### CARMAN'S COUNTRY KITCHEN
Map pp228-9 *Breakfast*
☎ 215-339-9613; 1301 S 11th St; brunch mains $12-13;
🕑 8am-2pm Thu-Mon; SEPTA Ellsworth-Federal Station, Bus 23, 64

Carman's cult following comes to feast on giant portions of experimental waffles (which will come with something like hazelnut butternut mocha sauce and kahlua whipped cream) and omelets with unusual fillings (fava and green beans). The small place has nearly zero seating, so there's a chance that guests will be invited to dine on resin furniture on the bed of a pickup truck parked outside. People drink out of mason jars while holding mismatched utensils, and reservations are taken over a pay phone. The fare ranges from amazingly good to surprisingly bland.

### MORNING GLORY DINER
Map pp228-9 *Breakfast*
☎ 215-413-3999; 735 S 10th St; breakfast, lunch and brunch mains $5-8, dinner mains $8-15, cash only;
🕑 7am-4pm Mon-Fri, 8am-3pm Sat & Sun; Bus 27, 40, 43

Good enough to warrant a tarp-covered patio in which diners wait for their names to be called, Morning Glory occupies a spiffed-up, hippie-esque diner and serves super-hot frittatas ( flavors include spinach and provolone as well as salmon, asparagus and goat cheese) that come with biscuits

---

## How to Order a Cheese Steak

Anyone will tell you it's a big no-no to follow the incorrect protocol when ordering a cheese steak. Those who screw up face some serious repercussions. Very often such rookies get served less meat. At Pat's King of Steaks (p116) offenders are sometimes told to head to the rear of the line. When it's 2am and 50 people are waiting behind you, it can be easy to panic. To avoid such a fate, follow these guidelines:

1. Before arriving at the spot where your order will be taken, determine the kind of cheese you want. The options are almost always Whiz (that's Cheese Whiz), provolone and American.
2. Determine if you want the steak 'wit' or 'witout' onions.
3. Get in line.
4. Never arrive at the window without already knowing your order. It is important to be quick. Visible decision-making is a punishable offense.
5. Order. For example, if you want a cheese steak with Cheese Whiz and onions, say, 'Could I have a Whiz wit?' If you want a provolone cheese steak with no onions, say, 'provolone witout.' If you don't want cheese, say either 'steak wit' or 'steak witout.'
6. Don't ask for other kinds of cheese. The few saps in history who asked for Swiss or Gouda still painfully remember the embarrassment of their hideous mistakes.
7. You won't get in trouble for being polite. It is acceptable to say 'please' and 'thank you.'

and stewed apples. If it's being served, the pecan waffle with whipped peach butter is hard to pass up. The coffee's good, the juice is fresh and the lunch sandwiches come loaded with vegetables.

### RALPH'S Map pp228-9 *Italian*
☎ 215-627-6011; 760 S 9th St; mains $14-20; 🕑 noon-10pm Sun-Thu, noon-11pm Fri & Sat; Bus 27, 40, 43

Established in 1900, Ralph's is a traditional Italian restaurant with simple and good main courses like baked lasagna. Ask for a table upstairs in the huge hall with traditional murals.

### SABRINA'S CAFE

Map pp228-9 *Modern American/Breakfast*
☎ 215-574-1599; 910 Christian St; breakfast mains $4-8, brunch mains $6-12, dinner mains $13-17; 🕑 8am-4pm Sun-Tue, 8am-9pm Wed & Thu, 8am-10pm Fri & Sat; Bus 23, 47, 63

Hipster hut meets grandma's kitchen in this popular spot known for its amazing daily brunch menu. Get your granola, egg whites, and blue cheese frittatas with spinach and big chunks of various mushrooms (that was three separate items, not one big gross one) here. Food comes in generous quantities. The coffee might be weak, but the juice is fresh.

### TRE SCALINI Map pp228-9 *Italian*
☎ 215-551-3870; 1533 S 11th St; mains $14-20, BYOB; 🕑 5-10pm Tue-Sat, 3:30-9pm Sun; Bus 23, 29

It looks like a collision between Graceland and an early Frank Lloyd Wright project, but this BYOB serves some of the best Italian food in South Philly. The simple penne in spicy tomato sauce is worth more than its $14, though our favorite dish remains a handmade black pasta with prawns and jumbo lump crab meat in a tomato sauce ($19). For decent weekend seating, make a reservation at least a week in advance.

## Top End
### PIF Map pp228-9 *French*
☎ 215-625-2923; 1009 S 8th St; dinner mains $18-26, BYOB; 🕑 5:30-10pm Tue-Sat; Bus 47, 64

Aggressively precious, this cute little bistro turns out some superlative escargot with garlic. Make reservations for the weekends and call ahead on weekdays – sometimes the entire place is booked for private parties.

### VICTOR CAFE Map pp228-9 *Italian*
☎ 215-468-3040; 1303 Dickinson St; mains $20-32; 🕑 5-10:30pm Mon-Thu, 5-11pm Fri-Sun; SEPTA Tasker-Morris Station, Bus 23, 29

A South Philly classic, Victor Cafe is renowned for its opera-singing waitstaff. They are often students from the nearby Curtis School of Music or moonlighting professionals, and they regularly burst into song, performing operas and arias. Reservations are recommended but the food is not.

# NORTHERN LIBERTIES

Though it contains only a handful of spots, nearly everything in this neighborhood provides good eating. Northern Liberties is definitely a part of town where the bars also provide good food options. Check out the menus at the Standard Tap (p136), Liberties (p136) and Abbaye (p136), the soba noodles at the Ministry of Information (p136) and the milkshakes at Silk City Diner (p109). A fancy Sunday brunch is unavoidable – nearly every place has one.

### IL CANTUCCIO Map p230 *Italian*
☎ 215-627-6573; 701 N 3rd St; lunch mains $8-9, dinner mains $14-16, BYOB, cash only; 🕑 11:30am-10pm; Bus 57

This corner trattoria fills up early on the weekends on account of its small size, homey atmosphere and simple, flavorful meals. The ravioli is made daily, with the filling determined by the mood of the chef after rolling out of bed. The stuffed fettuccine with mushrooms and peas comes in a top-notch sauce and is sized for hearty eaters. A word of caution: as the menu warns, do *not* try to put cheese on your fish. You will definitely be reprimanded.

### LAS CAZUELAS Map p230 *Mexican*
☎ 215-351-9144; 426 W Girard Ave; mains $9-15, BYOB; 🕑 11am-9pm Mon-Thu, 11am-10pm Fri & Sat, 11am-8pm Sun; Bus 15, 57

If you bring the tequila and the mix, they'll give you ice and a pitcher. For those who don't feel hungry enough for the excellent mole poblano, the quesadillas and taco appetizers cost a bit less and are nearly as filling.

### NORTH 3RD Map p230 *Modern American*
☎ 215-413-3666; www.norththird.com; 801 N 3rd St; mains $10-20; 🕑 5pm-2am, brunch 11am-3pm Sun; Bus 57

Another newcomer to the Northern Liberties scene, this arty place is both a bar and restaurant, serving up items such as macaroni and cheddar, beef medallions with asparagus and blood-orange margaritas. After dusk it gets very dark inside, with candles as the primary means of lighting all the crazy stuff on the walls. Present in the eclectic decor are Christmas lights, tacky ornaments, tiki masks and a giant cloth eagle suspended over the bar. There is a small stage in a side room where obscure movies are played on Tuesday.

### PIGALLE Map p230 *French*
☎ 215-627-7772; 702 N 2nd St; brunch mains $7-13, café items $8-12, mains $19-24; 🕐 5-10pm Tue-Thu, 5-11pm Fri & Sat, 5-9pm Sun, brunch 11am-3pm Sun; Bus 57

The SUV and BMW set comes to Northern Liberties to dine at this new and glitzy brasserie. Try dishes such as crispy arctic chard salad or potato-crusted halibut. At the bar, a pork loin wrapped in bacon with onion rings and mashed potatoes goes great with beer. Some desserts are made to order; in particular, we recommend Pigalle's airy *clafoutis* (a custardlike puffed pastry).

### RAT PACK CAFÉ Map p230 *Café*
☎ 215-974-7300; 631 N 3rd St; coffee $1.50; 🕐 7:30am-10pm; Bus 57

This small place looks a little tacky and garish. Even so, it actively wants you to stay and relax, and provides some plush couches toward the back for this purpose. A single computer terminal provides free Internet access.

# FAIRMOUNT PARK
Within Fairmount Park's thousands of acres, find the following spot hidden next to a wooded creek.

### VALLEY GREEN INN
Map pp220-1 *Modern American*
☎ 215-247-1730; www.valleygreeninn.com; Valley Green Rd at Wissahickon Creek; lunch mains $8-12, dinner mains $15-25; 🕐 noon-9pm Mon-Thu, noon-10pm Fri & Sat, 10am-9pm Sun; P

In the midst of a giant park is an old colonial inn facing the Wissahickon Creek. This is the Valley Green Inn, where you can enjoy a very leisurely prix-fixe brunch ($19) either on a shady porch or in the roadhouse's parlor. Other meals also score big points.

# UNIVERSITY CITY & WEST PHILADELPHIA
A few high-end options as well as dozens of cheap food trucks exist around the universities. West Philly is a center for new immigrants, testified to by the many inexpensive ethnic restaurants. In particular, Baltimore Ave is home to numerous worthy Ethiopian eateries.

## Budget
### BIG GEORGE'S STOP N DINE
Map pp220-1 *Southern*
☎ 215-748-8200; 52nd & Spruce Sts; $6-10; 🕐 7am-6pm Mon-Fri, 8am-4pm Sat, 9am-4pm Sun; SEPTA 52nd St Station, Bus 42, 52

When Bill Clinton came to town, this is where he ate. Saunter up to the cafeteria line and fill up a plate with Salisbury steak, fatback, fish, sausage, fried chicken and collard greens. When done, head to a booth and enjoy your pile of delicious grease under a neon glow. Avoid the dessert.

### BUBBLE HOUSE Map p225 *Teahouse/Asian*
☎ 215-243-0804; 3404 Sansom St; lunch mains $7-9, dinner mains $7-12; 🕐 noon-10pm Sun-Thu, noon-11pm Sat & Sun; SEPTA 34th St Station, 21, 30, 42

This is University City's *premier* place for tapioca balls added to iced specialty teas flavored with nondairy powder. Bubble House also offers traditional loose-leaf teas and entrées such as tempura tofu and Thai-styled red coconut curry. The waitstaff? Cute as a button.

### Top Five Vegetarian Spots
Check out these options if your stomach disagrees with cheese steaks. Some of these places serve meat and fish, but vegetarianism is well represented on all of their menus.

- **Charles Plaza** (p108) One of Chinatown's friendliest institutions
- **Citrus** (p124) A high-end Chestnut Hill BYOB
- **Essene** (p104) A health food store with a tasty café in the back
- **Gianna's Grille** (p114) Top-notch vegan cakes and pizza
- **White Dog Cafe** (p121) Local produce and artful preparation

## Top Five Pizza Joints

This town is covered in pizzas, but few are as good as the pies served in these places.

- **Gianfranco Pizza Rustica** (p105) Thin-crusted beauties by the slice
- **Joe's Pizza** (Map pp222-3; ☎ 215-569-0898; 122 S 16th St; slice $2; ☽ 8am-7pm Mon-Fri, 10am-7pm Sat) Hot slices keep downtown office workers alive.
- **Lombardi's** (p109) Allegedly the country's oldest pizzeria
- **Marra's Restaurant** (Map pp228-9; ☎ 215-463-9249; 1734 E Passyunk Ave; pies $12-18; ☽ 11:30am-10pm Tue-Thu, 11:30am-midnight Fri & Sat, 2-10pm Sun) A traditional mom-and-pop South Philly place with wooden booths and no slices
- **Tacconelli's** (p124) So good you need to order a dough three days in advance

**BUCKS COUNTY** Map p225      Café
☎ 215-387-6722; 3430 Sansom St; coffee $1-2; ☽ 7am-6pm Mon-Fri, 8am-4pm Sat, 9am-4pm Sun; SEPTA 34th St Station, 21, 30, 42
This café has good coffee and pastries to get you started in the morning. If you feel like reading, plenty of tables are provided, though the rigid chairs might propel you outside earlier than anticipated.

**DAHLAK** Map p225      Eritrean/Ethiopian
☎ 215-726-6464; 4708 Baltimore Ave; mains $6-8; ☽ 4-10:30pm; Bus 34
Under the same ownership since it opened in 1983, Dahlak serves devoted customers very generous portions. Its two rooms are dimly lit, with seating comprised of small chairs and large cubelike cushions clustered around little tables. Live music (not necessarily Eritrean) is sometimes played on the weekend.

**SAM'S PLACE** Map p225      Café
☎ 215-222-2926; 405 S 45th St; coffee $1; ☽ 7am-9pm Mon-Fri, 8am-9pm Sat & Sun; Bus 21, 42
This tiny convenience store attracts crust-punks and bespectacled kids with designer glasses through the merits of its makeshift coffee enterprise. The shop's interior lacks ambience, but some nicely weathered tables and chairs provide for the needs of chess players and layabouts.

**SITAR INDIA** Map p225      Indian
☎ 215-662-0818; 60 S 38th St; mains $7-13; ☽ lunch 11:30am-3pm Sun-Thu & 11:30am-4pm Fri & Sat, dinner 4:30-10pm Sun-Thu, 4:30-11pm Fri & Sat; SEPTA 40th St Station, Bus 21, 30, 40
Penny-pinching Penn students favor this joint, largely because it offers an affordable, all-you-can-eat buffet seven days a week. The lunchtime version costs $6, while the dinner buffet is $9.

**VIENTIANE** Map p225      Laotian/Thai
☎ 215-726-1095; 4728 Baltimore Ave; mains $7-10; ☽ 11am-3pm & 5-10pm Mon-Sat; Bus 34
Longstanding devotees remember when this place operated under a blue tarp next to a house. Now the owners have overcome questionable legality by moving to an actual storefront. Vientiane serves spicy yellow, red and green curries as well as Pad Thai, green papaya salad and a few more simple, clean-tasting dishes.

## Mid-Range

**LEMON GRASS** Map p225      Thai
☎ 215-222-8042; 3626-30 Lancaster Ave; mains $9-19; ☽ lunch 11:30am-2pm Mon-Fri, dinner 5-9pm Sun-Thu & 5-10pm Fri & Sat; SEPTA 34th St Station, Bus 10
Very few Thai restaurants exist in Philadelphia, making Lemon Grass a valued commodity. The vegetarian options are numerous and include the eggplant salad, a moderately spicy dish in a tomato vinaigrette, whose texture and taste is enhanced with cubes of crispy tofu.

**NAN** Map p225      French/Thai
☎ 215-382-0818; 4000 Chestnut St; mains $15-20; ☽ lunch 11:30am-2:30pm Tue-Fri, dinner 5-10pm Tue-Thu & 5-11pm Fri & Sat; SEPTA 40th St Station, Bus 21, 30, 40
Nan doesn't look like much – its beige walls and teal accents are vaguely reminiscent of a *Miami Vice* set – but foodwise it delivers the goods. Chef Kamol Phutlek has been working in the kitchens of Philly's better restaurants since the 1970s, and this new addition to the food scene reflects his culinary expertise. Meats are especially well prepared and presented. Try simpler fare like a lamb chop or more complicated items such as a sautéed sweetbread in a puff pastry over creamed leeks with a port-wine sauce.

### RX Map p225 *Modern American*
☎ 215-222-9590; 4443 Spruce St; mains $15-20; ⓨ lunch 11am-2:30pm Tue-Fri, dinner 5:30-9pm Tue-Thu & 5:30-10pm Fri & Sat, brunch 10am-2pm Fri & Sat; Bus 34, 42

The big windows and pleasant corner location of this former drugstore make Rx a comfortable spot for a leisurely meal. And leisurely it often is, as the friendly waitstaff is not especially speedy. Rx uses organic ingredients when possible and serves many vegetarian dishes.

### WHITE DOG CAFE
Map p225 *Modern American*
☎ 215-386-9224; 3420 Sansom St; lunch & brunch mains $8-12, dinner mains $16-25; ⓨ lunch 11:30am-2:30pm Mon-Fri & 11:30am-2pm Sat, dinner 5:30-10pm Sun-Thu & 5:30-11pm Fri & Sat, brunch 11:30am-2:30pm Sun, bar open until 2am daily; SEPTA 34th St Station, Bus 21, 30, 42

The White Dog looks kind of like a ski lodge, or kind of like a B&B that got rid of all its rooms and turned them into table space. Its menu, which changes seasonally, attempts to be as organic as possible. About a third of the entrées are made from land animals, another third from fish and the last from vegetarian ingredients. In addition to food functions, owner Judy Wicks stages lectures and seminars on political and social issues. She has also published her own cookbook, *The White Dog Cafe Cookbook: Multicultural Recipes and Tales of Adventure from Philadelphia's Revolutionary Restaurant.* The Sunday brunch is popular.

## Top End
### LA TERRASSE Map p225 *French*
☎ 215-386-5000; 3432 Sansom St; mains $20-30; ⓨ lunch 11:30am-2:30pm Mon-Fri, dinner 5:30-9pm Mon-Thu & 5:30-10pm Fri & Sat; SEPTA 34th St Station, Bus 21, 30, 42

Formerly a Penn hangout, this place got a makeover a few years back and reopened as a bistro with a sauce-laden menu. It stocks traditional staples such as crème brûlée, as well as inventive stuff. If you find the price tag prohibitive, you can save some cash by ordering from the café menu at the bar. People go mad over eating under the indoor tree.

### POD Map p225 *Japanese*
☎ 215-387-1803; 3636 Sansom St; dinner $20-30; ⓨ 11am-11pm Mon-Fri, 4pm-midnight Sat, 4-10pm Sun; SEPTA 34th St Station, Bus 21, 30, 42

Entirely white with the exception of artfully positioned circles of pastel light, POD looks exactly like a *Star Trek* movie set, or maybe a scene from *The Jetsons*, with chunky modeled chairs and uniformed servers. More than any of Stephen Starr's other restaurants, POD privileges exceptional decor over food. Definitely avoid the conveyor-belt sushi and stick to the menu items. POD also serves a rainbow of cocktails and an impressive selection of sake.

# MANAYUNK
Most restaurants in Manayunk overlook cute Main St. Those that don't, overlook the charming canal and Schuylkill River.

## Budget
### CHLOE'S CORNER Map p230 *Water Ice*
☎ 215-482-5600; 4162 Main St; water ices $1.50-3; ⓨ 11am-11pm Sun-Thu, 9am-3am Fri & Sat, May-Sep; SEPTA R6 Manayunk Station, Bus 35, 61

The red, green and white awnings of this popular snack stand offer a welcoming reward to hot bicyclists arriving in Manayunk from the south. Chloe's water ice comes in dozens of flavors and is considered some of the best in Philadelphia. There is outdoor seating only.

### LA COLOMBE Map p230 *Café*
☎ 215-483-4580; 4360 Main St; coffee $1-2; ⓨ 7:30am-6:30pm Mon-Fri, 8:30am-6:30pm Sat & Sun; SEPTA R6 Manayunk Station, Bus 35, 61

Though it doesn't feel overwhelmingly trendy like its Rittenhouse Square sister (p109), this café still serves the same great coffee. An added bonus is a choice of decent panini sandwiches ($5 to $6).

### Eat from a Truck
Philadelphia's food culture involves shiny, stainless steel trucks that vend cheap eats from sidewalks all over the city. There are several spots in town where they congregate. Catering to the city's office workers is a bunch of trucks near 20th and Market Sts. Near Penn they line up around 36th and Spruce Sts, 34th and Spruce Sts, and 36th and Walnut Sts. Common food offerings include fruit salad, falafels, burgers and burritos.

**MAINLY DESSERTS** Map p230     *Café*
☎ 215-487-1325; 4247 Main St; dessert $3-5, lunch mains $6, dinner mains $12-16; ☯ 11am-4pm Tue, 11am-10pm Wed & Thu, 11am-midnight Fri & Sat, 11am-9pm Sun; SEPTA R6 Manayunk Station, Bus 35, 61
Located on the 1st floor of a cute Victorian building, Mainly got its start making desserts and wedding cakes and has lately added savory foods to its repertoire. For lunch try a wrap or a Greek salad pita. For dinner eat a filling piece of grilled chicken breast marinated in olive oil, lemon and white wine. Most people usually end up stuffing a tart in their mouths, too.

**SORRENTINO'S DELI** Map p230     *Deli*
☎ 215-487-0559; 4361 Cresson St; sandwiches $3.40-4.50; ☯ 7am-10pm; SEPTA R6 Manayunk Station, Bus 35, 61
From the street Sorrentino's doesn't look like more than a generic corner store. For those who enter, it will look (both architecturally and in the selection of items for sale) more like a corner store circa 1930. And first-timers ordering a cheese hoagie will be shocked at how good it is. You can eat in the pink back room until around dark; after then it's take-out only.

# Mid-Range & Top End

**CARMELLA'S** Map p230     *Italian*
☎ 215-487-1400; 1 Leverington Ave; lunch mains $8-15, dinner mains $16-25, bar food $8-12; ☯ lunch

---

## Dining Alfresco

From sidewalk seating to a porch in the woods, Philadelphia has fine outdoor seating – well, until winter.

- **Azafran** (p114) You can't see it from the street, but there's a secluded garden out back.
- **Effie's** (p112) The low-key, quiet patio sits next to a shady alley.
- **Valley Green Inn** (p119) The porch overlooking the Wissahickon Creek can't be beat.
- **The Inn Philadelphia** (p112) This romantic locale is hidden among the quiet alleys of the Gayborhood.
- **Last Drop** (p112) This café's sidewalk tables can be used for endless hours.
- **Rouge** (p110) Eat and be seen on this piece of Rittenhouse sidewalk.

---

11am-3pm Mon-Sat, dinner 5-10:30pm Mon-Thu, 5-11pm Fri & Sat & noon-10pm Sun; SEPTA R6 Manayunk Station, Bus 35, 61
At the edge of town, Carmella's occupies a narrow island between the Schuylkill and the canal. Carmella's best feature, aside from ample parking, is a broad deck that wraps around the 2nd-floor bar, offering a pleasant view. The interior dining room feels like a chain restaurant and is decorated with large B&W portraits of angry-looking Italians. Enjoy decent fried calamari, shrimp scampi or pasta with red clam sauce.

**GRASSHOPPER** Map p230     *French*
☎ 215-483-1888; 4427 Main St; mains $18-23; ☯ 6-10pm Tue-Thu, 6-10:30pm Fri & Sat; SEPTA R6 Manayunk Station, Bus 35, 61
This romantic 10-table spot with salmon-colored walls and a worn pine floor claims to be French with Chinese influences. While stuff like a free-range veal steak flavored with cider, mushrooms, demi-glace and a light cream sauce comes off really well, it's sometimes hard to detect the Chinese motif (excepting an eggplant dish with spicy garlic sauce). Nearly all the dishes involve meat.

**HIKARU** Map p230     *Japanese*
☎ 215-487-3500; 4348 Main St; lunch mains $9-11, dinner mains $14-18, dinner Teppan $18-36; ☯ lunch 11:45am-2:30pm Wed-Fri & noon-3pm Sat & Sun, dinner 5-10pm Mon-Thu, 5-11pm Fri, 4:30-11pm Sat & 3-9:30pm Sun; SEPTA R6 Manayunk Station, Bus 35, 61
Passing by Hikaru on the street, one might correctly think, 'Hey look, that's a live sushi-bar monitor.' The monitor projects the action of the sushi chefs working on the 2nd floor of this restaurant. On the 1st floor Teppan specialties (hibachi lobster tail or chicken) are offered by a highly entertaining chef who prepares your meal at tableside. Folks who want more conventional fare like tempura and donburi don't get a show but they pay less.

**JAKE'S** Map p230     *Modern American*
☎ 215-483-0444; 4365 Main St; lunch mains $12-15, dinner mains $24-30; ☯ lunch 11:30am-2:30pm Mon-Fri, dinner 5-9:30pm Sun-Thu & 5-10pm Fri & Sat; SEPTA R6 Manayunk Station, Bus 35, 61
Yet another pale yellow bistro of excellent quality, Jake's dishes out lobster salad comprised of citrus-marinated tails and tempura-fried claws mixed with a spicy cabbage slaw, roasted trout and hot blueberry

cobbler. A three-course prix-fixe menu is offered for lunch ($20) and dinner ($35).

### KANSAS CITY PRIME Map p230 *Steakhouse*
☎ 215-482-3700; 4417 Main St; seafood mains $25-35, meat mains $22-45; ⏱ 5-11pm Mon-Sat, 5:30-11pm Sun; SEPTA R6 Manayunk Station, Bus 35, 61
You can get some seafood entrées (jumbo shrimp, salmon fillets), but the main attraction is 'prime entrées.' All meats on this list (veal loin chop, NY strip sirloin, a massive rib steak served on the bone) are certified USDA prime and are dry-aged for a minimum of 21 days.

# CHESTNUT HILL
Almost all of Chestnut Hill's restaurants lie along Germantown Ave, and the villagelike neighborhood has more bakeries than it knows what to do with.

## Budget
### BREDENBECK'S ICE CREAM PARLOUR & BAKERY Map p231 *Ice Cream/Bakery*
☎ 215-247-7374; 8126 Germantown Ave; cone $2-4; ⏱ ice cream parlor 11am-10pm, bakery 6am-7pm Mon-Sat & 8am-5pm Sun; SEPTA R8 Chestnut Hill West, R7 Chestnut Hill East, Bus 23
The ice cream shop sits in the right half of this building, and the bakery sits in the left half. In the parlor you can take a spiral staircase to seating on the 2nd floor or step outside to eat on a pair of benches with pastel cones painted on them. In the bakery you can buy a wide range of specialty cookies.

### CAKE Map p231 *Dessert*
☎ 215-247-6887; 184 E Evergreen Ave; sweets $1-4; ⏱ 7am-5pm Mon-Fri, 8am-5pm Sat, 8am-noon Sun; SEPTA R8 Chestnut Hill West, R7 Chestnut Hill East, Bus 23
For a really stellar chilled cupcake, stop in here. Cake also sells full-size cakes plus some cookies and bars. It's got a nice café space where you can eat and watch the action in the bakery behind the counter.

### CHESTNUT HILL FARMERS MARKET
Map p231 *Market*
8829 Germantown Ave; ⏱ 9am-6pm Thu & Fri, 8am-5pm Sat; SEPTA R8 Chestnut Hill West, R7 Chestnut Hill East, Bus 23
Located in a small iron-framed warehouse,

this farmers market is home to a flower shop, a produce stand, a coffee vendor, a chocolatier and a soup guy. It's a good place to grab a cheap lunch, particularly at **Shundeez**, a Middle Eastern spot, or **Yassime's Garden**, which serves Mediterranean cuisine. Both stores are operated by the same owner, and both sell prepared foods (it's hard to understand how a vegetable curry rice or a lentil salad can taste that good) for about $3.25 per half pound.

### EXPRESSLY VEGETARIAN CAFE
Map p231 *Vegetarian*
☎ 215-247-6700; 8700 Germantown Ave; $2.25-6.25; ⏱ 11am-2pm Mon-Fri; SEPTA R8 Chestnut Hill West, R7 Chestnut Hill East, Bus 23
Located in the rear of a Seventh-Day Adventist Church, this café is accessed through a door facing Rex Ave. Menu items include flat-bread sandwiches with lettuce, tomato, artichoke hearts, olives, basil, grilled tofu and soy mayo, veggie burgers, meatless hot dogs and cheese steaks made with braised gluten and eggplant. A filling bowl of carrot ginger soup runs $2.25.

### PIANTA Map p231 *Pizza/Juices*
☎ 215-248-4557; 8513 Germantown Ave; pizzas & paninis $7-9, juices & smoothies $3.50-4.50; ⏱ 10am-10pm Mon-Fri, 10am-11pm Sat, 11am-9pm Sun; SEPTA R8 Chestnut Hill West, R7 Chestnut Hill East, Bus 23
This long and narrow place serves some pretty tasty individual-size pizza in an environment reminiscent of a high-end food court. The stuff that comes out of the juicer is usually very good, with the possible exception of the pineapple-based drinks, which one hippie claims 'tastes like it was made using canned pineapple chunks.'

### ROLLER'S EXPRESSO
Map p231 *Classic American*
☎ 215-247-7715; 8341 Germantown Ave; $3-8; ⏱ 7:30am-4pm Tue-Fri, 8am-4pm Sat, 8:30am-3pm Sun; SEPTA R8 Chestnut Hill West, R7 Chestnut Hill East, Bus 23
Roller's Expresso looks like a former ice cream parlor reworked to become a breakfast spot. Inside is nice and bright, with 12 huge, thick glass lamps hanging by chains from a painted-white tin ceiling. Come for fantastic scones as well as ice cream and dessert. More substantial menu items include Mexican chicken lasagna, omelets, PB&J, and brie and tomato sandwiches.

## TOP OF THE HILL  Map p231  *Farm Stand*
☎ 215-248-6009; 186 E Evergreen Ave; deli items $4-6; ☽ 6am-6pm Mon-Fri, 7am-6pm Sat; SEPTA R8 Chestnut Hill West, R7 Chestnut Hill East, Bus 23

Outside find wooden baskets full of locally grown fruit, plenty of potted flowers for sale and some pleasant summer and autumn seating. Inside find good coffee as well as take-out sandwiches and prepared items.

## Mid-Range

### AL'DANA  Map p231  *Middle Eastern*
☎ 215-247-3336; 8630 Germantown Ave; lunch mains $6-10, dinner mains $8-12; ☽ lunch 11am-2pm Tue-Thu & Sun, dinner 5:30-10pm Tue-Sat & 5-9pm Sun; SEPTA R8 Chestnut Hill West, R7 Chestnut Hill East, Bus 23

Aside from serving some well-prepared sandwiches (sautéed spinach with onions and feta cheese, or fried eggplant with tomato and cucumber), this joint also offers a lunch buffet for $8. The drawback: plastic plates. The dinner entrées are more elaborate than the luncheon sandwiches.

### CINCIN  Map p231  *Chinese/French*
☎ 215-242-8800; 7838 Germantown Ave; lunch mains $6-10, dinner mains $10-20; ☽ lunch 11:30am-3pm Mon-Sat, dinner 3-10pm Mon-Thu, 3-11:30pm Fri & Sat & 2-10pm Sun; ⓟ ; SEPTA R8 Chestnut Hill West, R7 Chestnut Hill East, Bus 23

CinCin's medium-size dining room's pink and green decor combine with the parking lot outside to create the feel of a distinctly suburban dining experience. However, the food – such as the gingery gunpowder shrimp or the merlot veal scallops – is as fancy-time-urban as any city place.

### CITRUS
Map p231  *Modern American/Vegetarian*
☎ 215-247-8188; 8136 Germantown Ave; mains $15-17, BYOB, corkage $2; ☽ 5-9:30pm Tue-Thu, 5-10:30pm Fri & Sat; SEPTA R8 Chestnut Hill West, R7 Chestnut Hill East, Bus 23

Diners at Citrus contend with two things: no fewer than six edicts printed on the menu and in the bathroom that collectively give one the idea that this is an overly self-righteous place, and some of the best food in town. Everything from airy herbed bread served before meals to inspiring entrées (whether they're fish-based,

vegetarian or vegan) to desserts like green tea crème brûlée couldn't be better. Animal welfare is an active theme of the restaurant; you won't eat cheese with animal rennet or gelatin derived from animals. Citrus forbids diners from wearing fur and from making reservations.

### WOMEN'S EXCHANGE  Map p231  *Teahouse*
☎ 215-247-5911; 8419 Germantown Ave; $8; ☽ 11am-3pm Tue-Sat weather & season permitting; SEPTA R8 Chestnut Hill West, R7 Chestnut Hill East, Bus 23

At the rear of Chestnut Hill's Women's Center, whose framed charter proclaims that it was founded in 1919, there remains a garden in which well-behaved men and women partake in an old-fashioned afternoon tea, complete with tiny tea sandwiches, scones with lemon curd, petits fours, cookies and either hot or iced tea. The hours are somewhat informal.

# GERMANTOWN & ELSEWHERE

Unless it's eggs on a styrofoam plate from one of numerous breakfast spots, Germantown doesn't present many options, with one very notable exception: Rib Crib. If Germantown doesn't catch your fancy, then trek through Northeast Philadelphia to find one of the most popular pizza spots on the earth's crust.

### RIB CRIB  Map p231  *BBQ*
☎ 215-438-6793; 6333 Germantown Ave; ribs $8.50; ☽ 11am-1am Thu, 11am-2am Fri & Sat; Bus 23

This small, bunkerlike crib is covered with pictures of notable African Americans and turns out pork so perfectly done that meat falls off the bone with zero effort. The sauces are tangy, and the messy food is strictly to go.

### TACCONELLI'S  Map pp220-1  *Pizza*
☎ 215-425-4983; 2604 E Somerset St; pizzas $10-20; ☽ 4:30-9pm Wed & Thu, 4:30-10pm Fri & Sat, 4:30-9pm Sun; Bus 54, 89

As testimony to the possibility that Tacconelli's serves the best pizza in town, those who eat here have to reserve a dough several days in advance. An amazing feat, underscored by the fact that the joint sits in a remote, dingy part of town.

# Entertainment

# Entertainment

A top-shelf hub of entertainment, Philadelphia packs in every kind of option imaginable. Equal parts high-class and lowbrow, this is the kind of town where you can take in a ballet in the nation's oldest grand opera house, and then knock back a Pabst and a shot of swill for three bucks. Throughout the city, the cheap, the historic and the trendy cohabitate. Numerous worthwhile dive bars remain as a symbol of the city's traditional blue-collar roots, old jazz clubs still crank out the tunes and slick cover-charging lounges have sprung up in response to recent good fortune. Even terminally discouraged hipsters have plenty of fringe areas to which they can retreat.

Classical music is well represented by the Kimmel Center and the Curtis Institute, while theatergoers have the run of the town, despite Philly's geographic location a mere 100 miles south of Broadway. Film buffs should definitely check out the offerings at the International House, or maybe try to track down the mysterious Secret Cinema.

When in town, pick up the free weeklies (*City Paper* and *Philadelphia Weekly*) to check out listings and special events.

## THEATER & COMEDY

Theater in Philly ranges from traveling Broadway shows to prestigious experimental works. Yet given the city's proximity to New York, Philadelphia's theater companies can't help partaking in an ongoing identity crisis. This pressure results in two usual consequences: overacting or the drive to create fantastic shows. Either of these results is entertaining in its own way.

### ARDEN Map pp226-7

☎ 215-922-1122; www.ardentheater.org; 40 N 2nd St; tickets $24-40; ☺ box office 10am-6pm Mon-Sat, extended hrs on performance dates; SEPTA 2nd St Station, Bus 48, 57, 76

A slick, modern stage and well-designed seating set the tone for one of the finest theater experiences in Philadelphia. The house holds 360 seats, and even those in the back have an acceptable view. Arden stages wonderful revivals mixed in with ambitious contemporary productions. Expect to see stuff like *Rosencrantz & Guildenstern Are Dead*, *Cafe Puttanesca* or a literary adaptation of *Hard Times*. Arden also does fantastic kids' programming, where you can see shows like *Bunnicula*.

### FREEDOM THEATRE Map pp220-1

☎ 215-765-2793; www.freedomtheatre.org; 1346 N Broad St; tickets $25-30; ☺ box office hrs vary; SEPTA Girard Station, Bus 15

Founded in 1966, this theater stages potent dramas drawing on the African American experience. The annual *Black Nativity* has become a longstanding tradition; other shows include *Kofifi* and *Lazarus, Unstoned*. Freedom Theatre operates out of the mansion of Edwin Forrest (Philly's first celebrity stage actor), which was built back when N Broad St was a center of wealth. Recently renovated, the theater contains 299 seats.

### LAFF HOUSE Map pp228-9

☎ 215-440-4242; www.laffhouse.com; 221 South St; tickets $5-15; ☺ box office noon-6pm Tue, noon-11pm Wed & Thu, noon-midnight Fri & Sat; Bus 12, 40, 57

The only comedy club in Center City, the Laff House is so confident in its acts that there isn't a drink minimum. The club attracts local talents and national performers (the latter sell out early). Recent comedians include Ralph Harris and Mike Brooks, and Wednesday is open mic night. You must be 18 to enter.

### MUM PUPPETTHEATRE Map pp226-7

☎ 215-925-7686; www.mumpuppet.org; 115 Arch St; tickets $25-35; ☺ phone sales 10am-5pm Mon-Fri; SEPTA 2nd St Station, Bus 48, 57, 76

Having won 12 Barrymore Awards for excellence since its founding in 1985, the Mum Puppettheatre is more then just child's play, though such elements certainly factor. Productions here can be dark and otherworldly, beautifully crafted creations of silent fantasy worlds that fully captivate both adults and kids. There's a family series (*The*

*Velveteen Rabbit, Father Goose Tales)* and a more sophisticated evening series *(The Visit, Séance, A Christmas Carol)*. Tickets can be ordered through the website or over the phone; there's no formal box office. Preview shows (only $7) are offered occasionally.

## PIG IRON THEATRE COMPANY
☎ 215-627-1883; www.pigiron.org
Pig Iron combines techniques from silent film, vaudeville and shadow puppetry. Shows are well done, slightly surreal, somewhat intellectual, darkly funny and definitely not to be missed. The company plays in a variety of venues and is a **Fringe Festival** (p26) favorite. Call for a schedule and tickets.

## PLAYS & PLAYERS THEATER Map pp222-3
☎ 215-985-1400 ext 100; www.phillytheatreco.com; 1714 Delancey St; tickets $30-45; ☷ box office hrs vary; SEPTA Lombard-South Station, Bus 2, 40
This charming turn-of-the-century theater sits on a quiet residential street south of Rittenhouse Square. Presently it's home to the Philadelphia Theatre Company, which produces high-end contemporary plays with regional actors. August Wilson, the country's most famous African American playwright, recently opened his *King Hedley II* with the company. Other shows include *Nickel and Dimed, Bunny Bunny* and *Master Class*. World premieres are guaranteed each season. Limited discount tickets are available for students; call to inquire.

## PRINCE MUSIC THEATER Map pp222-3
☎ 215-569-9700; www.princemusictheater.org; 1412 Chestnut St; mainstage tickets $30-48, cabaret tickets $30-35, film tickets adult/student/senior/child $8.50/7/7/5; ☷ box office 10am-6pm Mon-Fri, 10am-5pm Sat, noon-5pm Sun plus 1hr before show time; SEPTA 15th St Station, City Hall Station, Bus 9, 21, 27, 32, 42
This theater stages decent versions of Broadway hits and, as the name suggests, performs musicals, musical comedies and some more artsy fare. The Prince Music Theater also operates an informal cabaret out of its upstairs venue, the Independence Foundation Black Box.

One of the theater's best contributions to Philly's art scene is a film series projected on the largest screen in the city. Numerous classical, historic, bizarre, local and international films, and documentaries are screened here, as are silent films with orchestra accompaniment. A particularly popular event in the film series is

*Release the Bats,* a Dracula film and cultural festival presented with the **Rosenbach Museum** (p73).

## STAGECRAFTERS THEATER Map p231
☎ 215-247-8881; www.thestagecrafters.org; 8130 Germantown Ave; tickets $15; SEPTA R8 Chestnut Hill West, R7 Chestnut Hill East, Bus 23
A house and a Revolution-era smithy were combined and enlarged to make this interesting, barnlike playhouse. The Stagecrafters, a community theater group founded in 1929, perform in the space. They put on about six shows each year, ranging from *Cat on a Hot Tin Roof* to *Arsenic and Old Lace*. In terms of quality of acting and costuming, expect a range that's possible only with a community troupe.

## WALNUT STREET THEATRE Map pp222-3
☎ 215-524-3550; www.wstonline.org; 825 Walnut St; mainstage tickets $40-60, Independence Studio on 3 tickets $24, Theatre for Kids tickets $10-14; ☷ box office 10am-6pm Mon-Sat, extended hrs on performance dates; SEPTA 8th St Station, Bus 9, 21, 42, 47
Don't expect greatness from America's oldest theater's main stage, where you can catch musicals and Broadway numbers such as *Annie*, the *Philadelphia Story* and *Hello Dolly*. Performance quality varies; often actors, directors and sometimes even costumers are second-rate. A plus is that the main theater is small, so you'll be very close to the stage. For mainstage shows, a handful of seats at the rear of the mezzanine cost only $10.

Better results can be had at the theater's **Independence Studio on 3**, which stages experimental productions in an intimate space. For children, the **Theatre for Kids** is a worthwhile stop. Representative performances include *The Little Engine That Could* and *A Christmas Carol*.

Though the building opened in 1806, it's hard to be cognizant of this fact once you enter. A 'renovation' in the 1970s largely ruined the original decor. Ford and Carter held their first presidential debate at the Walnut Street Theater.

## WILMA THEATER Map pp222-3
☎ 215-456-7824; www.wilmatheater.org; 265 S Broad St; tickets $30-48; ☷ box office 10:30am-6pm, extended hrs on performance dates; SEPTA Walnut-Locust Station, Bus 9, 12, 21, 27, 32, 42
A top Philadelphia theater company since the 1970s, Wilma has hosted a number of avant-garde productions. In the fall of 2003

Arthur Miller's *Resurrection Blues* made its East Coast premiere here. Wilma's quality of performance is up and down, though the theater earns big points for consistently doing edgy stuff.

In addition to plays, Wilma also produces a stellar dance series, *Danceboom!*, for a few weeks each winter. It's curated by **Fringe Fest** (p26) guru Nick Stuccio and exposes groundbreaking local performers.

On some Sundays students can buy tickets for $7; call ahead for details. Wilma discourages children under 12 from attending shows.

# DANCE

The city of Philadelphia makes a commendable effort to bring high 'cultcha' to the masses. The three companies listed here are excellent, and dozens of other troupes are intermittently active in the city. Pick up a *City Paper* for listings. Keep your eye on the **Prince Music Theater** (p127), **Kimmel Center** (p129), **Annenberg Center** (p128), **Wilma** (p127), **Arden** (p126) and **Painted Bride** (p63), all of which program dance.

## Tickets & Reservations

Ticket Philadelphia (☎ 215-893-1999; www .ticketphiladelphia.org; 🕑 9am-8pm) offers tickets for events at the Mann Center, Kimmel Center and Academy of Music. There is a service fee of $4.50 per ticket.

### KORESH DANCE COMPANY Map pp222-3
☎ 215-751-0959; www.koreshdance.org; 104 S 20th St; tickets $15-30

Based in Philadelphia and performing only a few times a year, this explosive troupe blends ballet, modern and jazz into a frenetic masterpiece. Don't pass up an opportunity to see them.

### PENNSYLVANIA BALLET
☎ 215-551-7000; www.paballet.org; Broad & Locust Sts; tickets $19-94; 🕑 main box office at Kimmel Center (p000), Academy of Music box office open 2hrs before performance; SEPTA Walnut-Locust Station, Bus 9, 12, 21, 27, 32, 42

Recent shows by this excellent dance company, whose home is the beautiful Academy of Music, include *The Taming of the Shrew*, *Swan Lake*, *Dracula* and *The Nutcracker*. The troupe also hosts the occasional premiere.

### THE PHILADELPHIA DANCE COMPANY
Philadanco!; ☎ 215-893-1999; www.philadanco.org; 9 N Preston St; tickets $20-40; SEPTA Walnut-Locust Station, Bus 9, 12, 21, 27, 32, 42

This 30-something-year-old company provides top-shelf, dizzying exhibitions of grace, strength and movement. Nationally acclaimed Philadanco! uses only the best choreographers, who frequently use modern dance and ballet to explore issues of black experience. Philadanco! is the resident dance company at the Kimmel Center, where it performs for a few days each season.

# OPERA & CLASSICAL MUSIC

Philadelphia is one of the best cities in America to see classical music, not only because of the high caliber of tunes, but also because several of the venues are breathtaking. The Kimmel Center and the Academy of Music are stunning, and since some shows sell out, you may want to purchase tickets in advance.

## Tickets & Reservations

Ticket Philadelphia (☎ 215-893-1999, www .ticketphiladelphia.org; 🕑 9am-8pm) books tickets for events at the Mann Center, Kimmel Center and Academy of Music. There is a $4.50 per ticket service fee.

### ANNENBERG CENTER FOR THE PERFORMING ARTS Map p225
☎ 215-898-3900; www.pennpresents.org; 3680 Walnut St; adult $10-50, discounts available for student & senior; 🕑 box office 10am-6pm Mon-Fri, noon-6pm Sat; SEPTA 36th St Station, Bus 30, 40

A sweet spot to catch theater, dance and music, the Annenberg puts on most of its shows from September through May. The offerings are diverse: depending on the schedule, you might catch a Senegalese percussion orchestra directed by Doudou N'Diaye Rose, '70s rocker Patti Smith giving a lecture and acoustic set, a classical recital, some jazz or a William Shakespeare play. Most Annenberg Center shows occur in one of three performance venues: **Zellerbach Theatre** or **Harold Prince Theatre** (both in the main Annenberg Center building) or the **Irvine Auditorium**

(3401 Spruce St). Depending on availability, student rush tickets are occasionally sold.

## THE CURTIS INSTITUTE OF MUSIC
Map pp222-3

☎ 215-893-7902; 1726 Locust St; www.curtis.edu; opera $30-46, symphony orchestra $5-77, alumni recitals $25, student recitals admission free; SEPTA Walnut-Locust Station, Bus 2, 12, 17

One of the finest music conservatories in the world, the Curtis Institute and its students consistently deliver the goods. The institute accepts only those who demonstrate nearly limitless musical talent; once accepted, each student receives a full-tuition scholarship. The institute's policy of accepting only one applicant per instrument per year fosters an unbelievably competitive admissions process.

Curtis puts on four categories of performance – opera, symphony orchestra, alumni recitals and **student recitals** ( ☎ 215-893-5261; Mon, Wed & Fri during the school year). Because the students choose recital pieces based on the needs of their training, audiences get exposed to stuff beyond the standard Mozart and Brahms.

## THE DELAWARE VALLEY OPERA COMPANY

☎ 215-725-4171; www.libertynet.org/dvoc; Hermit Ln; adult/child $15/7.50; ☯ box office opens 6:30pm on performance dates; Bus 32

Grab a chair, flashlight and picnic basket and head over to the Hermitage mansion in the Wissahickon section of Fairmount Park (p83) to enjoy some fantastically bucolic opera in an outdoor theater-in-the-round during warm months. In the winter, the company moves off the lawn and performs inside the Hermitage. Call or visit the website for directions.

## KIMMEL CENTER FOR THE PERFORMING ARTS Map pp222-3

☎ 215-790-5800; www.kimmelcenter.org; Broad & Spruce Sts; ☯ 10am-6pm, open later performance dates; SEPTA Walnut-Locust Station, Bus 9, 12, 21, 27, 32, 42

Philadelphia's most active center for fine music, the Kimmel Center organizes a vast array of performances. Visit the website or see the Neighborhoods chapter (p51) for more information.

## THE MANN CENTER FOR THE PERFORMING ARTS Map pp220-1

☎ 215-893-1999; www.manncenter.org; 52nd St &

Parkside Ave; tickets $10-130; ☯ 10am-5pm Mon-Sat; Bus 38, 40

A large outdoor performance space, the Mann Center seats 4000 under a pavilion with 10,000 additional seats on a grassy lawn. In addition to being the summer home of the **Philadelphia Orchestra** (p129), the Mann's summer season presents just about everything: a flamenco series, the Mormon Tabernacle Choir, Weird Al Yankovic, filmmaker Spike Lee and his music director, and big-name jazz, rock and blues acts.

## THE OPERA COMPANY OF PHILADELPHIA

☎ 215-893-1999; www.operaphilly.org; Broad & Locust Sts; tickets $7-155; ☯ main box office at Kimmel Center (p129), Academy of Music box office open 2hrs before performance; SEPTA Walnut-Locust Station, Bus 9, 12, 21, 27, 32, 42

Housed in the Academy of Music, Philly's opera company is lucky to perform in such a nice building, especially because this company usually delivers a mediocre performance. They seem to have a tough time getting all four leads to be of similarly high quality, which makes aficionados wince. The opera gives students a 10% discount on advance tickets and a 50% reduction on tickets purchased within two hours of show time.

## THE PHILADELPHIA CHAMBER MUSIC SOCIETY

☎ 215-569-8080; www.philadelphiachambermusic .org; 135 S 18th St; tickets $15-21; main box office at Kimmel Center; SEPTA Walnut-Locust Station, Bus 9, 12, 21, 27, 32, 42

This company programs exceptional chamber ensembles, pianists, jazz players, vocalists, string recitals and special musical attractions for an unbeatable price. The society organizes a busy schedule of world-renowned talent in a range of similarly renowned venues, including the Kimmel Center, **St Mark's Church** (1625 Locust St), the Philadelphia Museum of Art, the Curtis Institute of Music, the Samuel Fleisher Art Memorial and others.

## THE PHILADELPHIA ORCHESTRA

☎ 215-790-5800; www.philorch.org; Broad & Spruce Sts; tickets $10-130; main box office at Kimmel Center; SEPTA Walnut-Locust Station, Bus 9, 12, 21, 27, 32, 42

The city's orchestra, founded in 1900, still plays with polish, and Beethoven and Berg sound sweet at the Kimmel Center, where the orchestra resides. While most of their shows occur here, they also do a summer series at the Mann Center and occasionally revisit their old home in the Academy of Music. Christoph Eschenbach's recent appointment as music director is generating excitement.

At the time of writing, a special was on offer at the Kimmel Center box office: from 5:30pm to 6:30pm before evening subscription concerts and 12:30pm to 1:30pm before 2pm matinees, a ticket anywhere in the house is $10.

# FILM

Center City contains several venues – the most prominent being the three Ritz's – that show arty films. For more popular fare, folks need to head to South Philly, Manayunk or West Philadelphia.

## THE BRIDGE: CINEMA DE LUX

Map p225

☎ 215-386-3300; www.thebridgecinema.com; S 40th St at Walnut St; admission regular/matinee $10/7.25; SEPTA 40th St Station, Bus 21, 30, 40

This new-fangled cinema houses six screens with stadium seating. It also features wireless Internet access, a loungy waiting area seemingly furnished by Ikea and a darkened 'Media Immersion Room' with six plasma screens of vague purpose. There is also a bar, the 12 Lounge, in case you need a little liquid courage before viewing your blockbuster of choice.

### Ssh! It's a Secret Cinema

A beloved grass-roots kind of Philadelphian, film geek Jay Schwartz created an itinerant love-child called **Secret Cinema** (www.users.voicenet.com/~jschwart), whose mission is to retain history's projected images in spite of a cultural shift witnessing the gradual demise of repertory cinema. This translates into Mr Schwartz racing around town with a 16mm projector, stacks of folding chairs and reels of fascinating and bizarre film. In various, not-so-secret locations (some big, some little) throughout the city, Secret Cinema screens teen exploitation flicks, forgotten noir, thematic events like 'The Sugar-Charged Saturday Morning Supershow' featuring those cartoons from the '70s you'd rather not remember, serious documentaries and camp several times a month (since 1992). The website has detailed information; otherwise look for ads in the weekly papers.

## FILM @ INTERNATIONAL HOUSE

Map p225

☎ 215-895-6575; www.ihousephilly.org; 3701 Chestnut St; adult/student $6/5; SEPTA 36th St Station, Bus 21, 30, 40

Multiple times each week during the school year, International House presents some excellent screenings, often thematically organized. This might result in miniature Cuban film festivals (I am Cuba, Goodbye Dear Love), 'French Wednesdays' of contemporary Franco-cinema, and events like 'Masters of International Animation.' Frequently directors and performers are present to talk about their work. For advance tickets, stop by a TLA video store; otherwise just show up before a show.

## RITZ FIVE Map pp226-7

☎ 215-440-1184; www.ritzfilmbill.com; 214 Walnut St; adult/student/senior/matinee $8.50/5.50/5.50/5.50; SEPTA 2nd St Station, Bus 21, 42, 57

The combined 12 screens of the three Ritz theaters – other branches are **Ritz East** (Map pp226-7; ☎ 215-925-2501; 25 S 2nd St; SEPTA 2nd St Station, Bus 21, 42, 57) and **Ritz at the Bourse** (Map pp226-7; ☎ 215-440-1181; 4th & Ranstead Sts; SEPTA 5th St Station) – show independent, art, foreign and mainstream movies in conventional rooms. The sound is decent, the seats are comfortable and kids under six are prohibited. All Wed shows cost $5.50, and the first showings on Sat, Sun and holidays cost $6.

## ROXY THEATER Map pp222-3

☎ 215-923-6699; 2023 Sansom St; tickets $8; 19th St Station, Bus 9, 17, 12, 21, 42

This rickety, two-screen art-house favorite shows classics, cults and any other kinds of film it feels like.

## UNITED ARTISTS MAIN ST 6

☎ 215-482-6230; 3720 Main St; adult/student/senior/matinee $8.50/6/6/6; Bus 35, 61

This giant mother and its sister theater, **United Artists Riverview Plaza 17** ( ☎ 215-755-2353; 1400 S Delaware Ave; Bus 64), show the most popular flicks Hollywood can dish out, and both come with gargantuan parking lots.

# BARS & PUBS

Philly's bars have an unusual relationship with food. Almost every bar, no matter how gross or cool it looks, serves food, and sometimes the line distinguishing a restaurant from a bar gets a bit hazy. Also hazy is the distinction between bar and club. At the moment most bars in town feature DJs at least a couple of nights each week. So that place that looked like a typical Irish watering hole last Tuesday might be chockful of butt shakers on Friday night.

It's hard to say why, but compared to the locals in other American cities like New York and San Francisco, Philadelphians are extra-friendly and outgoing. Congenial conversations with strangers are a regular part of drinking in Philly, especially if you're seated at the bar.

Remember to bring photo identification, because if you look under 30 you will be asked for ID. The strictly enforced drinking age in Pennsylvania is 21. Bars close at 2am.

# OLD CITY

Outside of New Orleans, this neighborhood boasts the highest concentration of liquor licenses in the US, and the following selections represent only a glimpse of what's there. On a warm weekend night, thousands of young people descend on S 2nd and S 3rd Sts, filling every bar and club to capacity. Don't even try to drive a car near the hot spot, or you will get stuck in a gridlock. The scene is a bit bridge-and-tunnel, with about half the crowd commuting in from Jersey and the Philly suburbs.

## ANTHONY'S OLDE CITY PUB

Map pp226-7

☎ 215-922-1954; 226 Market St; 🕓 11:30am-2am; SEPTA 2nd St Station, Bus 17, 21, 33, 42, 76
One day, regular-Joe-style Anthony's woke up, and the city's hottest nightlife had surrounded it. Anthony's responded by completely ignoring this new set of circumstances. Today its booths and mirrors combine to look something like a Burger King dining room.

## BUFFALO BILLIARDS Map pp226-7

☎ 215-574-7665; 118 Chestnut St; table $12/hr; 🕓 11-2am; SEPTA 2nd St Station, Bus 17, 21, 33, 42, 76
Those who want to escape the Euro trends found in the rest of Old City's clubs often head here. It's kind of a jock place, but it's a place where jocks cultivate an appreciation for velour upholstery, at least in the expansive lounge upstairs. There are 10 pool tables in great shape, three dartboards and big TVs

playing sports. There's no satellite, so the only games shown are local.

## EULOGY BELGIAN TAVERN Map pp226-7

☎ 215-413-2354; 136 Chestnut St; 🕓 11am-2am; SEPTA 2nd St Station, Bus 17, 21, 33, 42, 76
Full of yellow paint, brass and reddish-stained chairs, Eulogy presents a warm picture on a chilly day. It also presents one of the most laid-back scenes in Old City, which is perhaps surprising since one of the owners used to be a 'Real World' star. As the name suggests, there's a good selection of Belgian beer.

## GLAM Map pp226-7

☎ 267-671-0840; 52 S 2nd St; 🕓 5pm-2am; SEPTA 2nd St Station, Bus 17, 21, 33, 42, 76
This snazzy club attracts boatloads of well-dressed African Americans, including basketball superstar Allen Iverson. Glam is glamorous, with plenty of pink neon, dramatically lit bottles of booze, cool metal finish, a disco ball and VIPs arriving in extravagant cars and limousines.

## IL BAR Map pp226-7

☎ 215-922-7800; 14 N Front St; 🕓 5:30-10pm Mon-Thu, 5:30-11pm Fri & Sat, 5-9pm Sun; SEPTA 2nd St Station, Bus 25, 48, 57, 76
Find one of the world's largest wine-preservation systems at the bar of this restaurant, where you can order by the glass from more then 120 varieties.

## PLOUGH AND STARS Map pp226-7

☎ 215-733-0300; 123 Chestnut St; 🕓 11:30am-2am; SEPTA 2nd St Station, Bus 17, 21, 33, 42, 76
A lot of the bridal parties that drunkenly

Entertainment – Bars & Pubs

traipse through Old City on weekend nights begin their evenings in this big Irish place before setting their eyes on more urbane dance floors elsewhere. Anticipate plenty of Guinness, the usual Irish touches and some gussied-up shepherd's pie.

### THIRTY TWO Map pp226-7
☎ 215-627-3132; www.32lounge.com; 12 S 2nd St; ☽ 6pm-2am; SEPTA 2nd St Station, Bus 17, 21, 33, 42, 76

Thirty Two made a splash on the Old City scene when it began offering European bottle service. Long and narrow, Thirty Two tries in vain to accommodate the weekend crowds of 20-somethings squeezing into the bar. Some think their best and tremendously expensive bet is to book a table in the VIP lounge, where they have slightly more space to bust it to whatever the DJ is spinning.

# CENTER CITY
Philadelphia's oldest bars lie throughout the streets and alleys of Center City. As this is a big place, we've broken it down into more manageable neighborhoods: Avenue of the Arts, Rittenhouse Square, Washington Square, and the Parkway and Museum Area.

# Avenue of the Arts
Along Broad St and around corners, the following bars present theatergoers with good options for pre- and post-show decadence.

### FRANK CLEMENT'S TAVERN Map pp222-3
☎ 215-568-3131; 1421 Sansom St; ☽ 11am-2am; SEPTA 15th St Station, City Hall Station, 9, 12, 21, 27, 32, 42

A smoky, dark and cluttered place, this tavern attracts almost all the city's trial lawyers and judges. It's kind of like a movie set, and in fact, was recently used to film an episode of Hack.

### LIBRARY LOUNGE Map pp222-3
☎ 215-893-1776; Broad St at Walnut St; bar food $12-15; ☽ 3pm-midnight; SEPTA Walnut-Locust Station, Bus 9, 12, 21, 27, 32, 42

The underused drinking and smoking lounge on the 19th floor of the Bellevue is aggressively Anglophile in character. It struts its stuff with the darkest possible wood, shelves of books, leather upholstered chairs, classical-style

marble busts and a fireplace that burns actual wood. Fittingly, a good selection of scotches and cigars is sold, but prices are a bit inflated. Library Lounge is very small for a hotel bar and would be exceptionally cozy were it not for the hideously out-of-character television yapping over the barman.

### MCGILLIN'S Map pp222-3
☎ 215-735-5562; 1310 Drury St; ☽ 11am-2am Mon-Sat; SEPTA 13th St Station, Bus 9, 12, 21, 27, 32, 42

Philadelphia's oldest continually operated tavern displays framed copies of all its liquor licenses behind the bar with empty spaces for the Prohibition years (it remained open as a speakeasy). Despite its illustrious history, McGillin's is used more by regulars than tourists. An older lunch crowd fills it up during the day, with younger bucks arriving at night. Watch out for St Patrick's Day, when entry is next to impossible.

# Rittenhouse Square
Not long ago, there was no nightlife in Rittenhouse Square. Now the following bars, along with Loie (p142), give stylish boys and girls a reason to dry-clean their designer clothes. Most of the action takes place north and east of the square.

### THE BARDS Map pp222-3
☎ 215-569-9585; 2013 Sansom St; bar food $9; ☽ 11:30am-2am; SEPTA 19th St Station, Bus 9, 12, 17, 21, 42

Its location next to a new place that unsubtly calls itself The Irish Pub makes the Bards appear more legitimately Irish than it otherwise might. The place is a must for anyone interested in indoor thatched roofs and decorative black kettles pretending to cook in a fireplace lit with red lights. Fish and chips as well as shepherd's pie are served.

### BAR NOIR Map pp222-3
☎ 215-569-9333; 112 S 18th St; ☽ 5pm-2am; SEPTA 19th St Station, Bus 2, 9, 12, 21, 42, 76

Appropriately housed in a cellar below street level, the popular Bar Noir is really two places. Before 10pm it's a tame neighborhood bar where you can grab a decent bite to eat. By midnight things change, and it feels like Pennsylvania's entire population has crammed itself into the bar, while the entire population of New Jersey stands in line outside. The closer it gets to 2am, the more exciting it is to be inside. A Philly institution since the punk '70s, Bobby Startup is the talented DJ.

## DENIM Map pp222-3

☎ 215-735-6700; 1712 Walnut St; cover $10; ⏰ 5:30pm-2am Wed-Sat; SEPTA Walnut-Locust Station, Bus 2, 9, 12, 42

Loved and hated, Denim comes packed with its own brand of elitist attitude. When it starts to get busy, a line forms outside. Those in the know get admitted quickly; others might be in for a long wait (show up early to avoid this fate). If you manage to get inside, you'll find a swanky lounge and a pretentious VIP space.

## L'HEXAGONE Map pp222-3

☎ 215-569-4869; 1718 Sansom St; ⏰ 11am-2am Tue-Sun; SEPTA Walnut-Locust Station, Bus 2, 9, 12, 42

This slick bar, whose owner and patrons want very much for it to be a dance club, is a bit small to comfortably accommodate the bodies, typically clad in Euro-fashion, attempting to gyrate to the DJ of the evening. Through the crowd, which begins to thicken around 10:30pm, see polished metal furniture with wood accents. During the day, L'Hexagone serves lunch from 11am to 2pm.

## MONK'S CAFE Map pp222-3

☎ 215-545-7005; 264 S 16th St; bar food $9-15, beer $3.50-25; ⏰ 11:30am-2am; SEPTA Lombard-South St Station, Bus 2, 27, 32, 40

The Monk's Cafe debuts more beer than any other place in the US. The place takes beer so seriously that it publishes a multiple-page 'Beer Bible' (that you can purchase) to accompany and explain its extensive menu of more than 200 brews. Each beer is served at an appropriate temperature and in an appropriately shaped glass. The Trappist leanings of the beer menu match the medieval decor, which includes broad beams overhead, low ceilings and wall-mounted tapestries. In terms of food, token vegan items make an appearance on the bar menu, as does rabbit terrine. Huzzah!

## NODDING HEAD BREWERY & RESTAURANT Map pp222-3

☎ 215-569-9525; 1516 Sansom St; ⏰ 11am-2am; SEPTA 15th St Station, Bus 9, 12, 21, 27, 32, 42

This microbrewery turns out a changing selection of well-crafted beers and, compared with the other bars in the neighborhood, doesn't get deafeningly loud or overly

crowded on weekends. The pub menu includes vegan burgers and stew, nonvegan BBQ ribs and spicy mussels.

# Washington Square West

Lovers of dive bars love this section of town. Washington Square is home to some long-term favorites, especially Dirty Franks and McGlinchey's. This district also contains the Gayborhood, whose nine blocks house most of the city's gay bars and clubs. The north and south boundaries of the Gayborhood are Walnut and Pine Sts. The east and west boundaries are 11th and Broad Sts.

## BIKE STOP Map pp222-3

☎ 215-627-1662; www.thebikestop.com; 206 S Quince St; ⏰ 11am-2am; SEPTA Walnut-Locust Station, Bus 9, 12, 21, 23, 42

Though it shoots for the bad-ass leather-daddy theme, most of the guys and bears who hang here are pretty welcoming. More often than not, Monday's jockstrap night is all about older dudes talking about gardening while hanging in a jock. On weekends, the four floors thump with DJs.

## BUMP Map pp222-3

☎ 215-732-1800; 1234 Locust St; ⏰ 5pm-2am; SEPTA Walnut-Locust Station, Bus 9, 12, 21, 23, 42

Design-school geometric patterns, slick lights and smooth open spaces give swanky Bump and the boys who hang here big style points. No guarantees about the longevity of this drink special, but this gay favorite serves a mean $3 martini from 9pm to 11pm nightly. Should that fantastic deal vanish, fear not: there's always the 'beef and drag' brunch on Sundays, which is pretty self-explanatory.

## DIRTY FRANK'S Map pp222-3

☎ 215-732-5010; 347 S 13th St; ⏰ 11am-2am Mon-Sat; Lombard-South Station, Bus 23, 40

A dingy dive bar favored by art students, this dark hole eases sorrows with sweet beer. Sit at the rectangular bar or in a booth. In the back, find the classic video game Ms Pac-Man; the well-used machine is in excellent condition.

## DR WATSON'S PUB Map pp222-3

☎ 215-922-3427; 216 S 11th St; upstairs cover $5-10; ⏰ 11am-2am; SEPTA 11 St Station, Walnut-Locust Station, Bus 9, 12, 21, 23, 42

This pub has reinvented itself on the merits of

two chicks who book music (rock, bluegrass, miscellany) on Friday and Saturday night (we don't vouch for quality on other evenings). A visit to this bar is like going to two distinct places. The 1st floor looks and feels like a mildly grim neighborhood bar full of fraternity brothers. Walk upstairs to find a pool table and a cramped performance area full of misguided youths with tasseled hair.

### FERGIE'S PUB Map pp222-3

☎ 215-928-8118; www.fergies.com; 1214 Sansom St; 🕙 11am-2am Mon-Sat, 5pm-2am Sun; SEPTA Walnut-Locust Station, Bus 9, 12, 21, 23, 42

This cozy Irish place tries hard to be an authentic pub, and the effort pays off. During the day, the main room has a nice draw of conversational types. During nights, there might be pub quizzes, Irish music or big weekend crowds. There's a firm 'no TV' policy.

### LOCUST BAR Map pp222-3

☎ 215-627-8550; S 10th & Locust Sts; 🕙 11:30am-2am; SEPTA Walnut-Locust Station 12, 23

A haven for nearby Thomas Jefferson University students, the Locust Bar attracts a mixture of medical students, regular Joes and cool kids. The place has the look of a dive bar minus the edginess created by the possibility of danger. Sunday is karaoke night.

### LUDWIG'S GARTEN Map pp222-3

☎ 215-985-1525; 1315 Sansom St; 🕙 11am-2am; SEPTA Walnut-Locust Station, Bus 9, 12, 21, 23, 42

Feast on spätzle and schnitzel at this tavern, Philadelphia's Oktoberfest epicenter. There's an outstanding selection of beer, a stuffed game head and some unfortunate waitresses wearing 'traditional' breast-enhancing German garb.

### MCGLINCHEY'S Map pp222-3

☎ 215-735-1259; 259 S 15th St; 🕙 10am-2am; SEPTA Walnut-Locust Station, Bus 9, 12, 27, 32

The price of a mug of porter remains the same for more than 11 years: $1.45. For this and other reasons, many find this dark and smoky dive to be Center City's finest asset. The rectangular bar, lined with stools, provides ample opportunity to stare at patrons seated opposite. Additional seating comes in the form of small tables.

### MORIARTY'S Map p222-3

☎ 215-627-7676; 1116 Walnut St; bar food $6-9; 🕙 11am-2am; SEPTA 11th St Station, Bus 9, 12, 21, 23, 42

This popular pub is covered in old taps, bottles, posters, and framed photos of former good times. The huge menu lists tons of snacks, sandwiches, bar food, Mexican specialties and elaborate drinks. Most of the slightly dim lighting emerges from old brass fixtures.

### SISTERS Map pp222-3

☎ 215-735-0735; 1320 Chancellor St; 🕙 5pm-2am Mon-Sat, noon-2am Sun; SEPTA Walnut-Locust Station, Bus 9, 12, 21, 23, 32, 42

Philadelphia's only lesbian bar, Sisters provides a floor to shake some tail and some tables to shoot some stick. The club serves food, including particularly cheap burgers and a Sunday brunch.

### TAVERN ON CAMAC Map pp222-3

☎ 215-545-0900; 243 S Camac St; 🕙 noon-2am Mon-Fri, 4pm-2am Sat & Sun; SEPTA Walnut-Locust Station, Bus 9, 12, 21, 23, 32, 42

Thought to be Philadelphia's oldest gay bar, Tavern on Camac attracts patrons through the merits of its active piano. Any day of the week, expect to hear show tunes and Broadway numbers, with the possibility of an infectious sing-along on busy weekend nights. Upstairs is host to dancing, cabarets and DJs. In the basement from Tuesday through Sunday, a subterranean pub serves conventional American entrées.

## Parkway & Museum Area

If Eastern State Penitentiary gave you the shakes, calm your nerves at these spots.

### BISHOP'S COLLAR Map pp222-3

☎ 215-745-1616; 2349 Fairmount Ave; 🕙 11am-2am; Bus 7, 48

The name refers to the look of a freshly poured Guinness, which is the favorite drink at this casual Irish tavern that offers sidewalk seating in nice weather. Their veggie burger tastes great.

### JACK'S FIREHOUSE Map pp222-3

☎ 215-232-9000; 2130 Fairmount Ave; 🕙 11am-2am; Bus 7, 33, 48

You can sit at a pretty wooden bar in this old firehouse converted into a bar and restaurant, and stare at the grim walls of **Eastern State Penitentiary** (p76) across the street. The setting is unique; the food is not.

# SOUTH STREET & AROUND

The bars along and around Philly's counter-cultural thoroughfare provide some quality options.

### ARTFUL DODGER Map pp228-9
☎ 215-922-7880; 400 S 2nd St; ☾ 11am-2am; Bus 12, 40, 57

Knock back a few Newcastles at this cozy, wood-paneled tavern. Attached is a small dining room, where acoustic bands play on some evenings.

### BOB & BARBARA'S Map pp222-3
☎ 215-545-4511; 1509 South St; ☾ 3pm-2am; SEPTA Lombard-South Station, Bus 2, 27, 32, 40

Just about every sexual orientation known to humankind packs into this seedy-looking bar for an immensely popular low-budget drag show on Thursdays. It's easy to make friends in the long bathroom line. Other nights, check out Nate Wiley and the Crowd Pleasers, an ancient jazz band populated by some oldsters who like to flirt with the younger ladies in attendance. Tuesday is Philly's best Ping-Pong night. In the bar you'll find cheap tables, brown industrial carpeting, walls covered in Pabst posters and neon signs, and almost everyone drinking canned Pabst Blue Ribbon.

### DOWNEY'S Map pp228-9
☎ 215-625-9500; 526 Front St; ☾ 11:30am-2am; Bus 12, 40, 57

Downey's is a large Irish place with turn-of-the-century furnishings imported from the old country. Its walls – and there's a lot of surface area to cover – are jam-packed with Celtic-inspired memorabilia. There's decent food (dinner 5-10pm, bar food until closing) and a rooftop deck and balcony overlooking the Delaware River. A guy wearing black is likely to bang at the ivories on weekends.

### NEW WAVE CAFÉ Map pp228-9
☎ 215-922-8484; 784 S 3rd St; mains $7-15; ☾ noon-2am; Bus 12, 40, 57

This bar continually recruits top chefs to oversee its kitchen. So while the place looks like nothing special, the stuff that emerges from the back assuredly is. It's weird to have such a great salad in so noisy and ugly a bar.

### O'NEAL'S Map pp228-9
☎ 215-574-9595; 3rd & South Sts; ☾ 11am-2am; Bus 12, 40, 57

Expect to find this small pub packed with vocal Eagles fans during any Birds game. O'Neal's has six televisions, a satellite connection and a huge number of microbrews. Plus, it's hard for a place to go wrong when it's got such a lovable bartender.

### TATTOOED MOM'S Map pp228-9
☎ 215-238-9880; 530 South St; ☾ 11am-2am; Bus 12, 40, 57

The upstairs portion of this two-story bar is the preferred South Street hangout for guys with metal disks in their ears, white girls with dreadlocks and dirty pants, and those with enough tattoos to justify the existence of all the parlors around the corner. The walls are completely covered in graffiti, and a few derelict bumper cars sit around to complete the look. Oh yeah, and the hardcore – and *Pixies* – playing jukebox is loud.

## SOUTH PHILADELPHIA

As you might expect, beer often serves as a necessary chaser following a cheese steak binge. Knowing this, South Philly delivers the goods at the following places.

### LOW BAR Map pp228-9
☎ 215-465-5505; 947 E Passyunk Ave; ☾ 5pm-2am; Bus 23, 47

A bar has operated out of this spot for a long, long time, though under a different name. Today ownership has passed to some trendy youths who retained the dirty, divey interior and pour tall, cheap drinks – a glass of Makers Mark the size of a double is $3.50. And that's not even happy hour! Occasionaly the beer hosts a heavy-metal karaoke for all those Scorpions fans out there.

### PHILADIUM TAVERN Map pp220-1
☎ 215-271-5520; 1631 Packer Ave; ☾ 11am-2am; SEPTA Pattison Stadium Station, Bus 23

Personally recommended by the Philly Phanatic himself, this small tavern has been a favorite of local sports fans for several decades. It's older then most sports bars, as evidenced by the age of some of the memorabilia on the walls. The kitchen serves a decent chicken parm sandwich.

### ROYAL TAVERN Map pp228-9
☎ 215-389-6694; 937 E Passyunk Ave; ☾ 5pm-2am Mon-Fri, 11am-2am Sat & Sun; Bus 23, 47

Young urban professionals really dig this tavern because it's pretty mellow and serves some quality food until 1am. Due to some unfortunate acoustics, it gets deafeningly loud when busy. (This is an amazing feat, since the jukebox's volume isn't cranked and there's no live music).

# NORTHERN LIBERTIES

Most of Northern Liberties' bars sit near a stretch of N 2nd St that looks vaguely an old cowboy town from the American West. The oldest bar is Liberties, while the Standard Tap and 700 Club are largely credited with jump-starting the neighborhood's march toward cool. Check out The Fire (p140), which operates a great bar in addition to its live music enterprise.

### 700 CLUB Map p230
☎ 215-386-3408; 700 N 2nd St; ☽ 3:30pm-2am Mon-Sat; Bus 57

This is one of the places that helped to establish Northern Liberties as a hip destination, where tattooed bartenders play the latest in trendy music from behind a bar partially made of frosted glass backlit with colored lights. DJs spin in the small upstairs lounge (p141) every night but Sunday.

### ABBAYE Map p230
☎ 215-627-6711; 637 N 3rd St; ☽ 11:30am-2am; Bus 57

If you're feeling a bit Flemish, head over to the Abbaye, which stocks a wide selection of Belgium beers as well as double- and triple-fermented brews from other countries.

### LIBERTIES Map p230
☎ 215-238-0660; 705 N 2nd St; ☽ 5pm-2am; Bus 57

An older crowd has been hanging at this bar since long before the neighborhood became fashionable. Though the inside has been renovated recently, the digs still look like they haven't changed much since 1925. Here you can drink under an ornamented, lofty ceiling at a long wooden bar and receive pours from bartenders who know a thing or two about the way things were. Cheap pub food is served (hot Buffalo wings are $4.95).

### MINISTRY OF INFORMATION Map p230
☎ 215-925-0999; 447 Poplar St; ☽ 5pm-2am Mon-Sat; Bus 57

It's useful to know that this spot was once a neighborhood bar called the J&B, 'cause the hipsters who now run it haven't changed a thing inside, and they certainly haven't added a sign out front with the new name. Look forward to cheap drinks and a chill place full of chill people.

### STANDARD TAP Map p230
☎ 215-238-0630; 901 N 2nd St; mains $8-20; ☽ 4pm-2am, kitchen 5pm-1am; Bus 57

This proper dimly lit pub is made with plenty of dark wood and has two floors, the second of which features a working fireplace. The tavern serves well-prepared burgers with marinated mushrooms, a cheap fried flounder sandwich and other good stuff. Draught beer, most of which is brewed in the Pennsylvania vicinity, comes from both conventional and hand-pumped taps. Refreshingly, the only racket you'll hear is the band, or a selection from the fantastic jukebox – there are no TV sets whatsoever. All this and noise isn't a problem? You just might have to come here more than once.

# UNIVERSITY CITY & WEST PHILADELPHIA

The fellas at Trophy Bikes (p146) will correctly tell you that it's pretty easy to crash a frat party during the fall semester rush, so

## Gay & Lesbian Venues

Most of Philadelphia's gay and lesbian options fall within the Gayborhood, a small neighborhood that lies between Broad and 12th Sts and Walnut and Pine Sts.

- **12th St Air Command** (p142) A large place with several dance floors and pinball machines
- **Bike Stop** (p133) This is the place for those who like bears and leather daddies.
- **Bob & Barbara's** (p135) Thursday night's drag show attracts an amazing crowd.
- **Bump** (p133) If you brought nice duds, wear them to this swanky place.
- **Shampoo** (p143) Every week Shampoo hosts a gay event unambiguously titled 'Shaft Friday.'
- **Sisters** (p134) This one's for the ladies.
- **Tavern on Camac** (p134) Sometimes all a fella needs is a comfortable bar and some show tunes.
- **Woody's** (p143) Philly's most famous gay club

long as you look reasonably young. For those who are respectful that such an option exists but too horrified to actually participate, there are several bars around Penn worth attending.

### CAVANAUGH'S Map p225
☎ 215-396-4889; S 39th & Sansom Sts; ⏲ 11am-2am, closed Sun mid-Jun–Aug; SEPTA 40th St Station, Bus 30, 40

Easily the best place in the city to watch college football, Cavanaugh's hooks up patrons with dozens of televisions. Since the bar has a satellite connection, it shows almost every sporting event possible. During big tournaments, the sets are labeled in advance so you can figure out where to sit. Tip: don't root against Penn, lest a flurry of backwards-turned baseball caps descend upon you in a perfectly curved rage.

### CHERRY TREE INN Map p225
☎ 215-386-1444; 4540 Baltimore Ave; ⏲ 10am-2pm; Bus 34

This unpretentious bar is a neighborhood favorite. It's small and narrow with a long, well-worn counter. Aside from being a good bar that isn't overrun with students, there's an Ethiopian restaurant, positioned upstairs from the bar, called Gojjo.

### FIUME Map p225
229 S 45th St; ⏲ 6pm-2am; SEPTA 46th St Station, Bus 21, 42

King of all holes-in-the-wall (there's not even a telephone), this undecorated place has eight stools at its 4ft bar, no taps and four or so small tables. It's on the floor above the Abyssinia Ethiopian Restaurant (which has a bigger, less interesting bar as well as cheap food). To find Fiume, enter on Locust St under the sign that says 'restaurant entrance' and head straight up the stairs to the 2nd floor. You want the place that looks like a bedroom that's been converted into a bar. On some evenings acoustic bands shoehorn themselves into a bay window.

### NEW DECK TAVERN Map p225
☎ 215-386-3408; 3408 Sansom St; ⏲ 11am-2am; SEPTA 34th St Station, 21, 30, 42

Popular with students, this Irish American bar first opened in 1933. The oldie interior is packed with worn brick arches, chipped mortar and plenty of mahogany. The huge

menu looks similar to that of a Chili's or other such national chain. Bands play on weekends.

### SMOKEY JOE'S Map p225
☎ 215- 222-0770; 210 S 40th St; ⏲ 11am-2am; SEPTA 40th St Station, Bus 30, 40

Penn's perennial undergraduate bar, this rah-rah place is completely covered with old photos of college athletics. It can be quiet on weeknights. Overheard: crossbar analysis of the *Peanuts* (Charles Schulz) greatest hits and misses. All agreed 'Peanuts' is a dumb name.

# MANAYUNK
By day Manayunk is a cute main-street community situated next to a historic canal. By night students bored with University City flock to the little village's numerous bars. Don't overlook Castle Roxx (p140), a bar that offers live music.

### THE BAYOU BAR & GRILL Map p230
☎ 215-482-2560; 4245 Main St; bar food $5-8; ⏲ 11am-2am; R6 Manayunk Station, Bus 35, 61

It might seem far-fetched to believe that a Mardi Gras–style crowd (we refer to volume and enthusiasm, but not to the costumes and decor) could successfully be re-created weeknight after weeknight, but somehow the folks at the Bayou manage to do it – and to attract enormous throngs of young revelers to their two-story place at very unlikely times. On weekends the impressive scene amplifies to ridiculous levels: it's virtually impossible to push through the crowd, and forget about trying to order anything to eat (too bad for you, 'cause the Cajun catfish sandwich goes pretty good with a beer).

### CRESSON INN Map p230
Gay & Cresson Sts; bag of chips 75¢; ⏲ 11am-2am; SEPTA R6 Manayunk Station, Bus 35, 61

A grumpy sign out front proclaims that this is 'where the "real" Yunkers drink.' One of the 'Yunkers' drinking inside must be a sales rep for a company making faux-wood paneling, because there's about six different (mismatched) kinds mounted lazily on all kinds of surfaces. One makes an appearance on top of the bar while another is attached to the base of the bar. The bar has two separate kinds of fake wainscoting.

## MANAYUNK BREWERY & RESTAURANT Map p230

☎ 215-482-8220; www.manayunkbrewery.com; 4120 Main St; bar food $7-9; ⊙ 11am-2am, bar food 5-11pm Tue-Thu & 5-11pm Fri & Sat; SEPTA R6 Manayunk Station, Bus 35, 61

This large place was formerly one of Manayunk's many textile mills. Today it serves some pretty good brews and has an excellent outdoor seating area a few feet from the bank of the canal that once serviced the mill. The cavernous interior holds three separate bars and attracts a frat-boy/sorority-girl kind of crowd. Live music is played many nights, and an 'adult' magician makes the rounds on Friday and Saturday early-evenings.

## PITCHER'S PUB Map p230

☎ 215-482-2269; 4328 Main St; bar food $4-6; ⊙ noon-2am; SEPTA R6 Manayunk Station, Bus 35, 61

Nearly every possible surface of this narrow bar is packed with neon signs, gaudy ads for popular American beer and sporting memorabilia. So why not have a Yuengling or a Coors Light, bask in the glow of one of many TVs, and watch the Eagles, Phils or Sixers take on whatever chumps they might be facing? You'll have plenty of male company and a racially mixed crowd, plus maybe even a dollar-drinks special.

## US HOTEL Map p230

☎ 215-483-9222; 4439 Main St; bar food $8-10, dinner mains $17-19; ⊙ 11am-2am, dinner 5-10pm Sun-Wed, 5-11pm Thu-Sat; SEPTA R6 Manayunk Station, Bus 35, 61

For a while, this 1903 bar was the only attraction on Main St. Though the Manayunk scene has undergone great change through its emergence as a center for nightlife, the US Hotel remains nearly the same. They took out the trough that the fellas used to pee into, and ladies no longer enter through the back. Even so, the locking drawers to which gunslingers would have relinquished their arms are still present, as is the original ceiling and marble floor. Nowadays the chef makes a mean mixed green, pear and goat cheese salad.

## CHESTNUT HILL

While most of the nightlife in sleepy Chestnut Hill is confined to the restaurants that line Germantown Ave, the area does have a few bars worth checking out.

## MCNALLY'S TAVERN Map p231

☎ 215-247-9736; 8634 Germantown Ave; ⊙ 11:30am-11:30pm Mon-Sat, noon-8pm Sun; SEPTA R8 Chestnut Hill West, R7 Chestnut Hill East, Bus 23

McNally's got its start in 1921 as a Prohibition-era tavern, largely because Mr McNally, a trolley car operator, was irritated that there was no good place in Chestnut Hill (the end of his line) to grab lunch. Today McNally's has a ton of pewter mugs hanging from the ceiling and a few claims to fame. One of them is a legendary sandwich called the Schmitter ($5.25) – a cheese steak with extra cheese, fried onion, tomato and a secret homemade dressing. Another is that McNally's was one of the first taverns in Philadelphia to serve African Americans. Pints come in Imperial sizes and smoking is not allowed.

## TOWEY'S TAVERN Map p231

☎ 215-247-4532; 7829 Germantown Ave; ⊙ 11am-2am; SEPTA R8 Chestnut Hill West, R7 Chestnut Hill East, Bus 23

Contractors, construction workers and guys sporting black eyes seem to prefer Towey's to the other bars in town. This is definitely a diamond in the rough, or maybe just a pile of rough. The men's room is clean, but you have to do all of your business in front of other guys. There's a pool table, a pinball machine and one of Philly's best cheese steaks. It costs a ridiculously low $3, but is served only from 11am to 2pm.

# LIVE MUSIC

Philly gives you plenty of incentive to pack ear plugs in your luggage.

## Tickets & Reservations

You can purchase tickets to most major events through Ticketmaster (☎ 215-336-2000; www.ticketmaster.com). Alternatively, drop by Sherry Ticket Office.

## SHERRY TICKET OFFICE Map pp222-3

☎ 215-561-5544; 146 S 15th St; ⊙ 11am-5pm Mon-Sat; SEPTA 15th St Station, Bus 9, 21, 42, 27, 32

This operation sells tickets to professional sporting events and performances at the Tweeter Center, Mann Music Center, Wachovia Center, First Union Spectrum, Lincoln Financial Field, Citizen's Bank Park and Tower Theater.

# JAZZ, BLUES & FOLK

The town that fostered Dizzy Gillespie, John Coltrane and Grover Washington Jr is still going strong. Some of Philly's most interesting clubs specialize in jazz. It's not every day you can see great bands jam under the massive taxidermied head of a buffalo, whose head flirtatiously peers toward his club's entrance, as at Ortlieb's Jazzhaus. Try to avoid making eye contact. It's impossible.

Aside from these listings, check out the schedule at the **Kimmel Center** (p129).

## CHRIS' JAZZ CLUB Map pp222-3
☎ 215-568-3131; 1421 Sansom St; cover $5-10; ☽ 11am-2am Mon-Sat; SEPTA Walnut-Locust Station, Bus 9, 12, 21, 27, 42

Showcasing local talent along with national greats, Chris' Jazz Club features a 4pm piano happy hour Tuesday through Friday with free hors d'oeuvres, and good bands Monday through Saturday nights. The space is intimate, and parking rates across the street at the Union League get reduced after 7pm. For a club, Chris' has an admirable dinner menu. As if the owner signed a special pact with the city, the stretch of Sansom St that the club occupies remains appropriately dingy for a jazz house, even in the face of new development nearby. Nevertheless Nicolas Cage recently caught a show here.

## CLEF CLUB OF PHILADELPHIA
Map pp222-3
☎ 215-893-9912; www.clefclubofjazz.8m.com; 736 S Broad St; ☽ hrs vary; Bus 27, 32, 63

One of Philadelphia's most historically important institutions, the Clef Club, established in 1966, evolved out of the Local 274, a black musicians' union formed in 1935 when racism and segregation prohibited African Americans from joining the city's other union for musicians. The unbelievable membership log includes greats such as John Coltrane, Dizzy Gillespie, 'Philly' Joe Jones and Grover Washington Jr. There are several jazz and blues performances each month.

## ORTLIEB'S JAZZHAUS Map p230
☎ 215-922-1035; 847 N 3rd St; occasional cover $5; ☽ 5pm-2am, shows 8pm-midnight; Bus 6, 57

Once a ramshackle lunchroom for the Ortieb brewery (that boarded-up, bombed-out old factory next door), Ortlieb's hasn't changed much of the original decor. The club kept the stuffed buffalo head and the lunchroom's Bavarian appearance, and added a jazz lineup that's among the most respected in town. The Tuesday house band has a stellar reputation. Ortlieb's also maintains a respectable dining room.

## TIN ANGEL Map pp226-7
☎ 215-928-0978; www.tinangel.com; 20 S 2nd St; cover $8-25; ☽ 6pm-2am; SEPTA 2nd St Station, Bus 17, 21, 33, 42, 76

This spot draws top-flight folk, soul and blues performers, such as Odetta, members of the Buena Vista Social Club, Dar Williams and Lloyd Cole. Located above the Serrano restaurant, Tin Angel is an intimate café environment where you can chill out, have a coffee, wine or dessert, and be impressed.

## TRITONE Map pp222-3
☎ 215-545-0475; 1508 South St; cover free-$10; ☽ 5pm-2am; SEPTA Lombard-South Station, Bus 2, 27, 32, 40

This bar offers down-and-dirty jazz, DJs and free jukebox nights – and pours some stiff drinks. Check out a weekly paper to see what's on.

## WARMDADDY'S Map pp226-7
☎ 215-413-2354; www.warmdaddys.com; 4 S Front St; ☽ 5:30pm-1am Tue-Sat, 3pm-midnight Sun; SEPTA 2nd St Station, Bus 17, 21, 33, 42, 76

A blues and gospel dinner club, Warmdaddy's slings spicy ribs, crispy fried chicken and fish in its Southern kitchen, while noisy down-home bands set the tone. Sundays are usually gospel, Tuesdays feature an open blues jam, and the rest of the week varies depending on the schedule of events. Consult the website for show times.

## ZANZIBAR BLUE Map pp222-3
☎ 215-732-4500; www.zanzibarblue.com; 200 S Broad St; cover $5-30; ☽ 5pm-2am; SEPTA Walnut-Locust Station, Bus 9, 12, 21, 27, 32, 42

While some jazz clubs charm us through their gritty patina, Zanzibar Blue woos with class and elegance. With an upscale dining room and bar filled with attentive listeners, it's no wonder that Nancy Wilson, Chick Corea and Chuck Mangione call it home. Usually national acts play on weekends and local bands perform weekdays. Either way, there's jazz seven nights a week.

# INDIE & ROCK

Philly's rock clubs range from dirty pits to massive stadiums with expensive nosebleed seats. Not all of the following clubs are exclusively about rock; at the smaller venues you may also catch hip-hop or spoken word. **Fiume** (p137), one of West Philadelphia's bars, occasionally hosts tiny shows. **Dr Watson's Pub** (p133), in the Washington Square District, does good weekend events.

## CASTLE ROXX Map p230

☎ 215-669-7406; 105 Shurs Lane; ⏰ 11am-2am; SEPTA R6 Manayunk Station, Bus 35, 61

At first, this place seems like your average slightly upscale wooden bar, until you start noticing some details. For example, there's a giant, incongruous china vase behind the counter, the mirrors in the bathrooms are designed to look like medieval coats of arms and the exterior has been done up to look like a castle. Blues, funk and rock bands play here throughout the week.

## ELECTRIC FACTORY Map pp222-3

☎ 215-336-2000; 421 N 7th St; tickets $15-40; ⏰ box office noon-6pm Mon-Sat; SEPTA Chinatown Station, Bus 47

This Clear Channel venue books big acts (Something Corporate, Rancid, Insane Clown Posse, Cake, Liz Phair), but it really needs to revamp the awful sound system.

## THE FIRE Map p230

☎ 267-671-9298; 412 W Girard Ave; music cover $5; ⏰ 5pm-2am; Bus 43, 57

With Schmitt's on tap and one of Philly's most engaging barmen, it's hard to have a bad time in this narrow, dingy place. One side is a watering hole (where there is no cover to drink) and the other is a music venue. The extraordinary The Trouble with Sweeney have been known to rock it up in this tiny room.

## GRAPE ST PUB Map p230

☎ 215-483-7084; 105 Grape St; cover $5-10; ⏰ 6pm-2am; SEPTA R6 Manayunk Station, Bus 35, 61

Though you can occasionally see live music by the likes of DJ Jazzy Jeff and G Love and Special Sauce, most of the acts that play here are exceptionally forgettable bands that need a bit more practice and creativity. Rock bands tend to play downstairs, while DJs spin

upstairs. The place has a dirty feel and a bunch of dark corners to hide in.

## KHYBER Map pp226-7

☎ 215-238-5888; 56 S 2nd St; cover $5-15; ⏰ 5pm-2am Tue-Sun; SEPTA 2nd St Station, Bus 17, 21, 33, 42, 76

Devoted to ROCK, this dirty old bar's nightly schedule of live music and its clientele contrast strongly with the rest of Old City's scantily clad denizens. The Strokes made it big while they were the Khyber's resident band.

## NORTH STAR Map pp220-1

☎ 215-684-0808; 2639 N Poplar St; cover $5-15; ⏰ 6pm-2am; Bus 7, 15, 32, 48

Consistently booking fantastic bands, the North Star manages a combination of neighborhood street cred, rock and cleanliness. One side of the bar serves food and has two tables for shooting stick; the other side, an intimate performance space, earns props by allowing short people to see via a balcony, high stage and staggered floor.

## R5 PRODUCTIONS

www.r5productions.com

This slightly mysterious, independent, low-budget production company (well, it's not so much of a company – it's more like a hyperactive guy who likes to program bands and then have them play in different spots throughout Philly) consistently works with excellent bands (Lightning Bolt, Polyphonic Spree). Nearly all R5 shows are staged in the basement of the First Unitarian Church at 22nd and Chestnut Sts. The really big shows go on in the chapel upstairs. These all-ages affairs seem to attract every single black-clad vegan in town. Advance tickets are sold at **Spaceboy Records** (p156).

## SILK CITY LOUNGE Map p230

☎ 215-592-8838; 435 Spring Garden St; music cover $5-10; ⏰ 5pm-2am; Bus 43, 57

Live music draws every variety and ethnicity of hipster into this lounge. Depending on the night, the club hosts indie rockers, house-spinning DJs, rockabilly acts, and just about anything else that's experimental and cool. From the outside it looks like a squat brick bunker with an oversized pagoda stuck on the entry. The dark and smoky interior is lit only by a variety of Chinese lamps, all red. If you need to get a snack, head next door to the **Silk City Diner** (p109).

### TLA Map pp228-9
**Theater of Living Arts;** ☎ **215-238-0660; 334 South St; tickets $12-40;** ☾ **box office noon-6pm Mon-Sat; Bus 40, 47**

The TLA was a performance space for an acting troupe in the '60s and a movie theater in the '70s, and lately it's been a medium-size live music venue. TLA's previous life as a movie theater means that the floor slopes gently toward the stage (the seats are gone – this is a general admission place) so views of the band tend to be pretty good. Some shows sell out early.

### TROCADERO Map pp222-3
☎ **215-922-5483; www.thetroc.com; 1003 Arch St; tickets $7-25;** ☾ **box office noon-6pm Tue-Fri, noon-5pm Sat (also open during most performances); SEPTA Chinatown Station, Market East Station, Bus 23, 48, 61**

Another former movie theater serving as a rock 'n' roll hall, the Trocadero (or Troc, as Philadelphians call it) is a great midsize place (it fits about 1000 people) that hosts acts such as Guided by Voices, Cat Power and Great Big Sea. On Mondays films are screened and entry is $3 (and can be used toward the purchase of booze!).

# HIP-HOP & HOUSE

Most Philadelphians who listen to hip-hop regularly don't have a favorite club – they have a favorite DJ. Such affection does tend to follow the DJ from venue to venue. So in addition to checking out these fine clubs, you might want to pick up a *City Paper* and read the excellent 'DJ Nights' column to see who's hot and where they are due to spin. Most likely it will be at one

---

## Major Rock Venues

Hold up a lighter and join the herd.

- **The Mann Center** (p129) Who doesn't like to see Weird Al play outdoors? Okay, maybe Aretha Franklin instead.
- **The Tweeter Center** (Map pp220-1; ☎ 215-336-2000 tickets; Mickle Blvd & Riverside Dr) Just over the river in Camden, watch Pearl Jam or Bruce Springsteen while sitting on a lawn with 24,999 other people.
- **Wachovia Center & Wachovia Spectrum** (p144) When the Flyers aren't flying, come here to hear Joe Cocker.

---

of the following locations, but sometimes other clubs and underground events enter the fray.

### 700 CLUB Map p230
☎ **215-386-3408; 700 2nd St;** ☾ **3:30pm-2am Mon-Sat; Bus 57**

After 10pm, DJs take over the cozy upstairs room of this neighborhood bar and get the crowd moving. Many nights they get some sweet DJs (including the guy who does the music for all the Urban Outfitters stores in the US), though it's kind of odd to see a room full of white people dancing to hip-hop.

### AQUA LOUNGE Map p230
☎ **215-769-5114; 323 Girard Ave; cover $10;** ☾ **9pm-2am Wed-Sat; Bus 15, 57**

Hard to detect unless you know its there, the Aqua Lounge is identifiable through an inconspicuous sign affixed above the entrance and through a telltale enormous doorman. Frequently nominated for best nightclub by the weekly newspapers' readers' polls, the smoothly cool Aqua is divided in two: one side is for the bar and lounge, and the other invariably contains an excellent hip-hop, house or techno-spinning DJ entertaining hipsters who know how to dress and how to dance. Usually there is enough couch and chair space for you to be a wallflower or to make out.

### THE FIVE SPOT Map pp226-7
☎ **215-574-0070; 5 S Bank St; cover $5-10;** ☾ **9pm-2am Tue-Thu, 6pm-2am Fri & Sat, 9pm-2am Sun; SEPTA 2nd St Station, Bus 17, 21, 33, 42, 76**

Tuesday night at this club features an event called 'Black Lily,' an acclaimed showcase for female DJs and hip-hop artists. Other evenings host more DJs, an occasional comedy act, a drag king or possibly a band. There are two floors (with the possibility of two acts), plenty of lounging space and some slightly dated decor. Upstairs on Thursday night is currently a Latin dance event. The Five Spot started as a swing club, and every now and then it returns to its roots.

### FLUID Map pp228-9
☎ **215-629-0565; 613 S 4th St; cover $5-10;** ☾ **9pm-2am; Bus 12, 40, 57**

Young crowds who like to bust it end up at this smallish hot spot, but not until after midnight. Depending on the evening, DJs play hip-hop, house or sometimes techno. While almost everyone ends up dancing, a really dark balcony overlooks the floor for the comfort of wallflowers and voyeurs. The unmarked entrance to the club is easy to miss: look for a blue door on Kater St.

### LOIE Map pp222-3
☎ 215-568-0808; 128 S 19th St; ☾ 11:30am-2am; SEPTA 19th St Station, Bus 9, 17, 21, 42, 33
This is a favorite haunt for the group of people who never leave Rittenhouse Square. A well-dressed young crowd with nice hair shows up around 10pm to hear the DJ of the evening. Loie attracts some of the finest spinners in town, and there's usually a hip-hop night at least once a week.

### SOMA Map pp226-7
☎ 215-873-0222; 33 S 3rd St; ☾ 8pm-2am; SEPTA 2nd St Station, Bus 17, 21, 33, 42, 76
Those with more discerning tastes in DJs head to Soma over most other clubs in Old City. Depending on the night, quality talents spin hip-hop, deep house, drum and bass, or reggae. And there's the occasional battle. The room is small, square and full of sweaty people. Tuesday through Thursday the dancing crowd is lively but thin enough for you to do your thing.

## LATIN
Aside from the clubs listed below, Latin lovers might want to shimmy their way over to **Alma de Cuba** (p109), **Rock Lobster** (p143) and **The Five Spot** (p141), all of which regularly offer Latin dancing.

### BRASIL Map pp226-7
☎ 215-413-1700; 112 Chestnut St; cover $5-10; ☾ 6pm-2am; SEPTA 2nd St Station, Bus 17, 21, 33, 42, 76
An Old City favorite for those who want to dance salsa instead of merely grind into somebody else, Brasil offers various evenings of Latin, Brazilian and Caribbean music and dance. On Wednesdays, group lessons are available from 9pm to 10pm, before the band. There's a long-running Brazilian jazz event on Sunday evening.

### CUBA LIBRE Map pp226-7
☎ 215-627-0666; 10 S 2nd St; ☾ 4pm-2am; SEPTA 2nd St Station, Bus 17, 21, 33, 42, 76
Cuba Libre, which makes the city's tastiest mojito, operates as both a restaurant and

a nightclub. Done up with an over-the-top Cuban theme, the interior contains scenic wall paints, potted trees, iron balconies and giant tropical ceiling fans. It's one of Old City's most popular spots, particularly on its weekly Latin dance night.

# DANCE CLUBS
Plenty of dancing occurs at the hip-hop venues previously mentioned; this section lists the places to go when you're looking to have fun with hundreds or even thousands of other people. There's a cluster of giant clubs along the Delaware River north of the Benjamin Franklin Bridge. These places frequently change hands – Egypt and Rock Lobster have managed to survive. The Delaware clubs can be a pain to get to on foot, as they are a bit isolated from the rest of the city. A cab ride might be just the thing. The Gayborhood presents another cluster of worthy treats, which are more accessible then their friends on the river.

### 12TH ST AIR COMMAND Map pp222-3
☎ 215-545-8088; 254 S 12th St; ☾ 4pm-2am Mon-Fri, 2pm-2am Sat & Sun; SEPTA Walnut-Locust Station, Bus 9, 12, 21, 23, 42
Attracting all ages of gay men, this three-story club provides a variety of romper rooms to suit anyone's fancy. The 1st floor features a karaoke stage (used on Wednesdays), a rectangular bar and a restaurant. Levels two and three variously hold a space for pool tables, a disco-styled dance floor, more bars, arcade games and a rooftop deck that can be either intimate or rowdy, depending on the size of the crowd, which just might be

## Top Five Clubs
Each of these clubs consistently books top DJs.
- **Aqua Lounge** (p141) Aqua's lounge
- **The Five Spot** (p141) The decor might look a bit dated, but Tuesday's 'Black Lily' forces you not to care.
- **Fluid** (p141) Hidden off South St, dark Fluid is small, but the dance floor takes up the entire room.
- **Loie** (p142) At night this Rittenhouse restaurant dumps the chefs, and a line forms out the door.
- **Shampoo** (p143) Philly's favorite giant club, Shampoo attracts thousands of clubgoers.

Entertainment – Dance Clubs

participating in a wet underpants contest. Cash only.

## EGYPT Map pp226-7
☎ 215-922-6500; www.egypt-nightclub.com; 520 N Columbus Blvd; cover $5-15; ⏰ 11:30am-2am; SEPTA Spring Garden Station, Bus 25, 43

One of Philly's oldest massive nightclubs, Egypt hosts a variety of specialty nights. Many of these cater to teenyboppers, and the minimum age to enter can be as low as 17. Saturday is typically 21 and over, and some Sundays (during the summer and when a public holiday falls on a Monday) host an event called 'Spoiled Rotten,' a party exclusively for those aged 14 to 18.

## FINNEGAN'S WAKE Map p230
☎ 215-574-9317; 537 N 3rd St; weekend cover $5-15; ⏰ 5pm-2am; SEPTA Spring Garden Station, Bus 43, 57

Formerly used for 19th-century casket manufacturing, this mind-bogglingly popular Irish-themed entertainment complex can get pretty packed on the weekends, which is quite a feat considering it's got three enormous floors. Bands (invariably Irish) play from Thursday through Saturday on the main floor, and there is a big dance space on the next level up. Adjacent to the dance floor are the doors behind which Abraham Lincoln's body lay when his corpse stopped by Philly for an overnighter en route to Illinois.

## LA TAZZA Map pp226-7
☎ 215-922-7322; 108 Chestnut St; cover $5; ⏰ 5pm-2am Tue-Sun; SEPTA 2nd St Station, Bus 17, 21, 33, 42, 76

Offering one off the city's few regular Goth nights, La Tazza attracts plenty of vamps after the sun sets on Thursday. Other nights are all about DJs who wear more than black. Food is served until 1:30am.

## ROCK LOBSTER Map pp226-7
☎ 215-627-7625; www.rocklobsterclub.com; 221 N Columbus Ave; cover $0-15; ⏰ 11:30-2am; SEPTA 2nd St Station, Bus 25

Large and endearingly tacky, Rock Lobster's outdoor decks enjoy excellent views of the Benjamin Franklin Bridge and the Delaware River. By day it operates as a New England–inspired lobster shack. Wednesday through Saturday night, cover bands and local radio station DJs play to huge crowds. On Sunday there's a live salsa band and free lessons. The crowd is very bridge and tunnel.

## SHAMPOO Map pp222-3
☎ 215-922-7500; www.shampoooonline.com; Willow St btwn 7th & 8th Sts; cover $7-12; ⏰ 9pm-2am Wed-Sun (occasionally 6am); Bus 47, 61

Home to foam parties, hot tubs and velvet seating, this giant nightclub hosts an immensely popular gay night on Friday, a long-standing Wednesday engagement for those who dig the Cure and Skinny Puppy, and a conventional free-for-all on Saturday. Many nights are all-ages (some run until 6am), and there's a dress code that prohibits T-shirts and work boots. Shampoo is an enormous place, with multiple DJs and an interesting maze of rooms. On weekdays it draws 600 to 800 people; on weekends that number increases to 2000 to 3000.

## TRANSIT Map p230
☎ 215-925-8878; www.transitnightclub.com; 600 Spring Garden St; cover $10; ⏰ 12pm-3:30am Wed, 10pm-3:30am Thu-Sat; Bus 43, 47, 61

Remember that crazy bar from *Star Wars* with all the different kinds of aliens in which Han Solo kills Jaba's emissary? Well, that bar is like a smaller version of Transit, only Transit is way more crowded, with more pronounced diversity. An after-hours club that stays open very late (on special occasions, until a remarkable 8am), Transit occupies multiple floors of a former bank in a gritty section of town. There are cavernous ceilings, big dance floors, big lighting effects and big DJs (funk, trance and hip-hop).

## WOODY'S Map pp222-3
☎ 215-545-1893; www.woodysbar.com; 202 S 13th St; ⏰ 11am-2am; SEPTA Walnut-Locust Station, Bus 9, 12, 21, 23, 42

Even my mom has heard of Woody's, and she's neither gay nor has she ever been to Philadelphia. This nightclub – Philly's most famous gay club – is totally hot, totally packed and mostly full of spruced-up boys, though ladies are definitely welcome too. Inside, find free Internet access, food and enough services that people don't need to leave except for sleep.

# SPORTS, HEALTH & FITNESS

Philadelphia provides plenty of sporting action, whether you want to get fit yourself or intend to eat a pile of nachos while

## Hoagie Ban!

Over the summer of 2003 Philadelphians heard unthinkable news: The Eagles' new home, Lincoln Financial Field, decided to prohibit fans from bringing food into the stands, hoping instead to guide hungry bodies towards expensive concessions. Outraged, Philadelphians and the local media began referring to the awful decision as 'the Hoagie Ban.' Protests ensued, letters were written and the angry citizens organized. The city hadn't dissented this strongly since King George decided to begin imposing taxes on his colonists in an attempt to recover losses from the Seven Years War.

Several months later Lincoln Field wisely lifted the ban, reuniting fans with their favorite game-time sandwich. Hoagies are now allowed in the stadium, though they must be wrapped tightly in clear plastic wrap.

Go Eagles!

watching someone else do the work. It's a four-team town, meaning that Big League football, baseball, basketball and hockey are all treats you can enjoy during your visit, depending on the season. The city also sponsors nationally regarded events in cycling and crew (see the Calendar, p13), while the University of Pennsylvania and Temple University field collegiate teams of every variety.

If you've got time and you can manage to score tickets, try to catch the Eagles or the Phillies during a home game. Not only will you get to experience the overwhelming intensity of Philadelphia's die-hard fans, but you'll get to sit in one of two excellent new stadiums.

If the weather is nice, be sure to rent a bike and explore the Schuylkill River Trail and Wissahickon Park, both of which provide many miles of fantastic – and often surprisingly rustic – scenery.

# SPECTATOR SPORTS
## Football
**PHILADELPHIA EAGLES** Map pp220-1
Lincoln Financial Field; ☎ Ticketmaster 215-336-2000; www.ticketmaster.com; SEPTA Pattison Station, Bus 17
The NFC East's Eagles play in spanking-new, state-of-the-art Lincoln Field. For many Philadelphians, emotional stability depends on the outcome of the games played here.

The NFL season runs from August through January, with home games occurring twice each month, usually on Sundays. Viewing a live game among Philadelphia's intense fans can be an interesting anthropological experiment, but tickets are notoriously hard to come by. If you don't get them well in advance, your best hope of entry is by paying high prices to a ticket broker or scalper. No matter the team, when dealing with scalpers, the best strategy is to wait until after games begin, when prices drop. A note of warning: scalping is technically illegal and you'll want to inspect your ticket carefully to avoid getting scammed.

## Baseball
**PHILADELPHIA PHILLIES** Map pp220-1
Citizen's Bank Park; ☎ Ticketmaster 215-336-2000; www.ticketmaster.com; tickets $15-40; ⊙ box office 9am-5pm Mon-Fri, 9am-1pm Sat; SEPTA Pattison Station, Bus 17
Lately, the Phillies have been teasing fans with potential for greatness. Not that it matters, because their die-hard fans will go to watch anybody who happens to be on the field. The National League team plays 81 home games from April to October. Though it was possible to score last-minute seats when the Phillies played at never-quite-sold-out Veterans Stadium, this will almost definitely change with the opening of Citizen's Bank Park in 2004. Aside from beautiful views onto distant downtown Philadelphia, this stadium boasts stands with great sightlines and close proximity to the field. The catch? There are now 43,000 seats instead of 67,000. Games will sell out, so purchase tickets early.

## Basketball
**PHILADELPHIA 76ERS** Map pp220-1
Wachovia Center; ☎ 215-339-7676, 800-462-2849 ticket sales; www.nba.com/sixers; 3601 S Broad St; tickets $15-62; ⊙ box office 9am-6pm Mon-Fri, 10am-4:30pm Sat; SEPTA Pattison Station, Bus 17
The Sixers can be inspiring to watch, particularly when Allen Iverson, the team's superstar, performs at his best. The storied team, which has won several championships and whose past players include Wilt Chamberlain, Julius 'Dr J' Erving and Charles Barkley, plays 41 home games from late October through April.

# Hockey

**PHILADELPHIA FLYERS** Map pp220-1
Wachovia Center; ☎ 215-218-7825, 215-336-2000
ticket sales; www.philadelphiaflyers.com; 3601 S Broad
St; tickets $23-85; ☽ box office 9am-6pm Mon-Fri,
10am-4:30pm Sat; SEPTA Pattison Station, Bus 17

These bruisers are itching for a Stanley Cup, which they haven't won since their bookend victories in 1974 and 1975. Perhaps the team isn't the same without crooner Kate Smith. Back in 1969 the team played her recording of 'God Bless America' before beating the Toronto Maple Leafs 6-3. The song became a good luck charm. Her record? 64 wins, 15 losses and 3 ties. Unfortunately, Smith died in 1986. Win or lose, the Flyers draw big crowds. The season runs from October through early April, with 44 home games.

## Crewing the Schuylkill

The flat Schuylkill River provides old-school Ivy Leaguers and their pals ample opportunity to excel at their favorite idiosyncratic sport. In fact, many rowers think the Schuylkill is one of the best courses in existence. The picturesqueness

---

## Interviewing the Philly Phanatic by John Spelman

One day during the fall, a man wearing a large costume of green fuzz allowed me to hang out in his locker room and shadow him for the length of a baseball game. Man and costume combined to form a powerful force: the Philly Phanatic, mascot of the Phillies. I have attended many professional baseball games in many stadiums throughout the US, but my experiences elsewhere did not prepare me for what would amount to be one of the most rewarding moments I would have during my research in Philadelphia.

A bit of history and description: the Phanatic is the first official mascot of any American major league team, and was created in 1978. He's 6-and-a-half-feet tall with a big round gut and a cone-shaped beak, covered in super-bright green fur. Basically a giant Muppet (indeed, his costume was designed by Jim Henson's studio) with a man inside, the fictive character hails from the Galapagos Islands. The arrival of the Phanatic in Philly changed baseball forever. Other teams appreciated Philadelphia's novel figure and attempted to create their own. Now, most teams have mascots.

In the Phanatic's room, I admired his numerous accessories (tiny piano, supersoaker, sombrero, large sunglasses, fake guitars) while his handler helped him into costume. Soon thereafter it was time to frantically follow him through the crowds, where high-fives were bestowed lightning-fast, bald heads were rubbed, popcorn was stolen, men were kissed and unwitting spectators were coerced into becoming dance partners. None of this behavior was met with protest.

One surprising thing I discovered was that people sincerely like the Phanatic. A lot. And not just kids, but fans of all variety. Upon his third-inning entrance into the stands, four entire sections of seating simultaneously erupted, jumping to their feet, screaming. Little kids began rushing over, drunken fraternity brothers pounded him on the back, teenage girls begged for a hug and my jaw dropped. Not one of these people seemed to be engaging the Phanatic with any sort of irony. This was legitimate affection.

Being a slightly cynical person who usually lives in a town with a crappy mascot nobody over the age of five cares about, I had to ask, 'why?' Back in his locker room, the Phanatic provided some explanation. After removing his head and drinking a few cups of water, his sweaty personage said that, unlike with most other teams, the Phillies give their mascot wide creative latitude and don't impose many restrictions on his behavior. The Phanatic makes up his own acts; they aren't prescribed. His freedom engenders greater spontaneity in the stands, and this spontaneity allows for a more robust, less structured relationship with fans. During his performances, the Phanatic visibly enjoys both his role and the crowds in the stands.

The Phanatic theorizes that his Henson-crafted costume might also have something to do with the affection people feel toward him. Aside from looking entirely nonthreatening and goofy, it possesses a head that actually moves, which allows for lifelike gesturing. The limited movement of other mascots seems clumsy by comparison.

When asked how he handles his iconic role, the Phanatic said he understands that 'the Phanatic's a great ambassador for the city. When you come to the airport, you see a picture of him. So I try to make the Phanatic embody Philly's spirit. The Phanatic has attitude, but he remains friendly with a neighborhood feel.' When asked why sports are such an important part of the city's overall makeup, he replied, 'It's indicative of the great northeast sports towns. You were born here. Your dad was, and so was his. Sports get passed down.' This answer might help explain why the fans love him so much. Since the Phanatic has been around since 1978, the kids who watched him cavort during his first years are now having kids of their own, and possibly recalling their earliest baseball memories through the ageless monster.

Being a travel guidebook writer, I also had a few unrelated-to-baseball questions for the Phanatic. What's the best sports bar in the city? 'The Philadium.' Have you ever touched the bell in costume? 'No. I tried, but they kicked me out.'

of the sport is complemented on the shore by pretty **Boathouse Row** (p84). Grab a picnic basket and head for a grassy patch on the east side of the river. Throughout the year, several regattas are held, the most famous being the Dad Vail. For more information, check out the Schuylkill Navy's website, www.boathouserow.org, and see our Calendar section (p13).

# OUTDOOR ACTIVITIES
## Cycling

Philadelphia contains some fantastic options for cyclists, especially once you get off the mean streets. The closest and most popular option is the paved **Schuylkill River Trail** (see tour, p100), which runs on both the west and east banks of that river. It connects with a network of gravel trails in beautiful, wooded Wissahickon Park. In here, you'll forget that cars exist.

For the daring and strong, the Schuylkill River Trail connects with the scenic Manayunk towpath, running along an old canal. This connects to another trail, leading to Valley Forge National Park. All told, it's 22 carless miles from Center City to Valley Forge along converted railroad tracks, with only 1 mile of that journey shared with vehicles.

The knowledgeable folks at Trophy Bikes are experienced cyclists and advocates. They can give you free maps outlining both the city and the region's bike routes. If you know where you want to go, they are happy to detail any confusing connections that might exist.

Another good resource is **The Bicycle Club of Philadelphia** ( ☎ 215-735-2453), founded in 1979. You can join their organized weekend rides (for all experience levels), and they can give you more information about the area's bike paths.

### BIKE LINE OF MANAYUNK Map pp230
☎ 215-487-7433; 4151 Main St; bike rental hour/day/ weekend/week $8/25/45/75; ⏰ 11am-8pm Mon-Fri, 10am-6pm Sat, 10am-4pm Sun; SEPTA R6 Manayunk Station, Bus 35, 61
Bike Line sits at the southern end of the 'Main St USA' bit of Manayunk and rents Trek hybrids and Trek mountain bikes. There's also a good selection of Treks and Cannondales for sale, plus a repair shop.

### TROPHY BIKES Map pp226-7
☎ 215-625-7999; 311 Market St; bike rental day/ half day $25/20; ⏰ 11am-7pm Mon-Fri, 9am-5pm Sat & Sun; SEPTA 2nd St Station, Bus 17, 21, 33, 42, 76
For rentals, this bike shop stocks the latest 21-speed Fugi hybrids and a couple of tandems. The staff specializes in touring. One of the guys working here describes the 50-mile trail from Center City to Perkiomen so well that you might want to just listen to him talk about it and skip the exercise. Come here for maps and info about tricky trail connections.

## Running

As Rocky Balboa proved, running is quite the Philadelphia treat. One of the best options is along either bank of the **Schuylkill River** (see tour p100). The remainder of Fairmount Park offers thousands of acres of good running terrain. Beautiful as the river trail and the park are, their more remote sections have seen some crime recently, so it's best to run with a partner.

Other options include a run along a narrow park that lies next to Front St in Queen Village and Society Hill. Checking out pugs along the way, cut across Old City and then, if you've got the stamina, head over the Benjamin Franklin Bridge.

Or you could be like Rocky himself and run on the city streets. Center City is compact, pretty, and historically and architecturally interesting, so a sidewalk run comes with plenty of entertainment. Such a run is best accomplished early in the morning, before downtown gets clogged with suits. Don't forget to charge up the steps of the **Philadelphia Museum of Art** (p77).

The informal, friendly Fairmount Running Club is a good resource for information on running in Philadelphia, particularly Fairmount Park. The group organizes weekly free runs, and can be reached through www.runfairmount.org.

## Inline Skating

Your best bet close to town is to use the Schuylkill River Trail; see Cycling.

### DRIVE SPORTS Map pp222-3
☎ 215-232-7368; 2601 Pennsylvania Ave; $8/hr; ⏰ 11am-7pm Mon-Fri, 10am-5pm Sat, 10am-4pm Sun; Bus 7, 32, 48, 76
Renting both blades and bikes, Drive Sports

is conveniently located near the Schuylkill River Trail. During warmer months the shop also sets up temporary operations near 1 Boathouse Row, just steps away from all the rivery goodness.

## Tennis

There are dozens of municipal tennis courts in town, but not many in Center City. Head over to West Fairmount Park, and you'll find more then a few. Call ☎ 215-686-0152 to sign up to use one.

## Golf

Philly has five city-run golf courses, all of them reasonably priced. While we outline the city's best public course in the listing below, the others are all worth your time, particularly Wissahickon Park's Walnut Lane ( ☎ 215-482-3370; $21), which was designed by Alex Findlay. Check out www.golfphilly.com for information about each course.

### COBBS CREEK
☎ 215-877-8707; 7200 Lansdowne Ave; weekend/weekday $32/27, club rental $15; ☻ 6am-dusk
Cobbs Creek was designed by legendary course architect Hugh Wilson (who more famously crafted nearby Merion, which is closed to the public). The pretty creek that winds through the front nine looks picture perfect, but you'll probably be cursing Wilson over your lost balls and subsequent penalty strokes unless you've got a very precise shot. There's a reason why the course gave Arnold Palmer troubles. Not long ago *Golf Week Magazine* named it the sixth-best municipal course in the country. It's best to set a tee-time a week in advance.

## Rowing

For those interested in rowing on the Schuylkill, your options are limited. As the sport is complicated, expensive and difficult to master, you can't just rent equipment for the day and tool around. People who live in town access the river by joining one of several clubs (usually based out of one of those charming Boathouse Row buildings). For information about becoming a member of a club, contact the Schuylkill Navy (www.boathouserow.org).

For those who have never rowed before and will be in Philly for a decent part of the summer, several camps are offered. There's PA Rowing Camps (www.parowing .com), which is run out of the Temple boathouse. Mount Airy Learning Tree (www.mt airylearningtree.org) organizes a learn-to-row camp through Vesper, one of the rowing clubs.

## Ice-Skating

Feel like a Philadelphia Blade at one of these two venues.

### CLASS OF 1923 SKATING RINK Map p225
☎ 215-898-1923; 3120 Walnut St; entry $4.50, rental $2.50; SEPTA 30th St Station
In University City, this indoor rink is open from mid-September to early April. Though there are public skating hours everyday, these hours vary. Call ahead.

### BLUE CROSS RIVERRINK Map pp226-7
☎ 215-925-7465; www.riverrink.com; Chestnut St at Columbus Blvd; entry $6, rental $3; ☻ 6-9pm Mon-Thu, 12:30pm-1am Fri & Sat, 12:30-9pm Sun late Nov–Mar; SEPTA 2nd St Station
As an alternative to Class of 1923, there's outdoor skating here, on Penn's Landing.

## HEALTH & FITNESS
## Gym & Fitness Centers

Most hotels have some kind of gym or fitness room on site. If you happen to be staying at the Park Hyatt at the Bellevue, then you're in particularly good luck: lodgers have access to The Sporting Club. This top-notch facility is open only to members, one of whom is Governor Ed Rendell; some others are members of the Philadelphia Ballet.

### 12TH STREET GYM Map pp222-3
☎ 215-985-4092; www.12streetgym.com; 204 S 4th St; day/week pass $20/49; ☻ 5:30am-11pm Mon-Thu, 5:30am-10pm Fri, 8am-8pm Sat, 9am-7pm Sun; SEPTA Walnut-Locust Station, Bus 9, 12, 21, 23, 42
For one of the friendliest gyms in the city, look here. The eight-level facility is over 60,000 sq ft and has every variety of equipment available and over 35 personal trainers on site. The super-nice staff keeps the goods spotless and clean.

## Yoga & Pilates

There's nothing like a bit of meditation and stretching to prepare body and mind for an oncoming cheese steak.

### YOGA 105 Map pp222-3

☎ 215-751-9642; www.yoga105.com; 1611 Walnut St, 4th fl; class $15; ☺ open daily with varying class schedules; SEPTA Walnut-Locust Station, Bus 9, 12, 21, 27, 32, 42

If you're ready for Bikram-style yoga and the 105°F temperatures associated with it, stop by this studio. It's got plenty of natural light, and if you can't stand the heat, try the classes in the Ashtanga tradition.

### YOGA ON MAIN Map p230

☎ 215-482-7877; www.yogaonmain.com; 4363 Main St; class $15; ☺ open daily with varying class schedules; SEPTA R6 Manayunk Station, Bus 35, 61

This studio is run by David Newman, who has been teaching hatha and Bhakti yoga since 1992. It might feel a bit cramped, but the slightly congested quarters are made up for in the high quality of the instructors. Private training is also offered, though this will cost you more.

## Massage & Day Spas

There's nothing like a deep massage to help body and mind after they struggle to digest an enormous cheese steak.

### BODY RESTORATION Map pp222-3

☎ 215-569-9599; www.bodyrest.com; 1611 Walnut St, 3rd fl; 1hr massage $65-75; ☺ by appt; SEPTA R6 Manayunk Station, Bus 35, 61

This nice-looking place offers Swedish, Shiatsu, deep-tissue and aromatic massages, as well as La Stone therapy, facials, waxing and various body treatments.

### TERME DI AROMA Map pp226-7

☎ 215-829-9769; www.termediaroma.com; 32 N 3rd St; 1hr massage $65-85; ☺ 1-9pm Tue, 11am-9pm Wed-Fri, 9am-7pm Sat, 10am-4pm Sun; SEPTA 2nd St Station, Bus 17, 21, 33, 42, 76

This relaxing Old City day spa offers an extensive menu of massages and spa packages. A facial, aromatherapy massage and ½-hour reflexology package lasts about three hours and costs $165. You can drop by to check out the wellness store, but you need to make an appointment before having some bodywork done.

# Shopping

# Shopping

At first glance, a unique shopping experience in Philadelphia might seem hard to find, with chains like the Gap, Abercrombie & Fitch and many others snagging prominent real estate. Study the city a bit, and a new pattern emerges. Philly boasts plenty of unique, locally based boutiques, multiple historic shopping districts and one of America's grandest and oldest department stores, where a holiday shopping experience features an organ with 30,000(!) pipes playing in the background. We give you a glimpse; there's much more to discover.

Those desperate to see Philadelphia's offerings of material goods could – provided they brought stamina, water and running shoes – make a 5-mile shopping circuit through Center City, catching most of the hot spots without doubling back. Begin in Old City's gallery district, where you'll find numerous artist-run stores, then head south to Walnut St, where you'll turn west and walk for about a mile and a half along one of Philly's most important commercial corridors. Things will get ritzier as you approach Rittenhouse Square: be sure to save time to wander around this glamorous 'hood before returning east along Pine St, experiencing the electric stores of Antique Row. When you hit 8th St, go south for a couple of blocks, and then go east on South St, Philadelphia's epicenter of kitsch.

## OLD CITY

The gallery district has a positive impact on Old City shopping: there's a nice range of cool, handmade stuff for sale, particularly north of Market St.

**AKA** Map pp226-7                    *CDs & Records*
☎ 215-922-3828; 7 N 2nd St; ⏰ 11am-11pm Mon-Sat, noon-6pm Sun; SEPTA 2nd St Station, Bus 48, 57, 76
Stocking an encyclopedic inventory of music,

### Top Five Shopping Areas

- **Walnut St** For those who want to feel historically relevant, the stretch linking Rittenhouse Square and Washington Square is loaded with trendy chains and some boutiques.
- **South St** Check out teenagers checking out weirdly colored kitsch. There are plenty of comic, clothing and record stores here too.
- **Italian Market** Vendors and stalls fill the sidewalks in this century-old traditional market (p81). Find fresh produce, cheese, meat and more than a few Italian Americans.
- **Old City** The gallery district along 2nd and 3rd Sts immediately north of Market contains the most arty and artist-run stores. Check out the custom-made handbags at **Viv Pickle** (p151) or the handmade messenger bags at **Reload** (p151).
- **Chestnut Hill** A stroll along tony Germantown Ave reveals a dense cluster of tiny, cute shops.

AKA deals in conventional rock, indie, electronica, hip-hop and more. The vinyl is upstairs, and CDs are downstairs. AKA's used section is small but well considered.

**BIG JAR BOOKS** Map pp226-7              *Books*
☎ 215-574-1650; 55 N 2nd St; ⏰ 10am-9pm; SEPTA 2nd St Station, Bus 48, 57, 76
An immensely pleasant browsing experience can be had at this shop, because it has a diverse selection of used books and because a simple café operates up front. It's so comfortable and relaxed that if it didn't close, some people might not ever leave.

**FOSTER'S URBAN HOMEWARE**
Map pp226-7              *Home Accessories*
☎ 267-671-0588; 124 N 3rd St; ⏰ 10am-8pm Mon-Sat, noon-5pm Sun; SEPTA 2nd St Station, Bus 48, 57, 76
Pick from 20 brightly patterned shower curtains at Foster's, where stainless steel toothbrush holders, vividly colored lamps, hot pink trashcans and a great selection of glassware abound. Also up for grabs are plates, candles, clocks and yellow bowling balls that light up. Foster's also operates a store for quality cookware in **Reading Terminal Market** (☎ 215-925-0950; 8:30am-6pm Mon-Sat).

**ME & BLUE** Map pp226-7              *Clothing*
☎ 215-592-7898; 311 Market St, 2nd fl; ⏰ 11am-7pm Mon-Fri, 10am-6pm Sat, noon-5pm Sun; SEPTA 2nd St Station, Bus 48, 57, 76
New items mix with vintage stuff in this

loft-like boutique, easy to miss in its 2nd-floor space. If stuff doesn't move fast, it gets moved to a super-cheap sales rack. Who wants a party frock that won't break the bank? On **First Fridays** (p62) Me & Blue hosts special trunk parties while the galleries do their gallery thing.

### MODE MODERN

Map pp226-7                                *Furniture*
☎ 215-627-0299; www.modemodern.com; 159 N 3rd St; ☽ noon-6pm Tue-Sat, 1-5pm Sun; SEPTA 2nd St Station, Bus 48, 57, 76
Mostly stocking the great designers of the '50s, this fantastic furniture store contains pieces from as early as 1920, along with some contemporary stuff. As the goods tend to be in beautiful condition, prices tend to be high.

### RELOAD

Map pp226-7                          *Messenger Bags*
☎ 215-922-2018; 142 N 2nd St; ☽ 11am-5pm Mon-Fri, noon-6pm Sat; SEPTA 2nd St Station, Bus 48, 57, 76
The two people working in this shop hand-make super-durable, super-cute bike messenger bags. On the 1st floor is a display gallery; below that is the workshop where the duo does their thing. Bags run from $80 to $200.

### SCARLET ALLEY Map pp226-7          *Gifts*
☎ 215-592-7898; 241 Race St; ☽ 11am-7pm Mon-Fri, 10am-6pm Sat, noon-5pm Sun; SEPTA 2nd St Station, Bus 48, 57, 76
This pleasant, nice-smelling gift shop feels like Christmas year-round. Find tasteful music boxes, arty cards, fashion accessories and home accessories. There's a dollop of baby books and clothes in the back.

### SHANE CANDIES Map pp226-7          *Candy*
☎ 215-922-1048; 110 Market St ☽ 9am-5:30pm Mon-Sat; SEPTA 2nd St Station, Bus 9, 17, 21, 42, 48, 76
One of several shops throughout the nation that claims to be America's oldest candy store, Shane's still looks much like it did back in 1911. Come here for truffles, almond bark, caramels and fudge.

### SODAFINE

Map pp226-7              *Vintage & Handmade*
☎ 215-574-9112; 37 N 3rd St; ☽ 11am-7pm Mon-Sat; SEPTA 2nd St Station, Bus 48, 57, 76
This little shop, in the small backroom of

---

## Top Five Vintage Stores

- **Buffalo Exchange** (p154) Outlets of this chain sprout up in most cool American cities.
- **Jennie's Vintage** (p156) Find hip stuff for sale in the rear of a former synagogue.
- **Retrospect** (Map pp228-9; ☎ 267-671-0116; 534 South St; ☽ noon-10pm Mon-Sat, noon-7pm Sun) This shop has the biggest selection of vintage clothes in Center City.
- **Vagabond & Sodafine** (p151) Two trendy shops support each other in one small location.
- **Village Thrift** (Map pp220-1; ☎ 215-639-6930; Broad & Lehigh Sts; ☽ 9am-7pm Mon-Fri, 10am-5pm Sun) So cheap that other thrift stores buy their stuff from here, Village Thrift has several branches throughout some dodgy parts of town.

Vagabond, carries a frequently changing cast of corsage pins, fuzzy boots, knit legwarmers, silk-screened tank tops, graffitied hats and other such items made by consignors from the Philly arts community. Also find a few racks of vintage clothes and shoes, including a minuscule boys' area.

### VAGABOND

Map pp226-7                   *Clothing & Knitting*
☎ 267-671-0737; 37 N 3rd St; ☽ 11am-7pm Mon-Sat, 11am-5pm Sun; SEPTA 2nd St Station, Bus 48, 57, 76
Sweetly priced threads, knitting lessons and overall cuteness make Vagabond a favorite Old City hipster destination. Aside from yarn, Vagabond sells handmade hats and scarves, little vintage purses, old jewelry, and all the pants, shirts and coats a plucky girl needs to avoid the Gap. Dog lovers enjoy petting large, placid Kodiak, a big white laze-about.

### VIV PICKLE Map pp226-7          *Handbags*
☎ 215-922-5904; www.vivpickle.com; 21 N 3rd St; ☽ noon-7pm Wed-Fri, noon-6pm Sat; SEPTA 2nd St Station, Bus 48, 57, 76
A quirky little handbag shop, Viv Pickle allows you to order colorful custom bags. Just select the shape, fabric (pick from about 150), handles and lining, and specify any added features. A design consultant is on staff to help. The process takes four weeks, with each bag costing an amazing $30 to $60. Strapped for time? Just pick out a ready-made job from the front of the store.

# CENTER CITY

Center City contains Philadelphia's principal department stores, the usual chains and several malls (Liberty Place, the Bellevue and the Gallery). Rittenhouse Square and Walnut St present some of Philadelphia's most fashionable clothing boutiques. Center City also contains two oldies but goodies: Antique Row and Jeweler's Row.

## RITTENHOUSE SQUARE

The epicenter of Philadelphia's fashion world, this is the place to find the most expensive offerings. As a rule of thumb, the closer you get to the square, the bigger the price tag gets.

### ADRESSE Map pp222-3          *High Fashion*
☎ 215-985-3161; 1706 Locust St; ☖ 11am-7pm Tue-Sat; SEPTA Walnut-Locust Station, Bus 2, 12
Philadelphia's premier lifestyle boutique, this husband-and-wife-run shop presents artful designers not found elsewhere in the city. Etro, Malo, Paul Smith, Moncler and more clothe men and women; Lambertson Truex and Bottega Veneta add handbags and shoes. There's a touch of high-end furniture and fine crystal, and lotions and shaving cream come from an 800-year-old Italian pharmacy. This is an expensive place (bordering on pretentious), obsessed with classic beauty and elegance.

### AIA BOOKSTORE & DESIGN CENTER
Map pp222-3          *Books & Gifts*
☎ 215-496-7215; www.aiabookstore.com; 117 S 17th St; ☖ 10am-6pm Mon, Tue & Thu-Sat, 10am-8pm Wed; SEPTA Walnut-Locust Station, Bus 2, 9, 21, 42
This small favorite features gifty, design-oriented stuff like models of Baroque churches, slick cards and a ton of colorful doodads that both adults and children find appealing. The other side of the store contains shelves of books that expound upon urban studies and beautiful places.

### BLACK'S BAGS & BAGGAGE
Map pp222-3          *Luggage*
☎ 215-496-7215; 117 S 17th St; ☖ 10am-6:30pm Mon-Fri, 10am-6pm Sat; SEPTA Walnut-Locust Station, Bus 2, 9, 21, 42
Baggage mishandled by the airlines? Black's offers rapid repair service. The store is full of all kinds of containers with collapsible handles and little wheels, as well as wallets, briefcases, umbrellas and travel gear.

### BORN YESTERDAY Map pp222-3          *Children*
☎ 215-568-6556; 1901 Walnut St; ☖ 10am-6pm Mon, Tue & Thu-Sat, 10am-7pm Wed, noon-5pm Sun; SEPTA 19th St Station, Bus 9, 21, 33, 42
People with hip babies shop here for infant clothing, Lamaze soft toys, and all kinds of fluffy pink, yellow and blue items. For girls who learned to walk and need to fit into the Rittenhouse Square fashion scene, there are some tiny designer velvet and wool skirts and pants.

### BOYD'S Map pp222-3          *Men's & Women's*
☎ 215-564-9000; 1818 Chestnut St; ☖ 9:30am-6pm Mon-Sat; SEPTA 19th St Station, Bus 9, 21, 33, 42
Men find this store a haven and a blessing. This classic, multifloored haberdashery has 45 tailors on site and plenty of beautiful suits to match. A shopping experience in here comes with Corinthian columns and a grand marble staircase. Look forward to extraordinarily attentive service. Boyd's also carries inventory for conservatively dressed women.

### THE CHILDREN'S BOUTIQUE
Map pp222-3          *Children*
☎ 215-732-2661; 1702 Walnut St; ☖ 10am-6pm Mon, Tue & Thu-Sat, 10am-7pm Wed, noon-5pm Sun; SEPTA Walnut-Locust Station, Bus 9, 21, 33, 42
This store has two big floors of conventional shoes and clothes for babies and kids, and an additional level devoted to toys. While most of these toys are for kids aged eight and under, bigger fellas will get all worked up over baking soda and vinegar rockets, junior telescopes and a levitating metallic top.

### COEUR Map pp222-3          *Lingerie & Swimsuits*
☎ 215-972-0373; 132 S 17th St; ☖ 10am-6pm Mon, Tue & Thu-Sat, 10am-7pm Wed; SEPTA Walnut-Locust Station, Bus 9, 21, 33, 42
A comfortable, serious store for intimates, Coeur carries bras and panties from European designers, Rosa Chá swimsuits and more exotic items. For its holiday public service, Coeur sometimes installs live models in its window; crowds of up to 80 men are often parked on the steps of the church across the street.

### DANIELLE SCOTT
Map pp222-3          *Women's Shoes*
☎ 215-545-9800; 1718 Walnut St; ☖ 10am-6pm Mon, Tue & Thu-Sat, 10am-7pm Wed, noon-5pm Sun; SEPTA Walnut-Locust Station, Bus 9, 21, 33, 42
A tiny boutique in the back of **Knit Wit** (p153), this store doesn't carry much, but what it does

have is totally chic. Younger ladies go wild over Marc Jacobs, while the more mature crew digs Jimmy Choo and Christian Lacroix.

### EVANTINE DESIGN Map pp222-3 *Home Gifts*
☎ 215-545-6883; 210 West Rittenhouse Square; ⏰ 10am-6pm Mon-Sat; Bus 12, 17
Expect a small selection of fancy umbrellas, flowers, glassware, vases and wooden handbags that look like cigar boxes. People annually pop into this store, on the 1st floor of **The Rittenhouse** hotel (p166), when birthdays of hard-to-shop-for people arise.

### HEAD START SHOES
Map pp222-3                           *Women's Shoes*
☎ 215-567-3247; 126 S 17th St; ⏰ 10am-6pm Mon, Tue, Fri & Sat, 10am-7pm Wed & Thu, noon-5pm Sun; SEPTA Walnut-Locust Station, Bus 9, 21, 33, 42
This shoe store has a big selection of popular fashion and carries many brands. The range includes, boots, chunky stuff, plenty of colors, and things that look fragile. There's a token half-dozen pairs for men.

### JOAN SHEPP
Map pp222-3        *Women's Clothing & Shoes*
☎ 215-735-4080; 1616 Walnut St; ⏰ 10am-6pm Mon, Tue & Thu-Sat, 10am-8pm Wed, Sun noon-5pm; SEPTA Walnut-Locust Station, Bus 9, 21, 33, 42
All about women's fashion, Joan Shepp's friendly staff deals in shoes by Prada, Mui Mui and Trippen, while Jean Paul Gaultier and Dries Van Noten dominate the clothing choices.

### JOSEPH FOX Map pp222-3                    *Books*
☎ 215-563-4184; 1724 Sansom St; ⏰ 9:30am-6pm Mon, Tue & Thu-Sat, 9:30am-7pm Wed; SEPTA 19th St Station, Bus 2, 9, 21, 42
A generalist's store for new books, Joseph Fox exhibits strength of catalogue in its children's books and in its architecture, landscape architecture and design section, which surprisingly carries a better inventory than **AIA** (p152).

### KITCHEN KAPERS
Map pp222-3                          *Kitchen Supply*
☎ 215-546-8059; www.kitchenkapers.com; 213 S 17th St; ⏰ 10am-6pm Mon, Tue & Thu-Sat, 10am-8pm Wed, noon-5pm Sun; SEPTA Walnut-Locust Station, Bus 9, 21, 33, 42
This New Jersey chain has 15 outlets, with this one in Center City offering an all-encompassing selection of gear that aspiring chefs need to make any item they want.

### KNIT WIT Map pp222-3        *Women's Clothing*
☎ 215-564-4760; 1718 Walnut St; ⏰ 10am-6pm Mon, Tue & Thu-Sat, 10am-7pm Wed, noon-5pm Sun; SEPTA 19th St Station, Bus 2, 9, 21, 42
This Walnut St favorite for personal service features conservative clothes with a twist. Knit Wit favors European designers (Paul Smith, Blue Marine and Mr & Mrs Macleod), and its stock ranges from dressy to casual and sporty. Knit Wit features My People, a Philly company that does trendy monogramming (in baby blue, hot pink and more) on tee shirts, hoodies, yoga pants and track shorts.

### PETULIA'S FOLLY
Map pp222-3   *Women's Clothing & Housewares*
☎ 215-569-1344; 1710 Sansom St; ⏰ 10am-6pm Mon, Tue & Thu-Sat, 10am-7pm Wed; SEPTA 19th St Station, Bus 2, 9, 21, 42
One half of this boutique deals in pretty housewares such as Middle Kingdom Porcelain, and the other is comfortable and spacious – a pleasant room to browse for Joie pants and sweats.

### PLAGE TAHITI
Map pp222-3                           *Women's Clothing*
☎ 215-569-9139; 128 S 17th St; ⏰ 10am-6pm Mon, Tue & Thu-Sat, 10am-7pm Wed; SEPTA Walnut-Locust Station, Bus 9, 21, 33, 42
Known for stocking the hottest jeans (FRX, Citizen's of Humanity, many others) in Center City, this cute boutique and the friendly girls who work here watch your back with Juicy sweats and some estate jewelry. It draws a pre–midlife-crisis crowd.

### STILETTO Map pp222-3            *Women's Shoes*
☎ 215-972-1393; 124 S 18th St; ⏰ 11am-6pm Mon & Tue, 10am-7pm Wed & Fri, 10am-6pm Thu, 10am-5pm Sat; SEPTA 19th St Station, Bus 2, 9, 21, 42
For the thinnest, tallest heels, check out this expensive high-fashion shop, so well regarded that it attracts folks like Patti Labelle and the Eagles' wives. Among the pointy items for sale are models by Gianmarco Lorenzi, Gianni Bravo and Roberto Cavalli.

### TOWN HOME Map pp222-3 *Home Accessories*
☎ 215-972-5100; 126 S 19th St; ⏰ 10am-6pm Mon, Tue & Thu-Sat, Wed 10am-8pm; SEPTA 19th St Station, Bus 2, 9, 21, 42
For mother-of-pearl cheese cutters, fancy display trays, stationery and Simon Pearce glassware, head into one of Rittenhouse Square's newer stores.

Shopping – Center City

# WASHINGTON SQUARE WEST

Many of this area's shops – particularly Afterwords and Giovanni's Room – cater to the gay community. Washington Square is also the place to find the store with Philadelphia's largest selection of beer. Move east along Market St, and shopping options get a tad sleazy. Around Market and 8th Sts is where to go to buy cheap knock-off electronics.

## AFTERWORDS

Map pp222-3                          *Magazines & Novelties*
☎ 215-735-2393; 218 S 12th St; ☺ 11am-10pm
Mon-Sat, 11am-7pm Sun; SEPTA Walnut-Locust Station, Bus 9, 12, 21, 23, 42

With a selection ranging from the risqué to the regular, Afterwords stocks nearly every kind of magazine. If you aren't in the mood for some light reading, check out the collection of kitsch, greeting cards and faux vintage lunch boxes.

## BAUM'S THEATER & DANCE SHOP

Map pp222-3                                  *Dancewear*
☎ 215-923-2244; 106 S 11th St; ☺ 9am-5:15pm
Mon-Fri, 9:30am-5pm Sat; SEPTA 11 St Station, Bus 9, 12, 21, 23, 42

Outfitting thespians since 1887, Baum's is a fourth-generation family-owned business. The large store carries ballet shoes, tap shoes, ballroom shoes, leotards, makeup, boas and a ton of wigs. If it has sequins, it's probably here.

## BUFFALO EXCHANGE

Map pp222-3                               *Used Clothing*
☎ 215-627-4647; 1109 Walnut St; ☺ 11am-7pm

## Shopping Malls

**The Bellevue** (Map pp222-3 ☎ 215-875-8350; 200 S Broad St; ☺ 10am-7pm Mon-Sat, noon-5pm Sun) Swanky, small and marbled, the mall includes Williams-Sonoma and others.

**The Gallery at Market East** (Map pp222-3; ☎ 215-925-7162; 9th & Market Sts; ☺ 10am-7pm Mon-Sat, noon-5pm Sun) This big concrete box from the '70s contains the usual mall staples and is positioned directly over a principal transportation hub.

**The Shops at Liberty Place** (Map pp222-3; ☎ 215-851-9055; 16th & Chestnut Sts; ☺ 9:30am-7pm Mon & Tue, 9:30am-8pm Wed, 9:30am-7pm Thu-Sat, noon-6pm Sun) A pinwheel of shops, it's got a Rand McNally, J Crew, Ann Taylor and other conventional clothiers.

Mon-Sat, noon-5pm Sun; SEPTA Walnut-Locust Station, Bus 9, 12, 21, 23, 42

This growing vintage chain buys and sells a good selection of used clothing and shoes for men and women. The prices are pretty good for hipsters needing cheap threads.

## THE FOODERY Map pp222-3                      *Beer*
☎ 215-928-1111; 324 S 10th St; ☺ 9am-midnight; SEPTA Lombard-South Station, Bus 23, 40

Philadelphia's best place to buy beer by the bottle, the Foodery, which doesn't look like anything special on the outside, is a small convenience store that somehow manages to stock a staggering selection of brews. To find what you need, consult the handy directory, which will point you to the right cooler and shelf. Sadly, there's no Double Diamond; for that, head over to the **Monk's Cafe** (p133).

## GIOVANNI'S ROOM Map pp222-3          *Books*
☎ 215-923-2960, 800-222-6996; 345 S 12th St; ☺ 11:30am-7pm Mon-Thu, 11:30am-10pm Fri, 10am-10pm Sat, 1-7pm Sun; SEPTA Lombard-South Station, Bus 23, 40

At Philadelphia's most comprehensive gay bookstore, the sections include lesbian literature, gay literature, art, politics, sadomasochism and more. Also look for CDs, a bunch of rainbow-colored bric-a-brac and a super-friendly staff. The store is a great place to pick up flyers advertising local events of interest.

## HELLO WORLD Map pp222-3          *Accessories*
☎ 215-545-7060; 340 S 12th St; ☺ 11am-7pm
Mon-Fri, noon-5pm Sat & Sun; SEPTA Lombard-South Station, Bus 23, 40

In this corner store you'll find a sweet selection of enviable youth-culture handbags as well as picture frames, candlesticks and well-designed lamps and jewelry.

## I GOLDBERG Map pp222-3              *Army/Navy*
☎ 215-925-9393; 1300 Chestnut St; ☺ 10am-5:45pm Mon, Tue, Thu & Sat, 10am-6:45pm Wed & Fri; SEPTA 13th St Station, Bus 9, 21, 23, 42

Cheap surplus gear and clothes sleep in the basement, with new uniforms, jackets, jeans, fatigues, boots and camping equipment neatly organized in the three floors above it.

## JUST HATS Map pp222-3                          *Hats*
☎ 215-627-7470; 130 S 12th St; ☺ 9:30am-5:30pm
Mon-Sat; SEPTA 11th St Station, Bus 9, 21, 23, 42

In the city where the Stetson was born, hat

shops like this old-school remnant, on a gritty stretch of 12th St, are virtually extinct. Come here for various shapes, sizes and colors of felt hats. The shop carries Stetson, Kangol, Dobbs and, if you're lucky, maybe even some made from beavers.

### LORD & TAYLOR

Map pp222-3          *Department Store*
☎ 215-241-9000; 1300 Market St; ◷ 10am-7pm Mon, Tue, & Thu-Sat, 10am-8pm Wed, noon-5pm Sun; SEPTA 11th St Station, Bus 9, 21, 23, 42
Occupying the former home of Wanamaker's, this department store boasts an atrium that's arguably the most stunningly beautiful place in Philadelphia, particularly around the December holidays (p14).

### MALE EGO Map pp222-3     *Sex Paraphernalia*
☎ 215-925-3233; 1206 Chancellor St; ◷ noon-7pm Sun-Wed, noon-11pm Thu-Sat; SEPTA Walnut-Locust Station, Bus 9, 21, 23, 42
With only two tiny floors, this store manages to offer a bit of everything: leather harnesses, sex accessories, gay porn and a small selection of club clothes and swimsuits.

### NEAT STUFF Map pp222-3     *Vintage Toys*
☎ 215-545-6883; 341 S 13th St; ◷ 1:15-5pm Mon-Sat; SEPTA Lombard-South Station, Bus 23, 40
Buying and selling toys from the 1950s through the '90s, this cluttered hole-in-the-wall also specializes in dust. There isn't any apparent organization system, and shoppers are often overheard saying, 'What the hell is that?' This is an excellent stop for those nostalgic about their childhood: a favorite memento is bound to be present.

### ROBIN'S BOOKS Map pp222-3     *Books*
☎ 215-735-9600; 110 S 13th St; ◷ 10am-8pm Mon-Sat, noon-8pm Sun; SEPTA Walnut-Locust Station, Bus 9, 21, 23, 42
This bookstore boasts a huge African American Studies section and a bookcase or two of quality travel guides in addition to generalist stock.

### SCARLETT Map pp222-3     *Cosmetics*
☎ 215-875-9408; 104 S 13th St; ◷ 11am-5pm; SEPTA Walnut-Locust Station, Bus 9, 21, 23, 42
Tread across a leopard-print carpet to pick up cosmetics, makeup, lotions and more at this boutique whose products recently were applied to Mandy Moore in a recent *Teen Magazine* cover appearance.

## Wanamaker's

Designed by Daniel Burnham back when department stores were an innovative breakthrough, this magnificent building (now home to Lord & Taylor; see p155) was visited in 1911 by President Taft, who declared it 'a revolution for the common man.' The store encircles a massive five-story grand court with a polychromatic vaulted ceiling, and every inch is covered in opulent materials. The grand court, the focal point of the store, becomes impossibly magnificent when the world's largest pipe organ booms to life at regular intervals during the Christmas season. Those who have never experienced the overwhelming power of the organ suddenly stiffen and stop, stunned. How could such sound and physical beauty be combined in a place where people innocently come to shop?

With over 2 million sq ft, this landmark (1902–11) is the largest building in the city. The organ dates from 1904, made for the St Louis World's Fair. It took 13 freight cars to transport it to Wanamaker's, and it was enlarged upon arrival. For more information, check out www.wanamakerorgan.com.

### SPIROS DOULIS Map pp222-3     *Jewelry*
☎ 215-922-1199; 136 S 11th St; ◷ 11am-5pm Mon-Fri; SEPTA 11th St Station, Bus 9, 12, 21, 23, 42
An ancient place run by an ancient guy, this small, disorderly shop is full of grandma's jewelry, baubles, clocks, watches and dusty relics. The man himself does repairs.

# SOUTH STREET & AROUND

Very young and very colorful, South Street east of 6th is packed solid with stores selling crazy stuff, dusty books, used records and body piercings.

### GILY JEAN'S Map pp228-9     *Western Wear*
☎ 215-592-9926; 320 South St; ◷ 11am-7pm Mon-Sat; Bus 40, 57, 63
If you happen to be a rough-riding rodeo freak, cowboy or cowgirl, then stop by this Western outfitter to satisfy your craving for oversized belt buckles and shiny boots.

### GREEN STREET CONSIGNMENT SHOP

Map pp228-9     *Rag Shop*
☎ 215-733-9261; 700 South St; ◷ 11am-8pm Mon-Thu, 11am-9pm Fri & Sat, 11am-7pm Sun; Bus 40, 47
With the bare look of a thrift store and the prices

## Shopping Rows

Philly has three unique shopping districts of the old-school pedestrian variety, where shops purveying similar items cluster together. All three – Antique Row, Fabric Row and Jeweler's Row – are cute enough to visit even without the intent to spend dough.

- **Antique Row**, running along Pine St between 9th and 17th Sts, is home to more than a dozen stores doing a trade in the old, with a collective inventory ranging from grandfather clocks to cheap metal TV trays. Find everything from the work of notable cabinetmakers to estate jewelry to all sorts of chintzy trinkets. Most places are open Monday through Saturday.

- **Fabric Row** runs along 4th St between Bainbridge and Catherine Sts. This row has been here since the late 1800s, and nearly every store along the strip deals in textiles. The place is a physical reminder that Philly was once the 'Workshop of the World.' You'll also find a small army of tailors.

- **Jeweler's Row**, on Sansom St between 7th and 8th Sts, is a single, festive block, slightly faded since its glory days in the early 20th century. It's easy to spot – just look for a charming street paved with red brick, a bunch of diamond sellers and plenty of patina.

of a consignment shop, it's possible to find a really cool dress or some linen pants for only a few dollars more than an actual bargain.

### HOUSE OF TEA Map pp228-9      Tea
☎ 215-923-8327; www.houseoftea.com; 720 S 4th St; ⏰ 10am-6pm Thu-Sat; Bus 40, 47

Founded by Nathaniel Litt, an architect who ran away to become (variously) a circus clown, a magician, and a **Le Bec-Fin** (p111) pastry chef (and whose story was interesting enough to be pictured on the cover of *Life* magazine), this shop stocks around 200 varieties of loose teas. Also for sale are tea accessories and a variety of Yixing teapots.

### PHILADELPHIA RECORD EXCHANGE
Map pp228-9      Records
☎ 215-925-7892; 618 S 5th St; ⏰ noon-8pm; Bus 40, 47

Don't be surprised if you see a sign stating, 'If we don't have it, you're an idiot.' This place means business, stocking vast selections of used jazz, R&B, rock (in the basement) and more. The various rooms are so cluttered that walking around with a backpack can be a challenge. Prices are fair.

### SOUTH ST ANTIQUES MARKET
Map pp228-9      Antiques & Vintage
☎ 215-592-0256; 615 S 6th St; ⏰ noon-7pm Wed & Thu, noon-8pm Fri & Sat, noon-7pm Sun; Bus 40, 47

Occupying a former synagogue, this place houses a selection of vintage clothing, jewelry, furniture and other items. Particularly good is **Jennie's Vintage**, located at the back of the 1st floor.

### SPACEBOY RECORDS Map pp228-9    CDs
☎ 215-925-3032; 409 South St; ⏰ noon-10pm Sun-Thu, noon-midnight Fri & Sat; Bus 40, 57, 63

This South St stalwart stocks many categories of music but focuses mostly on alternative stuff. While it carries vinyl, CDs remain the main attraction, and shoppers can listen to nearly anything before making a purchase. Spaceboy sells advance tickets to shows at some venues, including **R5 Productions** (p140).

### TIME ZONE Map pp228-9    Shoes & Clothing
☎ 215-592-8266; 535 South St; ⏰ noon-11pm Mon-Fri, 11am-11pm Sat, noon-9pm Sun; Bus 40, 47, 57, 63

Vintage clothes are stocked upstairs, coolie trends downstairs. There is a pretty wide selection of military-style boots, colorful leather shoes and nonathletic sneakers. Brands indicative of the shoe offerings are John Fluevog and Camper.

### ZIPPERHEAD Map pp228-9      Kitsch
☎ 215-928-1123; 407 South St; ⏰ noon-11pm Sun-Thu, noon-midnight Fri & Sat; Bus 40, 57, 63

Referenced in the Dead Milkmen song 'Punk Rock Girl,' this place has been drawing Philly's bleak teenagers since the '80s. They come to flirt with cute punk-rock staffers and buy hair dye and pins.

# SOUTH PHILADELPHIA

The Italian Market dominates the shopping scene in South Philadelphia.

### 9TH STREET RECORDS Map p228-9    Vinyl
☎ 215-922-2352; 820 S 9th St; ⏰ 11am-5pm Tue-Sat, 11am-2pm Sun; Bus 23, 47, 64

A musty, one-room hole-in-the-wall with an eclectic selection of used records, this shop specializes in jazz and experimental music. Milk crates are the principle organizing devices, and the owner is trying to cultivate a stock of cassettes, reasoning that they are now an endangered species.

## DI BRUNO'S BROTHERS

Map pp228-9        *Cheese*
☎ 215-922-2876; 930 S 9th St; ☽ 8am-6pm Tue-Sat,
8am-2pm Sun; Bus 23, 47, 64

Cheese with truffles? No problem. If this cheese shop, here since 1939, doesn't stock what you need, it's time to book a flight to Italy.

## FANTE'S KITCHEN WARES SHOP

Map pp228-9        *Kitchen & More*
☎ 215-922-5557; www.fantes.com; 1006 S 9th St;
☽ 9am-5pm Tue-Sat, 9am-1pm Sun; Bus 23, 47, 64

Family-run, nationally renowned Fante's has operated since 1906 and sells everything for the cook from wooden spoons to copper saucepans.

# UNIVERSITY CITY

University City has several decent bookstores, as if you couldn't have guessed that. Most shopping options are very close to campus, and east of 40th St.

## BLACK CAT Map p225      *Gifts*
☎ 215-386-6664; 3426 Sansom St; ☽ 11am-8pm;
SEPTA 36th St Station, Bus 21, 30, 42

Specializing in beautifully made, earth-friendly crafts, this is an ideal shop for anyone who likes either hippies or cats. Look for darling knit dolls, handmade kitty bowls, Fair Trade coffee that comes in a bag dressed up with a Zapatista mask and more.

## THE LAST WORD BOOKSHOP

Map p225        *Used Books*
☎ 215-386-7750; 3925 Walnut St; ☽ 10am-10pm;
SEPTA 40th St Station, Bus 21, 30, 40

A used bookstore with really beat-up couches, the Last Word welcomes lingering browsers. The only drawback is that the mood of the place is set by industrial carpets and lighting.

## PENN BOOK CENTER

Map p225        *Books*
☎ 215-386-7750; 130 S 34th St; ☽ 10am-10pm;
SEPTA 36th St Station, Bus 21, 30, 42

This small, well-stocked academic bookstore features a comprehensive 'human settlement/built environment' section, in addition to others. It's been a Penn institute since 1962.

## UNIVERSITY OF PENNSYLVANIA
## BOOKSTORE Map 225     *Books*
☎ 215-898-7595; 3601 Walnut St; ☽ 9am-10:30pm

Mon-Sat, 11am-8pm Sun; SEPTA 36th St Station, Bus 21, 30, 42

The official bookstore of the university, this place carries almost everything, including trinkets with Penn's logo printed on them. The travel section kicks ass.

# MANAYUNK

Picturesque Main St in Manayunk makes for a pleasant stroll through a valley of boutiques.

## AFRICA ON MAIN Map p230   *African Art*
☎ 215-483-3373; 4460 Main St; ☽ 11am-9pm Tue-Sun; SEPTA R6 Manayunk Station, Bus 35, 61

This friendly husband-and-wife-run gallery features masks, large wooden animal sculptures, jewelry and paintings, most of which they acquire during their frequent travels to sub-Saharan Africa. They also sell work rendered in shona stone.

## AMERICAN PIE Map p230    *Shoes*
☎ 215-487-3747; 4305 Main St; ☽ 11am-7pm Mon-Wed, 11am-8pm Thu-Sat, 11am-6pm Sun; SEPTA R6 Manayunk Station, Bus 35, 61

It's worth stopping in here if only to see the color palette of the various knickknacks for sale. Items include clocks, small furniture, some beautiful glass menorahs, some tacky glass menorahs, mirrors, ceramics and jewelry made by various American artisans. The staff encourages pets to enter.

## BEANS Map p230      *Beauty*
☎ 215-487-3333; www.beansbeauty.com; 4405 Main St; ☽ 10am-6pm Mon, Tue & Thu, 10am-9pm Wed, Fri & Sat, noon-6pm Sun; SEPTA R6 Manayunk Station, Bus 35, 61

Beans stocks a staggering assortment of cosmetics, soaps, hair clippers, combs, dyes and just about anything else that ever touches anyone's hair, skin or nails. It's the brainchild of a guy who's been styling hair for more than 20 years; his studio is upstairs.

## BENJAMIN LOVELL SHOES

Map p230        *Shoes*
☎ 215-487-3747; 4305 Main St; ☽ 11am-7pm Mon & Tue, 11am-8pm Wed & Thu, 11am-9pm Fri & Sat, noon-6pm Sun; SEPTA R6 Manayunk Station, Bus 35, 61

This shoe store, which operates another shop on **South Street** (Map pp228-9; ☎ 215-238-1969; 318 South St; ☽ 11am-8pm Mon-Thu, 11am-9pm

## Sales Tax

Neither Philadelphia nor Pennsylvania charges a sales tax on clothing, which amounts to a 7% discount on new apparel. Nearby states New Jersey and Delaware don't charge sales tax on clothes either, which might explain Philly's shopper-friendly policy.

Fri & Sat, 11am-5pm Sun), stocks shoes for men and women. Men's brands include Mephisto, Ecco, Naot and Camper, while women can add Dansko and more exotic fare to that list. As usual, the ladies have more choices.

### BIAS Map p230 *Clothing*
☎ 215-483-8340; 4442 Main St; ☺ 11am-7pm Mon-Tue, 11am-9pm Wed-Sat, noon-6pm Sun; SEPTA R6 Manayunk Station, Bus 35, 61
This tiny, glass-fronted boutique has a super small selection of cutesy skirts, pants and tank tops. Lately it's been attempting to cultivate a vaguely Japanese look.

### DOWN 2 EARTH
Map p230 *Earth-Friendly Miscellany*
☎ 215-482-4199; 4371 Main St; ☺ 11am-6pm Sun-Tue, 11am-9pm Wed-Thu, 11am-10pm Fri, 10am-10pm Sat; SEPTA R6 Manayunk Station, Bus 35, 61
Down 2 Earth sells a diverse number of recycled and all-natural products. Among the choices are a bunch of baby accessories, including some tiny tank tops with Philadelphia printed on them, quilted clothes hangers with smiling pigs and frogs on them, and pink and blue clocks. Other items are dog toys, novelty martini glasses, drinking equipment and picture frames. Burt's Bees products and their pals abound.

### THE EYEGLASS WORKS Map p230 *Eyewear*
☎ 215-487-2711; 4407 Main St; ☺ 10am-6pm Tue, Thu & Fri, 10am-8pm Wed, 10am-4pm Sat, noon-5pm Sun; SEPTA R6 Manayunk Station, Bus 35, 61
For one of Philadelphia's finest selection of colorful, plastic frames (yeah, they've got wire, too), people with eye trouble will love to stop in here. With a lab on site, the staff can cut most prescriptions pretty quickly.

### LEEHE FAI Map p230 *Women's Clothing*
☎ 215-483-4400; 4340 Main St; ☺ 11am-7pm Mon, Tue & Fri, 11am-9pm Wed & Thu, 10am-7pm Sat, noon-6pm Sun; SEPTA R6 Manayunk Station, Bus 35, 61
On the main floor of this upscale, expensive and colorful shop is a wide range of boutique

clothing (Tocca, Jaunty) plus a few handbags. On the 2nd floor, a great selection of formal and evening wear lies on an interior balcony overlooking the main level. Leehe Fai maintains a second store on **Rittenhouse Square** (Map pp222-3; ☎ 215-564-6111; 133 S 18th St; ☺ 10am-7pm Mon-Fri, 10am-9pm Sat, noon-6pm Sun).

### MAINLY SHOES Map p230 *Shoes*
☎ 215-483-8000; 4410 Main St; ☺ 11am-7pm Mon & Tue, 11am-8:30pm Wed & Thu, 11am-9:30pm Fri & Sat, noon-6pm Sun; SEPTA R6 Manayunk Station, Bus 35, 61
For men, this store stocks a bunch of Prada, Cole Hann, Puma and Bacco Bucci. Women luck out with a bigger selection (surprise!), also featuring Prada, Robert Clergerie and others.

### PUBLIC IMAGE Map p230 *Women's Clothing*
☎ 215-482-4008; 4390 Main St; ☺ 11am-6pm Mon & Tue, 11am-7pm Wed-Sat, noon-5pm Sun; SEPTA R6 Manayunk Station, Bus 35, 61
With an eye that spots young fresh talent in New York before it gets to the Bergdorf Goodman level, those in charge of Public Image make it a good spot for new fashion. They also have a great collection of upper-middle-price-range stuff that's pretty hard to come by in Philly, such as Tocca, Vivienne Tam and Cynthia Rowley. It's like SoHo next to a bike path.

### TAG Map p230 *Clothing*
☎ 215-482-9656; 4358 Main St; ☺ 11am-8pm Mon-Sat, 11am-7pm Sun; SEPTA R6 Manayunk Station, Bus 35, 61
TAG's offerings are all about trendy urban clothes for men and women. It sells a ton of Von Dutch, Guess and other big names.

### UNIQUE EYEWEAR
Map p230 *Glasses & Bags*
☎ 215-483-5300; 4257 Main St; ☺ 11am-6pm Mon-Sat; SEPTA R6 Manayunk Station, Bus 35, 61
The main attraction of this store seems not to be its small selection of designer frames, which is dominated by Fendi, but rather its stock of well-displayed shoulder bags, which is dominated by Manhattan Portage.

### WHY BE BOARD Map p230 *Games*
☎ 215-483-8800; 4333 Main St; ☺ 10am-6pm Mon-Sat, noon-6pm Sun; SEPTA R6 Manayunk Station, Bus 35, 61
A colorful store stocking hard-to-find puzzles and toys, Why Be Board specializes in an excellent (if disorganized) selection of games,

including a number of items for adults. If you happen to be looking for something electronic, you'd better not stop in here.

# CHESTNUT HILL

Almost everything commercial lies along Germantown Ave. Warning: the cuteness of the little boutiques, stone Victorian homes and babies in strollers might be overwhelming.

## ARTISANS ON THE AVENUE

Map p231 *Clothing & Home Accessories*
☎ 215-381-0582; 8428 Germantown Ave; ☽ 11am-5pm Tue-Sat; SEPTA R8 Chestnut Hill West, R7 Chestnut Hill East, Bus 23

Seven women own and operate this shop and Artisans, Too!, down the street. They make everything they sell in the store, from kids' clothes to dresses to sweaters to painted furniture.

## CALEB MEYER STUDIO

Map p231 *Jewelry & Crafts*
☎ 215-248-9250; 8520 Germantown Ave; ☽ 10am-5:30pm Tue-Fri, 10am-5pm Sat; SEPTA R8 Chestnut Hill West, R7 Chestnut Hill East, Bus 23

There are two types of things for sale at this jewelry studio: those handmade by the Caleb Meyer people, and those handmade by American artisans who work independently of the studio. The folks at Caleb Meyer work with platinum and gold, and the craftspeople they host deal with everything from silver to wood to colored glass. Expect high quality and matching prices. Also expect a really sleepy old dog to be lying around.

## CHESTNUT HILL CHEESE SHOP

Map p231 *Cheese*
☎ 215-242-2211; 8509 Germantown Ave; ☽ 9am-5:30pm Mon-Sat, noon-4pm Sun; SEPTA R8 Chestnut Hill West, R7 Chestnut Hill East, Bus 23

A dark cheese shop with nice old shelves and some of that old-school Chestnut Hill patina, this place offers the area's best selection of quality cheeses. It also sells various specialty goods, such as caviar, jams and things that have been pickled.

## CHESTNUT HILL SPORTS

Map p231 *Sporting Goods*
☎ 215-242-6167; 8628 Germantown Ave; ☽ 9am-7pm Mon-Fri, 9am-6pm Sat, 10am-4pm Sun; SEPTA R8 Chestnut Hill West, R7 Chestnut Hill East, Bus 23

Another decades-old Chestnut Hill store, this one sells a wide range of athletic equipment. It has a particularly good selection of cleats and La Crosse gear. In terms of apparel, there's a bunch of styles of Speedos, shorts and sweatshirts. The store makes it very easy to find whatever Phillies, Flyers, Sixers or Eagles jersey you might need, even if you happen to be an infant.

## EL QUETZAL
Map p231 *Women's Boutique*
☎ 215-247-6588; 8427 Germantown Ave; ☽ 10am-6pm Mon-Sat, noon-5pm Sun; SEPTA R8 Chestnut Hill West, R7 Chestnut Hill East, Bus 23

This women's clothing and home goods store specializes in washable linens and comfortable easy wear. Representative brands include Flax and Fresh Produce. If you want shoes and you intend to buy them here, be prepared to select from one of five styles of Naot.

## FRENCH LEMON

Map p231 *Accessories & Shoes*
☎ 215-247-6177; 8442 Germantown Ave; ☽ 10am-5pm Tue-Sat; SEPTA R8 Chestnut Hill West, R7 Chestnut Hill East, Bus 23

This small, eclectic, sort-of French-themed store carries men's bow ties, crystal candlestick holders, a few enviable modern watches and a plethora of color. The French Lemon's most consistent draw is its selection of women's shoes, some of them by Amy J Gladstone and Lacoste, others by more obscure makers.

## INTERMISSION

Map p231 *Performing Arts & CDs*
☎ 215-242-8515; 8405 Germantown Ave; ☽ 10am-6pm Mon-Sat, 11am-5pm Sun; SEPTA R8 Chestnut Hill West, R7 Chestnut Hill East, Bus 23

This store sells CD recordings of opera, the Philadelphia orchestra, jazz, blues, Broadway soundtracks and classical music. It also stocks scripts, theatrical posters and various other trinkets. A selection of carnivalesque marionettes and other kinds of puppets hangs from the ceiling.

## KILIAN HARDWARE COMPANY

Map p231 *Hardware*
☎ 215-247-0945; 8450 Germantown Ave; ☽ 8:30am-5:30pm Mon-Fri, 8:30am-5pm Sat; SEPTA R8 Chestnut Hill West, R7 Chestnut Hill East, Bus 23

It's hard to believe that places like this still exist in America. Kilian, established in 1913, is a large hardware store with overflowing shelves reaching all the way to some very high ceilings. Without bragging too much, the folks at Kilian can rightly claim that 'if we don't have it, it probably doesn't exist.' Don't expect to find anything yourself; very likely, you'll need to find both a guide and a ladder. Among the goods stocked are banjos, mulch, decent kitchen knives and working antique phones.

### LA VIE CREATIF Map p231 *Home Accessories*
☎ 215-248-5000; 8609 Germantown Ave; ☽ 10am-5:30pm Tue-Sat, noon-4pm Sun; SEPTA R8 Chestnut Hill West, R7 Chestnut Hill East, Bus 23

Nice smells, dried flowers, wooden fruit and select furniture abound in this somewhat cluttered three-room American crafts place. Check out the lamps designed by the Kinzig sisters. They cost around 500 bucks, but as one browsing local said, 'In a world where finding a decent lamp is like finding an accurate pirate map pointing to treasure buried near your home, these shiny friends are a steal.'

### MANGO Map p231 *Girls' Boutique*
☎ 215-248-9299; 8622 Germantown Ave; ☽ 10am-5:30pm Mon-Sat, noon-5pm Sun; SEPTA R8 Chestnut Hill West, R7 Chestnut Hill East, Bus 23

The one Chestnut Hill boutique catering to the younger female crowd vends journals, incense, inexpensive silver jewelry and plenty of gifty stuff. It also sells dresses and sweaters.

### MONKEY BUSINESS Map p231 *Thrift Store*
☎ 215-248-1835; 8624B Germantown Ave; ☽ 9:30am-4pm Tue-Fri, 10am-4pm Sat; SEPTA R8 Chestnut Hill West, R7 Chestnut Hill East, Bus 23

This volunteer-run store selling 'gently worn' upscale stuff donates all proceeds to a Chestnut Hill hospital. Men will have better odds finding a decent suit here than in any place on South St. The shop isn't directly on Germantown Ave; head down a little driveway to find it sitting behind the buildings that front the street.

### O'DOODLES Map p231 *Toys*
☎ 215-247-7405; 8335 Germantown Ave; ☽ 9:30am-6pm Mon-Fri, 11am-5pm Sun; SEPTA R8 Chestnut Hill West, R7 Chestnut Hill East, Bus 23

The owners of O'Doodles formerly ran a stationery store out of this building until a Staples opened down the street. Rather than compete with that monster, they switched operations and now run perhaps Philadelphia's finest toy store (at least for those 12 and

under). The selection is a mixture of conventional games, creativity products, toys and more obscure upscale stuff. Kids are always eager to enter the exceedingly colorful innards; they are always exceedingly reluctant to leave.

### THE PHILADELPHIA PRINT SHOP
Map p231 *Antiquated Maps & Prints*
☎ 215-242-4750; 8441 Germantown Ave; ☽ 10am-5pm Mon-Sat; SEPTA R8 Chestnut Hill West, R7 Chestnut Hill East, Bus 23

Run by two guys who make regular appearances on PBS's *Antiques Roadshow*, this gallery has an excellent collection of old maps, 19th-century bird's-eye views of various cityscapes, and engravings of natural science specimens from the Age of Enlightenment. Also for sale are rare books. If something needs paper restoration, take it here.

### THE PIPE RACK Map p231 *Tobacconist*
☎ 215-242-3625; 8433C Germantown Ave; ☽ 10am-5pm Mon-Sat; SEPTA R8 Chestnut Hill West, R7 Chestnut Hill East, Bus 23

The barely legible wooden sign out front, whose paint has nearly all peeled away, indicates that this tobacconist has been in operation since 1920. The selection of loose leaves is pretty good, the selection of pipes could use improvement and the lazy organization inside comforts many visitors.

### QUELQUE CHOSE
Map p231 *Women's Accessories*
☎ 215-248-6022; 8437 Germantown Ave; ☽ 10am-5pm Mon-Sat; SEPTA R8 Chestnut Hill West, R7 Chestnut Hill East, Bus 23

Quelque Chose stocks novelty bubble bath, a small assortment of toiletries, scarves and solid-colored jackets ranging from bright orange to brown. There's also a good selection of handbags of numerous sizes, fabrics (none are leather) and patterns.

### STYLOS Map p231 *Accessories*
☎ 215-753-1118; 8436 Germantown Ave; ☽ 10am-5pm Tue & Thu-Sat, 10am-7pm Wed, noon-4pm Sun; SEPTA R8 Chestnut Hill West, R7 Chestnut Hill East, Bus 23

This boutique caters to older ladies and those with more traditional tastes. Among the items carried are Brighton shoes, sweaters, knits, scarves, wallets and other miscellany.

# Sleeping

# Sleeping

Philadelphia's range of accommodation reflects its age and history as an important American urban center. There are B&Bs built before the Revolutionary War (one of which is on the campus of the Independence Mall), a hostel in a converted Fairmount Park mansion, numerous hotels built during Philadelphia's industrial boom and a number of steel-frame modern monsters in the Museum District. Most recently, new facilities – one of them big enough to house a small town – have been built for conventioneers. Nearly all hotels, B&Bs and even hostels are located in Center City, with a few options near University City and the requisite enclave of towers and motels in the asphalt jungle surrounding the airport.

There are a good number of guesthouses and B&Bs, at which you can expect intimacy and camaraderie but not an ice machine down the hall. If you intend to stay at a B&B, it's best to make reservations in advance; if you simply show up and ring the bell, there might be anyone there to answer. Note that many B&Bs operate out of row houses that have a lot of stairs and poor handicapped access. Budget travelers should be warned that there are only a few hostels in town, and these come with a curfew.

National chains run most of the hotels in town. Several of them – notably the Radisson, the Park Hyatt at the Bellevue, the Ritz-Carlton and the Best Western at Independence Park – occupy beautiful old buildings and thus come with more character than their names suggest. Most hotels have some kind of parking service. Usually it involves a valet and costs about $25 per day. The Park Hyatt at the Bellevue and the Holiday Inn Historic District only charge $16, but you park for yourself.

> ## Top Five Places to Sleep
>
> - **Park Hyatt at the Bellevue** (p164) Welcome to the Gilded Age
> - **La Reserve** (p165) Friendly B&B with sweet antiques
> - **Ritz-Carlton** (p164) Militarily crisp service in a hotel attached to a model of the Pantheon
> - **Sheraton Rittenhouse Square** (p165) The nation's first 'environmental hotel' overlooking the eminent square
> - **Shippen Way Inn** (p168) Affordable, colonial and cute

The tourism and marketing folks at www.gophila.com intermittently offer a deal where travelers can get two nights for the price of one, plus free parking. Peek at their website to check for specials before booking your room.

## OLD CITY

Many of the lodging options in this neighborhood sit directly across the street from the Independence National Historical Park. If you're south of Market St, the closer you get to 2nd St, the closer you are to Old City's potent bar and club scene. Head north of Market, and you're in the midst of a gallery and cultural district.

### Budget

**BANK ST HOSTEL** Map pp226-7     *Hostel*
☎ 215-922-0222; 2 S Bank St; dm $20; ⊠ ; SEPTA 2nd St Station, Bus 9, 12, 21, 42, 57
A clean, comfortable hostel in Old City, this place has separate men's and women's dormitories. There is a large, well-equipped kitchen and dining area with free tea and coffee, a pool table, washer-dryer facilities and a TV lounge. The hostel is closed between 10am and 4:30pm, but you can drop off your bags during this time. There's a 12:30am curfew Sunday to Thursday, 1am on Friday and Saturday.

**SOCIETY HILL HOTEL** Map pp226-7     *B&B*
☎ 215-925-1919; www.societyhillhotel.com; 301 Chestnut St; r $80-100, ste $120-150; SEPTA 2nd St Station, Bus 9, 12, 21, 42, 57
This building opened in 1832 to provide lodging for longshoremen. Today the 12-room inn sits atop a congenial restaurant and bar, which gets popular at lunchtime. The complimentary

breakfast consists of juice, coffee and warmed breads. There's no elevator.

## Mid-Range

### BEST WESTERN – THE INDEPENDENCE PARK HOTEL

Map pp226-7                                      *Boutique Hotel*
☎ 215-922-4443, 800-624-2988; www.independence
parkhotel.com; 235 Chestnut St; r $129-189; SEPTA 2nd
St Station, Bus 9, 12, 21, 42, 57

Once a dry goods store and shop for a doll manufacturer, this mid-19th-century building is now a small, 36-room boutique hotel. While much of the charm of the old rooms has been retained, some of the decorating flair is a little tacky. There's a decent breakfast in the morning with fresh waffles and fruit. Some evenings the hotel hosts a fireside wine-and-cheese reception in the lobby.

### HOLIDAY INN – HISTORIC DISTRICT

Map pp226-7                                               *Hotel*
☎ 215-923-8660, 800-843-2355; www.holiday-inn
.com; 400 Arch St; r $99-149; P ; SEPTA 5th St Station,
Bus 48, 57, 76

This hotel does the job for those who want to sleep close to the Liberty Bell. It's a modern, eight-story structure with an outdoor pool and mediocre breakfast.

### OMNI HOTEL  Map pp226-7                        *Hotel*
☎ 215-925-0000; www.omnihotels.com; 401 Chestnut
St; r $150-200; P ; SEPTA 5th St Station, Bus 9, 12,
21, 42, 57

While the Omni's rooms are somewhat lackluster, many of them have really great views of Independence National Historical Park. That and the great location explain why the Omni can get away with charging a slightly inflated price. The lobby comes off much better than the rooms, and its fireplace is big, active and cozy during winter months.

### PENN'S VIEW HOTEL

Map pp226-7                                      *Boutique Hotel*
☎ 215-922-7600, 800-331-7634; www.pennsview
hotel.com; Front & Market Sts; r without/with Jacuzzi
$165/185; P ; SEPTA 2nd St Station, Bus 48, 57, 76

This beautiful old hotel overlooks the Delaware River – too bad about that expressway out front, though. Some of the 27 rooms have fireplaces and Jacuzzis, and a continental breakfast is included. Ask for something on the top floor, as this provides the best possible

view and the greatest distance from the interstate. The hotel also contains the impressive **Il Bar** (p131), which offers 120 wines by the glass.

### THOMAS BOND HOUSE

Map pp226-7                                                *B&B*
☎ 215-923-8523; www.winston-salem-inn.com/
philadelphia; 129 S 2nd St; r $95-115, ste $145-175;
SEPTA 2nd St Station, Bus 9, 12, 21, 42, 57

This is it – your big chance to sleep in a house that Benjamin Franklin visited. Owned by the National Park Service and part of Independence National Historical Park, this home was built by Thomas Bond, a surgeon and buddy of Franklin, who played an instrumental role in founding the Pennsylvania Hospital. The building dates from 1769, with later additions made in 1824 and 1840. The rooms may be small, but they are laden with history (plenty of framed documents mounted throughout the house repeatedly explain and underscore this point). Breakfast is light on weekdays and substantial on weekends. The place is well maintained, having undergone restoration in 1988.

# SOCIETY HILL & PENN'S LANDING

Staying in Society Hill is a good deal. It's a quiet, residential neighborhood with the most popular historic sites only a few blocks away. South Street and its counter-cultural offerings are nearly as close. Penn's Landing is a bit noisier, and you have to walk over the freeway every time you want to come into town.

### SHERATON SOCIETY HILL

Map pp226-7                                               *Hotel*
☎ 215-238-6000; www.sheraton.com; 1 Dock St;
r $129-179; P ; Bus 12, 40

Set in a safe, quiet spot in one of Philadelphia's toniest neighborhoods, this four-story modern contraption holds 365 rooms. A few have windows that overlook the interior lobby, which indeed means that other hotel guests can see into these rooms unless the curtains are drawn. All of the equipment in the exercise room was replaced in the fall of 2003, so it's in great shape, even if you aren't. There's also a heated indoor pool, three restaurants and a slightly grumpy staff.

## Brave New Rooms

For the cheapest deals on the swankiest rooms, the Internet has become a traveler's best friend. Generally you can get the lowest possible room rates when using a 'bid-for-travel' website such as www.priceline.com or www.hotwire.com. At Priceline, you specify a geographic area within the city you'll be staying, select the type of hotel you're looking for (4, 3, 2 or 1 stars) and enter a bid, which they'll accept or reject. At Hotwire, you pick from quoted prices. More often than not, the rate you'll win is significantly less than those offered by the hotels directly. It's conceivable to stay at the Ritz-Carlton for $60 per night!

However the 'bid-for-travel' sites come with risks. For example, bidders forfeit control over choosing a specific hotel – if you know in advance that you want to stay exclusively at the Bellevue, then these sites are not for you. If you are unsure about your dates of travel, note that room reservations come with a strict no-cancellation policy. The fabulous website www.biddingfortravel.com provides a FAQ that thoroughly explains the pitfalls of name-your-price websites and can walk first-time bidders through the process while outlining strategies.

For those who find the randomized hotel selection of Priceline and Hotwire unpalatable, the Internet can help you, too. Sites like www.hotels.com, www.hoteldiscounts.com, www.travelocity.com and www.expedia.com allow you to be your own travel agent: you enter your travel dates, and a list of available hotels pops up, generally arranged from cheapest to most expensive. Because these sites handle millions of reservations every year, hotels regularly give them reduced rates. They are great clearinghouses for rooms at well below published rates.

Additionally, many hotels post special prices on their own websites, where the tariffs offered will often be less than the rates quoted by the people who man front desks. Like airlines, they often give Internet users a better deal if rooms are purchased at least two weeks in advance.

### HYATT REGENCY AT PENN'S LANDING Map pp226-7 _Hotel_

☎ 215-928-1234; www.pennslanding.hyatt.com; 201 S Columbus Blvd; r $129-199; Ⓟ ; Bus 25

While enjoying a beautiful view of the waterfront and Benjamin Franklin Bridge, this Hyatt suffers the same fate as everything else on Penn's Landing – it feels (and is) cut off from the rest of the city. The rooms are nice, though, and come with complimentary Internet access.

# CENTER CITY

The different neighborhoods of Center City present very distinct lodging experiences. Generally you're in for a more entertaining nighttime experience if you are sleeping south of Market St. As you get closer to Pine St, things get increasingly residential and increasingly genteel, particularly around Rittenhouse Square.

## AVENUE OF THE ARTS

Sleeping along Broad St is a fine idea, especially since it means you're probably staying in one of the nicest hotels in the city. It also means most theater options are on your doorstep, and both Rittenhouse Square and the Gayborhood are only a few blocks away. Though Broad St can get a bit loud, rooms are so high up it doesn't really matter.

### PARK HYATT AT THE BELLEVUE

Map pp222-3 _Hotel_

☎ 215-893-1234, 800-778-7477; www.park philadelphia.hyatt.com; Broad St at Walnut St; r $125-275, average $159; Ⓟ ; SEPTA Walnut-Locust St Station, Bus 12, 27, 32

Modeled after works of the French Renaissance and topped with an enormously complicated mansard roof, this grand dame, designed by the Hewitt brothers, was once considered among the finest hotels in the country. Its status was greatly reduced in the 1970s, when bacteria from the hotel's ventilation system killed 29 guests, and the hotel became _the_ place to contract Legionnaires' disease. Due to fear over Legionnaires' and a general decline in demand for lodging in Philadelphia, the hotel now operates only on the top seven floors of the building. The remaining rooms are magnificent. In America, where old hotels were systematically stripped of their interior character during postwar renovations, the Bellevue somehow managed to escape that terrible fate. The wallpaper alone is reason enough to stay here.

### RITZ-CARLTON Map pp222-3 _Hotel_

☎ 215-523-8000; www.ritzcarlton.com/hotels/ philadelphia; 10 Avenue of the Arts; r $200-300; Ⓟ ; SEPTA 15th St Station, Bus 21, 27, 32, 42

This Ritz possesses one of the most lavish hotel lobbies in North America. Built between 1905 and 1908 by McKim, Mead and White, it was modeled after the Pantheon and boasts a marble dome spanning over 100ft with an oculus about 140ft from the floor (it's not an exact reproduction – don't expect the Pantheon's Attic placage). During the afternoon, a formal afternoon tea is held in the rotunda. The 331 rooms contained in a pre-WWII adjoining tower, formerly used as a bank, are the usual high-end Ritz stuff. As the hotel just opened in 2000, the spacious, marble-clad bathrooms feel about as clean as an operating room.

# RITTENHOUSE SQUARE

This is the safest and most fashionable part of town. Rooms that overlook the square directly are hard to beat. A stretch of hotels along 17th St is close to nightlife, and Pine St's La Reserve is nice and quiet.

# Budget

### LA RESERVE Map pp222-3                      B&B
☎ 215-735-1137, 800-354-8401; www.centercity bed.com; 1804 Pine St; r $85-110; ✕ ; SEPTA Lombard-South St Station, Bus 40, 17

Though this elegant 1868 row house looks completely formal and French, the guy who runs it – Bill Buchanan – couldn't be more laid-back. Aside from the considerable collection of good antiques, there's a garden and fattening breakfasts. La Reserve is in a quiet, safe neighborhood close to lots of Philly hot spots. Guests tend to come from academic and creative circles, and often end up being repeat customers. For entertainment, lodgers either hit the town or play the Steinway in the front room. There are no TVs and parking can be tricky. Rooms have shared baths.

# Mid-Range

### LATHAM HOTEL Map pp222-3 Boutique Hotel
☎ 215-563-7474; www.lathamhotel.com; 135 S 17th St; r $109-149; P ; SEPTA Walnut-Locust St Station, Bus 2, 7, 12, 21, 42

This European-style oldie sits close to Rittenhouse Square, and a few of the rooms on the highest floors provide a glimpse of the park. Often there's a package deal: for an additional $20 or so, you get parking and breakfast for two. For an additional $10, guests get a room with a bay window and better views (not necessarily of the square). The staff is very friendly, but the bed coverings are very red.

### RADISSON PLAZA – WARWICK HOTEL
Map pp222-3                                    Hotel
☎ 215-735-6000, 800-333-3333; www.radisson.com; 1701 Locust St; r $110-190; P ; SEPTA Walnut-Locust St Station, Bus 2, 7, 12, 21, 42

Known as the Warwick Philadelphia until recently, this 1926 'English Renaissance' beauty has attracted many celebrities over its years. Sly Stallone lived here for two years, OJ Simpson did some time here as well, and President Clinton and both Bushes visited, too. Rumors claim that Joe Louis' first professional boxing match was held in the ballroom. Because of the age of the building and the fact that it was once an apartment building, the 545 rooms – many of which overlook Rittenhouse Square – are oversized, and they're not cookie-cutter. The hotel is cool about pets so long as they weigh less than 50lb.

### SHERATON RITTENHOUSE SQUARE
Map pp222-3                                    Hotel
☎ 215-546-9400, 800-325-3535; www.sheraton.com; 18th St at Locust St; standard $129-199; park view $144-214; ✕ P ; SEPTA Walnut-Locust St Station, Bus 2, 7, 12, 21, 42

The first 'environmentally smart' hotel in the US, originally built in the early 20th century as a men's athletic club, does not allow smokes or pets inside. Staples, not glue, hold down the carpets, which are cleaned with non-toxic products. The bedding is organic, and most of the furniture is made from recycled shipping pallets – not that you could tell by looking at it. Folks with allergies often stay here, as the air-filtration system is state-of-the-art, creating a mold- and pollen-free environment. Many of

Sleeping – Center City

---

## Top Five Hotel Bars

- **Il Bar** (p131) Sample over 120 wines by the glass at Penn's View Hotel's bar/restaurant.
- **Library Lounge** (p132) Don't forget to bring a pipe and smoking jacket to this watering hole in the Bellevue.
- **Loews** (p167) On the 1st floor of the PSFS building (aka Loews Philadelphia Hotel) is this art-deco–inspired, clublike bar that gets packed when conventions come to town.
- **POD** (p121) Hang with the undergrads at The Inn at Penn bar and feel like an astronaut.
- **Ritz-Carlton** (p164) Take your pick: smoke a cigar in a former bank vault or enjoy a cocktail in McKim's model of the Pantheon.

the rooms have excellent views of Rittenhouse Square, though a few of the parkside rooms have only one small window. Avoid these, and ask for digs with more substantial glass.

### SOFITEL Map pp222-3 *Hotel*
☎ 215-569-8300; www.sofitel.com; 120 S 17th St; r $129-279; Ⓟ; SEPTA 15th St Station, Bus 2, 7, 12, 21, 42

The staff at this recently renovated hotel behave like actual people instead of courteous robots, which is one of the ways Sofitel stands apart from its neighbors. The 306 modern rooms are warmly designed using a subdued color palette, comfortable beds and cherry furniture. Eight rooms are specially designed to cater to the needs of disabled travelers. There's a gym and pets are welcome. Unlike other hotels that are trying to be European, this French-owned job actually is.

## Top End

### THE RITTENHOUSE Map pp222-3 *Hotel*
☎ 215-546-9000; www.rittenhousehotel.com; 210 W Rittenhouse Square; r $250-350; Ⓟ; SEPTA 19th St Station, Bus 12, 17

There is a reason why the Rittenhouse's website and brochure don't show an exterior image of the building it inhabits: its 20th-century ugliness is entirely out of character with the rest of the surrounding 19th-century square. However, exterior unsightliness vanishes inside with 98 exceptionally appointed rooms and massive windows specially angled to provide amazing views of the park. There's a full-size swimming pool, excellent spa and very attentive service. During peak season, book your bed a month in advance.

### RITTENHOUSE SQUARE BED & BREAKFAST
Map pp222-3 *B&B*
☎ 215-546-6500; www.rittenhousebb.com; 1715 Rittenhouse Square; s $179-229, ste $229-299; ✉; SEPTA Walnut-Locust St Station, Bus 2, 12

Exceedingly formal, the staff at the Rittenhouse behave more like they work in a hotel than in a B&B. The precious place occupies a beautifully renovated carriage house and feels like it might have been one of Louis XIV's properties. Oprah Winfrey stays here when she comes to town. Kids under 12 are not permitted.

## WASHINGTON SQUARE WEST

Up along Market St is the worthy Loews Philadelphia Hotel in the former PSFS

building. Almost everything else is clustered around Antique Row and the Gayborhood.

## Budget

### ANTIQUE ROW B&B Map pp222-3 *B&B*
☎ 215-592-7802; 341 S 12th St; r $65-110; ✉; SEPTA Lombard-South St Station, Bus 23, 40

In a lovely, comfortable house, this B&B's offerings range from small rooms to apartments with private bathrooms and kitchens. Most rooms have telephones (local calls are free), a few have shared baths and all have cable TV. Fixings for breakfast are provided, and guests can make what they like (eggs, toast, cereal). Barbara Pope is the friendly host; if she has no vacancies, she'll help you book rooms elsewhere. Discounts are available for longer stays.

### UNCLES UPSTAIRS INN Map pp222-3 *B&B*
☎ 215-546-6660; www.unclesinn.com; 1220 Locust St; r standard/deluxe $85/105; SEPTA Walnut-Locust St Station, Bus 23, 40

Occupying a nicely restored 19th-century row house and positioned above a popular bar, Uncles attracts a largely gay following. The breakfast is good, and most lodgers end up hanging out at the bar downstairs for at least a portion of the evening, which often helps to create a sense of camaraderie between the guests. The rooms on the top floor are quieter than those directly above the bar, which can get quite loud.

## Mid-Range

### ALEXANDER INN Map pp222-3 *Hotel*
☎ 215-923-3535; www.alexanderinn.com; 12th & Spruce Sts; s/d/king $99/109/139; SEPTA Walnut-Locust St Station, Bus 12, 23

Though the outside is an odd combination of old brick walls accented with vinyl-sided bay windows, the rooms at this inn look and feel pretty good. The partially successful design intent was to model the rooms in a pseudo-art-deco fashion, 'reflecting the great cruise ships of the '40s.' As at many hotels, the designers did a better job in the lobby than in the rooms themselves. Thankfully, whoever decorated prefers actual art to 'tasteful' renderings of fruit. Continental breakfast and gym use are complimentary. If vacancies exist, this place is a good bet during peak tourist season, as it never inflates room rates.

Sleeping – Center City

## LOEWS PHILADELPHIA HOTEL

Map pp222-3                                    *Hotel*

☎ 215-627-1200; www.loewshotels.com/hotels/
philadelphia; 1200 Market St; r $125-195; **P** ; SEPTA
Market Station East, Bus 23, 38, 42

On the inside, the new Loews Hotel shoots
for an art-deco design theme that attempts
to match the exterior brilliance of the building it occupies: the PSFS, an International-style
masterwork (and National Historic Landmark)
by Howe and Lescaze. Expect limited success.
While architects swoon over the famed curving
lines of the building's base at 12th and Market
Sts, and lodgers sleeping inside might get a few
more style points than those staying at the Marriott across the street, the rooms really aren't that
much different. However, the list of amenities offered is extensive. Feel like a sauna? Also, pets get
the royal treatment, with walking and grooming
services, toys and vet-approved room service.

## TEN ELEVEN CLINTON Map pp222-3   *B&B*

☎ 215-923-8144; www.teneleven.com; 1011 Clinton
St; r $145-175; Bus 23, 47

Comfortably situated on a quiet side street, this
five-room B&B lives in a big brick building from
1836. Currently the rooms are a bit floral, though a
redesign is in the works. Guests have access to an
absolutely silent patio. The makings for breakfast
are provided, but guests have to put in the labor.
Rooms contain a private kitchen and bath.

# Top End

## THE INN ON LOCUST Map pp222-3   *Hotel*

☎ 215-985-1905; www.innonlocust.com; 1234 Locust
St; r $175-250, multilevel ste $375; SEPTA Walnut-
Locust St Station, Bus 12, 23

A law firm until the owners decided to make
it an inn, this is the place to be for business
types. Each of the 24 rooms has been tastefully
modernized, featuring simple designs and ergo-
nomic furniture that coexists nicely with turn-of-
the-century brick walls, tall ceilings and French
windows. There are DVD players, Ethernet connections and a staff that will roll your bed out of
your room and replace it with a conference table
and chairs, should you be meeting with up to 18
of your associates. Rooms vary in size, and there's
a public parking lot across the street.

# PARKWAY & MUSEUM AREA

This neighborhood is largely made up of
office towers and hotels. At night, after people
go home, it can be a bit of a ghost town.

# Budget & Mid-Range
## BEST WESTERN CENTER CITY

Map pp222-3                                    *Hotel*

☎ 215-568-8300; www.bestwestern.com; 501 N 22nd
St; r $99-129; **P** ; Bus 7, 32, 38

On the backside of the **Rodin Museum** (p78),
this place looks and feels like a motel. It's a
bit distant from most of the action in Center
City, but it does have the rare advantage of
free parking.

## COURTYARD BY MARRIOTT

Map pp222-3                                    *Hotel*

☎ 215-496-3200; www.marriott.com/courtyard;
21 N Juniper St; r $99-200; **P** ; SEPTA 13th St Station,
Bus 23, 38, 42

Mostly visited by corporate types wearing
Brooks Brothers suits, this is one of several
in Philly's collection of super-tall buildings on
the historic registry that are now operated as
hotels by national chains. Directly across from
City Hall, it's about as close to the geographic
center of town as one can get. There's an
attractive, old-school hotel bar that's hardly
used. The small lobby, with cathedral ceiling
and original chandeliers, is breathtaking, but
the service is decidedly not.

## EMBASSY SUITES

Map pp222-3                          *Hotel & Residence*

☎ 215-561-1776; www.embassysuites.com; 1776
Benjamin Franklin Parkway; ste $129-179; **P** ; SEPTA
Suburban Station, Bus 32, 76

Especially large suites are the main draw at the
otherwise bland and clean Embassy Suites,
now around 30 years old. Many rooms have
balconies, and the hotel's amenities include
a sauna and fitness room. A majority of the
guests are business people staying long-term.

## PHILADELPHIA MARRIOTT
## DOWNTOWN Map pp222-3          *Hotel*

☎ 215-625-2900; www.marriott.com; 1201 Market
St; standard $140-200, deluxe $289-389; **P** ; SEPTA
Market Station East, Bus 23, 61

If it was built in 1996 and holds 1408 rooms,
then it must be this hotel, which employs
over 1000 people and somehow manages
to sell out (thanks largely to conventioneers).
Rooms with decent views are on the 11th floor
or higher, so be sure to ask for one of those.
Or if you want to be historic, take one of the
210 deluxe rooms contained in the former
Reading Terminal Station, connected by an

enclosed bridge to the main building. The tall ceilings will alert you that you're in an older room, though most old-time detailing has been stripped away with renovation. In the enormous complex are three restaurants, two lobby bars, a sports bar, a Kinko's, a hair salon, a health club, a flower shop and a pool.

**THE WESTIN** Map pp222-3 *Hotel*
☎ 215-563-1600; www.westin.com; 17th & Chestnut Sts; r $165-195; P ; SEPTA 19th St Station, Bus 2, 9, 21, 42
Despite the fact that this hotel is part of the modern Liberty Place complex, the interior comes close to achieving the elegant atmosphere of bygone days. The lobby, which you enter through an elevator from the valet parking area, is comparable to a series of formal, comfortable living rooms full of couches and pianos. The rooms themselves are more generic, but the beds are comfortable and clean.

## Top End
### FOUR SEASONS HOTEL
**PHILADELPHIA** Map pp222-3 *Hotel*
☎ 215-963-1500; www.fourseasons.com/philadelphia; 1 Logan Square; r $220-300; P ; SEPTA 19th St Station, Bus 2, 9, 21, 42
For the crispest, most formal service in town, head over to this high-end chain to see if it's possible to open the front door without assistance. The building is a somewhat squat Modernist job that wraps itself around a central courtyard whose landscaping contains a Modernist waterfall. Just about any service and amenity a hotel can offer is on site. The hotel has 364 spiffy rooms and contains the notable Fountain Restaurant.

# SOUTH STREET
You've got one option, and it's fabulous. And it's just far enough away from South Street to avoid being overrun by the gallivanting young crazies.

**SHIPPEN WAY INN** Map pp228-9 *B&B*
☎ 215-627-7266, 800-245-4873; 418 Bainbridge St; r $85-120; Bus 40, 57
Tall folks should watch their heads near yesteryear's low thresholds in this nine-room B&B, one of the oldest houses in town for bunking down. Two-thirds of the place was built around 1750; a 20th-century addition in

the back comprises the rest. There's a pleasant, private garden, and an active fireplace in the living room. Breakfast equals muffins, tea and fruit, while afternoons signal wine and cheese.

# UNIVERSITY CITY & FAIRMOUNT PARK
Most of these options are adjacent to Penn's campus. The Gables B&B is a bit distant from Penn and a tad close to sketchy bits of town. The hostel in beautiful Chamounix Mansion is in the middle of Fairmount Park.

## Budget
### CHAMOUNIX MANSION
Map pp220-1 *Hostel*
☎ 215-878-3676; www.philahostel.org; 3250 Chamounix Dr, West Fairmount Park; dm adult/ HI member/child $18/15/7.50; P X ; Bus 38
This hostel operates out of a restored mansion and carriage house, both from 1802. The buildings are set in an attractive park setting but a fair distance from downtown. If the hostel isn't busy, a smaller dorm can be used as a private room for couples or families. There's a kitchen, snack- and drink-vending machines, TV lounge, tennis courts, free bikes and free parking. It's closed between 11am and 4:30pm and has a midnight curfew; it's also closed from December 15 to January 15. To avoid a wasted trip, especially July through September, reserve ahead. Chamounix is 30 minutes on bus No 38 from Market St to the corner of Ford and Cranston Rds in West Fairmount Park. From the stop sign, walk 1 mile on Ford Rd, then turn left onto Chamounix Dr and continue to the hostel at the end of the road. Women should not try this at night.

### DIVINE TRACEY HOTEL
Map p225 *Christian Hotel*
☎ 215-382-4310; 20 S 36th St; r daily $40-60, r weekly $80-150; X ; SEPTA 36th St Station, Bus 21
Run by a Christian sect that once enjoyed some clout in Philadelphia (and whose tenets include beliefs that all people should live strictly celibate lives and that the future of the world requires a universal American culture), this clean, 100-room hotel has a friendly staff and very quiet guests. The hotel has strict rules: no smoking, no alcohol, no swearing, separate floors for men and women, and a modest

public dress code. Don't leave a tip for house-keeping – that's also a no-no. There isn't a curfew. Rates (payable by cash or traveler's check only) vary depending on a room's size and whether or not it comes with a private bathroom.

### GABLES Map p225 *B&B*
☎ 215-662-1918; www.gablesbb.com; 4520 Chester Ave; s $75-110, d $85-125; [P] [✗] ; Bus 13

Built in 1889 by noted area architect Willis Hale, this beautiful Queen Anne has a wraparound porch and, since it used to be part of the sub-urbs a very long time ago, a beautifully planted garden surrounding the house. Inside there's about as much elaborate woodworking as you'd expect from an über-Victorian structure that has won several awards for conscientious restoration (note: modern amenities do exist). Some of the 10 rooms share a bath. There's free parking in the driveway behind the house, free wireless Internet access and a full break-fast. Kids under 10 are not allowed.

### INTERNATIONAL HOUSE
Map p225 *Academic Housing*
☎ 215-387-5125; www.ihousephilly.org; 3701 Chestnut St; s w/shared bath $65, d $75; SEPTA 36th St Station, Bus 21, 40

Built in 1970, the International House provides long- and short-term lodging to students, prospective students, professors, conference attendees and professional trainees. Interna-tional House is not affiliated with any of the nearby universities; it's an independent insti-tute, founded over 90 years ago with a mission that's all about promoting internationalism. Many of those staying here come from conti-nents other than North America. International House sponsors a bunch of language and film programs (see p130), and is a good place to stay for those feeling disoriented in the New World. No kids allowed.

## Mid-Range & Top End
### THE INN AT PENN Map p225 *Hotel*
☎ 215-222-0200; www.theinnatpenn.com; 3600 Sansom St; r $129-199; [P] ; SEPTA 36th St Station, Bus 21, 40

This four-year-old Hilton boasts 238 clean, new rooms, a 24-hour gym and close proximity to Penn's campus. Reservations for stays during graduation (when rooms jump to $300) begin to be taken exactly one year before com-mencement, and the hotel usually sells out within a few hours.

### SHERATON UNIVERSITY CITY HOTEL
Map p225 *Hotel*
☎ 215-387-8000; www.starwood.com/sheraton; 36th & Chestnut Sts; r $180-260, ste $375; [P] ; SEPTA 36th St Station, Bus 21, 40

This postwar Sheraton is looking a bit run-down in comparison to its contemporaries. There's covered parking, a gym, an outdoor pool, 365 rooms and a funny smell. Room rates vary hugely depending on the goings-on at Penn. It is possible to get a rate cheaper than those listed above.

# CHESTNUT HILL
Cute as a button, villagelike Chestnut Hill has only pretty places to stay, but keep in mind you'll be about 9 miles from Center City.

## Budget
### ANAM CARA Map p231 *B&B*
☎ 215-242-4327; www.anamcarabandb.com; 52 Woodale Rd; r $85-125; SEPTA R7 Wyndmoor Station

The main building of this small B&B, whose name means 'soul friend,' contains only a few guest rooms, all exceedingly floral in their de-sign. The innkeeper, Teresa Vesey, is very Irish and very friendly, as is her dog. For those who need to stay for extended periods, Anam Cara offers reduced rates in a second building.

### SILVERSTONE Map p231 *B&B*
☎ 215-242-1471; www.silverstonestay.com; 8840 Stenton Ave; r $60-140; SEPTA R7 Chestnut Hill East Station, Bus 77

For those who want to sleep in an opulent Victorian-Gothic stone mansion built in 1877 for a Philadelphia industrialist, this is your best bet. The rooms (well, some of them), staircases, windows and porch were all de-signed to blow your mind. There are two- and three-room apartments available, and kids are actively welcomed.

## Mid-Range
### CHESTNUT HILL HOTEL
Map p231 *Boutique Hotel*
☎ 215-242-5905; www.chestnuthillhotel.com; 8229 Germantown Ave; r/ste $129/179; SEPTA R8 Chestnut Hill West Station, Bus 23

A colonial building left over from Chestnut Hill's 18th-century resort-area days, the hotel's exterior exudes more of a days-of-yore feel than the rooms, which have been redone over the years. They are charming, however, with four-poster beds, floral wallpaper and other 18th-century touches. With 28 rooms and suites, the hotel stands as the largest lodging house in the area, and is often used by people attending weddings. Travelers will be happy to know that the rates include a complimentary continental breakfast (served from 7-10:30am). There are also package deals; the 'Gardens Package' includes admission for two to the **Morris Arboretum** (p90) and a bottle of wine.

## SUGARLOAF CONFERENCE CENTER

Map p231                                          *Estate*

☎ 215-242-9100; www.sugarloafconfctr.com; 9230 Germantown Ave; r $129-199; Ⓟ

This conference center, run by Temple University, rents out leftover rooms that aren't being used by conference attendees. Though the rooms themselves are relatively new, they are part of a 32-acre estate on the Wissahickon River, whose tennis courts and swimming pool feel very old. Staying here will make you feel like a vacationing robber baron. Free parking!

## Near the Airport

For those who have early flights or can't sleep without the comforting knowledge that planes are taking off and landing overhead, we've compiled this handy list of lodging options in close proximity to the airport.

- **Philadelphia Airport Marriott** ( ☎ 215-492-9000; www.marriott.com; 1 Arrivals Rd; r $170-220; Ⓟ ) The closest. In fact, it's so close that it touches the tarmac.

About 1.5 miles north of the airport off I-95's exit 13, you'll find these two options:

- **Hilton Philadelphia Airport** ( ☎ 215-365-4150; www.hilton.com; 4509 Island Ave; r $140-130; Ⓟ )
- **Sheraton Suites** ( ☎ 215-365-6600; www.starwood.com/sheraton; 4101B Island Ave; r $120-160; Ⓟ ) Free airport shuttle

Head 3 miles south of the airport to find a cluster of cheap motels at I-95's exit 9A, in the town of Essington:

- **Motel 6** ( ☎ 610-521-6650; www.motel6.com; 43 Industrial Hwy; s/d $55/60; Ⓟ ) Small pets are welcome.
- **Comfort Inn** ( ☎ 610-521-9800; www.comfortinn.com; 53 Industrial Hwy; r $100-120; Ⓟ ) Free airport shuttle
- **Red Roof Inn** ( ☎ 610-521-5090; www.redroof.com; 49 Industrial Hwy; s $60-70, d $70-80; Ⓟ )
- **Holiday Inn** ( ☎ 610-521-2400; www.holiday-inn.com; 45 Industrial Hwy; r $100-145; Ⓟ ) Free airport shuttle
- **Ramada Inn** ( ☎ 610-521-9600; www.ramada.com; 76 Industrial Hwy; r $70-80; Ⓟ ) This Ramada has 292 rooms and a free airport shuttle.

# Excursions

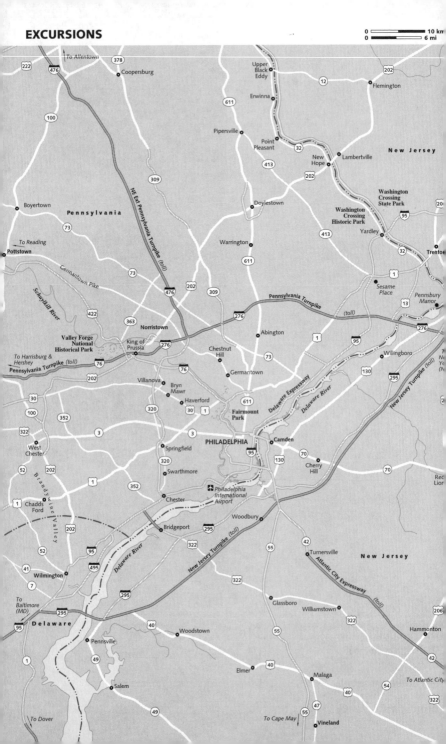

# EXCURSIONS

# Excursions

Escaping Philadelphia's concrete jungle for greener pastures is an easy trick, particularly if you have a car. Philadelphia is surrounded by rural hills, pretty farmland and cute towns, and it sits close to the Atlantic Ocean. So whether you want to have an Ichabod Crane experience dashing across a covered bridge, bob in the surf or shop for antiques, Philly's environs are your playground.

Before leaving for Bucks County and the Brandywine Valley, you might want to stop by the **Independence Visitor Center** (p55), which provides helpful maps and information about these regions.

## VALLEY FORGE

The site of the Continental Army's renowned winter encampment from December 19, 1777, to June 19, 1778, **Valley Forge National Historical Park** (Map p172; ☎ 610-783-1077; www.nps.gov/vafo; N Gulph Rd & Rte 23; admission free; ☯ sunrise-sunset) contains 5.5 sq miles of scenic beauty and open space 20 miles northwest of downtown Philadelphia. Not a battlefield, the site is nonetheless a symbol of bravery and endurance – 2000 of George Washington's 12,000 troops perished here from freezing temperatures, hunger and disease while the British occupied Philadelphia. Despite such losses, the army was reorganized and emerged to eventually defeat the British.

Full comprehension of the dramatic events that took place here is integral to enjoying the park as more than a bucolic valley. The 15-minute film *Valley Forge: A Winter Encampment* can help greatly with this task; it is on view at the **Welcome Center** ( ☎ 610-783-1077; ☯ 9am-5pm).

### Transport

**Distance from Philadelphia** 20 miles
**Direction** Northwest
**Bus** Catch SEPTA bus 125 at the corner of N 16th St and JFK Blvd or at 30th St Station. It goes to the Valley Forge Welcome Center. The trip takes about 40 minutes and costs $6.
**Car** Take I-76 (Schuylkill Expressway) west to exit 327. Make a right at the first traffic light. At the next light, make a right onto N Gulph Rd and follow the signs.
**Bicycle** It's a 20-mile ride but it's pretty. The Schuylkill River Trail beings in Philly and runs right through the park.

The Welcome Center also contains exhibits, and an information desk offers maps and brochures highlighting the park's major points of interest and the area's other attractions. Costumed reenactments of the Continental Army's training procedures are staged occasionally during warmer weather. If you have a car, you can buy a CD or tape from the Welcome Center that narrates a 10-mile tour of the park. Organized **bus tours** (adult/child $15.50/11.50; 90 minutes) periodically depart from the visitors center.

## Sights & Activities

Important sights include the **National Memorial Arch**, dedicated to the soldiers who endured the winter encampment, and the **Monument to Patriots of African Descent**, a bronze statue honoring the 5000 blacks who died in the war. The **Isaac Potts House** (tour $3; ☯ 9am-5pm April-Nov), built in 1774, was used as Washington's headquarters and is furnished with period reproductions. You can also visit the sites of various artillery positions and **Varnum's Quarters**, the 18th-century farmhouse used by General Varnum that overlooked the parade ground where General von Steuben whipped the Continental Army into efficiency and discipline.

In addition to the sights, there are miles of pretty hiking, biking and equestrian trails. Bring a picnic basket.

# BUCKS COUNTY

Philadelphia's neighbor to the north, tranquil Bucks County is all about cute towns and scenic countryside. Here, you can sleep in an artist's village, drive across numerous covered bridges, admire the changing leaves of fall and float down the Delaware River (as well as visit the site where Washington crossed it).

## WASHINGTON'S CROSSING

The **Washington Crossing Historic Park** (Map p172; ☎ 215-493-4076; www.fwchp.org; Rtes 32 & 532, Washington Crossing; adult/senior/child $5/4/2; ☼ 9am-5pm Tue-Sat, noon-5pm Sun) marks the site where George Washington's army crossed the Delaware River into New Jersey on Christmas night, 1776, to surprise and defeat an encampment of Hessian mercenaries of the British Army at Trenton. It was a turning point in the war. A reenactment of the crossing takes place every Christmas.

The park is divided into two parts. The **visitors center**, in the lower park, has a short film on the events (and an exhibition of paintings by New Hope painters). Nearby, next to the bridge, **McConkey Ferry Inn** is where Washington dined before the crossing. In the upper park, toward New Hope, the 110ft **Bowman's Hill Tower** affords a great view of the Delaware Valley. Washington used the hill as a lookout. North of the tower is the **Bowman's Hill Wildflower Preserve** (☎ 215-862-2924; www.bhwp.org; 1635 River Rd (Rte 32); adult/senior/child $5/3/2; ☼ 8:30am-sunset), home to numerous species of plants native to Pennsylvania. The 100 acres have plenty of trails.

Across the river in New Jersey is the **Washington Crossing State Park** (Map p172; ☎ 609-737-0623), very much like its Historic Park counterpart in Pennsylvania, with a friendly welcome to picnic baskets and bicycles. In the visitors center you can check out the oldest known American dog tag, and the **Ferry House** (☎ 609-737-2515) is the building where Washington and his officers planned the attack. It's been restored to resemble a farmhouse of the period.

## Getting There & Away

There's no public transportation to the park, but the SEPTA R3 train stops at Yardley, about 5 miles south. By car, take I-95 N from Philadelphia to exit 31 and follow Rte 32 north for 3 miles. At the junction with Rte 532, turn right for the visitors center, or left for Bowman's Hill Tower and **New Hope** (p175).

## DOYLESTOWN

Driving north from Philadelphia to Doylestown, the seat of Bucks County, you will exchange urbanity for an increasingly bucolic landscape. Within this sleepy terrain sits an amazing collection of attractions, along what is called 'the Mercer Mile.' Each attraction is the legacy of Henry Mercer, who made his fortune designing handcrafted tiles during the years when industrial standardization was causing the demise of artisanship.

The **Fonthill Museum** (☎ 212-348-9461; www.fonthillmuseum.org; E Court St & Rte 313; adult/child $7/2.50; ☼ 10am-5pm Mon-Sat, noon-5pm Sun), once Mercer's home, is a giant, 42-room mansion modeled after European castles and built at the height of the Arts and Crafts movement. It's made entirely of poured concrete with an interior covered in exotic tiles (some designed by Mercer and some from around the world, including some rare Babylonian tablets). Devotion to craftsmanship demonstrates itself in this tiling and in the fact that no two windows are alike. The puzzling building is oddly designed: among the many strange attributes are stairways that lead nowhere. The exhibitions sprawl throughout the house. Aside from the thousands of embedded tiles, enjoy the interesting collection of American decorative arts typical of the period when Mercer was alive. You can only see this museum by taking part of a guided tour. A reservation is strongly recommended.

### Transport

**Distance from Philadelphia** 35 miles
**Direction** North
**Bus** SEPTA's R5 regional train terminates at Doylestown.
**Car** Bucks County, with hundreds of scenic square miles, is best visited by car. I-95 runs northeast through the eastern edge of the county. Rtes 132 and 32 are the major paths connecting I-95 to the bulk of the county. Rte 32 follows the edge of the Delaware River for about 30 miles.

Nearby, the six-story **Mercer Museum** ( ☎ 212-345-0210; www.mercermuseum.org; 84 S Pine St; adult/child $6/2.50; ☽ 10am-5pm Mon & Wed-Sat, 10am-9pm Tue, noon-5pm Sun), a second concrete behemoth, was built in 1916 and inspired by the castle of yore. Inside you're sure to have one of America's more unusual museum experiences. True to Mercer's interests, the museum contains a supremely rich collection (easily the best in America) of preindustrial folk artifacts. Some of the splendid rooms feel more like a barn than a noble building, with walls covered with thousands of old woodworking tools, agricultural implements, baskets and textiles; the tools of over 50 vanished trades are represented here. Suspended from the rafters are carriages, a Conestoga wagon, a whaling boat and an antique fire engine.

## Getting There & Away
### CAR
To get to Doyleston, take 1-95 N to Street Rd (Rte 132), then Street Rd W to Rte 611 N. Follow this to Doylestown (avoiding the Rte 611 bypass) and take the Doylestown exit on the right. Follow the blue and white Cultural District signs. The trip takes about an hour.

To go to the Mercer Museum, follow signs to the first traffic light and turn right on Ashland St. Take an immediate right on Green St; the museum is on your left.

To go to Fonthill, continue past Ashland a few blocks until you arrive at Court St, where you turn right. Fonthill will be on your left.

### TRAIN
Take SEPTA's R5 Lansdale/Doylestown line to Doylestown Station ($5.50 one way, 80 minutes), located at Clinton Ave and Ashland St. Walk along Ashland St E (turn right when coming out of the station) and, to go to Mercer, cross over Rte 611. Turn right on Green St; the museum is on the left. To go to Fonthill, turn left on Rte 611, and then right on Court St.

## NEW HOPE & LAMBERTVILLE
New Hope, about 26 miles north of Philadelphia, is a quaint, artsy town that sits on the Delaware River. It's edged with a long and peaceful towpath perfect for runners, cyclists and strollers. The town draws a large amount of gay folk, who feel comforted by the abundance of

### Detour: Sesame Place
Kids freak out over meeting Big Bird, Elmo and pals at **Sesame Place** (Map p172; ☎ 215-752-7078; www.sesameplace.com; 100 Sesame Rd, Langhorne; admission $38.95, kids under 2 free; ☽ 10am-8pm June-Aug with reduced hrs & days May, Sep & Oct), where pint-size, well-done amusement park rides are also offered. Many rides will get you wet, so be sure to bring a bathing suit (or buy one at the park). Throughout the day, live shows are staged featuring Sesame Street characters.

Take I-95 N to Morrisville exit 46A. Follow Rte 1 N, exiting at Oxford Valley. Turn right onto Oxford Valley Rd, then turn right at the third traffic light.

rainbow flags hanging outside of various businesses, as well as a gay anti-discrimination ordinance that was passed in 2002. The place gets swamped with visitors on nice summer weekends.

Stroll across a bridge spanning the Delaware to wonderful Lambertville, which smiles at New Hope from New Jersey. A bit less touristy then its sister town, the charming village presents a few antique shops and fine-dining experiences.

## Sights & Attractions
One of New Hope's most unique offerings is the mule-drawn canal boat rides in the Delaware Canal, a leftover from the canal-building era of the mid-19th century. Stop by the **New Hope Canal Boat Company** ( ☎ 215-862-0758; 149 Main St; adult/child $10/8; tours 12:30pm & 3pm May-Oct) for tickets.

For those who want to spend three picturesque hours floating slowly downstream in a tube or canoe, seek out **Bucks County River Country** ( ☎ 215-297-5000; www.rivercountry.net; 2 Waters Lane, Point Pleasant; tube/canoe $18/20; ☽ rent 9am-2:30pm, return by 5pm), about 8 miles north of New Hope on Rte 32. Though you'll be stuck with a $5 parking charge, the 80°F water of the Delaware is pretty awesome.

## Eating & Sleeping
A great daytrip from Philly, New Hope has a plethora of handsome B&Bs if you decide to make a weekend out of it.

**Fox & Hound Bed & Breakfast** ( ☎ 215-862-5082; www.foxhoundinn.com; 246 W Bridge St;

Excursions – Bucks County

175

r from $85; (P)) This B&B, one of the best, has cute rooms in an 1850 stone manor.

**Porches on the Towpath** (☎ 215-862-3277; www.porchesnewhope.com; 20 Fisher's Alley; r from $95; (P)) One of several gay-owned inns, this is another relatively good deal. It features elegant quarters and is tucked away on a quiet lane fronting the canal.

New Hope's Main St is filled with decent, affordable eateries. One of them is **Landing Inn** (☎ 215-862-5711; 22 N Main St; mains $8-14), a great romantic spot with a fireplace and waterfront views. In Lambertville try **Church Street Bistro** (☎ 609-397-4383; 11½ Church St; lunch mains $7-15, dinner mains $22-28; ⏱ 11:30am-10pm Wed-Mon), warmed by a wood-burning stove and serving a small menu featuring stuff like braised lamb with artichoke hearts.

# BRANDYWINE VALLEY

Straddling Delaware and Pennsylvania, the Brandywine Valley is about 25 miles southwest of Philadelphia and features a terrific collection of mansions, gardens, museums and art galleries. Fifteen miles wide and 35 miles long, it's a patchwork of wooded and rolling countryside, historic villages, ancient farmhouses and chateau estates.

It was after defeat at the Battle of Brandywine Creek on September 11, 1777, that George Washington's army spent the following winter camped at Valley Forge (p173). The valley is closely associated with the du Pont family, who came here after fleeing Napoleon's France, made money selling gunpowder to an expanding US, and went on to develop chemical factories, textile mills and landscaped gardens. Howard Pyle and Andrew Wyeth are two artists also closely connected with the area.

Most people's 'must-sees' include the Winterthur and Hagley estates; if time permits, you could also stop in at Longwood Gardens or Nemours and the Brandywine River Museum. The Brandywine's wealth of attractions is mostly in Delaware, while most country inns and restaurants are in Pennsylvania.

Christmas exhibitions and events at most Brandywine Valley museums run from Thanksgiving through New Year's Day.

## Information

The **Brandywine Valley Tourist Information Center** (☎ 610-388-2900, 800-228-9933; www.brandywinevalley.com; Rte 1; ⏱ 10am-6pm Apr-Sep, 10am-5pm Oct-Mar) sits outside the gates of Longwood Gardens in Kennett Square, PA. In Philadelphia, the **Independence Visitor Center** (p55) provides maps and extensive information for the valley.

## Sights & Activities

### LONGWOOD GARDENS

Samuel du Pont established these superb 1050-acre **gardens** (☎ 610-388-1000; www.longwoodgardens.org; Rte 1, Kennett Square; adult/child 16-20/child 6-15/child under 6 $14/6/2/free; ⏱ 9am-5pm) at the beginning of the 20th century. The gardens have beautifully maintained grounds and several large, heated conservatories. There are 11,000 different kinds of plants, roses and orchids in bloom year-round. In addition, there's an indoor children's garden with a maze, the historic Pierce du Pont House and one of the world's mightiest pipe organs. Nighttime (in summer) displays of illuminated fountains and festive lights

### Detour: Pennsbury Manor

When William Penn wanted to escape the rat race of the 2000 people living in Philadelphia, this was where he came. Though he spent most of the colony's early days dealing with legal troubles in England, he did find himself wandering this land, 25 miles up the Delaware River from Philadelphia, on two occasions: 1682 to 1684 and the summer of 1700.

Today's 43-acre plantation (Map p172; ☎ 215-946-0400; www.pennsburymanor.org; 400 Pennsbury Memorial Rd; tour adult/child $5/3; ⏱ 9am-5pm Tue-Sat, noon-5pm Sun) features costumed actors, a reconstruction of Penn's Manor (built on the original foundation), period outbuildings and furniture, and plenty of petable livestock to amuse those of the age where livestock petting amounts to a fit of entertainment.

To see the 17th-century splendor, take I-95 North to Rte 13. Continue for 2 miles, then turn right on Green Lane. Turn left onto Radcliffe St at the dead end and continue 4.6 miles to Pennsbury Memorial Rd.

# BRANDYWINE VALLEY

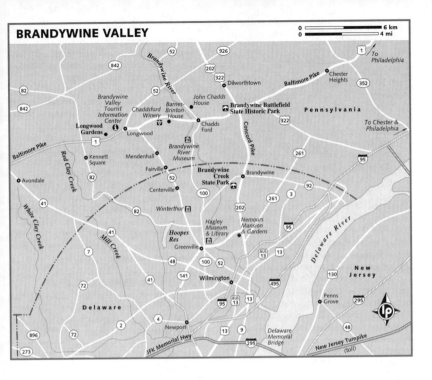

at Christmastime dazzle with their magnificence. The gardens also have many well-publicized seasonal events.

Longwood is frequently open later than 5pm, as season and holidays permit. On Tuesdays, adult entry drops to $8.

## BRANDYWINE BATTLEFIELD STATE HISTORIC PARK

This **park** ( ☎ 610-459-3342; Rte 1, Chadds Ford; admission free, guided building tours adult/child/senior $3.50/1.50/2.50; ☼ 9am-5pm Tue-Sat, noon-5pm Sun) lies on the north side of Rte 1, east of the Chadds Ford Bridge. The visitors center has an audiovisual display, exhibits, and pamphlets on the Battle of Brandywine Creek, which took place on farms north of the park. You can also visit the (restored) farmhouses that served as headquarters for the Revolutionary generals as well as for George Washington and his French comrade the Marquis de Lafayette, who came close to losing their bid for American independence at Brandywine.

'Revolutionary Times at Brandywine' is a two-day reenactment of the Battle of Brandy-

wine Creek. It occurs in mid-September; there are crafts and food then too.

## CHADDS FORD

This small, sleepy town takes its name from a shallow stretch of the Brandywine River where travelers once forded the river. In the 1730s John Chadds began a ferry service near this point and also opened a tavern, which exists today as the **Chadds Ford Inn** (p179), a restaurant full of trinkets.

Work up your appetite by visiting the **John Chadds House** ( ☎ 610-388-7376; www.chaddsfordhistory.org; Rte 100; adult/child $5/3; ☼ noon-5pm Sat & Sun May-Sep), the former home of the ferryman, farmer and tavern keeper, built around 1725. You can park nearby in the Chadds Ford Historical Society lot. Paying for admission also earns you access to the **Barns-Brinton House** (beside the Chaddsford Winery), originally built as a tavern in 1714 and restored to its original appearance.

A footpath from the Barns-Brinton House leads to the **Chaddsford Winery** ( ☎ 610-388-6221; www.chaddsford.com; 632 Baltimore Pike; ☼ noon-6pm). Operating from a

Excursions – Brandywine Valley

**Distance from Philadelphia** 35 miles
**Direction** Southwest
**Car** The Brandywine Valley's sites are diffused over many rustic miles, making a car necessary. Rtes 52 and 202 form the general eastern and western borders of the valley. I-95 goes to Wilmington, Delaware; Rte 52 joins Rte 1 and I-95. To get to sites around Chadds Ford, follow I-95 S to 322 W. Then take Rte 1 southwest to Chadds Ford, Brandywine Battlefield Park and Longwood Gardens.

renovated 18th-century barn, this boutique winery is on Rte 1, about 5 miles south of Rte 202. Producing small lots of varietal wines with grapes imported from the surrounding area, Chaddsford offers free guided and self-guided tours to see the grapes being crushed, fermented, barrel-aged and bottled. You're given a sample to taste when you first arrive, but a full tasting of around 10 wines costs $5. There are picnic tables around the barn.

Nearby you can also see a showcase of American artwork at the **Brandywine River Museum** ( ☎ 610-388-2700; Hwy 1 & Rte 100; adult/student/senior/child $5/2.50/2.50/2.50; ☼ 9:30am-4:30pm), which includes the work of the 'Brandywine School.' Housed in a 19th-century gristmill, the place is full of works by the Wyeth family, Howard Pyle, Maxfield Parrish, William Trost Richards and Horace Pippin, among hundreds of others.

### WINTERTHUR

One of the valley's most famous attractions, **Winterthur** ( ☎ 302-888-4600, 800-448-3883; Rte 52, Winterthur, DE; adult/senior/student/child $15/13/13/5; ☼ 10am-5pm Tue-Sun) was the country estate of Henry Francis du Pont until he opened it to the public in 1951. When du Pont inherited the estate in 1927, he moved the best of his American furniture collection here, doubling the size of the existing house and converting it to a showplace for the world's most important collection of early American decorative arts. During the next 20 years du Pont continued to increase his collection and the size of Winterthur.

The museum consists of two buildings, one with 175 period rooms and another with three exhibition galleries. These house over 89,000 objects made or used in America between 1640 and 1860, including

furniture, textiles, paintings, prints, pewter, silver, ceramics, glass, needlework and brass. The museum is surrounded by 980 acres, 60 of which are beautifully planted with native and exotic plants.

For an additional fee (usually $5), excellent guided tours are available, such as 'Private Spaces & Gaming Places, Elegant Entertaining, Stylish Suites,' and, seasonally, 'Yuletide.' Call ahead to find out the offerings and to make a reservation – they fill quickly. Some tours are better for kids than others, so be sure to ask.

Winterthur is 6 miles northwest of Wilmington, Delaware, on Rte 52, 10 minutes off I-95 via exit 7 (Delaware Ave, Rte 52 N). If you're coming from Chadds Ford, drive west 3 miles on Rte 1 to Rte 52 S; from Longwood Gardens, Rte 52 S is 1 mile east on Rte 1.

### HAGLEY MUSEUM & LIBRARY

Beautifully situated on the banks of the Brandywine River, this **museum and library** ( ☎ 302-658-2400; www.hagley.org; Rte 141, Wilmington, DE; adult/senior/student/child $11/9/9/4; ☼ 9:30am-4:30pm daily Mar 15–Dec, 9:30am-4:30pm Sat & Sun and a tour each weekday at 1:30pm Jan–Mar 14) is another 'must-see.' This 240-acre outdoor museum, on the site of the birthplace of the DuPont Company, tells the story of the du Ponts as part of the broader history of America's Industrial Revolution. DuPont started operations here as a gunpowder manufacturer in 1802. You can also explore the ruins of the original mills, and visit restored buildings and millraces with exhibits, models and live demonstrations.

Allow at least three to four hours for your visit. Hagley is a large site with great natural beauty, and lots of things to see and do. The museum offers guided tours (included in the price of admission).

Hagley is on Rte 141, north of Wilmington, Delaware. From Philly, take exit 8B from I-95 (Rte 202 N) to Rte 141 S and follow the signs to the Hagley Museum. From Chadds Ford, take Rte 100 S to Rte 141 N.

### NEMOURS MANSION & GARDENS

This vividly opulent **attraction** ( ☎ 302-651-6912; Rockland Rd at Rte 202, Wilmington, DE; tour $10; ☼ tours 9, 11am, 1 & 3pm Tue-Sat, 11am, 1 & 3pm Sun May-Oct with limited hrs Nov & Dec) is the estate of Alfred I du Pont. It's named after the site of the family's ancestral home in north-central France. Surrounded by 300 acres of gardens and natural woodlands, the Louis XVI–style chateau was built in 1909–1910 and has 102 rooms. Today it contains fine examples of antique furniture, Oriental rugs, tapestries and paintings dating back to the 15th century. Nemours' exhibits illustrate the du Ponts' lavish lifestyle, including vintage cars, a billiards room and bowling alley. The grand French gardens stretch almost one-third of a mile along the main vista from the mansion.

Visitors must be 12 years of age or older. Tours are required. They last a minimum of two hours and include the mansion followed by a bus tour through the gardens. You need to arrive at reception (the building in the parking lot) a good 15 minutes before the start of the tour. Reservations are recommended; the office is open 8:30am to 4:30pm Monday to Friday.

# Eating

**Buckley's Tavern** ( ☎ 302-656-9776; 5812 Kennett Pike, Centerville, DE; main dishes $6-14; 🕑 11:30am-1pm Mon-Sat, 9:30am-1pm Sun) This is one of the region's most popular drinking spots. There's a small pub with a dining room and garden at the back. Everyone from gentry to farmers is a regular here, and the place is usually packed. The hearty menu ranges from healthy salads to deep-fried red snapper.

**Chadds Ford Inn** ( ☎ 610-388-7361; junction of Rtes 1 & 100, Chadds Ford; lunch mains $7-14, dinner mains $16-25; 🕑 lunch 11:30am-2:30pm Mon-Fri, 11:30am-4pm Sat, dinner 5:30-9:30pm Mon-Thu, 5-10pm Fri & Sat, 2:30-9pm Sun, brunch 11am-2:30pm Sun). Over the centuries, the tavern evolved into a popular restaurant, furnished with colonial antiques and three generations of Wyeth paintings. The international cuisine served is up-to-date.

Another popular historic restaurant is **Dilworthtown Inn** ( ☎ 610-399-1390, 1390 Old Wilmington Pike, Dilworthtown, PA; mains $22-36; 🕑 5:30-9:30pm Mon-Thu, 5-9:30pm Fri & Sat, 3-8:30pm Sun). This wood, stone and brick structure with fireplaces and gas lamps dates back to 1758 and serves modern American cuisine. The proprietor stocks an excellent wine cellar. To find the inn, head north on Rte 202 from the junction with Rte 1. After a mile and a half, turn left at the second traffic light. After about 200 yards

## The Battle of Brandywine Creek

The British Army nearly ended the American Revolution when it attacked and overwhelmed the American forces at Brandywine Creek on September 11, 1777.

In August George Washington learned that 13,000 British and 5000 Hessian mercenaries (from Hesse, Germany) under General William Howe had landed at the head of the Chesapeake Bay. They had been advancing slowly through Delaware, gathering intelligence and securing supply lines for an attack on Philadelphia, the new national capital.

In defense of Philadelphia, Washington moved 11,000 troops to the Wilmington area. Realizing that the Brandywine Valley presented a geographical obstacle to Howe, Washington and his French supporter, the Marquis de Lafayette, set up the bulk of their defenses along the high ground east of the creek at Chadds Ford, the most likely place for the British to cross. In addition, American troops covered two other fords on the Brandywine in hopes of forcing Howe to fight at Chadds Ford.

Howe anticipated Washington's plans and on September 11, using intelligence from local British sympathizers, he sent the bulk of his troops on a long march to the north around Washington's right flank, under the cover of darkness and fog. Back at Chadds Ford, when the fog lifted, Howe's generals made a decoy attack and marched a few columns back and forth among the hills to give Washington's scouts the impression that the main British force was gathering at Chadds Ford for a charge. Washington didn't realize until mid-afternoon that Howe, with 11,000 redcoats, had nearly encircled his army. After brutal fighting, the remains of the American force escaped to Chester, Pennsylvania. British troops suffered 600 dead and wounded; the Americans had 900 casualties and lost 400 men as prisoners of war.

Fifteen days later Howe's troops marched into Philadelphia unopposed. Although Washington had been defeated, the battle helped persuade the French to make a formal alliance with the Americans, an alliance that would prove crucial to the final outcome of the Revolution. In the meantime, Washington was able to regroup (at Valley Forge) to fight again the following year. As he reported to Congress following the battle: 'Notwithstanding the misfortune of the day, I am happy to find the troops in good spirits; and I hope another time we shall compensate for the losses now sustained.'

you come to a stop sign; turn right, and the restaurant is the building on your right.

## Sleeping

Accommodations in Wilmington, New Castle and Philadelphia are within easy reach of the Brandywine Valley. However, there are also options – a few very charming – that are closer. Rte 202 (Concord Pike) contains several hotels and motels, and most of them offer good-value packages (especially on weekends) that include a room and admission to Brandywine Valley museums.

The 41-room, 1987-built **Brandywine River Hotel** ( ☎ 610-388-1200; www.brandywine riverhotel.com; junction of Rtes 1 & 100, Chadds Ford; r/ste $125/169) is not a piece of antiquity, but it is nicely designed to blend in with the surroundings, with colonial-style interiors.

The luxurious and top-end **Fairville Inn** ( ☎ 610-388-5900; www.fairvilleinn.com; 506 Kennett Pike, Mendenhall, PA; r $150-190) contains a main house, built in 1826, and a rear carriage house and barn. Seven of the 15 rooms have fireplaces, and the entire place is beautifully decorated. A substantial continental breakfast and light but delicious afternoon tea are included.

### Covered Bridges

This little driving tour will lead you through five of Bucks County's remaining covered bridges. Begin at the intersection of Rte 413 and Stump Rd in Hinkletown. Take Stump Rd east for a mile, turning left onto Wismer Rd and passing through **Loux Bridge**. Half a mile past the bridge, turn right onto Dark Hollow Rd. After 1 mile, turn right on Covered Bridge Rd. Experience the thrill of **Cabin Run Bridge** after just half a mile. Pull a U-turn and pass back through the bridge. Follow Covered Bridge Rd past your buddy Dark Hollow Rd and continue for almost 3 miles. Take a left on Cafferty Rd, and you'll soon hit **Frankenfield Bridge**. Enjoy driving through it, and soon take a right onto Hollow Horn Rd. After a mile go right onto Headquarters Rd (stay left at curve) and continue for another mile. Turn left at Giegel Hill Rd, soon arriving at **Erwinna Bridge**. Admire and then turn around. Turn left onto Rte 32 and, after about 1.5 miles, turn left on Uhlerstown Rd to arrive at **Uhlerstown Bridge**. When you're bridged out, head back to Rte 32 and make a right. This will bring you to lunch in **New Hope** (p175) or **Lambertville** (p175).

From Rte 1 west of Chadds Ford, take Rte 52 S to Mendenhall; Fairville is almost a mile past Mendenhall on the left side.

# Pennsylvania Dutch Country

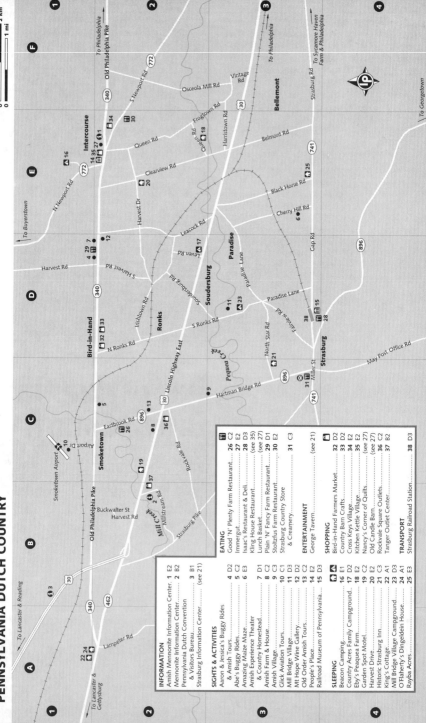

# Pennsylvania Dutch Country

Pennsylvania Dutch Country is home to a community of Amish (*Ah*-mish), Mennonites and Brethren collectively known as 'plain people.' The Old Order Amish in particular – with their distinctive clothing, old-school habits and beautiful farmscapes – are a major draw for tourists; the area is one of the most visited in Pennsylvania. Consequently, people whose forefathers immigrated to the New World to escape the attention and persecution of others find themselves the object of intense curiosity by camera-toting tourists. To maintain their privacy, some have moved to other, less developed parts of the state.

Most Pennsylvania Dutch live on carefully manicured farms, but because of rising population, urbanization and other outside pressures, many also work in small-scale industries producing quilts, furniture and crafts that are sold to tourists. Others work in family-style restaurants, sell produce at farmers markets or offer buggy rides to visitors. There *are* tourist traps, but you can escape some of the commercialism by staying on an 'English'-operated (the Amish refer to anyone outside their community as 'English,' wherever they're from) farm or at one of the more remote tourist homes, or by visiting the

back roads, where you'll see Amish people doing their daily farm work. See the boxed text 'Amish, Mennonites & Brethren' (p185) for more information about the plain people.

The region is famous for its large meals, served in a number of restaurants 'family style,' with diners often sitting together at long tables and eating as much as they please. Meals are huge and hearty, and they generally include three meats (usually chicken, beef, and ham or sausage), applesauce, pepper cabbage, candied sweet potatoes, corn, hardboiled eggs soaked with pickled radishes, string beans, noodles and shoofly pie (the lack of a top crust on this gooey molasses concoction attracts flies, hence its name). In addition, Pennsylvania Dutch Country is famous for its soft and hard pretzels. You can visit pretzel-making operations in Lititz, and there are small hand-rolling shops everywhere. Lititz also has a chocolate factory (and museum). Another popular food item is Lebanon bologna.

There are ample campgrounds, motels, hotels and B&Bs in the area. An alternative to the usual accommodations is to stay on one of the many local farmhouses, which often rent rooms for around $50. The dairy farms and other farms that rent rooms welcome kids, and guests are generally welcome to milk the cows (although it's usually done by machine) and sometimes to feed the calves. Some of these places are listed in this chapter, and the names of more are available from the visitors centers.

Many roads in the area, especially Rtes 30 and 340, are lined with craft shops. Popular items for sale are quilts, wooden furniture, faceless dolls, tools and candles. Also prominent are hex signs: found on barns and quilts, these were originally used to ward off bad luck and evil, but today they're merely decorative. The farmers markets in Lancaster and Bird-in-Hand and near Reading are popular for their selection of pies, jams, meat, preserved vegetables and fresh fruit and vegetables. Many people visit Reading simply for the bargains available at its factory outlet stores, but there is an increasing number of factory outlets throughout the region.

The region's landscape presents a picture of dueling settlement patterns. Those places that the plain people control exhibit the best in picturesque, rolling farmland. The beauty can truly inspire awe. Contrasted against this are the 'English'-owned thoroughfares in the form of strip malls, which provide many of the facilities needed by visitors and modern users of the land and can be tacky and ugly.

# Orientation

The core of the Pennsylvania Dutch region is a string of towns, farms and sights spread out over an area of perhaps 20 miles by 15 miles, about 80 miles west of Philadelphia. These lie to the east of Lancaster – the area's main city and more or less its western boundary. Lancaster has a popular farmers market, an interesting museum and some historic sights, including the home of President Buchanan.

East of Lancaster, the road most traveled by tourists is Rte 340 (Old Philadelphia Pike), along which are the towns of Bird-in-Hand and Intercourse. South of this, and also running east-west, is Rte 30 (Lincoln Hwy), which becomes increasingly commercialized as one travels toward the city of Lancaster. Rte 896 (Hartman Bridge Rd) runs north-south between Rtes 30 and 340, meeting Strasburg to the south at the junction with Rte 741. To get off the beaten track, take any one of the side roads between Rtes 30 and 340.

To the north of this core is the town of Lititz, home of the country's first commercial pretzel bakery, and to its northeast is Ephrata, where the Ephrata Cloister was the site of an 18th-century ascetic religious community called the Pietists.

Though really separate, Reading, to the northeast of the true Pennsylvania Dutch region, is usually discussed as part of it. Most visitors to Reading go there to shop for factory-outlet bargains, but the Daniel Boone Homestead to the east and the Hawk Mountain Sanctuary to the north are other lures. The towns of Palmyra and Lebanon, west of Reading, are also included in the region.

# Organized Tours

## AIR

Glick Aviation Tours (Map p182; ☎ 717-394-6750, Airport Dr) at Smoketown Airport, a mile west of Bird-in-Hand, does a 15-minute flyover of Lancaster County (two/three passengers $33/50). There's also a 25-minute version for a bit more cash. Weather permitting, planes fly Monday to Saturday 9am to 5pm and Sunday 1pm to 5pm.

## BUS

Amish Country Tours ( ☎ 717-768-3600, PO Box 414, Bird-in-Hand, PA 17505; adult/child $21/ 12) is the largest bus-tour operator in the area. This company runs several narrated tours from the Plain 'N' Fancy Farm (p191), on Rte 340 midway between Bird-in-Hand and Intercourse. The 2¼-hour tour takes the back roads past farmlands and homes, visits an Amish farm stand for your cider-purchasing needs, and stops at Amish shops and at the Mt Hope Wine Gallery (Map p182) for a tasting. From April to October it leaves twice daily Monday to Saturday and once on Sunday; in November it leaves once daily; from December to March, there are tours on weekends only.

The Pennsylvania Dutch Convention & Visitors Bureau (p186) runs similar tours.

Connective Tours ( ☎ 215-925-8687; www.philly tour.com) offers daytrips to the area from Philadelphia. You travel by train to Lancaster and from there, a bus takes you on a guided tour of Amish country. Trips are available April to October, last 10 hours and cost $95.

## PERSONAL GUIDES

Personal guides are a good way to see the region because they direct you (literally – they sit in your car while you drive) to communities and homes away from the commercial areas.

The friendly Old Order Amish Tours (Map p182; ☎ 717-299-6535; 63 Eastbrook Rd), on Rte 896 near Ronks, takes individuals or small groups on private tours of Amish farms and homes. You're not allowed to take photographs. The rate for a two-hour tour is $20 per person.

The Mennonite Information Center (p187) provides visitors with a personal guide at $26 for two hours. The center also provides other tourist information.

# Getting There & Around

Pennsylvania Dutch Country is about a 90-minute drive west of Philadelphia on Rte 30. If you're coming from farther north, take I-76 (Pennsylvania Turnpike) to Rte 222 South, which runs directly into Lancaster. Rte 422 North, off I-76 near Valley Forge, will take you to Reading. You can reach Lancaster and Reading by plane, bus or train, but to explore the region adequately, you'll need a car, motorcycle or bicycle.

Note: the Amish use their horses and buggies as a means of transportation, so if you're driving, at times you'll need to slow down considerably and travel at their pace for a while.

# AMISH, MENNONITES & BRETHREN

The Old Order Amish are the most distinctive of the Pennsylvania Dutch people of Lancaster County, but the Amish are just one of three major groups – the Amish, the Mennonites and the Brethren – who are themselves further divided into various smaller churches and groups with differing beliefs. (It's actually more correct to say Pennsylvania German, since the use of 'Dutch' is a corruption of 'Deutsche,' meaning German; many of the early settlers came from German-speaking parts of Europe.)

The Amish, Mennonites and Brethren all trace their origins to 16th-century Switzerland. A religious sect calling itself the Brethren began in Zurich in 1525. They believed that a church should be made up of a group of individuals baptized as adults, because only adults can repent from sin and confess their faith in Christ before they are baptized. The name 'Anabaptist,' which means 'baptized again,' was applied to them by their opponents, who persecuted them. Some Anabaptists became known as Mennonites because of Menno Simons, a Dutchman who was formerly a Roman Catholic priest before becoming an early leader of the group. In 1693 a Swiss Mennonite bishop named Jacob Ammann split from the Anabaptists, and his followers eventually became known as the Amish. The first colony of Mennonites settled in 1683 in Germantown, now a neighborhood in Philadelphia, and the first large groups of Amish arrived in Pennsylvania in the early 18th century.

The Amish, Mennonites and Brethren are unified on the issues of separation of church and state, a Bible-centered life, voluntary adult membership and a 'forgiving love' that translates into conscientious objection to military service and even lawsuits. Where they differ is in dress, use of technology, some Biblical interpretation and language (the Amish speak Pennsylvania Dutch, a German dialect, at home, and the others speak English).

Most of Lancaster's Brethren and Mennonites are indistinguishable from the rest of the county's worldly folk in dress, although their clothing emphasizes modesty. The distinctive Old Order Amish and Old Order Mennonites dress similarly (but not quite the same) and have certain prohibitions on the use of technology. Then there are other groups of Mennonites, Brethren and even Amish – the Amish Mennonites, or 'Beachy Amish' – who wear distinctive clothing but use 'worldly' items. The Old Order Amish, who make up the bulk of the local community, are farmers who generally travel by horse and buggy, wear distinctive clothing and prohibit certain technology.

Old Order Amish men wear unlapelled dark suits, suspenders, solid-colored shirts, black socks and shoes, and broad-brimmed straw hats. Women wear dresses of solid-colored fabric that cover their arms and go past their knees. These dresses are covered by a cape and apron. Women wear their hair in a bun on the back of the head. Single women wear black prayer coverings for church services and, after they get married, switch to white prayer coverings. Single men wait to grow beards (but never mustaches) until after they are married. Though they are generally less strict than their Amish cousins, many Mennonites dress using a very similar code. For most visiting 'English,' the clothes of the two groups are almost indistinguishable.

Amish bishops make decisions about technology based on whether the item in question is too 'worldly' and whether its use may result in the disintegration of the closely knit community. For example, telephones, back when they were a new commodity, were once allowed inside Amish homes. In time the bishops felt that they were being used too often for frivolous gossip, and issued a ban of telephones inside of houses. Heeding the bishops' edict, all phones were removed. However, many families built sheds (they look like outhouses) on their front lawns in which new phone lines were installed. These have not yet been banned, as the community has used them responsibly. No official ruling on the use of cell phones has been passed, and, therefore, they are still allowed. Any prohibitions are constantly under reinterpretation.

While many Amish won't drive cars, they'll ride with friends or hire vehicles to take them somewhere, and bus travel is acceptable. This brings us to the wheel. Bicycles, which encourage young people to go far from their homes, are not used. Rubber wheels are permitted on wagons, tricycles and scooters but not on large farm equipment. The most obvious example is the tractor, which must have steel wheels. Tractors are permitted around the barn and to power machinery but are not allowed in the fields. The tractor speeds up farming and eliminates the need for labor, which is considered beneficial.

Electric power is acceptable if it comes from batteries or some fuel generators; gas lanterns are fine. Electricity is not acceptable if it comes from the 'English'-operated power grid. Oddly, kids can be spotted playing with handheld video games as they work at their family's roadside farm stand.

Children attend one-room Amish schoolhouses until the eighth grade and learn the basics in reading, writing and arithmetic. They're exempt from the usual compulsory US school attendance to age 16. Any other education they receive is in the form of on-the-job training. In their late teens, Amish youngsters have a choice to stay or leave the community – about 85% choose to stay. The community is divided into church districts of 150 to 200 people. There's no central church – the district members gather at a different home every second Sunday for a three-hour service of hymn singing (without music) and scripture reading.

Lancaster County has around 15,000 Amish, most of whom live east of the city of Lancaster. Owing to the shortage of farms, some move to other parts of Pennsylvania or to other states; there are large communities of Amish in Ohio and Indiana.

You shouldn't take photographs of the Amish; they prefer that no one makes what they consider graven images of them. Don't even ask whether they mind; they do and will be uncomfortable about being approached.

# LANCASTER

Lancaster (population 56,000) is a pleasant town 57 miles west of Philadelphia. Settled first by Swiss Mennonites around 1700, it was originally called Gibson's Pasture. In the mid-18th century, it was renamed after the birthplace (in Lancashire, England) of Lancaster County's first commissioner, John Wright. Lancaster is noted for having been the capital of the US for a day (September 27, 1777) when Congress fled Philadelphia after George Washington's defeat at the Battle of Brandywine (p179). They stopped here overnight before continuing to York, Pennsylvania.

Prior to the Civil War, Lancaster was a staging post on the Underground Railroad, and Thaddeus Stevens (1792–1868), a Republican politician and opponent of slavery, is buried here. James Buchanan (1791–1868), following his term as the 15th president of the US (1857–61), made his home in Lancaster.

Today the town is known for its farmers market, some historic buildings and its outlet stores. As a cute, pedestrian-friendly urban center, Lancaster provides some bars, restaurants and nightlife for those who need a little action after a day of bucolic farm gazing.

## Orientation

Penn Square, with its Soldiers & Sailors Monument, is the town's central point. King St (between Water and Duke Sts) and Queen St (between Orange and Vine Sts) mark the main downtown commercial area. Queen St is the city's east-west divider; Orange St divides it north-south. A one-way system operates downtown: Rte 222 runs north along Lime St and south along Prince St; Rte 462 runs east along King St and west along Orange St; Rte 23 runs east along Chestnut St and west along Walnut St.

## Information

The **Pennsylvania Dutch Convention & Visitors Bureau** (Map p182; ☎ 717-299-8901, 800-723-8824; www.padutchcountry.com; 501 Greenfield Rd, Lancaster, PA 17601; ⏰ 8:30am-5pm Sun-Thu, 8:30am-6pm Fri & Sat Sep-Jun, 8am-6pm daily Jul & Aug) is the tourist office for the region. It's on the northeast

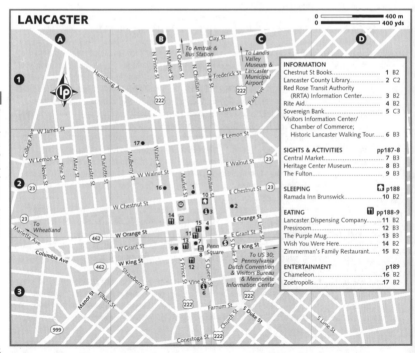

LANCASTER

| | | |
|---|---|---|
| 0 | | 400 m |
| 0 | | 400 yds |

**INFORMATION**
Chestnut St Books............................ 1 B2
Lancaster County Library.................. 2 C2
Red Rose Transit Authority
    (RRTA) Information Center........... 3 B2
Rite Aid........................................... 4 B2
Sovereign Bank................................ 5 C3
Visitors Information Center/
    Chamber of Commerce;
    Historic Lancaster Walking Tour.... 6 B3

**SIGHTS & ACTIVITIES**                    pp187-8
Central Market.................................. 7 B3
Heritage Center Museum.................... 8 B3
The Fulton........................................ 9 B3

**SLEEPING**                                      p188
Ramada Inn Brunswick......................10 B2

**EATING**                                        pp188-9
Lancaster Dispensing Company........11 B2
Pressroom....................................... 12 B3
The Purple Mug............................... 13 B3
Wish You Were Here........................ 14 B2
Zimmerman's Family Restaurant...... 15 B2

**ENTERTAINMENT**                             p189
Chameleon......................................16 B2
Zoetropolis......................................17 B2

side of the city, off Rte 30 West at the Greenfield Rd exit. It has a 15-minute audiovisual display about the region, called *People, Places & Passions*, which gives a basic overview of what you can see in the area. Get a copy of the free *Pennsylvania Dutch Country/Lancaster County Map & Visitors Guide;* it contains discount coupons for attractions, accommodations and restaurants.

The **Mennonite Information Center** (Map p182; ☎ 717-299-0954; www.mennoniteinfoctr .com; 2209 Millstream Rd, Lancaster, PA 17602; ☉ 8am-5pm Mon-Sat with reduced winter hrs) has general tourist advice and is a center for information (with a wide selection of books) about the Mennonites. The center shows a 20-minute film, *Postcards from a Heritage of Faith*, which explains the beliefs of the Mennonites and the Amish, as well as the differences between them.

Lancaster's downtown **Visitors Information Center/Chamber of Commerce** ( ☎ 717-397-3531; 100 S Queen St; ☉ 8:30am-5pm Mon-Fri, 9am-4pm Sat, 10am-3pm Sun) sells a map of the area for $6 and is also the point of departure for the Historic Lancaster Walking Tour.

For books, check out **Chestnut St Books** ( ☎ 717-393-3773; 11 W Chestnut St; ☉ 10am-5pm Tue-Sat), a quiet shop selling used books and a few rare editions, maps and prints. There's also the **Lancaster County Library** ( ☎ 717-394-2651; 125 N Duke St; ☉ 9am-9pm Mon-Thu, 9am-5:30pm Fri & Sat).

**Sovereign Bank** (23 E King St) has several locations in Lancaster, including the main location on E King St.

Postal services are available at the **main post office** (W Chestnut & N Prince Sts; ☉ 7:30am-4:30pm Mon-Fri, 8am-noon Sat) and at the **Rite Aid** drugstore (cnr N Queen & E Orange Sts; ☉ 7am-6pm Mon-Sat).

# Sights & Activities
## CENTRAL MARKET
One of the country's earliest publicly owned **farmers markets** ( ☎ 717-291-4723; Penn Square; ☉ 6am-4pm Tue-Fri, 6am-2pm Sat), this place has been operating since the early 18th century. The redbrick building housing the market dates from 1889, making this also one of the oldest covered markets in the US. On sale is a good selection of fruit,

vegetables, meat, baked goods and crafts, many of them from Amish farms.

## HERITAGE CENTER MUSEUM
Located in Lancaster's old city hall, this excellent **museum** ( ☎ 717-299-6440; 13 W King St; admission free; ☉ 10am-4pm Tue-Sat May-Dec) contains 18th- and 19th-century paintings, quilts, pewter items, furniture and other craftwork and fine art by local artisans and artists. It features a series of changing exhibitions on the ground floor. Check out the barrel vault on the 2nd floor, added in a 1933 renovation and covered in colorfully stenciled cloth. The museum's store smells nice and stays open year-round.

## WHEATLAND
An 1828 Federal mansion located about a mile northwest of downtown, **Wheatland** ( ☎ 717-392-8721; www.wheatland.org; 1120 Marietta Ave (Rte 23); adult/senior/student/ child $5.50/4.50/3.50/1.75; ☉ 10am-4pm Apr-Oct) was once home to James Buchanan, America's only bachelor president. Surrounded by 4 acres of gardens, the restored mansion features Buchanan's furnishings, many of which were gifts from foreign heads of state. Buchanan was a fairly active entertainer and palled around with the likes of Andrew Johnson, America's second favorite impeached president, in this very building.

## LANDIS VALLEY MUSEUM
This 16-acre outdoor **museum** ( ☎ 717-569-0401; www.landisvalleymuseum.org; 2451 Kissel Hill Rd; adult/senior/student/child $9/7/7/6; ☉ 9am-5pm Mon-Sat, noon-5pm Sun), about 2.5 miles northeast of town, is composed of homes, workshops and stores dating from 1760 to the early 20th century. The buildings have been assembled in one place to re-create the Pennsylvania Dutch rural life and work of that period. You can see presentations of blacksmithing, leather working, spinning, basket weaving, tinsmithing, lace making and chair caning.

From downtown Lancaster, take Lime St (Rte 222) north to the exit for Rte 272. Turn right and follow Rte 272 to the traffic light just past the Quality Inn. Turn left at this light onto Kissel Hill Rd. The entrance to the museum is about 300 yards down, on the right.

## THE FULTON

On the site of a former prison yard sits Lancaster's **opera house** ( ☎ 717-397-7425; www.atthefulton.org; 12 N Prince St; tickets adult $17-45 & student/child $15/12, tours adult/student/child $7/5/5; ☺ box office 9am-5pm Mon-Fri, 10am-4pm Sat, tours 11am Mon-Fri), built more than 150 years ago and older than Philadelphia's Academy of Music. The beautiful building is well preserved and still active. You can catch pop theater (such as *Joseph and the Amazing Technicolor Dreamcoat* and *A Christmas Carol*) or the Lancaster Symphony Orchestra.

## Organized Tours

**Historic Lancaster Walking Tour** ( ☎ 717-392-1776; 100 S Queen St; tour adult/senior/child $7/6/4; ☺ 1pm Mon, Wed, Thu & Sun, 10am & 1pm Tue, Fri & Sat), located in the downtown Visitors Information Center, does daily walking tours from April through October. They last 90 minutes, include a short film and are conducted by an interpreter in colonial costume, who will point out old churches, stables and cornices.

## Sleeping

You can't stay in town cheaply, but if you go southeast on Rte 462/30, there's a commercial strip with plenty of hotels and motels, and farther out into Pennsylvania Dutch Country there are campgrounds and farmhouses surrounded by more pretty farmland than your mind can parse.

**O'Flaherty's Dingeldein House** (Map p182; ☎ 717-293-1723, 800-779-7765; www .dingeldeinhouse.com; 1105 E King St (Rte 462); r $95-160) Two miles east of town before the intersection with Rte 30, O'Flaherty's is one of two B&Bs in the Lancaster area. It's small and comfortable, with five rooms. The common areas have gas fireplaces, and there's parking in back.

**King's Cottage** (Map p182; ☎ 717-397-1017, 800-747-8717; www.kingscottagebb.com; 1049 E King St; r $150-200) Near O'Flaherty's, the area's other B&B occupies a large, airy, Spanish-style mansion from 1913 with a library, fireplace and afternoon tea. Its eight rooms have private baths, wooden floors, good carpet, big beds and antique furniture.

**Garden Spot Motel** (Map p182; ☎ 717-394-4736; 2291 Rte 30; s/d $55/70 in peak season) This good-value motel is 5 miles east of Lancaster. It has 18 clean, well-lit rooms and a coffee shop on the premises.

**Ramada Inn Brunswick** ( ☎ 717-397-4800, 800-821-9258; www.hotelbrunswick.com; 151 N Queen St; r $99-109) If you want to stay downtown, it'll have to be at this 225-room hotel. The exterior is an unattractive mix of concrete and brick with rooms that contain fully functional furniture of the ugly variety. Bonus: free parking. Visit the hotel's website for special deals and other information.

## Eating

In addition to fresh food from the phenomenal **Central Market** (p187), you can buy prepared Middle Eastern food from **Saife's** in the market; spinach or meat pies are $2, and the vegetarian *kibbe* (made of bulgur, potato, parsley and peas) is $1.85.

**Lancaster Dispensing Company** ( ☎ 717-299-4602; 3335 N Market St; mains $6-9; ☺ 11am-2pm Mon-Sat, 1-10pm Sun) This pub has a varied menu of sandwiches, seafood and pasta salads; it also has a good selection of vegetarian and Mexican dishes. The atmospheric, dark and wooden taproom is a great spot in which to begin tomorrow's headache.

**Pressroom** ( ☎ 717-399-5400; 26 W King St; lunch mains $7-10, dinner mains $16-22; ☺ lunch 11am-3:30pm Mon-Sat, dinner 5-9:30pm Mon-Thu, 5-10:30pm Fri & Sat) Located in an old building that used to house one of the nation's first hardware stores, the Pressroom looks and feels like a locale for pulp writers of the 1940s to sling their dirt. Why not indulge? Have some lobster tails.

**The Purple Mug** ( ☎ 717-393-8099; 25 N Prince St; sandwiches $5-6; ☺ 8am-3pm Mon, 8am-11pm Tue-Sat, 11am-5pm Sun) Staff pour strong coffee in this café environment and prepare ham, turkey and roast beef sandwiches dressed with tasty stuff like brie and sun-dried tomatoes.

**Wish You Were Here** ( ☎ 717-299-5157; 108 W Orange St; breakfast $2.25-6; ☺ 8am-2pm Wed-Fri, 8am-1:30pm Sat & Sun) Come here for excellent breakfasts, particularly the 'Swedish' oatmeal pancakes. Traditional luncheon sandwiches are served, and the kitchen will try to make food vegan when possible. To find it, look for grandma's white lace curtains in the window.

## Detour: Hershey

The home of Milton S Hershey's chocolate empire, this town began in 1903 as an attempt to provide a model, moral community for those working in what was the largest chocolate factory in the world. Today the town offers numerous chocolate-related attractions. You might want to take your sweetie to **Hershey Park** ( ☎ 717-534-3900; www.hersheypa.com/attractions/hersheypark; adult/senior/child 3-8 $36/20/20; ☺ 10am-10pm Mon-Fri, 10am-11pm Sat & Sun Memorial Day–Labor Day, also open some weekends in May & Sep) for a kiss. It's a 90-acre landscaped amusement park that Milton Hershey originally established in 1906 as a recreation area for his workers. It now has over 50 rides, several of which can make you wet, dizzy or sick. Opening hours are fairly complicated; those above are general, so call or check the website to confirm. To avoid enormous crowds, go on a weekday. There is a fee for parking.

Visitors can't tour the actual Hershey's chocolate factory due to health regulations, but there is a free tour through **Chocolate World** ( ☎ 717-534-4900; www.hersheyschocolateworld.com). It's a mock factory, served by the same parking lot as Hershey Park, where visitors sit in little plastic cars that move along a conveyor past exhibits telling the story of the making of chocolate. At the end you get a free sample. Young kids love it, but others might be disappointed by the tackiness. Naturally, you exit through a candy store selling Hershey products, and a food court. As with Hershey Park, hours are elaborate. Chocolate World is open at 9am daily year-round, but closing hours vary: May through September it closes mostly at 10pm and generally at 5pm the rest of the year.

To get to Hershey from Philadelphia, take I-76 West to exit 266. Turn left onto Rte 72 North and follow it to Rte 322 West, which leads you (after about 12 miles) into Hershey. Alternatively, take Rte 30 West to Lancaster, then Rte 283 West to Rte 743 North to Hershey.

---

Zimmerman's Family Restaurant ( ☎ 717-394-6977; 66 N Queen St; main dishes $3-6; ☺ 5:45am-4pm Mon-Sat) Those seeking a 65¢ cup of coffee and a 1970s diner, look no farther. This is the place for grilled cheese sandwiches, milkshakes, some Greek fare and plenty of seating in booths or on swiveling stools.

## Entertainment

Chameleon ( ☎ 717-393-7133; 223 N Water St; cover $0-15; ☺ doors open at 6 or 8pm, depending on the show) Esteemed by rock musicians everywhere, Lancaster's finest has an 18-year history of attracting very big names to its tiny space (with a sweet balcony overlooking the stage). Among the many to plug in are the Pixies, Cat Power, Kid Rock, Moby, Anthrax and the Reverend Horton Heat. Live grew up playing at this venue. Chameleon still nurtures emerging local bands, and asses shake to DJs on Friday and Saturday night.

Zoetropolis ( ☎ 717-394-8272; 235 W Lemon St; tickets $5; ☺ shows generally start 7pm) A haven for local art students and creative-types, Zoetropolis' makeshift theater gallery and coffeehouse screens independent films and hosts vaudeville acts, lectures and snake-charming displays, and there's an impressive list of even weirder events.

## Getting There & Away

### BUS

Capitol Trailways ( ☎ 800-333-8444) operates from the Amtrak station. There's one bus daily to Philadelphia ($16.25, 90 minutes) and one to Atlantic City ($24, three hours).

### TRAIN

The Amtrak station ( ☎ 717-291-5080, 53 McGovern Ave) is about a mile north of downtown. There are 10 one-way trains daily to Philadelphia ($16, 80 minutes) and eight to New York ($55, three hours).

### CAR & MOTORCYCLE

The quickest way to Lancaster from Philadelphia is via the Pennsylvania Turnpike (I-76); at exit 286 (old exit 21) take Rte 222 South into town. Northward, Rte 222 leads to Reading; southeast of town it leads to Maryland. Another option from Philadelphia is to take Rte 30 West, which passes through the heart of Pennsylvania Dutch Country. From Lancaster, Rte 30 continues southwest to York and Gettysburg. Rte 283 leads northwest from Lancaster to Harrisburg, and Rte 501 heads north to I-78.

## Getting Around

Red Rose Transit Authority (RRTA; ☎ 717-397-4246; www.redrosetransit.com) is Lancaster

County's bus service; you can get info and buy tickets at its **information center** (47 N Queen St; ⏰ 8:15am-5:15pm Mon-Fri, 10am-2pm Sat). Lancaster County is divided into five fare zones, with the city of Lancaster as the central, or base, zone. One-way fares range from $1.15 to $2.25.

# INTERCOURSE & AROUND

This small town (population 1200) along Rte 340 (Old Philadelphia Pike), 8 miles east of Lancaster, was founded in 1754 and was originally called Cross Keys. No one knows for sure how it obtained its current name, but its residents have been doomed to a lifetime of excellently bad jokes bestowed upon them from folks living in adjacent towns with unfunny place-names. As tormented as they are, the good citizens of Intercourse are very pleased not to live in Blue Ball, Pennsylvania (not covered in this book), which might contain the United States' most systematically humiliated adolescents. The reason usually given for Intercourse's name is that the town stands at the intersection of the old King's Hwy (Rte 340) and the old Newport Rd (Rte 772). Another possible explanation is that the name evolved from a sign at the entrance to an old racing track on King's Hwy that read 'Enter Course.' Regardless, Intercourse became the town's official name in 1814.

Almost all of Intercourse's commercial action lies along Rte 340. The town possesses numerous opportunities to shop for crafts as well as some sights cashing in on Amish culture. Here as elsewhere, plenty of pretty farmland surrounds the strip.

## Information

The **Amish Mennonite Information Center** (Map p182; ☎ 717-768-0807; 3551 Old Philadelphia Pike; ⏰ 11am-4pm Mon-Sat Apr-Oct), near the Kitchen Kettle Village shopping center, has tourist information as well as information on the Amish and Mennonites.

## Sights & Activities

### PEOPLE'S PLACE

A cultural center that gives visitors a sensitive introduction to Amish and Mennonite life, **People's Place** (Map p182; ☎ 717-768-7171; www .thepeoplesplace.com; 3513 Old Philadelphia

Pike; theater adult/senior/child $5/4/2.50, theater & museum adult/senior/child $8/7/4; ⏰ 9:30am-5pm Mon-Sat Sep-May, 9:30am-8pm Mon-Sat Jun-Aug) is very informative and has parts that are geared toward children. It screens *Who Are the Amish?*, an intelligent, beautifully photographed show (running 30 minutes) about Amish life from birth to death. It also operates a 20 Questions Museum, with a display of questions and answers for adults and children about Amish and Mennonite life. There are also exhibits on clothing, buggies and religious practices.

The bookstore has a wide selection of books on the Amish and the Mennonites, and you can purchase a video of *Hazel's People*, a film about the Mennonite community starring Geraldine Page.

### AMISH EXPERIENCE THEATER & COUNTRY HOMESTEAD

This **theater and home** (Map p182; ☎ 717-768-8400; www.amishexperience.com; theater adult/child $7/4.50, theater & house adult/child $11.50/7.50; ⏰ 9am-5pm Mon-Sat Apr-Jun, 9am-8pm Mon-Sat, 11am-6pm Sun Jul-Oct, abbreviated hrs other months) are at the **Plain 'N' Fancy Farm Restaurant** and shopping area (p191), on Rte 340 between Intercourse and Bird-in-Hand. The theater shows the film *Jacob's Choice*, which deals with a young Amish man's dilemma – whether to stay and follow the traditional way of life, or to enter the world of the 'English.'

There are 40-minute tours of the nearby Amish Country Homestead, a fairly accurate replica of an Old Order Amish home. From April to June the tours run from 9:45am to 4:15pm Monday to Saturday and 10:45am to 4:45pm Sunday; from July to October they run 9:45am to 6:15pm Monday to Saturday and 10:45am to 4:45pm Sunday. On-site are **Aaron & Jessica's Buggy Rides** (Map p182; ☎ 717-768-8828; ride $10), and **Amish Country Tours** (see p184).

## Sleeping

**Beacon Camping** (Map p182; ☎ 717-768-8775; www.beaconhillcamping.com; Newport Rd (Rte 772 West); RV/tent $27/24; ⏰ Apr-Nov) is a half-mile northwest of Intercourse, on a quiet hilltop overlooking the farmlands. There are 46 sites, and only a few are for tents.

**Eby's Peaquea Farm** (Map p182; ☎ 717-768-3615; 459A Queen Rd; r $65-90 incl breakfast) This farm home has two buildings: a house from 1814 and a modern Cape Cod cottage (which is handicapped accessible). Among the 100 acres you'll find a covered bridge on the premises, and kids get pumped over feeding cows by hand. Sometimes a stay includes dinner with the Eby's Amish neighbors. No booze allowed. From town, follow Queen Rd south off of Rte 772.

**Harvest Drive** (Map p182; ☎ 717-768-7186; www.harvestdrive.com; 3370 Harvest Dr; r $80-100) Rooms here have a TV, phone and private bath. It's a plain, clean motel with some excellent views of corn from many of its windows. Take Rte 340 West half a mile to Clearview Rd, then go south about 0.8 miles to Harvest Dr, then turn west.

## Eating

On the main street (Rte 340), **Immergut** (Map p182) – the name means 'always good' in German – sells soft and hand-rolled pretzels starting at 90¢. The **Lunch Basket** (Map p182; ☎ 717-768-3462; 3551 Old Philadelphia Pike; dishes $2-5), next to the Amish Mennonite Information Center, is a simple but popular sandwich-and-pizza shop that also does good ice cream.

**Kling House Restaurant** (Map p182; ☎ 717-768-2746; 3529 Old Philadelphia Pike; sandwiches $5, breakfast mains $4-8, lunch mains $6-7, dinner mains $8-16; ☼ breakfast 8-11am Mon-Sat, lunch 11am-4pm Mon-Sat, dinner 4-7pm Thu-Sat Easter-Thanksgiving) Kling House, in the Kitchen Kettle Village shopping area, serves breakfasts of egg, sausage and potato ($5) or peach melba pancakes in raspberry syrup ($5). Desserts are also good here.

**Stoltzfus Farm Restaurant** (Map p182; ☎ 717-768-8156; 3761A Old Philadelphia Pike; family-style adult/child $14/7; ☼ 11:30am-8pm Mon-Sat May-Oct, 11:30am-8pm Fri & Sat Apr & Nov) One block southeast of Intercourse on Rte 772, in a large barnlike building behind the Stoltzfus meat factory, is one of the least commercial (but it still gets a hefty share of visitors) of the family-style places. The Stoltzfus Market, next door, sells meat and baked goods.

**Plain 'N' Fancy Farm Restaurant** (Map p182; ☎ 717-768-4400; 3121 Old Philadelphia Pike; family-style meal adult/child $15/7; ☼ noon-8pm) This restaurant is on Rte 340 between Intercourse and Bird-in-Hand. It's open year-round as a monument to America's caloric intake: trucks unload massive shipments of food out back, while buses unload massive shipments of people out front. The huge, all-you-can-eat enterprise significantly helps the area belt-making trade.

## Shopping

Intercourse is the epicenter of shopping for Pennsylvania Dutch goods. There are stores in town selling quilts, handmade wooden furniture, decoys (wooden ducks), pewter, fudge, brass, clothing and more. It's hard to choose one over another – look around.

**Kitchen Kettle Village** (Map p182; www.kitchenkettle.com; Rte 340) is a collection of shops at the west end of town. In the 'village' **The Pewter Shoppe** (☎ 717-768-2783; ☼ 9am-5pm Mon-Sat) sells pewter lamps, mugs and knickknacks, while **Pepper Lane Fudge** (☎ 866-753-8343; ☼ 9am-5pm Mon-Fri, 9am-5:30pm Sat) makes sweets, fudge and confections.

A little farther east, at the intersection of Rtes 340 and 772, **Cross Keys Village** (Map p182) is a smaller shopping center; across the road you can watch candle-making downstairs at the **Old Candle Barn** (Map p182; ☎ 717-768-8926; 3551 Old Philadelphia Pike; ☼ 8am-4pm Mon-Sat). For quilts, try **Nancy's Corner of Quilts** (Map p182; ☎ 717-768-8790; 3503 Old Philadelphia Pike; ☼ 8am-4pm Mon-Sat).

On Rte 772, for several miles northwest of Intercourse, there are a number of places selling wooden furniture, quilts and secondhand wares.

## Getting There & Away

RRTA bus No 13 from Duke St in Lancaster stops up to nine times daily (Monday to Saturday) on Rte 772 (N Newport Rd) in Intercourse. By car from Lancaster, follow King St (Rte 462) east out of the city, then take the left fork onto Rte 340. If you're coming from Philadelphia, Rte 772 connects Rtes 222 and 30 with Intercourse.

# BIRD-IN-HAND & AROUND

Bird-in-Hand, a few miles east of Lancaster on Rte 340, was so named in 1734. Back then the town wasn't much of a town – it was more a place to stop for those traveling to or from Lancaster along the Pike. The name may have been taken from the sign at the town's then-prominent inn. Today the small town has many stores and restaurants, and a smaller proportion of teamsters and highwaymen. Just in case you were worried, don't be – Bird-in-Hand is also blessed with many miles of farms and Amish folk.

## Sights & Activities
### AMISH FARM & HOUSE
This is a reconstruction of an **Old Order Amish farm** (Map p182; ☎ 717-394-6185; 2395 Rte 30 East; adult/senior/child $7/6.25/4.25; ☻ 8:30am-5pm Sep-May, 8:30am-6pm Jun-Aug) with animals and buildings spread out over 25 acres. The ticket gets you a guided tour of the house, with a description of the Amish culture and way of life. After the tour you can wander solo around the farm, which contains a waterwheel, windmill, smokehouse, milk house and a blacksmith (he's there from April through October). Overall the operation is a tad cheesy.

### BIRD-IN-HAND FARMERS MARKET
The **farmers market** (Map p182; ☎ 717-393-9674; ☻ 8:30am-5:30pm Fri & Sat), on the main street (Rte 340), has fewer 'gourmet' items than Lancaster's Central Market but more Amish homemade jams, pies, pretzels, fudge and other foods. In addition to the year-round hours listed, from April through November the market is also open Wednesday, and from July through October it's also open Thursday. Skip the gifts from the gift shop connected to the market; you're better off shopping in the shops listed here, or in Intercourse.

### HORSE & BUGGY RIDES
**Abe's Buggy Rides** (Map p182; ☎ 717-392-1794; adult/child $12/6; ☻ 9am-6pm Mon-Sat Apr-Oct, 9am-3pm Mon-Sat Nov-Mar, closed Jan), on Rte 340, half a mile west of Bird-in-Hand, does a 2-mile tour in an Amish family carriage. It's pretty, but don't be fooled into thinking the drivers are actually Amish.

## Sleeping & Eating
**Country Acres Family Campground** (Map p182; ☎ 717-687-8014; www.bird-in-hand.com/countryacres; 20 Leven Rd; RV site $27-30, tent site $20-24) This campground is surrounded by farmland. It offers a handful of clustered tent sites; the rest is

all for RVs. The property contains a pool, laundry facility, horseshoes and a volleyball court. Included with the tariff is a two-hour complimentary tour of the area. To get here from Bird-in-Hand, take N Ronks Rd south to Rte 30, then go east to Leven Rd.

**Good 'N' Plenty Farm Restaurant** (Map p182; ☎ 717-394-7111; Eastbrook Rd (Rte 896); family-style meals adult/child 4-10 $16/8; ☻ 11:30am-8pm Mon-Sat Feb-Nov) This large family-style restaurant covers two floors of a former barn. Take Rte 340 west to Rte 896, then head south to the restaurant.

## Shopping
**Country Barn Crafts** (Map p182; Rte 340; ☻ 9am-5pm Mon-Sat), just east of Bird-in-Hand, is an Amish-owned store operated in a converted tobacco barn on an Amish farm. It has a good selection of carpets, quilts, dolls, wall hangings, pillows and carvings – all of which are made locally.

Two discount factory-outlet malls are south of town on Rte 30. **Rockvale Square Outlets** (Map p182; ☎ 717-293-9595) is at the intersection with Rte 896. **Tanger Outlet Center** (Map p182; ☎ 717-392-7260) is on the corner of Millstream Rd, opposite the Mennonite Information Center.

## Getting There & Away
RRTA bus No 13 from Duke St in Lancaster stops up to nine times daily (Monday to Saturday) in Bird-in-Hand. By car from Lancaster, follow King St (Rte 462) east out of the city, then take the left fork onto Rte 340. If you're coming from Philadelphia, Rte 772 connects Rte 222 and Rte 30 with Rte 340.

# STRASBURG & AROUND
Strasburg (population 2800), at the less-traveled southern end of Pennsylvania Dutch Country on Rte 741, makes for a pleasant visit. It's the most picturesque and least commercialized of the regional towns and has some interesting attractions for train buffs.

The **Strasburg Information Center** (Map p182; ☎ 717-687-7922) is at the reception desk in the **Historic Strasburg Inn** (p193). There's a **post office** ( ☻ 8am-4:30pm Mon-Fri, 9am-1pm Sat) near the intersection of Rtes 896 and 741.

# Sights & Activities

## AMAZING MAIZE MAZE
Every year farmers carve a 5-acre **maze** (Map p182; ☎ 717-687-6843; www.cherrycrest farm.com; 150 Cherry Hill Rd; adult/child $10.75/8.75; ☺ 10am-5pm Tue-Thu & 10am-dusk Fri & Sat Jul & Aug, 1pm-dusk Fri & 10am-dusk Sat Sep-Nov) into a big field of corn. The mazes are thematic – one recently celebrated the centennial of man's first flight – and clues, trivia and scenic bridges will comfort the lost.

## AMISH VILLAGE
This re-created **Amish village** (Map p182; ☎ 717-687-8511; adult/child $6.50/2.50; ☺ 9am-5pm Mon-Sat, 10am-5pm Sun) is composed of about six major buildings, including an Old Order Amish house, a blacksmith shop and a schoolhouse. The grounds have peacocks, mules and a mother sow with her piglets (well, until the piglets become pigs and the piggies become bacon). It is on Rte 896, 2 miles north of Strasburg.

## MILL BRIDGE VILLAGE
The most elaborate of the replicas, **Mill Bridge Village** (Map p182; ☎ 717-687-8181; www.millbridge.com; adult/child $5/3; ☺ 10am-5pm Apr-Oct), 2 miles south of Ronks on S Ronks Rd, is a re-created colonial 'village' that includes an Amish house, a school, a covered bridge, a blacksmith shop, a log cabin, a broom maker, a stone and timber grist mill from 1728, a barnyard and a zoo. Often there's someone working in each building who can tell you how that building functioned in the 18th century. Buggy rides (adult/child $10/5) are also available. If you camp here, you get free admission to the village.

## RAILROAD MUSEUM OF PENNSYLVANIA
Opposite the Strasburg Railroad station is this huge **museum** (Map p182; ☎ 717-687-8628; www.rrmuseumpa.org; adult/senior/child $7/6/5; ☺ 9am-5pm Mon-Sat, noon-5pm Sun Apr-Oct, closed Mon Nov-Mar). Spanning the history of Pennsylvania railroads since 1825, it features a collection of steam locomotives and railcars from different periods, as well as artifacts such as uniforms and engineers' tools.

## STRASBURG RAILROAD
From the **Strasburg Railroad station** (Map p182; ☎ 717-687-7522; www.strasburgrailroa d.com; Rte 741; adult/child $9.25-15.25/ 5.75-10.75), a mile east of town, a steam train does a 45-minute, 9-mile roundtrip scenic tour through the countryside to the village of Paradise. The beautifully restored train, one of America's oldest short-liner steam trains, runs up to 10 times daily April through November (weekends only December through March). The fare varies depending on the opulence – some of it mind-blowing – of the Victorian-era car (coach, parlor, dining or lounge) in which you travel. There are special Easter, Halloween and Christmas trains, featuring guests like the Easter bunny and St Nick; these sell out early.

# Sleeping & Eating
**Mill Bridge Village Campground** (Map p182; ☎ 717-687-8181; site $25-35) has fishing, free buggy rides and free admission to Mill Bridge Village.

**Rayba Acres** (Map p182; ☎ 717-687-6729; www.raybaacres.com; 183 Black Horse Rd; farmhouse r $70 for 2 people, extra person $5, house r $65) About 3 miles east of Strasburg, off Rte 741, this dairy farm has been in the family for over 100 years. Rooms are available in the old and new houses. The old farmhouse has six large carpeted rooms with shared bathroom; the new house has motel-style units.

**Sycamore Haven Farm Home** (Map p182; ☎ 717-442-4901; 35 S Kinzers Rd; d $50-65, extra person $5) Perhaps not surprisingly, this is a working farm next to a large sycamore tree. Take Rte 741 east for about 6 miles, then turn right on S Kinzers Rd. Go under the railroad bridge, and it's about 300 yards down, on the left.

**Historic Strasburg Inn** (Map p182; ☎ 717-687-7691, 800-872-0201; www.historicstrasburginn .com; 1 Historic Dr; r from $130) Parts of this building date back to 1793, and its 102 rooms are nicely appointed with colonial reconstruction furniture. The inn is set in 58 peaceful acres off Rte 896, north of town. It has a pool, restaurant and pub (the **George Tavern**). Guests are offered bike rentals ($15/day).

**Isaac's Restaurant & Deli** (Map p182; ☎ 717-687-7699) Isaac's is part of a small shopping mall on Rte 741, just east of Strasburg. Fitted out like an old railroad carriage, it mostly serves sandwiches and pizzas ($4.95-6.95), and has a good vegetarian selection.

**Strasburg Country Store & Creamery** (Map p182; ☎ 717-687-0766; 1 W Main St) Plenty of homemade ice cream is dished out to give your kids a quick sugar rush before they pass out in the back seat during the drive home. The store is in the center of town, at the intersection of Rtes 741 and 896.

## Getting There & Away

Strasburg is at the intersection of Rtes 741 and 896, about 3 miles south of Rte 30. There's no public transportation from Lancaster, although RRTA bus No 14 stops several times daily at Rockvale Square, about 3 miles to the north, at the intersection of Rtes 896 and 30.

# LITITZ

A pretty town with many 18th- and 19th-century redbrick buildings, Lititz (population 9020) was founded in 1756 by Moravians who had fled religious persecution in Europe. In 1861 Julius Sturgis established the first commercial pretzel bakery in the US here. At the **Sturgis Pretzel House** ( ☎ 717-626-4354, 800-227-9342; www.sturgispretzel.com; 219 E Main St; admission $2; ☺ 9am-5pm Mon-Sat) you can take a 20-minute tour of the bakery and make your own pretzels. There are also a number of rooms full of all sorts of crafts.

West along Main St and around the corner is the **Wilbur Candy Americana Museum** ( ☎ 717-626-3249; www.wilburbuds.com; 45 N Broad St; admission free; ☺ 10am-5pm Mon-Sat). Though fairly small, it's probably more interesting for adults than **Hershey's Chocolate World** (p189). A two-room display of old chocolate-making equipment, including molds for Easter eggs, is at the rear of the chocolate shop. There's a store where you can buy all the chocolate your mouth needs.

RRTA bus No 10 from Lancaster stops up to 16 times daily (Monday to Saturday) in Lititz. Lititz is about 10 miles north of Lancaster on Rte 501.

# EPHRATA

Ephrata *(Eh*-fra-ta, population 13,230) is on Rte 322, approximately midway between Lancaster and Reading. The **Chamber of Commerce Visitor Center** ( ☎ 717-738-9010; www.ephrata-area.org; 77 Park Ave; ☺ 9am-2pm Mon-Fri) is located off Main St in a quiet residential neighborhood. The historic town's cloister serves as yet another example of religious tolerance in Pennsylvania, this time for a freaky pack of 18th-century celibates.

Ephrata (which means 'fruitful' or 'plentiful' in old Hebrew) is home to the **Ephrata Cloister** ( ☎ 717-733-6600; 632 W Main St; adult/senior/child $7/6.50/4; ☺ 9am-5pm Mon-Sat, noon-5pm Sun), founded in 1732 by Conrad Beissel, a Pietist (Pietism was a reform movement in the German Lutheran church in the 18th and 19th centuries). It was a communal society made up of religious celibates and ascetics of both sexes, as well as affiliated married householders; at its peak, it had about 300 people, and its last celibate member died in 1813.

Today the striking medieval-style buildings – tall, steep-roofed, wood-and-shingle structures – are in their original locations. The doors were made low to force people to bend 'in humility.' Members of the community lived and worked under a rigorous schedule and ate only enough food to maintain their strength. Note the bed made of a 15-inch-wide plank, with a wooden block for a pillow.

Many books were printed at the cloister, including a translation of the Mennonites' *Martyrs Mirror*. The cloister is also known for its Frakturschriften ('broken writing'), a script in which each letter is a combination of strokes, as well as for its beautiful *a cappella* singing. A slide show and guided tour are included in the price of admission.

RRTA bus No 11 runs Monday to Saturday between Lancaster and Ephrata. By car, take Rte 222 North from Lancaster or Rte 222 South from Reading to Rte 322 West.

# READING & AROUND

Reading *(Red*-ing, population 81,200) straddles the Schuylkill River about 45 miles northwest of Philadelphia. The Leni-Lenape people (Native Americans, not Amish), who fished the river, originally settled the area. The Dutch set up a trading post there in 1663, and European settlers began arriving toward the end of that century. The sons of William Penn (Thomas and Richard) laid out the town in the 1740s, and it was named after Penn's county seat in Berkshire,

England. During the 19th century, it became an important manufacturing and industrial center – a position it maintains today.

Reading itself doesn't have the attractions of the rest of Pennsylvania Dutch Country, but there are a few sights outside town, including Daniel Boone's birthplace. Reading is more noted for its huge collection of factory-outlet stores, and it modestly promotes itself as 'the outlet capital of the world.' The town gets busy in mid-September – when visitors combine a trip to see Pennsylvania's fall colors with some early Christmas shopping – and it stays frantic until after Christmas.

## Orientation

Downtown Reading is on the east bank of the Schuylkill River. Business Rte 422 East becomes Penn St, the main street in town, which leads west over the river to the suburbs of West Reading and Wyomissing, and to the factory outlets. Penn St divides the town into north and south segments. The north-south Business Rte 222 becomes 5th St in town.

### Daniel Boone Homestead

This folklore hero was actually a real guy. Born outside Reading, Daniel Boone caught a serious case of wanderlust and, along with a few others, set out on a two-year adventure, exploring the unmapped, unknown terrain that eventually became the state of Kentucky. While it's unlikely that 'he killed him a bear when he was only three,' his dad did give him his first rifle at the age of 12.

The famous outdoorsman was born and raised (until the age of 15) in a log house on the site of the present **homestead** ( ☎ 610-582-4900; www.danielboone homestead.org; 400 Daniel Boone Rd; adult/senior/child $4/3.50/2; ☯ 9am-5pm Tue-Sat, noon-5pm Sun) in Birdsboro, 9 miles east of Reading. The reconstructed house includes the original foundation, portions of the 18th- and 19th-century building material, period German and English furnishings and a spring in the basement. Inside the visitors center is a video of a fellow in old garb talking as though he knew Boone. The price of admission includes a guided tour. Around the homestead are 600 acres of land with hiking and biking trails.

Take Rte 422 East to the intersection with Rte 82; continue straight through the traffic lights, and after the sign for the homestead, turn left onto Daniel Boone Rd. The entrance to the property is about a mile from the turn.

## Information

The **Reading & Berks Visitors Bureau** ( ☎ 610-375-4085, 800-443-6610; www.readingberkspa .com; 352 Penn St; ☯ 9am-5pm Mon-Fri, 10am-2pm Sat) has lots of information about the factory outlets, plus other attractions and amenities. There's also a **visitors center** ( ☯ 9am-5pm Mon-Sat, 10am-5pm Sun) at the VF Factory Outlet. Most of its information is on the factory outlets, but it can help with other things, too.

In the heart of things is the main **post office** (N 5th St btwn Court & Washington Sts; ☯ 8am-5pm Mon-Fri, 8am-2pm Sat) and the **library** (cnr Franklin & S 5th Sts; ☯ 8:15am-9pm Mon-Wed, 8:15am-5:30pm Thu & Fri, 8:45am-5pm Sat).

## Sights

It's odd to see a Japanese pagoda in the middle of Pennsylvania, but there it is, red-and-gold, neon-lit at night and several stories high. Sitting on a hill in Mt Penn Forest Reservation, about 10 blocks east of the town's center and with good views across town, the **Reading Pagoda** ( ☎ 610-372-0553; admission free; ☯ 11am-5pm) was built by Wilan Witman at the turn of the 20th century as an apology to Reading for defacing Mt Penn through his rock quarrying operations. To find the pagoda, follow Duryea Dr up through the reservation.

## Sleeping

Reading is busiest from mid-September till after Christmas, so it's best to book ahead. During that time, room rates at the hotels and motels go up by as much as 40% to 50%. You can get a list of B&Bs from the visitors center. Of note, the central **Hunter House B&B** ( ☎ 610-374-6608; 118 S 5th St; r from $100) is a delightful townhouse that was built in 1847. It has several comfortable rooms.

In West Reading and Wyomissing, west of the river, most of the places are chain motels with standard, clean rooms and no surprises.

**Econolodge** ( ☎ 610-378-5105; www.econo lodge.com; 635 Spring St; r from s/d $50/57) This motel is at Park Rd, just off Rte 422 in Wyomissing.

**Lincoln Plaza Hotel & Conference Center** ( ☎ 610-372-3700; www.lincolnplaza.com; cnr 5th

& Washington Sts; r $110-120) Reading's top hotel has 104 rooms, its own restaurant and fitness center, and – though you can't tell from the outside – a beautiful bar (original leaded glass) converted from an old library and smoking room.

**Dutch Colony Inn & Suites** ( ☎ 610-779-2345, 4635 Perkiomen Ave (Business Rte 422); r from $68) The closest motel on the east side of town (5 miles from the center) has a restaurant, bar, laundry facilities, heated swimming pool and gym.

# Eating

The factory outlets have food courts inside, and there are chain restaurants around them. As delicious as that might sound, the town of Reading provides a few more interesting options.

**Reading Farmers Market** (cnr Penn & S 8th Sts; ☒ 10am-6pm Thu & Fri, 10am-2pm Sat) This emporium provides a helping hand, fruit and sausages to those looking to self-cater. While you'll feel like a local picking up what the vendors put down, you might shed a few tears over the limited hours.

**Jimmy Kramer's Peanut Bar & Restaurant** ( ☎ 610-376-8500; 332 Penn St; dinner mains $7-11; ☒ 11am-11pm Mon-Thu, 11am-midnight Fri & Sat) Established in 1924, this place is named after the free peanuts everyone gets. Just throw the shells on the floor. The place has good pub food, serving traditional stuff like beef stew and shrimp platters. Almost everything comes fried.

**May Belle's** ( ☎ 610-898-0101; 501 Washington St; breakfast & lunch $2.50-5, dinner & brunch $5-12; ☒ 7am-2:30pm Mon-Thu, 7am-8pm Fri, 8am-8pm Sat, 10am-4pm Sun), in the Berkshire Building on the corner of N 5th and Washington Sts, occupies a former banking room with super-tall ceilings. May Belle's is all about Louisiana soul food and prepares some stellar gumbo. For breakfast, the fried catfish, eggs and grits are what you want.

# Shopping

Reading's factory outlets, the town's biggest draw, spread out over Reading itself and Wyomissing, located west of town. They sell clothes (including designer labels and sportswear), crockery, cosmetics and other items at clearance prices (read: huge discounts).

**VF Factory Outlet** ( ☎ 610-378-0408; www.vffo .com/states/pa/pa.htm; 801 Hill Avenue; ☒ 9am-7pm Mon-Thu, 9am-9pm Fri, 9am-7pm Sat, 10am-5pm Sun) In the VF Outlet Village at Park Rd and Hill Ave, VF offers shoppers acres of discounts. The massive complex contains several enormous buildings with dozens of retailers, including Jones NY, Lee, Geoffrey Beene, Izod, Liz Claiborne, London Fog, Reebok and Tommy Hilfiger. Aside from piles of clothes, there are piles of shoes, accessories, leather and toys.

**Reading Outlet Center** ( ☎ 610-373-5495; www.outletsonline.com/roc; 801 N 9th St; ☒ 9:30am-6pm Mon-Sat, 11am-5pm Sun) This compound features Guess, Old Navy and Nautica.

**Outlets on Hiesters Lane** ( ☎ 610-921-8130; 755 Hiesters Lane; ☒ 9:30am-9pm Mon-Sat, 10am-5pm Sun) The biggest draw here is Burlington Coat Factory, though there's also a good selection of baby stuff (head to the 'Baby Depot'). The parents of older squirts can also find plenty of clothes at Hiesters Lane's 'Kids Depot.'

# Getting There & Away
## BUS
The **Reading Intercity Bus Terminal** ( ☎ 610-374-3182; 20 N 3rd St) is served by **Bieber Tourways**

## Detour: Hawk Mountain Sanctuary

The 2400-acre **Hawk Mountain Sanctuary** ( ☎ 610-756-6961, 610-756-6000; www.hawkmountain.org; adult/senior/child $5/4/3, weekends in fall $7/7/3; ☒ 9am-5pm Dec-Aug, 8am-5pm Sep-Nov) was established in 1934 to protect migrating hawks from hunters. Today it's a preserve for bald eagles, ospreys, peregrine falcons, hawks and other migrating birds, such as the swift and the swallow. Spring and fall bring thousands of birds to the sanctuary, and the best spot for viewing them is the 1521ft North Lookout. A 4-mile walking trail connects the sanctuary with the Appalachian Trail. You can rent binoculars at the visitors center, which is open daily. Bear in mind that the sanctuary gets busy on weekends. Also note that the sanctuary doesn't sell food, so packing a lunch is a good idea.

To find the sanctuary, take Rte 61 North; then Rural Rte 2 East. Hawk Mountain is in Kempton, 25 miles north of Reading.

( ☎ 610-375-0839) and **Capitol Trailways** ( ☎ 800-333-8444). Bieber Tourways goes to Philly (one way adult/child $20/12, 1¼ hours, four departures Mon-Fri, three departures Sat & Sun) as does Capitol Trailways (one way $10.50, 1¼ hours, four departures Mon-Fri, two departures Sat & Sun).

### CAR & MOTORCYCLE

From Philadelphia, take I-76 (Schuylkill Expressway) North to the Pennsylvania Turnpike, then head west to exit 298 (old exit 22). Then take I-176 North to Rte 422 and follow it west into downtown. From Harrisburg you can take either I-76 (Pennsylvania Turnpike) East to exit 21, then Rte 222 Northeast, or you can take Rte 322 and then Rte 422 East into Reading.

## Getting Around

The **Berks Area Reading Transportation Authority** (BARTA; ☎ 610-921-0601; 1700 N 11th St) is the county bus line. Most fares around town are $1.35.

# GETTYSBURG

As a consequence of Gettysburg's position at the junction of several roads and its proximity to the Mason-Dixon Line, it became the site of the bloodiest battle in US history. The battle – begun July 1, 1863

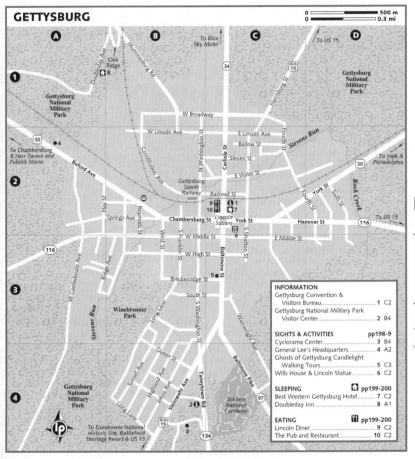

– was a turning point in the Civil War and helped inspire Abraham Lincoln's famous Gettysburg Address, delivered on November 19, 1863.

It also helped inspire today's busy tourist industry, which capitalizes on both the battle and the war. In spite of the commercialism in the town (population 8700), tranquil Gettysburg National Military Park is certainly worth visiting to see where the Union and Confederate Armies confronted each other. Over 51,000 soldiers on both sides were killed, wounded or captured during the three-day battle. Some believe that if the Confederates had defeated the Union army (and they definitely had the resources to do so), then they could have easily captured the important industrial cities of Philadelphia and Baltimore and, eventually, won the Civil War. The former home of President Dwight D Eisenhower is another nearby attraction. The town itself, with its many fine historic buildings, is small enough to walk around.

# Orientation

Gettysburg is about 55 miles southwest of Lancaster, 30 miles southwest of Harrisburg and 140 miles west of Philadelphia. The approximately 1.5 sq miles of Gettysburg are laid out around Lincoln Square. Several large roads converge in the town. Rte 30 (York and Chambersburg Sts in town) and Rte 116 (Hanover, York and W Middle Sts) cross east to west. Rte 97 enters from the south (Baltimore St) and leaves to the north as Rte 34 (Carlisle St). Business Rte 15 enters town as Steinwehr Ave from the southwest and exits in the northeast as Harrisburg St. Finally, Rte 134 enters from the south as Taneytown Rd and ends in town as Washington St.

Gettysburg National Military Park surrounds the town.

# Information

The **Gettysburg Convention & Visitors Bureau** (☎ 717-334-6274; www.gettysburg.com; 35 Carlisle St; ✆ 8:30am-5pm Mon-Fri) distributes a comprehensive list of local attractions.

The **Gettysburg National Military Park Visitor Center** (☎ 717-334-1124; www.nps.gov/gett; 79 Taneytown Rd; ✆ 8am-5pm Sep-May, 8am-6pm Jun-Aug), less than a mile south of Lincoln Square, is in the park off Taneytown

Rd. (There are, however, plans to move the center despite some local opposition.) Pick up the *Gettysburg Official Map & Guide,* which includes a self-guided driving tour (allow two to three hours) that follows a route that is marked by signposts (with a single large white star) that describe the battle action at important points.

Licensed battlefield guides charge $40 per carload (up to six people) for a two-hour tour. These tours are well worth it. The guides are available on a first-come, first-served basis, so you need to get to the visitor center early (except in the winter, when cold drives away the fragile, leaving plenty of space for the courageous). There are also free park-ranger-guided walks of the National Cemetery and High Water Mark Trail.

# Sights & Activities
## GETTYSBURG NATIONAL MILITARY PARK

This 8-sq-mile **park** (☎ 717-334-1124; www .nps.gov/gett; admission free; ✆ 6am-10pm) encompasses most of the area of the three-day battle. South of the visitors center along the High Water Mark Trail, Cemetery Ridge is the site of Pickett's Charge (see 'The Battle of Gettysburg' boxed text p199). Other hikes include the mile-long Big Round Top Loop Trail. There's also Devil's Den, a mass of boulders Confederate snipers used as a hideout. The **Cyclorama Center** (admission $2.50) is a 360-degree painting of the battle. At the visitors center, you can learn more through the extensive exhibits and the Electric Map, a kitschy relic that dramatizes battle formations with tiny light bulbs.

## OTHER SIGHTS

Other Gettysburg attractions include the **Eisenhower National Historic Site** (☎ 717-338-9114; www.nps.gov/eise; adult/child $7/4; ✆ 9am-4pm), Ike's former home. Visits are only via a shuttle bus that departs from the Gettysburg Military Park Visitor Center. Also in the area is the house that served as **General Lee's Headquarters** (☎ 717-334-3141; 401 Buford Ave; adult/child $2/free; ✆ 9am-5pm Mon-Fri, 9am-7pm Sat & Sun Apr-Oct). Lincoln prepared his Gettysburg Address in the **Wills House** (☎ 717-334-8188; Lincoln Square; $3.50;

10am-5pm Fri-Sun), now a museum. In the evening you can mingle with the battle spirits on the **Ghosts of Gettysburg Candlelight Walking Tours** ( ☎ 717-337-0445; www.ghostsofgettysburg.com; 271 Baltimore St; $6).

## Festivals & Events

The annual **Civil War Heritage Days** ( ☎ 717-334-6274) festival, taking place from the last weekend of June through the first weekend of July, features living history encampments, battle reenactments, a lecture series and book fair. Book early, as it's a popular event for history buffs (call for recorded information).

On November 19 check out the **Anniversary of Lincoln's Gettysburg Address** ( ☎ 717-334-6274), with memorial services at the National Cemetery, commemorating Lincoln's famous speech.

## Sleeping & Eating

Accommodations can get crowded during summer, and some places have a two-night minimum on select weekends. Rooms sell out quickly (like a year in advance) during Civil War Heritage Days, so book well ahead.

**Battlefield Heritage Resort** ( ☎ 717-334-1577; sites $17-24) Campers might try this campground, southwest on Business Rte 15.

**Blue Sky Motel** ( ☎ 717-677-7736; 2585 Biglerville Rd; d winter/summer $29/49) In a quiet location on Rte 34 heading north, Blue Sky has 16 rooms, a small picnic area and a heated pool. From town, take Rte 34 North for 4.5 miles.

**Doubleday Inn** ( ☎ 717-334-9119; www.doubledayinn.com; 104 Doubleday Ave; r $95-130) This large white house overlooks a quiet part of the battlefield and Gettysburg College. Five of the nine rooms have private baths with claw-footed tubs. On selected evenings a historian from the National Military Park Visitors Center comes to the house to speak and answer questions about the battle.

**Best Western Gettysburg Hotel** ( ☎ 717-337-2000; 1 Lincoln Square; r $70-140) Built in 1797 the renovated, 88-room hotel, in the center of town, has added Jacuzzis to what once felt like an old place.

**Herr Tavern and Publick House** ( ☎ 717-334-4332; 900 Chambersburg Rd; dinner mains

---

## The Battle of Gettysburg

The Battle of Gettysburg is the most famous battle of the Civil War. Some war buffs spend their lives studying the battle or only one day of it, and each year there are regular reenactments of events relating to this pivotal moment in US history. At Gettysburg, from July 1 to 3, 1863, the 75,000 men of Robert E Lee's Confederate Army met the 97,000 men of Union General George G Meade. The battle was the result of a chance sighting of some of Meade's troops by a group of Confederate troops who were sent to get supplies.

The battle began on July 1, with Confederate troops attacking Union troops on McPherson Ridge, west of Gettysburg. The Union troops held their position until the afternoon, when they were beaten back in a rout through town. Thousands were captured before they could regroup south of town on Cemetery Hill. The first day of battle ended with the Union troops, who had retreated, fortifying their positions while the bulk of Meade's army arrived to reinforce them.

By dawn of the second day the Confederate troops were laid out along an arc running through the middle of Gettysburg and along Seminary Hill. Facing them, a mile away to the east, was a smaller arc of Union troops on Cemetery Ridge. Lee ordered attacks against both flanks of the Union line. Confederate James Longstreet's attack smashed through the Union left flank at a peach orchard south of town and overran the Union position on Little Round Top. On the other flank, though, RS Ewell's attack didn't succeed in dislodging the Union troops and, ultimately, the Confederates couldn't exploit Longstreet's success.

On the third day, Lee's artillery bombarded Union positions on Cemetery Ridge and Cemetery Hill; the Union artillery responded. The sickening high point came when Confederate General George Pickett led a massive charge of 12,000 men across an open field toward the Union line at Cemetery Ridge. In less than an hour 10,000 of Pickett's men were dead or wounded, and the expression 'Pickett's Charge' entered the lexicon as a brave but futile attempt to defeat an enemy.

After the battle there were 51,000 dead, wounded and missing troops, and 5000 dead horses. Lee's invasion of the North had been stymied, and his army was exhausted. Union General Meade 'won' the battle but was too cautious (or too afraid) to pursue the Confederate Army. Although the war continued for two more years, the Confederacy never recovered from its losses at Gettysburg.

$18-27; ⊙ 11am-9pm Mon-Sat, 5-9pm Sun) Dine on upscale American cuisine for lunch and dinner in a historic setting.

**The Pub and Restaurant** ( ☎ 717-334-7100; Lincoln Square; burgers $7, mains $10.50-19; ⊙ 11am-1:30am Mon-Sat, noon-11pm Sun) Cheap sandwiches, soups and salads galore are served here.

**Lincoln Diner** ( ☎ 717-334-3900; 32 Carlisle St; dishes $3-10; ⊙ 24hr) Next to the railroad tracks, Lincoln is a sweet diner that's popular for lunch, serving hamburgers, iceberg lettuce salads and roast beef. Blueberry pie plus coffee equals pleasure.

## Getting There & Away

Incredibly, for a major tourist destination, there's no public transportation to or around Gettysburg. By car, it's accessible on Rte 30 from Philadelphia, Lancaster or York. From Philadelphia you can also take I-76 (Pennsylvania Turnpike) west to exit 17 and follow Rte 15 South.

---

### Antiquing in Lancaster County

Your antiquing pleasure comes in the form of huge and serious indoor/outdoor flea markets, usually held on Sunday. There are several big venues in a small geographic area in Lancaster County. **Renninger's** ( ☎ 717-336-2177; www.renningers.com; 2500 N Reading Rd, Adamstown; ⊙ 7:30am-4pm) is the reigning champ – it has about 400 vendors selling just about every weird thing ever made. Nearly as good and practically next door is **Stoudtburg Antique Mall** ( ☎ 717-484-4386; www.stoudtburg.com; N Reading Rd, Adamstown; ⊙ 5am-4pm Sun), whose complex also contains Pennsylvania's first modern microbrewery, Stoudt's Brewing Company. Also nearby is **Shupp's Grove** ( ☎ 717-484-4115; www.shuppsgrove.com; Rte 897, Adamstown; ⊙ 7am-5pm Sat & Sun Apr-Oct), which has been spreading itself over several acres since 1962. Put them all together, and the world of man-made items is pretty extensively represented.

To get to antiquing heaven, take I-76 West from Philadelphia to exit 286. Go right on Rte 272 N. Renninger's will be on the left. Stoudtburg also sits near this exit. To find Shupp's Grove, continue on Rte 272, turning right on Rte 897 S. Head south for a mile, finding Shupp's on the left side of the road.

**Directory**

# Directory

## TRANSPORTATION
### AIR
### Airlines
The following airlines serve the Philadelphia International Airport:

**Air Canada** (AC; www.aircanada.ca; ☎ 800-776-3000)
**Air France** (AF; www.airfrance.com; ☎ 800-237-2747)
**Air Jamaica** (JM; www.airjamaica.com; ☎ 800-523-5585)
**AirTran Airways** (FL; www.airtranairways.com; ☎ 800-825-8538)
**America West** (HP; www.americawest.com; ☎ 800-235-9292)
**American Airlines** (AA; www.aa.com; ☎ 800-433-7300)
**ATA – American Trans Air** (TZ; www.ata.com; ☎ 800-435-9282)
**British Airways** (BA; www.ba.com; ☎ 800-247-9297)
**Continental** (CO; www.flycontinental.com; ☎ 800-525-0280)
**Delta Air Lines** (DL; www.delta.com; ☎ 800-221-1212)
**Lufthansa** (LH; www.lufthansa.com; ☎ 800-645-3880)
**Midwest Express** (YX; www.midwestexpress.com; ☎ 800-452-2022)
**Northwest Airlines** (NW; www.nwa.com; ☎ 800-225-2525)
**Southwest Airlines** (SW; www.iflyswa.com; ☎ 800-435-9792) starting May 9, 2004
**United Airlines** (UA; www.ual.com; ☎ 800-241-6522)
**US Airways** (US; www.usairways.com; ☎ 800-428-4322)
**USA 3000** (U5; www.usa3000airlines.com; ☎ 800-872-3000)

### Airport
**Philadelphia International Airport** (Map pp220-1; ☎ 215-937-6800, 800-745-4283; www.phl.org; 8000 Essington Ave), 7 miles south of Center City, is served by direct flights from Europe, the Caribbean, Mexico and Canada, and offers connections to Asia, Africa and South America. Domestically, it has flights to over 100 destinations in the USA.

There's an information desk, ATM and currency exchange in every terminal. A few have post-office vending machines. Luggage carts can be rented for $3.

Fare for a taxi to Center City is a flat fee of $20. The airport is also served by SEPTA's regional service using the R1 line. The R1 ($5.50) will drop you off in University City or in numerous stops in Center City.

See Car, below, for information about renting a car at the airport. To drive to the airport, take I-95 South to the Philadelphia International Airport exit, or take I-76 East and follow the signs for the Philadelphia International Airport. Long-term parking at the airport costs $8 per day.

### LAND
### Bus
Greyhound and Peter Pan are the major carriers. Greyhound connects Philadelphia with hundreds of cities nationwide, while Peter Pan concentrates on the Northeast. Roundtrip fare to New York City is about $40 (2½ hours one way), to Atlantic City $12 (1½ hours) and to Washington, DC $40 (3½ hours).

**Greyhound** ( ☎ 800-229-9424; www.greyhound.com)
**Peter Pan Bus Lines** ( ☎ 800-237-8747; www.peterpanbus.com)
**Capitol Trailways** ( ☎ 800-444-2877; www.capitol trailways.com) Makes connections to Lancaster, Reading, New York City, and Washington, DC.
**NJ Transit** ( ☎ 215-569-3752 within Philadelphia, 800-772-2222 within NJ, 973-762-5100 out of state; www.njtransit.com) Carries you from Philly to points in New Jersey.

Another option is an enigmatic service known as the **'Chinatown Bus,'** run by slightly mysterious companies providing connection between Philly's, NYC's, DC's and Boston's Chinatowns. A return trip (two hours) costs $20. Consult www.ivymedia.com for details about this service.

### Car
Several interstate highways lead through and around Philadelphia. From the north and south, I-95 (Delaware Expressway) follows the eastern edge of the city beside the Delaware River, with several exits for Center City.

I-276 (Pennsylvania Turnpike) runs east across the northern part of the city and over the river to connect with the New Jersey Turnpike.

From the west, I-76 (Pennsylvania Turnpike/ Schuylkill Expressway) branches off the Pennsylvania Turnpike to follow the Schuylkill River to South Philadelphia and over the Walt Whitman Bridge into New Jersey, south of

Camden. Just north of downtown, I-676 (Vine St Expressway) heads east over the Benjamin Franklin Bridge into Camden itself. If you're coming from the east, take I-295 or the New Jersey Turnpike, which connects to I-676 over the Benjamin Franklin Bridge into downtown.

# Train

Beautiful **30th St Station** (Map pp222-3; ☎ 215-349-3196; www.30thstreetstation.com), beside the Schuylkill River in University City, is one of the biggest train hubs in the country. **Amtrak** (☎ 800-872-7245; www.amtrak.com) provides regional service from here. Philadelphia is on Amtrak's Northeast Corridor route, which runs between Richmond, Virginia ($120 roundtrip, 4¾ hours, 240 miles, 13 daily) and Boston ($148 roundtrip, six hours, 240 miles, 17 daily) via Washington, DC ($90 roundtrip, two hours, 135 miles, 36 daily) and New York City ($96 roundtrip, 90 minutes, 100 miles, 45 daily); there are also trains west to Lancaster ($29 roundtrip), Harrisburg, Pittsburgh and Chicago and south to Florida.

The above prices reflect conventional fares at time of press. Amtrak also operates the high-speed Acela train line between Washington, DC and Boston. Acela trains are brand-new, very comfortable and more expensive. The payoff? A trip from Philly to Boston is reduced to five hours; it's 70 minutes to New York City.

A cheaper but longer (adult/child $17.40/11.40; 2½ hours) way to get to New York City is to take the **SEPTA** R7 suburban train to Trenton in New Jersey. You can pick up this train from the Amtrak 30th St Station, Suburban Station or Market Street East Station. There you connect with **NJ Transit** (☎ 215-569-3752 within Philadelphia, 800-772-2222 within NJ, 973-762-5100 out of state; www.njtransit.com) to Newark's Penn Station, then continue on NJ Transit to New York City's Penn Station.

To buy your ticket to New York, you have two options. At 30th St Station, find one of the two NJ Transit ticket machines, which can issue you passes for both legs of the trip. At other stations in Philly, these machines do not exist. You'll have to buy the ticket for your second leg on the platform in Trenton. Warning: in Trenton, often you'll have only a minute or two before your connection departs for New York. While ticket-vending machines are conveniently located on the platform, there aren't that many of them. If long lines form, be ready to board the train without a pass and pay the $5 surcharge for a conductor-issued ticket.

NJ Transit also has a frequent rail service between 30th St Station and Atlantic City ($60 one way, 1½ hours).

The **Port Authority Transit Corporation** (PATCO; ☎ 215-922-4600; www.drpa.org/patco) has frequent subway trains to Camden, New Jersey, for $1.15. Stops in Philadelphia are 15th-16th St Station, 11th-12th St Station and 9th-10th St Station along Locust St, and 8th St Station at Market St. Then it's a scenic ride across the Benjamin Franklin Bridge to Camden.

# GETTING AROUND
## Bicycle

If you aren't straying too far from Center City, a bike is possibly the most efficient means of transport – it can be faster than driving a car or taking the bus. Since the city is relatively flat, it isn't even strenuous. However it's likely that you will have to contend with motorists who aren't very respectful of your right to be on the road.

Basic bike rules are to ride in the street (not on the sidewalk), and follow the same traffic laws as motorists. Philadelphia has marked a few bike lanes throughout Center City, many of them shared with public buses. Watch out for potholes and old trolley tracks. Always be sure to lock your bike, as theft is an issue.

Bicycle rentals (p146) can be had for around $25 a day.

## Bus

**SEPTA** (☎ 215-580-7800; www.septa.org) operates Philadelphia's municipal buses. Though extensive and reliable, the web of bus lines is difficult to make sense of, particularly since SEPTA's confusing website doesn't provide a comprehensive map of the 120 routes servicing Philly's 159 sq miles. To get such a map, you have to purchase SEPTA's *Official Philadelphia Transit & Street Map* ($7) either online or from a transit store.

The one-way fare on most routes is $2, for which you'll need the exact change or a token. Many subway stations and transit stores sell discounted packages of two tokens for $2.60.

If you're going to be doing a lot of traveling, SEPTA's Day Pass ($5.50) is a decent value. It gives you a day's unlimited riding on all local trains and buses, plus a one-way trip on the R1 airport rail line. It is available at regional rail stations or SEPTA sales outlets.

At time of boarding, you may purchase a transfer for 60¢ that entitles you to another ride.

# Car & Motorcycle

Driving isn't recommended in central Philadelphia; parking is difficult and regulations are strictly enforced. Downtown distances are short enough to let you see most places on foot, and a train, bus or taxi can get you to places farther out relatively easily. Park your car in a guarded lot and save it for trips out of the city or for evening trips. When booking a room with a hotel, ask about its parking facilities. Most Center City hotels have lots that charge a daily parking fee of around $20.

If you want to cross downtown east-west, remember that the I-676 (Vine St Expressway) runs under the city streets and can save you a lot of time. Most downtown streets have alternate one-way traffic. The exceptions are Broad St, with three lanes in both directions; Vine St; Benjamin Franklin Pkwy; and Market St between City Hall and Front St, and west of 20th St (between 20th and 15th Sts, it's one-way eastbound).

For emergency road service and towing, **American Automobile Association** (AAA; p207) members can call ☎ 800-222-4357.

### RENTAL

The main car-rental companies have desks at the airport (in addition to the offices listed below). Rates go up and down like the stock market, and it's always worth phoning around to see what's available. Booking ahead usually ensures the best rates, and web rates are usually better than when you book through a person. Typically a small car might cost $30 to $45 a day, or $150 to $250 a week. Most rates include unlimited mileage; if a rate is unbelievably cheap, there is probably a per-mile charge after a certain distance.

On top of that, add $9 to $12 a day for insurance, called a loss/damage waiver. Add another $20 for liability insurance if you are afraid you might run over someone. If you will be using your own insurance, don't forget to bring your policy information with you; without it the rental companies will make you use theirs.

**Avis** (Map pp226-7; ☎ 215-629-1333; www.avis.com; 201 S Columbus Blvd; ☽ 7am-7pm Mon-Fri, 8am-5pm Sat, 9am-4pm Sun; SEPTA 2nd St Station, Bus 25, 76)
**Budget** (Map pp228-9; ☎ 215-462-2055; www.budget.com; 841 S Christopher Columbus Blvd; ☽ 7:30am-7:30pm; SEPTA Bus 25)
**Enterprise** (Map p230; ☎ 215-592-9700; www.enterprise.com; 510 N Front St; ☽ 8am-6pm Mon-Fri, 9am-4pm Sat; SEPTA Spring Garden Station, Bus 5, 25, 43)

**Hertz** (Map pp222-3; ☎ 215-492-2951; www.hertz.com; 31 S 19th St; ☽ 7am-10pm Sun-Fri, 7am-6pm Sat; SEPTA 19th St Station, Bus 9, 17, 21, 33, 42)
**National** (Map pp222-3; ☎ 215-567-1760; www.nationalcar.com; 36 S 19th St; ☽ 7:30am-9:45pm Sun & Mon, 7:30am-7:15pm Tue & Wed, 7:30am-9:45pm Thurs & Fri, 7:30am-4:15pm Sat; SEPTA 19th St Station, Bus 9, 17, 21, 33, 42)

### ROAD RULES

Except where otherwise posted, the speed limit on Philadelphia's surface streets is 25mph (15mph in alleys and school zones). On highways, the speed limit ranges between 55 and 65mph. Drivers and passengers in the front seat must use seat belts. Pennsylvania law requires that children under four years of age be fastened in a child-passenger restraint system. Children ages four through seven are required to be in an appropriately fitting child booster seat. Children aged eight to 18 must wear a seat belt.

# Taxi

Philadelphia's cabs are carefully regulated and pretty cheap. Downtown and in University City you can hail a cab easily enough during the day, especially at 30th St Station, other train stations and around the major hotels. At night and in the suburbs you're better off phoning for one.

Fares are $1.80 for the first one-sixth of a mile, then 30¢ for each subsequent one-sixth plus 20¢ for every minute of waiting time. The fare from University City to Penn's Landing is about $7. The flat fare from Center City to the airport is $20. Cab companies to try are:

**Liberty Cab** ( ☎ 215-389-8000; 842 S 2nd St)
**Yellow Cab** ( ☎ 215-333-3333; 8125 Frankford Ave)

# Train

**SEPTA** ( ☎ 215-580-7800; www.septa.org) runs the most efficient public transport options in Center City: subway and trolley lines. These interchange at 30th St Station, 15th St Station and 13th St Station. See p232 for a route map.

### SUBWAY

SEPTA operates two subway lines in Philadelphia. The **Market-Frankford** line (also known as the El) runs east-west along Market St from 69th St in West Philadelphia to Front St, from where it heads north to Frankford. The **Broad St** line runs north-south from Fern Rock in North Philadelphia to South Philadelphia's Pattison Ave, near all three major sports stadiums.

The one-way fare on most routes is $2. See the Bus section, above, for SEPTA ticket and Day Pass details.

**PATCO** (p203) offers another convenient subway route across Center City.

### TROLLEYS
SEPTA also operates a trolley service. Routes 10, 11, 13, 34 and 36 begin underground at 13th St Station, on tracks running parallel to the Market-Frankford Line. This subway-surface line heads east-west along Market St from 13th St Station to 33rd St; there it emerges from the ground, with various routes forking northwest and southwest. It provides excellent service to University City and West Philadelphia. The fare is the same as the subway.

### REGIONAL RAIL
Philadelphia's regional rail network is also run by SEPTA, and connects downtown with the suburbs and surrounding counties. Seven major routes are divided into six fare zones radiating from the city. One-way fares range from $3 to $7 during peak periods; off-peak fares are 50¢ to 75¢ cheaper. The main downtown stations are 30th St Station in University City, Penn Center Suburban Station at JFK Blvd and N 16th St, and Market East Station at Market and N 10th Sts beneath The Gallery shopping complex.

Useful routes are R7 to Germantown and Chestnut Hill East, R8 to Chestnut Hill West, R6 to Manayunk, and R1 to the airport.

# PRACTICALITIES

## ACCOMMODATIONS
The average room rate is about $130, with some seasonal variations (lowest in January and February, highest in September and October). Rates tend to be higher on weekends and lower on weekdays. A budget room will run less then $100 per night, while a mid-range option will cost between $100 and $200. Jump the $200 barrier, and you've hit the top end.

You can book a room for many hotels through www.hoteldiscounts.com ( ☎ 800-715-7666). For tips on using the Internet to get cheap rates, see 'Brave New Rooms' (p164).

## ALCOHOL LAWS
Welcome to Byzantium. Pennsylvania's laws governing the purchase of booze are complex.

You can purchase beer by the case at beer distributors and by the bottle at a limited number of delis. Six-packs are available only as take-out from bars and restaurants, and at inflated prices. Wine and liquor can be purchased only at state-run stores (called Wine & Spirits Shoppes) or from wineries. Beer distributors and state stores are open 9am to 9pm Monday though Saturday, with a very limited number of state stores also open on Sunday. Many restaurants allow you to bring your own (BYOB) bottle of booze, which can greatly reduce the cost of a meal. Bars usually close at 2am. The legal drinking age is 21.

## BUSINESS HOURS
Most of Philadelphia's offices are open from 8:30am or 9am to 5pm or 5:30pm. Most shops are open from 10am or 11am to 6pm or 7pm seven days a week, noon to 6pm Sunday. Restaurants are usually open from 11:30am to 2pm for lunch, and about 5pm to 10pm for dinner at least six days a week (sometimes closed on Monday). Generally shops are open on public holidays (expect July 4th, Thanksgiving, Christmas and New Year's Day), but banks, schools and offices are usually closed.

For information on public holidays and closures, contact the **Independence Visitor Center** (p55) or the **Philadelphia Convention & Visitors Bureau** (Map pp222-3; CVB; ☎ 215-636-3300; www.pcvb.org; 1515 Market St).

## CHILDREN
Philadelphia is very child-friendly, particularly since many of the city's sites and museums were designed with children in mind (see 'Tops for Children,' p63). On SEPTA, children aged 11 and younger ride for free or 75¢, depending on the day and the child's height. If you aren't accustomed to traveling with small children, you might find some encouragement in Lonely Planet's *Travel with Children*.

### Babysitting
Many big hotels have babysitting services. If you are staying at one of said hotels, check with the front desk to inquire about rates and availability. If you are not, contact reputable **Your Other Hand** ( ☎ 215-790-0990; $15/20 per hr with/without 1-day advance notice), used by the Four Seasons and the Ritz-Carlton.

# CLIMATE

Summer is one of the busiest tourist periods. Heat and humidity can be sweltering and uncomfortable. Though some days can be lovely, relief frequently comes through large rain and thunderstorms. Bring an umbrella.

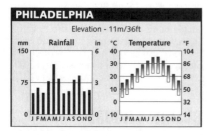

**PHILADELPHIA**

Elevation - 11m/36ft

The best times to visit Philadelphia are in the spring, after the winter has dissipated, and during the fall, when the city enjoys pleasant, mild weather. October in particular provides for some sweet visitation, as Pennsylvania's autumn leaves yield beautiful colors and the Pennsylvania Dutch Country enters into a harvest period. Winter can be surprisingly frigid, and snow is far more common here than a couple of hours south in DC. See www.weather.com for the latest forecasts.

# DISABLED TRAVELERS

Center City is a good destination for disabled visitors. Most museums and major sights are wheelchair accessible, as are most large hotels and restaurants. Smaller businesses housed in old buildings can sometimes have problematic staircases and narrow thresholds.

Public transport can be trickier. While 100% of SEPTA's buses are scheduled to be wheelchair accessible sometime in 2004, many subway stations are not. Market Street East and University City stations are accessible. To find out about others, contact **SEPTA** ( ☎ 215-580-4000). Disabled people who can't use public transit can use **Customized Community Transportation** (CCT), a door-to-door transport provider – apply for a pass by calling ☎ 215-580-7145.

Most sidewalks are in pretty good shape. All curbs are cut. Some hindrances include cobbled streets around Independence National Historical Park, Old City and Society Hill. Only a few crosswalks have audible crossing signals.

Many large hotels have suites for disabled guests, but call the hotel itself – not the

chain's 800 number – to check before you reserve. Larger car-rental agencies offer hand-controlled models at no extra charge. All major airlines, Greyhound buses and Amtrak trains allow service animals on board and frequently sell two-for-one packages if you need an attendant to accompany you.

The site www.phila.gov/aco provides key information about accessibility within the city. Also contact the folks at **Independence Visitor Center** (p55) for additional help.

Many organizations and tour providers specialize in helping disabled travelers, including the following:

**Mobility International USA** ( ☎ 541-343-1284; www.miusa.org; PO Box 10767, Eugene, OR 97440)

**Society for the Advancement of Travel for the Handicapped** (SATH; ☎ 212-447-7284; www.sath.org; 347 Fifth Ave, No 610, New York, NY 10016)

# DISCOUNT PASS

The **Philadelphia CityPass** ( ☎ 888-330-5008; www.citypass.net; adult/child $36/22) allows visitors to check out six popular attractions – the Franklin Institute, the Academy of Natural Sciences, the Philadelphia Zoo, the National Constitution Center, the Independence Seaport Museum and the Philadelphia Trolley Works – for 50% off admission prices (regular prices would total $71/45 adult/child). You can purchase CityPass at any of the above attractions. It's good for nine days.

# EMERGENCIES

Dial ☎ 911 for police, ambulance and fire emergencies; this is a free call from any phone.

Services in Philadelphia include the **Philadelphia Suicide & Crisis Center** ( ☎ 215-686-4420) and the **rape crisis center** ( ☎ 215-985-3333). **Traveler's Aid Society** (Map pp222-3; ☎ 215-523-7580; www.travelersaid.org; 1201 Chestnut St, 12th fl) is a nonprofit agency that helps stranded travelers in distress.

# GAY & LESBIAN TRAVELERS

Both gay men and lesbians have made the so-called Gayborhood (nine blocks between Walnut and Pine Sts, and 11th and Broad Sts) a safe and fun destination to be out. The rest of Center City is usually inclusive, though same-sex public displays of affection aren't often seen.

The excellent website www.gophila.com/gay lists useful information for both Philadelphia and the counties surrounding it. When in town, stop by **Giovanni's Room** (p154) for more information and to consult flyers outlining events. The free weekly *Philadelphia Gay News* is available in curbside stands throughout Center City.

## HOLIDAYS

Traveling during major holidays can cause prices to soar, as airline flights fill up and hotels sell out. The period surrounding Christmas and New Year's Day is the most frenzied, followed by Thanksgiving and Independence Day. Book early if you find yourself traveling at these times.

Following is a list of the major holidays observed in Philadelphia; note that on national public holidays (all those listed excluding St Patrick's Day and Halloween), banks, offices and many businesses close. If a public holiday falls on a weekday or weekend, it is often celebrated on the nearest Friday or Monday to create a three-day weekend. For information on festivals and events, see p13.

**New Year's Day** January 1
**Martin Luther King Jr Day** Third Monday in January
**Presidents' Day** Third Monday in February
**St Patrick's Day** March 17
**Easter** Date varies (a Sunday in March or April)
**Memorial Day** Last Monday in May
**Independence Day** July 4
**Labor Day** First Monday in September
**Columbus Day** Second Monday in October
**Halloween** October 31
**Veterans' Day** November 11
**Thanksgiving** Fourth Thursday in November
**Christmas** December 25

## INTERNET ACCESS

Internet access is widely available in hotels, usually for a daily fee of about $10. Free Internet access can be had at any branch of the Free Library of Philadelphia. The **Central Library** (Map pp222-3; ☎ 215-686-5322; 1901 Vine St; 🕙 9am-9pm Mon-Thu, 9am-6pm Fri, 9am-5pm Sat, 1-5pm Sun) is the largest and grandest. Many cafés in town offer terminals or wireless signals, sometimes for a fee, sometimes free. **Ing Direct** (Map pp222-3; ☎ 215-731-1410; 17th & Walnut Sts; 🕙 7am-7pm Mon-Fri, 10am-7pm Sat, 11am-6pm Sun) is a bank and café with free access. In Society Hill bring your laptop and a few bucks for the Wi-Fi at **Philadelphia Java Co** (Map pp228-9; ☎ 215-928-1811; 518 S 4th St; $2/hr; 🕙 7am-10pm Mon-Fri, 8am-11pm Sat, 8am-8pm Sun).

## LEGAL MATTERS

There is no reason to expect a run-in with the police during a visit to Philadelphia, unless you blatantly challenge local laws or commit a crime. Drinking alcoholic beverages outdoors is not officially allowed, though drinking beer and wine is often permissible at street fairs and other outdoor events; if vendors are selling it, it's safe to assume you can drink it. In Pennsylvania and New Jersey it is illegal to drive while intoxicated. In Pennsylvania, it is illegal to operate a motor vehicle when your blood alcohol content exceeds 0.08%; New Jersey allows drivers 0.10%.

Although attitudes toward jaywalking (crossing streets where there is no crosswalk) are relaxed and cops usually look the other way, it is illegal. Also note that the age of consent in Pennsylvania and New Jersey is 16.

If you are arrested for any reason, you have the right to remain silent. There is no legal reason to speak to a police officer if you don't wish to, but never walk away from an officer until given permission. All persons who are arrested are legally allowed (and given) the right to make one phone call. If you don't have a lawyer or family member to help you, call your consulate. The police will give you the number on request.

## MAPS

Free, excellent-quality paper maps of Center City are available at the **Independence Visitor Center** (p55). Members of **AAA** (Map pp222-3; ☎ 215-864-5050; www.aaamidatlantic.com; 2040 Market St; 🕙 8am-6pm Mon-Fri) can stop by the office for the best-available maps of Philadelphia and Pennsylvania.

For a good selection of pocket-size laminated maps and atlases, stop by either the **University of Pennsylvania Bookstore** (p157) or **Rand McNally** (Map pp222-3; ☎ 215-563-1101; www.randmcnally .com; 16th & Chestnut Sts, in Liberty Place; 🕙 9:30am-7pm Mon-Sat, noon-6pm Sun).

## MEDICAL SERVICES

Philadelphia is like most American cities when it comes to health care: excellent medical attention is readily available, and the only real concern is that a collision with the US health care system might seriously injure your wallet. Remember to buy health insurance before you travel. In the event of an emergency, dial ☎ 911 from any phone to summon medical help.

*continued on p210*

# INTERNATIONAL VISITORS
## Entering the Country

To enter the USA you must have a nonrefundable, roundtrip ticket, except when entering overland from Canada or Mexico (in which case sufficient funds for the duration of your stay must be shown).

Thanks to heightened security measures, travelers can expect long waits at immigration and security checkpoints. As of January 2004, all visitors with visas will be photographed and fingerprinted upon entry. The only exceptions are visitors from countries under the Visa Waiver Program, although they will eventually be subject to closer scrutiny as well. Check with the Department of Homeland Security at www.dhs.gov for current procedures and requirements.

No matter what your visa says, US immigration officers have an absolute authority to refuse or impose conditions on admission. Public health, customs and agricultural inspections may be carried out separately or together with immigration clearance.

No immunizations are required to enter the USA, but you should have adequate health insurance before setting out.

### PASSPORTS

Your passport must be valid for at least six months after your intended stay in the USA. Technically Canadians don't need a passport, but official proof of citizenship with photo ID is necessary.

### VISAS

The USA is overhauling its entry requirements as it establishes new national security guidelines. It is imperative that travelers double-check current regulations before coming to the USA, as changes will continue for several years. Check www.unitedstatesvisas.gov.

Under the Visa Waiver Program, citizens of certain countries may enter the USA without a visa for stays of up to 90 days. Currently, 27 countries are in the program, including most EU nations, Australia and New Zealand. For an updated list of countries included in the program, contact the **US State Department** ( ☎ 202-647-4000; www.travel.state.gov). All other travelers will need a visitor's visa. Visas can be obtained at most US consulate offices overseas; however, it is generally easier to obtain a visa from an office in one's home country.

### INTERNATIONAL DRIVER'S LICENSE

With few exceptions, you can drive legally in the US with a valid driver's license issued by your home country. If your home country license is not in English, you may be required to show an international driving permit.

## Customs

You must declare amounts in excess of $10,000 in cash, traveler's checks, money orders and other cash equivalents. Each visitor can import 1L of liquor, 200 cigarettes and 100 cigars (provided they are not Cuban), but you must be at least 21 years of age to possess alcohol and 18 years old for tobacco products.

## Electricity

Electrical current in the US is 110-115V, 60Hz AC. Outlets may accept flat two-prong or three-prong grounded plugs. If your appliance is designed for another electrical system, buy an adapter.

## Embassies & Consulates
### USA EMBASSIES & CONSULATES

In addition to those listed here, US embassies and consulates overseas can be found on the government's website (http://usembassy.state.gov).

**Australia** ( ☎ 02-6214-5600; Moonah Place, Yarralumla, ACT 2600)

**Canada** ( ☎ 613-238-5335; 490 Sussex Dr, Ottawa, ON K1N 1G8)

**France** ( ☎ 01-43-12-22-22; 2 avenue Gabriel, 75008 Paris)

**Germany** ( ☎ 030-8305-0; Neustädtische Kirchstrasse 4-5, 10117 Berlin)

**Ireland** ( ☎ 1-668-8777; 42 Elgin Rd, Dublin 4)

**Mexico** ( ☎ 01-55-5080-2000; Paseo de la Reforma 305, Col. Cuauhtémoc, 06500 Mexico, DF)

**New Zealand** ( ☎ 4-462-2000; 29 Fitzherbert Terrace, Thorndon, Wellington)

**UK** ( ☎ 20-7499-9000; 24 Grosvenor Square, London W1A 1AE)

### EMBASSIES & CONSULATES IN PHILADELPHIA

Consulates not mentioned here are likely to be found in New York or in Washington, DC.

**Austria** (Map pp222-3; ☎ 215-772-7630; 123 S Broad St, Philadelphia, PA 19109)

**Denmark** (Map pp222-3; ☎ 215-772-7454; 123 S Broad St, Philadelphia, PA 19109)

**Dominican Republic** (Map pp226-7; ☎ 215-923-3006; 437 Chestnut St, Philadelphia, PA 19106)

**Finland** (Map pp228-9; ☎ 215-465-5565; 112 Christian St, Philadelphia, PA 19147)

**Germany** (Map pp222-3; ☎ 215-568-5573; 1515 Market St, Philadelphia, PA 19102)

**Italy** ( ☎ 215-574-8168; 6 Saint & Chestnut Sts, Philadelphia, PA 19102)

**Mexico** (Map pp226-7; ☎ 215-922-4262; 111 S Independence Mall East, Philadelphia, PA 19106)

**Spain** ( ☎ 215-848-6180; 3410 Warden Dr, Philadelphia, PA 19129)

**Sweden** (Map pp222-3; ☎ 215-496-7200; 1628 JFK Blvd, Philadelphia, PA 19103)

# Money

## CURRENCY & CHANGING MONEY

The US dollar ($) is divided into 100 cents (¢) with coins of 1¢ (penny), 5¢ (nickel), 10¢ (dime), 25¢ (quarter), the relatively rare 50¢ (half dollar), and the equally elusive $1 coin. Bills come in denominations of $1, $2, $5, $20, $50 and $100. Gas stations, convenience stores and fast-food eateries may not accept bills over $20.

There are exchange bureaus in every terminal of the **Philadelphia International Airport** (p202). While this is convenient, the best rates are generally available at banks. Always ask about commissions and other surcharges when exchanging money. Most banks are open 10am to 5pm Monday to Thursday, until 6pm Friday, and sometimes for a few hours on Saturday morning.

Another exchange option is **American Express Travel Service** (Map pp222-3; ☎ 215-587-2300; www.americanexpress.com/travel; 1600 JFK Blvd; ☯ 9am-5pm Mon-Fri).

## ATMS

Almost all ATMs accept cards from the Cirrus, Visa, Star and Global Access networks. Machines are everywhere, especially at banks and convenience stores. Most ATMs charge a service fee of $1.50 per transaction for foreign bankcards, but exchange rates usually beat traveler's checks. ATMs at Wawa, a local chain of convenience stores, don't charge the service fee.

## TAXES

Except for clothing and food, which are exempt, the sales tax is 7%. This tax does, however, apply to food bought in cafés and restaurants. Philadelphia also charges a 7% city tax on accommodations, which means that you pay a total surcharge of 14% on the listed price for a room.

## TIPPING

Tipping in the US is not really optional – the service has to be absolutely appalling to consider not tipping. An unspoken protocol sets a minimum tip – even for a beer – at $1. Following is a guide:

Bars 15%
Cabbie 10%
Hotel porter $3-5

Restaurant 15-20%
Valet parking $2

## TRAVELER'S CHECKS

American Express, Visa and Thomas Cook are widely known issuers of traveler's checks. Restaurants, hotels and most shops readily accept US-dollar traveler's checks – same as cash – but small businesses, markets and fast-food chains may refuse them.

# Post

The **US Postal Service** (USPS; ☎ 800-275-8777; www.usps.gov) is reliable and inexpensive. Call for the nearest branch, including those that accept poste restante (General Delivery). Most post offices have after-hours stamp-vending machines. You can also buy stamps from hotel concierges, convenience stores and supermarkets.

At press time, first-class mail within the US is 37¢ for letters up to 1oz (23¢ each additional ounce) and 23¢ for postcards. International airmail rates are 80¢ for a 1oz letter and 70¢ for a postcard; both are 20¢ less to Canada or Mexico. Aerograms cost 70¢.

The **Philadelphia Main Post Office** (Map pp222-3; ☎ 215-895-8980; 2970 Market St; ☯ 6am-midnight) is impressively old and massive, occupying several city blocks. The **Penn Center Station** (Map pp222-3; ☎ 215-568-6452; 1500 JFK Blvd; ☯ 8am-5:30pm Mon-Fri) is centrally located, while the B Free Franklin Post Office (p57) postmarks stamps with Franklin's signature.

# Telephone

## DIALING CODES

Always dial ☎ 1 before toll-free (800, 888 etc) and domestic long-distance numbers (these include three-digit area codes). If you dial the area code when you shouldn't or don't dial it when you should, a recording from the phone company will set you straight.

International rates apply for calls to Canada, even though the dialing code (+1) is the same as for US long-distance calls. Dial ☎ 011 followed by the country code for all other overseas direct-dial calls.

## PHONES

Public pay phones are either coin- or card-operated; some also accept credit cards. Local calls usually cost 35¢ minimum and increase with the distance and length of call. Pay phones in airports and better hotels have data ports for laptop Internet connections.

The USA uses a variety of mobile phone systems, 99% of which are incompatible with the GSM 900/1800 standard used throughout Europe, Asia and Africa. Check with your cellular service provider before departure about using your phone in the US. Sometimes calls are routed internationally, while US travelers should beware of roaming surcharges (either way, it can become very expensive for a 'local' call).

## PHONE CARDS

Private prepaid phonecards are available at newsstands, convenience stores, supermarkets and pharmacies. Cards sold by major telecommunication companies like AT&T may actually offer better deals than upstart companies, whose cards have catchy names. Read the fine print.

## Time

Eastern Standard Time (EST) is five hours behind GMT. During Daylight Saving Time (from the first Sunday in April to the last Saturday in October), the clock moves ahead one hour. At noon in Philadelphia it's:

9am in Los Angeles
11am in Mexico City
noon in New York
5pm in London
6pm in Paris
3am (the next day) in Sydney

continued from p207
## Emergency Rooms

**Pennsylvania Hospital** Map pp222-3
☎ 215-829-3000; www.uphs.upenn.edu/pahosp; 8th & Spruce Sts; 🕑 24hr
**Children's Hospital of Philadelphia** Map p225
☎ 215-590-1000; www.chop.edu; 34th St & Civic Center Blvd; 🕑 24hr
**Thomas Jefferson University Hospital** Map pp222-3
☎ 215-955-6000; www.jeffersonhospital.org; 111 S 11th St; 🕑 24hr
**Graduate Hospital** Map p222-3
☎ 215-893-2353 emergency, 215-893-2000 general; 1800 Lombard St; 🕑 24hr
**University of Pennsylvania Medical Center** Map p225
☎ 215-662-4000; 3400 Spruce St; 🕑 24hr

## SAFETY

Like most big US cities, Philadelphia has its share of homelessness and crime, but prudent travelers are not at any undue risk. Certain neighborhoods are seedier than others and are considered 'unsafe.' These include Germantown, parts of West Philadelphia and South Philadelphia, and most of North Philadelphia. Though the majority of Center City and other touristed sections of the city are reasonably safe, travelers should be aware of their surroundings whenever they walk in the city. After dark, some of the city's parks – particularly Fairmount – host numerous crimes, some of them violent. Most tourists won't visit or even see Philly's most dangerous spots.

Standard urban common sense applies: leave valuables at home; avoid walking alone through poorly lit areas at night; and if you're lost and confused, try not to look lost and confused. If you find yourself somewhere you would rather not be, act confident and sure of yourself; then go into a store and call a taxi.

## TOURIST INFORMATION

The city of Philadelphia operates the stellar **Independence Visitor Center** (p55), near the Liberty Bell, to help travelers arrange accommodations and develop itineraries. Here you can get detailed information not only on Philadelphia but also on Bucks, Montgomery and Chester counties. Request a copy of the 'Official Visitors Guide.'

Also check out the **Greater Philadelphia Tourism Marketing Corporation** website (www.gophila.com). Consult it to learn about seasonal events, hotel packages, obscure museums and much more. Their Culture Files provide extensive information on just about every museum, dance troupe, park, garden and attraction in the city.

The following websites can provide additional trip-planning help:

http://philadelphia.citysearch.com
www.digitalcity.com
www.experiencepa.com

## WOMEN TRAVELERS

In general, Center City is safe for women travelers, while outlying neighborhoods can get sketchy. If you are unsure about which areas are considered dicey, ask at your hotel, or telephone the **Independence Visitor Center** (p55) for advice. Other women are a great source for the inside scoop, too.

At most hours the subway needn't be shunned by solo female travelers, though it's wise to ride in the operator's cars. As service winds down at the end of the night, it can get pretty lonely down there. Take a cab if you think you might be uncomfortable.

If you're out late clubbing or at a venue farther afield, consider stashing away money for the cab fare home. If you're ever assaulted, call the police (☎ 911).

# Behind the Scenes

## THE LONELY PLANET STORY

The story begins with a classic travel adventure: Tony and Maureen Wheeler's 1972 journey across Europe and Asia to Australia. There was no useful information about the overland trail then, so Tony and Maureen published the first Lonely Planet guidebook to meet a growing need.

From a kitchen table, Lonely Planet has grown to become the largest independent travel publisher in the world, with offices in Melbourne (Australia), Oakland (USA), London (UK) and Paris (France).

Today Lonely Planet guidebooks cover the globe. There is an ever-growing list of books and information in a variety of media. Some things haven't changed. The main aim is still to make it possible for adventurous travelers to get out there – to explore and better understand the world.

At Lonely Planet we believe travelers can make a positive contribution to the countries they visit – if they respect their host communities and spend their money wisely.

## THIS BOOK

This 1st edition of *Philadelphia & the Pennsylvania Dutch Country* was researched and written by John Spelman. The Food chapter was written by Francine Maroukian, and the History chapter was written by Ron Avery. This guide was commissioned in Lonely Planet's Oakland office and developed by:

**Commissioning Editors** Jay Cooke, Kathleen Munnelly
**Editor** Emily Wolman
**Cartographer** Bart Wright
**Assistant Cartographer** Kat Smith
**Designer** Candice Jacobus
**Layout** Shelley Firth
**Proofreaders** Jeff Campbell, Alex Hershey, Valerie Sinzdak
**Index** Ken DellaPenta
**Cover Designers** Pepi Bluck, Candice Jacobus
**Regional Publishing Manager** Maria Donohoe
**Project Manager** Kathleen Munnelly

**Cover photographs** by Lonely Planet Images: Statue of Benjamin Franklin at the Franklin Institute of Science, Richard Cummins; Robert Indiana's LOVE statue at LOVE Park, Richard Cummins (back).

**Internal photographs** by Lonely Planet Images All images are the copyright of the photographers unless otherwise indicated. Many of the images in this guide are available for licensing from Lonely Planet Images: www.lonelyplanetimages.com.

## ACKNOWLEDGMENTS

Many thanks to SEPTA for the use of its transit map © 2004 and to Elizabeth Fiend for the permission to reprint her recipe 'Philly Cheese Fakes' © 2000 on p29. A big thank you also to Cara Schneider of the GPTMC for all her help.

## THANKS
### JOHN SPELMAN

As everyone knows, first thanks always go to supportive mothers, and, in this case, they go to mine. My cantankerous brother and his excellent Philadelphia household – Brett, Mike, James Tantum, Jen and Amy, plus Lara, Rob and Cara – deserve thanks for the floor space, two wheels and insider orientation. I should have given you more than a shower curtain and booze in return.

Vivid gratitude goes to Cara Schneider and pal Gene, who showed me things that I still don't believe exist; to the entire Dubin family, particularly Eli, for providing help, support and a car when I needed it; to Chris, South Philly roommate and enjoyable rooftop companion; to my carpool; to Kyle, Catherine, Leah and future Representative Hohns, who welcomed a stranger and decisively separated yes from no; to Suzanne Biemiller; to Tom Burgoyne for kicking ass at Veterans Stadium; to the BiG TeA PaRtY crew; to collaborators Ron Avery, John McInerney and Francine Maroukian, who produced work better than I ever could; to Kathleen, Jay and Bart in Oakland, for doing a stellar job keeping me and this book on track; and to Emily Wolman (aka EKW), for making it comprehensible.

Two trusted friends, Erik and Robert, visited during this project, both providing observations necessary for its completion. Thanks especially to Lisa, for patience, kindness and furnishing our Berkeley apartment before my return.

**Published by Lonely Planet Publications Pty Ltd**
ABN 36 005 607 983

**Australia** Head Office, Locked Bag 1, Footscray
Victoria 3011, ☎ 03 8379 8000 fax 03 8379 8111
talk2us@lonelyplanet.com.au

**USA** 150 Linden St, Oakland, CA 94607
☎ 510 893 8556, toll free 800 275 8555
fax 510 893 8572, info@lonelyplanet.com

**UK** 72-82 Rosebery Ave, Clerkenwell, London,
EC1R 4RW ☎ 020 7841 9000, fax 020 7841 9001
go@lonelyplanet.co.uk

**France** 1 rue du Dahomey, 75011 Paris
☎ 01 55 25 33 00, fax 01 55 25 33 01 bip@lonelyplanet.fr,
www.lonelyplanet.fr

© Lonely Planet Publications Pty Ltd 2004
Food Chapter (pp31-8) © Francine Maroukian 2004

Photographs © photographers as indicated/Lonely Planet
Images 2004

Printed through SNP SPrint (M) Sdn Bhd

Printed in Malaysia

# SEND US YOUR FEEDBACK

We love to hear from travelers – your comments
keep us on our toes and help make our books better.
Our well-travelled team reads every word on what
you loved or loathed about this book. Although we
cannot reply individually to postal submissions, we
always guarantee that your feedback goes straight
to the appropriate authors, in time for the next
edition. Each person who sends us information is
thanked in the next edition – and the most useful
submissions are rewarded with a free book.

To send us your updates – and find out about LP
events, newsletters and travel news – visit our award-
winning website: www.lonelyplanet.com.

Note: We may edit, reproduce and incorporate
your comments in Lonely Planet products such as
guidebooks, websites and digital products, so let us
know if you don't want your comments reproduced
or your name acknowledged. For a copy of our
privacy policy visit www.lonelyplanet.com/privacy.

# Index

*See also separate indexes for Eating (p215), Entertainment (p216), Shopping (p217) and Sleeping (p217).*

Index

Index

215

ENTERTAINMENT

# SHOPPING

# SLEEPING

# Notes

## LEGEND

### ROUTES

| | |
|---|---|
| Tollway | Walking Path |
| Freeway | Unsealed Road |
| Primary Road | Pedestrian Street |
| Secondary Road | Stepped Street |
| Tertiary Road | Tunnel |
| Lane | One Way Street |
| Walking Tour | Walking Tour Detour |

### TRANSPORT

| | |
|---|---|
| Metro | Rail |

### HYDROGRAPHY

| | |
|---|---|
| River, Creek | Swamp |
| Intermittent River | Water |

### BOUNDARIES

| | |
|---|---|
| International | State, Provincial |

### POPULATION

| | |
|---|---|
| ○ CAPITAL (NATIONAL) | ◉ CAPITAL (STATE) |
| ● Large City | ● Medium City |
| ○ Small City | ○ Town, Village |

### AREA FEATURES

| | |
|---|---|
| Area of Interest | Land |
| Building | Market |
| + + + Cemetery | Park |

### SYMBOLS

| SIGHTS/ACTIVITIES | INFORMATION | SHOPPING |
|---|---|---|
| Beach | Bank, ATM | Shopping |
| Church | Embassy/Consulate | **TRANSPORT** |
| Monument | Hospital, Medical | Airport, Airfield |
| Museum, Gallery | Information | Bus Station |
| Picnic Area | Internet Facilities | Cycling, Bicycle Path |
| Point of Interest | Parking Area | General Transport |
| Ruin | Gas Station | Taxi Rank |
| Synagogue | Police Station | Trail Head |
| Skiing | Post Office, GPO | **GEOGRAPHIC** |
| Winery, Vineyard | Telephone | Lighthouse |
| Zoo, Bird Sanctuary | Toilets | Lookout |
| **SLEEPING** | **ENTERTAINMENT** | Mountain, Volcano |
| Sleeping | Café | National Park |
| Camping | Pub, Bar | )( Pass, Canyon |
| **EATING** | Theater | Shelter, Hut |
| Eating | | Waterfall |

*NOTE: Not all symbols displayed above appear in this guide.*

# Map Section

# PHILADELPHIA

A   B   C   D

**1**

476

76

Conshohoken

West
Conshohocken

23

Hector St

76

Old Gulph Rd

Matsonford Rd

Ridge Parkway

Lafayette
Hill

Germantown Pike

Butler St

Grove Rd

Joshua Rd

Elm St

Barren Hill Rd

Thomas Rd

Papei Mili Rd

Wyndmo

see Chestnut Hill map

R7 Chestnut
Hill East

Stenton Ave

R8 Chestnut
Hill West

Chestnut
Hill

Springfield Ave

Bells Mill Rd

Henry Ave

M
A

Germantown Ave

Mt Air

**2**

Villanova
University

Rosemont

Villanova

30

Rosemont
University

Spring Mill Rd

Old Gulph Rd

Morris Ave

Conshohocken State Rd

Roseglen

23

Gladwyne

Schuylkill Expressway

River Rd

SEPTA R6

Umbria St

Schuylkill River

Shawmont Ave

Ridge Ave

Henry Ave

9
Fairmount
Park

Valley
Green Rd

Allens Ave

Roxborough

Wissahickon Creek

Wissahickon Ave

see Manayunk map

Manayunk

Lincoln Dr

School House Ln

Philadel
Univers

Wissahi

**3**

476

Roberts Rd

Haverford

Havertown

Haverford
College

College Ave

Darby Rd

Ardmore Rd

Haverford Rd

Bryn Mawr
College

Robers Rd

Bryn Mawr

Ardmore

Lower
Merion

Narberth

Old Gulph Rd

Montgomery Rd

Conshohocken State Rd

23

SEPTA 100

SEPTA R5

Wynnewood Rd

Bala
Cynwood

St Joseph's
University

R6
Cynwood

1

Wynnefield

4

76

Kelly Dr

Chamounix Dr

13

**4**

3

Lawrence
Park

Springfield Rd

Lawrence Rd

Eagle Rd

Chester Pike

Penfield

Cobb Creek

Haverford Rd

Merion
Station

Penn
Wynne

City Ave

Morris
Park

30

SEPTA R6

Fairmount
Park

11

Concourse
Drive

Fairmount
Park

Kelly Dr

C
Mo
Av

13

1

Cobbs Creek
Park

69th Street
Terminal

M

3

Upper
Darby

see University City &
West Philadelphia map

SEPTA
Market-Frankford Line

Chestnut St

Walnut St

30

Lancaster St

43rd St

13

3

3

University of
Pennsylvania

Richland

Drexel
Hill

Township Line Rd

Drexel Ave

State Rd

Garrett Rd

Darby Rd

Burmont Ave

Landsdowne

Cobbs
Creek
Park

West
Philadelphia

5

13

Baltimore Ave

13

Baltimore Ave

**5**

476

3

Springfield Rd

Sproul Rd

Woodland Ave

Morton

Swarthmore

SEPTA R3

1

SEPTA R101

Clifton
Heights

Baltimore Pike

Clifton Ave

Collingdale

SEPTA R102

Darby

13

MacDade Blvd

Colwyn

Cobb Creek

Yeadon

Woodland Ave

Elmwood Ave

Lindbergh Ave

Elmwood

SEPTA R1

Passyunk Ave

Schuylkill River

76

S 26th St

Franklin De
Roosevelt P
& Golf Cou

95

**6**

Swarthmore
College

Rutledge

Glenolden

13

R102
Sharon
Hill

MacDade Blvd

Sharon
Hill

Delmar Dr

94th St

Cobb Creek

Eastwick

Island Ave

Philadelphia
International
Airport

Penrose Ave

Delaware Expressway

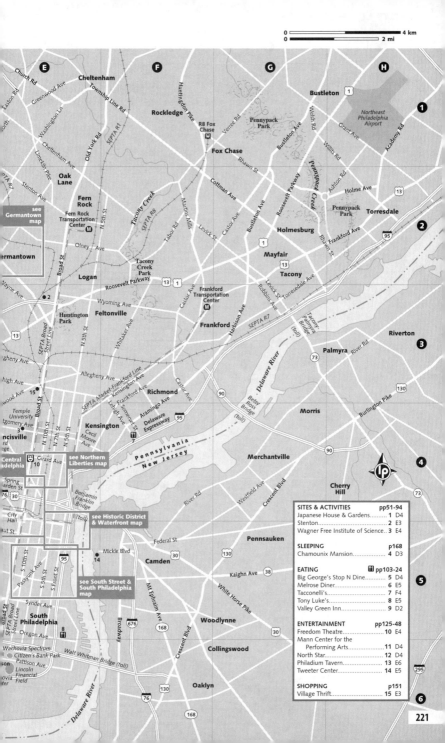

A  B  C  D

16
To North Star
57
Olive St
103
Eastern State Penitentiary
Fairmount Ave
114

Fairmount Park
Aquarium Dr
Art Museum Dr
Wallace St

30 / 76

17
Philadelphia Museum of Art

Vernon St
Green St
Brandywine St

S 33rd St
Garden St
N 31st St
Pennsylvania Ave
Pennsylvania Ave
W River Dr
Eakins Oval
N Spring Garden Ave
33

Hamilton St

13 / 13
Powelton St
Park Towne Place
Benjamin Franklin Parkway
26
99
Free Library of Philadelphia

Schuylkill River
Vine St Expressway
30 / 676
Winter St
Vine St

Parkway & Museum District
Race St
25
Franklin Institute Science Museum
Logan Circle & Square
21
Race St
29

30th St Station
Cherry St

Market St
Drexel University
30th St
M
John F Kennedy
19th St
Market St

Chestnut St
S 33rd St
S 32nd St
S 31st St
S 30th St
Schuylkill Expressway
76
22nd St
M
3
22
133
173
172
78
Ludlow St

Walnut St
University of Pennsylvania
Chestnut St
115
127 132
76
143 70 117
144
see inset left
170

Sansom St
Walnut St

Schuylkill River
S 24th St
S 23rd St
S 22nd St
Locust St
48
Rittenhouse Square
44

64
54 89
Rittenhouse Square
30 140
24

Spruce St
Delancey St
27
15
125
36
Pine St

Chestnut St
49
90
101
92
166
Ionic St
S 17th St
139
156
153
119
160
161
45
149
75
Sansom St
Moravian St
108
146
Walnut St
37
52
56 13
66
88
Rittenhouse Square
147 167
65
155
152
Chancellor St
Lombard St
53
South St
Bainbridge St
Fitzwater St
Catherine St

# CENTRAL PHILADELPHIA MAP KEY

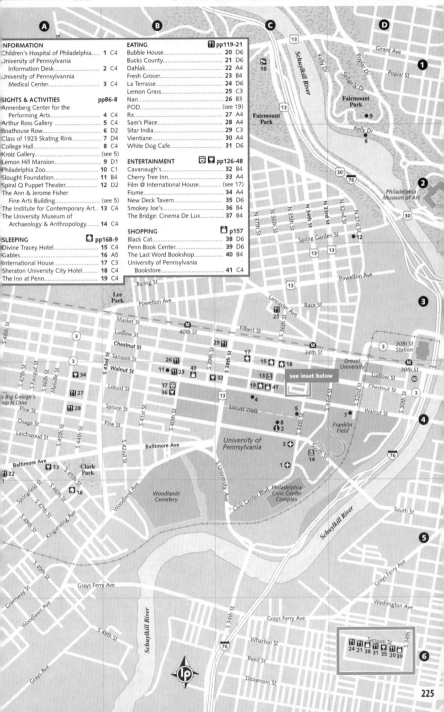

# UNIVERSITY CITY & WEST PHILADELPHIA

225

A  B  C  D

1

N 8th St
N Franklin St
Vine St
676
• 27
Race St
Florist St

Cherry St
Cherry St
• 21
N 7th St
Independence National Historical Park
US Mint
93
Appletree St
Race St
55
91
34
62
Arch St
N 6th St
Cherry St
59
15
Filbert St
Cherry St
89
61 36
92 24
Elfreth's Alley
20

2
8
75
Christ Church Burial Ground
42
5
N 5th St
N 4th St
Old City
N 3rd St
53
N 2nd St
Arch St
25
88
22
12
Cuthbert St
Commerce St
66
95
Columbus Blvd
5th St
Filbert St
33
95
13
2
96
60
11
7
Market St
56
American St
Church St
2nd St
87
38

3
Ranstead St
Market St
65
Ludlow St
90
82
45
S 7th St
Independence National Historical Park
63
81
69
64
32
18
Ranstead St
79
Franklin Court
40
84
86
35
Elbow Ln
83
85
77
58
49
19
Old City Hall
1
44
Chestnut St
4
51
47
Bank St
72
76
Congress Hall
3
41
73
Independence Hall
29
23
Strawberry St
Chestnut St
Library Hall
71 50
68 67 74 57
14
Second Bank of the US & National Portrait Gallery
10
Independence National Historical Park
Ionic St
17
Walnut St
Letitia St
43
S 6th St
James St
37
9
28
54
Welcome Park
Penn's Landing

4
Washington Square
Rose Garden
S 5th St
Sansom St
78
Walnut St
6
S 4th St
52
Dock St
46
97
Locust St
Willings Alley
26
S Washington Square
31
S 3rd St
St James Pl
16
Magnolia Garden
New Dock

5
Spruce St
Dock St
S Front St
International Sculpture Garden
City Park
S 7th St
Cypress St
Spruce St
39
Pine St
Delancey St
Society Hill
USS Olympia & Becuna
30

Pine St
Lombard St
Lombard St
LP

6
South St
Lombard St
95
South St
Columbus Blvd

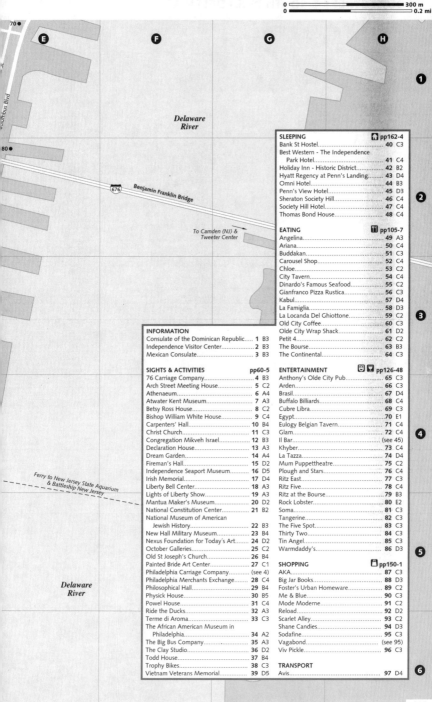

0 ――――――― 300 m
0 ――――――― 0.2 mi

**E**     **F**     **G**     **H**

70 ●

*Delaware River*

80 ●

676 Benjamin Franklin Bridge

To Camden (NJ) & Tweeter Center

Ferry to New Jersey State Aquarium & Battleship New Jersey

*Delaware River*

**1**
**2**
**3**
**4**
**5**
**6**

A B C D

1

Lombard-South M

Lombard St

Seger Park

Addison St

S 15th St

South St

Lombard St

Pine St

Rodman St

49

S 13th St

S 12th St

S 11th St

Bainbridge St

14

South St

44

65

Kater St

S 8th St

S 7th St

Fitzwater St

Bainbridge St

Palumbo Playground

2

33

Catherine St

Webster St

40

38

Fulton St

Christian St

26

60

13

7

Montrose St

23

Catherine St

39

29

Carpenter St

Salter St

Christian St

Montrose St

Hall St

Passyunk Ave

Broad St

62

Washington Ave

4

Carpenter St

3

Ellsworth-Federal M

Alter St

12

63

Kimball St

36

57

Kimball St

54

Ellsworth St

League St

42

Washington Ave

League St

S 6th St

Randolph St

Annin St

17

S 13th St

S 12th St

S 11th St

Federal St

S 10th St

S 9th St

4

Titan St

Wharton St

Wainock St

Alder St

Capitolo Playground

24

Federal St

Passyunk Square

15

Latona St

34

Reed St

Reed St

Wharton St

Gerritt St

48

Wilder St

Wilder St

Reed St

S Watts St

S Juniper St

S Clarion St

S 13th St

Dickinson St

Lion St

Wilder St

Dickinson St

South Philadelphia

5

Greenwich St

Tasker St

46

Cross St

Iseminger St

Camac St

S 12th St

Morris St

Tasker St

Fernon St

Mountain St

47

Castle Ave

Pierce St

Morris St

Moore St

32

6

S 11th St

S 10th St

S 9th St

S 8th St

S 7th St

S 6th St

S 5th St

228

To Melrose Diner

**SLEEPING** ⬆ p168

Shippen Way Inn..................................... 10 E2

**EATING** 🍴 pp114-118

Azafran................................................... 11 F2
Broad Street Diner.................................. 12 A3
Butcher's Cafe........................................ 13 C2
Cafe Izmir.............................................. 14 C2
Carman's Country Kitchen...................... 15 B4
Cedar's................................................... 16 F2
Center City Pretzel Co........................... 17 C3
Django.................................................... 18 E2
Dmitri's................................................... 19 E3
Essene.................................................... 20 E2
Famous 4th St Deli................................. 21 E2
Fez.......................................................... 22 F2
Fiorella Sausage..................................... 23 C3
Geno's Steaks......................................... 24 C4
Gianna's Grille........................................ 25 D1
Isgro Pastries.......................................... 26 C2
Ishkabibble's Eatery............................... 27 E2
Jim's Steaks............................................ 28 E2
John's Water Ice..................................... 29 D3
Judy's Cafe............................................. 30 F2
Mallorca................................................. 31 F2
Marra's Restaurant................................. 32 A6
Morning Glory Diner.............................. 33 C2
Pat's King of Steaks................................ 34 C4
Philadelphia Java Co.............................. 35 E2
Pif.......................................................... 36 C3
Pink Rose Pastry Shop............................ 37 E2
Ralph's.................................................... 38 C2
Sabrina's Cafe......................................... 39 C3
Sarcone's Bakery.................................... 40 C2
South Street Diner.................................. 41 F2
Taqueria la Veracruzana......................... 42 C3
Tartine.................................................... 43 E2
The Bean................................................ 44 D1
The Dark Horse Pub............................... 45 F1
Tre Scalini.............................................. 46 B5
Varallo Brothers..................................... 47 B6
Victor Cafe............................................. 48 A5
Whole Foods.......................................... 49 D1

**ENTERTAINMENT** 🎭 📺 pp126-48

Artful Dodger......................................... 50 F1
Downey's................................................ 51 F2
Fluid....................................................... 52 E2
Laff House............................................... 53 F2
Low Bar.................................................. 54 D3
New Wave Café...................................... 55 E3
O'Neal's.................................................. 56 F2
Royal Tavern.......................................... 57 D3
TLA......................................................... 58 E2
Tattooed Mom's..................................... 59 E2

**SHOPPING** 🛍 pp155-7

9th Street Records.................................. 60 C2
Benjamin Lovell Shoes............................ 61 E2
Di Bruno's Brothers................................ 62 C3
Fante's Kitchen Wares Shop................... 63 C3
Gily Jean's.............................................. 64 E2
Green Street Consignment Shop............. 65 E2
House of Tea........................................... 66 E2
Philadelphia Record Exchange................ 67 E2
Retrospect.......................................... (see 59)
South St Antiques Market/Jennie's
    Vintage............................................... 68 D2
Spaceboy Records................................... 69 E2
Time Zone.............................................. 70 E2
Zipperhead............................................. 71 E2

**TRANSPORT**

Budget.................................................... 72 G3

**INFORMATION**

Finnish Consulate.................................... 1 F4

**SIGHTS & ACTIVITIES**                    pp78-82

Gloria Dei (Olde Swedes') Church........ 2 F4
Isaiah Zagar House.................................. 3 D1
Mario Lanza Museum.............................. 4 C3
Mother Bethel AME Church.................... 5 D1
Mummers Museum.................................. 6 F4
Samuel S Fleisher Art Memorial............. 7 D2
Spector Gallery....................................... 8 E2
St Peter's Church.................................... 9 F1

229

# NORTHERN LIBERTIES

0 ⟩⟩⟩ 500
0 ⟩⟩⟩ 0.3 mi

| SIGHTS & ACTIVITIES | pp82-3 |
| --- | --- |
| Edgar Allan Poe National Historic Site.... | 1 B3 |
| Guild House........................................ | 2 B3 |
| National Shrine of St John Neumann..... | 3 C1 |
| Project Room...................................... | 4 B1 |
| Table Space........................................ | 5 B1 |

| EATING | 🍴 pp118-19 |
| --- | --- |
| Il Cantuccio....................................... | 6 D3 |
| Las Cazuelas...................................... | 7 C1 |
| North 3rd.......................................... | 8 D2 |
| Pigalle.............................................. | 9 D3 |
| Rat Pack Café.................................... | 10 D3 |
| Silk City Diner................................... | 11 C3 |

| ENTERTAINMENT | 😃 🎭 pp126-48 |
| --- | --- |
| 700 Club............................................ | 12 D3 |
| Abbaye.............................................. | 13 D3 |
| Aqua Lounge...................................... | 14 D1 |
| Finnegan's Wake................................ | 15 C3 |
| Liberties............................................ | 16 D3 |
| Ministry of Information....................... | 17 C2 |
| Ortlieb's Jazzhaus.............................. | 18 D2 |
| Silk City Lounge................................ | (see 11) |
| Standard Tap..................................... | 19 D2 |
| The Fire............................................. | 20 C1 |
| Transit.............................................. | 21 C3 |

| TRANSPORT | |
| --- | --- |
| Enterprise.......................................... | 22 D3 |

# MANAYUNK

0 ⟩⟩⟩ 500 m
0 ⟩⟩⟩ 0.3 mi

| SHOPPING | 🛍 pp157-9 |
| --- | --- |
| Africa on Main.................................. | 19 B1 |
| American Pie..................................... | 20 C2 |
| Beans............................................... | 21 B2 |
| Benjamin Lovell Shoes........................ | 22 C2 |
| Bias.................................................. | 23 B2 |
| Down 2 Earth.................................... | 24 C2 |
| Leehe Fai......................................... | 25 C2 |
| Mainly Shoes.................................... | 26 B2 |
| Public Image...................................... | (see 26) |
| TAG.................................................. | 27 B2 |
| The Eyeglass Works............................ | 28 B2 |
| Unique Eyewear................................. | 29 C2 |
| Why Be Board................................... | 30 C2 |

| SIGHTS & ACTIVITIES | p89 |
| --- | --- |
| Bike Line of Manayunk....................... | 1 D3 |
| Yoga on Main ................................... | 2 B2 |

| EATING | 🍴 pp121-3 |
| --- | --- |
| Carmella's.......................................... | 3 A1 |
| Chloe's Corner.................................... | 4 D3 |
| Grasshopper....................................... | 5 B2 |
| Hikaru.............................................. | 6 C2 |
| Jake's............................................... | 7 B2 |
| Kansas City Prime.............................. | 8 B2 |
| La Colombe....................................... | 9 B2 |
| Mainly Desserts................................. | 10 C2 |
| Sorrentino's Deli................................. | 11 C2 |

| ENTERTAINMENT | 🎭 pp126-48 |
| --- | --- |
| Castle Roxx....................................... | 12 D3 |
| Cresson Inn....................................... | 13 B1 |
| Grape St Pub..................................... | 14 C2 |
| Manayunk Brewery & Restaurant........ | 15 D3 |
| Pitcher's Pub..................................... | 16 C2 |
| The Bayou Bar & Grill........................ | 17 C2 |
| US Hotel............................................ | 18 B1 |

# CHESTNUT HILL

**ENTERTAINMENT** 🎭🎟️ pp126-48
McNally's Tavern...................... **19** C3
Stagecrafters Theater............... **20** C4
Towey's Tavern........................ **21** D4

**SHOPPING** 🛍️ pp159-60
Artisans on the Avenue............. **22** C3
Caleb Meyer Studio.................. **23** C3
Chestnut Hill Cheese Shop........ **24** C3
Chestnut Hill Sports................. **25** C3
El Quetzal.............................. **26** C3
French Lemon......................... **27** C3
Intermission........................... **28** C3
Kilian Hardware Company........ (see 27)
La Vie Creatif......................... **29** C3
Mango................................. (see 25)
Monkey Business.................... (see 25)
O'Doodles............................. **30** C3
Quelque Chose....................... (see 26)
Stylos.................................. (see 27)
The Philadelphia Print Shop....... (see 26)
The Pipe Rack........................ (see 26)

**INFORMATION**
...ors Center............................ **1** C3

**SIGHTS & ACTIVITIES** pp89-91
...estnut Hill Historical Society...... **2** B3
...na Venturi House.................... **3** C4
...odmere Art Museum................ **4** A2

**SLEEPING** 🛏️ pp169-72
...m Cara.............................. **5** D4
...stnut Hill Hotel..................... **6** C3
...erstone............................. **7** C2
...arloaf Conference Center........ **8** A2

**EATING** 🍴 pp123-4
...ana................................. **9** C3
...denbeck's Ice Cream Parlour..... **10** C4
...a Bakery............................ **11** C3
...stnut Hill Farmers Market........ **12** C3
...cin.................................. **13** D4
...us.................................. **14** C4
...essly Vegetarian Cafe............. **15** B3
...ta.................................. **16** C3
...er's Expresso...................... **17** C3
...of the Hill........................ (see 11)
...men's Exchange.................... **18** C3

# GERMANTOWN

**INFORMATION**
Germantown Historical Society
& Visitors Center....................... **1** C2

**SIGHTS & ACTIVITIES** pp91-3
Cliveden................................ **2** B1
Deshler-Morris House................. **3** C2
Ebenezer Maxwell Mansion......... **4** B2
Grumblethorpe......................... **5** C2
Johnson House......................... **6** B1
Upsala.................................. **7** B1
Wyck................................... **8** B1

**EATING** 🍴 p124
Rib Crib................................. **9** B1

# SEPTA Railroad & Rail Transit

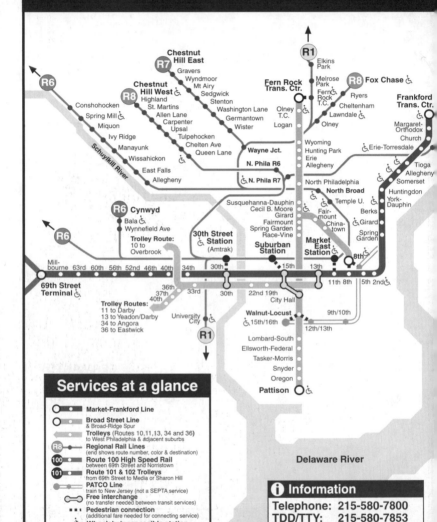

## Services at a glance

- **Market-Frankford Line**
- **Broad Street Line** & Broad-Ridge Spur
- **Trolleys** (Routes 10,11,13, 34 and 36) to West Philadelphia & adjacent suburbs
- **R8** **Regional Rail Lines** (end shows route number, color & destination)
- **100** **Route 100 High Speed Rail** between 69th Street and Norristown
- **101** **Route 101 & 102 Trolleys** from 69th Street to Media or Sharon Hill
- **PATCO Line** train to New Jersey (not a SEPTA service)
- **Free interchange** (no transfer needed between transit services)
- **••• Pedestrian connection** (additional fare needed for connecting service)
- **♿ Wheelchair accessible station**

© SEPTA 2004

### Delaware River

## ℹ Information

| | |
| --- | --- |
| Telephone: | 215-580-7800 |
| TDD/TTY: | 215-580-7853 |
| Internet: | www.septa.org |